ROCK PROPHECY

Sex & Jimi Hendrix in World Religions
The Original Asteroid Prediction & Microsoft Connection

by Michael Fairchild

Defining the Faith of Creation's Way:
Religion of the Freeks

First Century Press
P.O. Box 39606
Rochester, NY 14604

716 244-5552
mail@rockprophecy.com

Rock Prophecy

Copyright © 1995 by Michael Fairchild

First published in November 1999

Library of Congress Catalog Card Number: 99-96702

ISBN: 1-929342-02-0

Bookbinding by:
Olde Ridge Bookbindery, Rochester, NY
Printed in Rochester, NY, USA

Cover photo by Steve Grills

Cover design and book layout by:
Bash! Studios, Rochester, NY, USA

Acknowledgements

ᨃ

Editorial suggestions were made along the way by:
Charles Blass (spring 1995 draft)
Liz Kempf and Chuck Abreu (winter 1998 draft)
Ron Hein and Tammany Kramer (spring 1999 draft)
Brad Rosen offered key insights too.

We do not worship Jimi. The Hendrix story teaches us how destructive "worship" can be.[1]

This Child is destined...to be a sign that will be opposed so that the inner thoughts of many will be revealed.   – Luke 2:34-35

*Satan...[acts] for the specific purpose of blocking or obstructing human activity. The root **stn** means "one who opposes, obstructs, or acts as adversary." (The Greek term **diabolos**, later translated "devil," literally means "one who throws something across one's path.")*
                                                                – Elaine Pagels[2]

The point is: who is wrong and who is right, that's what the point is – not how many people.   – Jimi[3]

1. Michael Fairchild, Straight Ahead magazine, 8/94, p.16.
2. Elaine Pagels, *The Origin of Satan*, (New York: Random House, 1995), p.39.
3. Circus 3/69, p.40

This book is dedicated to the seers. We are the forerunners of the future. We are not "rejected" by the unfree elitist media. Reject = *defect*, an equation used to devalue us. We are not rejected. We are *obstructed*. "Obstruct" conveys the *unrighteousness* of those who oppose us.

"Success" for *Rock Prophecy* is defined not in terms of numbers of books sold. Success is measured by the Prophecy's survival.

Rock Prophecy is not a "Hendrix book." It is the Newest Testament which defines the faith of Creation's Way: religion of the *freek*s. The Prophecy is protected by title 17 of the U.S. Code, Public Law 94-553, 90 Stat. 2541 section 107 which permits "Fair Use" of excerpts of copyrighted lyrics and text for purposes of illustration, clarification or comment of the author's observations. The law regarding Fair Use allows reproduction of parts of lyrics and poems, to explain their meanings, without having the ideas expressed in this book held hostage by any owner of lyrics/poems, who might wish to obstruct use of excerpts.

Statements in this book are the opinion of the author, usage of attributed sources is in no way meant to express an endorsement by that person of the work.

Rock Prophecy carries the concepts that dominators are most concerned to obstruct and crush. The unjust monied among us – the so-called "rich" – will seek out and destroy every copy of this book that they can confiscate.

> *There's nothing we can explain to them. Most of it is from bitterness, there's no color part now, there's no black and white, it's very small...They have to relax and wait to go by the psychological feeling. If you start thinking negative, it switches to bitterness, aggression, hatred, whatever.*
>
> — Jimi[4]

---

4. L.A. Free Press 1969.

Immediate Precursor

ℐ

If one wishes to attribute the media's 1995-1999 asteroid craze to causes other than *Rock Prophecy,* or to events that transpired before *Rock Prophecy* was copyrighted in 1995, we could go all the way back to 1877 when Jules Verne wrote *Off On A Comet* and designate *that* book as the "trigger" for the blitz of reports about rocks from space in the late 1990s. Or we could go back just a couple decades to the 1978 film *A Fire In the Sky,* or the 1979 movie *Meteor,* or the 1984 film *Night of the Comet.*

The Timeline, which is an important part of the *Rock Prophecy* concept, is included in this book's Introduction as a review of the history of asteroid issues in recent popular culture, following the copyright date for this book.

Many of us are aware of occasional asteroid stories that caught the public's attention at some point over the past century or so (my favorite is the 1893 book *The Destruction of Atlantis* by Ignatius Donnally). And members of today's media will claim that the current asteroid craze was kicked off by comet impacts on Jupiter in 1994. But the main point of the Timeline in this book's Introduction is to prove *otherwise.*

Consider timing. There have been a handful of asteroid stories published at various points between 1877 and 1994. But as the Timeline explains, all of these stories produced minor "impacts" on popular culture. The actual asteroid craze in modern media – characterized by repeated and excessive/obsessive mass media blockbuster fixation, from *The New York Times* to all major TV networks and Hollywood films – is outlined in the Timeline. Nowhere else is this "wave" of reports chronicled. No one else was keeping track – except for me – because I was watching it all from the start as my brainchild was ripped off by media elites over the course of several years.

The media's unique wave of stories about rocks from space escalated in late 1995, about 6 months after *Rock Prophecy* was seen in D.C. at the Library of Congress (LOC). My manuscript arrived at the LOC at the height of the Hendrix lawsuit proceedings, which are described in the Introduction of *Rock Prophecy.*

PRIOR to 1995, all asteroid reports and media stories about space rocks are scattered haphazardly across the decades in disconnected isolation from each other. By contrast, the intense crescendo of reports triggered after *Rock Prophecy* was copyrighted, firmly identifies *RP* as the IMMEDIATE PRECURSOR to the frenzy in media, a blitz of reports which continued at an uninterrupted peak for three years (the most recent manifestation is a McDonalds' "asteroid" TV commercial which aired on the heels of the 1998 movies *Armageddon* and *Deep Impact*). *Rock Prophecy* appeared at precisely the right time prior to the media blitz, marking this book forever as the catalyst for that craze. There is NO OTHER directly connected event in 1995 prior to the media blitz about asteroids. A description of this fact is the point and purpose of the Timeline, and its eternal value.

Rock Prophecy preceded the craze, and many of the 1995-1999 media reports contain content similar with sections of this book (as the Timeline points out). The quality, intensity, and sheer number of major media reports about asteroids during this period is unprecedented in history. Never again can the attention of civilization be introduced to the threat of rocks in such a concentrated way.

Everyone on Earth has now been "trained" and conditioned to this issue. While most people shrug off the odds of an impact, most scientists who've studied the subject agree that a hit is inevitable, it's only a matter of *when*, and the odds indicate that we're long overdue for the next big one. This book is about Jimi's prediction of *when*, made at a time when only a tiny handful of people were even thinking about asteroids at all. By contrast, after *Rock Prophecy* was copyrighted in 1995, the asteroid issue was hyped up to the number one topic of discussion in the late 1990s, to such an extent that for me to come out today and claim *Rock Prophecy* as the trigger for this blitz will elicit indignant huffs of "How dare you!"

But it's true.

Consider how not a single media report listed in the Timeline mentions the occasional isolated book about asteroids, like *Lucifer's Hammer* (1977) or *The End of the Age* (1987). The few books such as these are not contenders against *Rock Prophecy* as "triggers" instigating the craze in media for asteroids in the late 1990s. And regardless, like I say in my March 11, 1998, letter (see Timeline): the whole issue of who triggered the blitz is just a sliver in *Rock Prophecy* anyway, just a small fraction of the book. *RP* is not a story about *who* started this fixation with space rocks. And it is not a book about how I personally was treated by the Microsoft dominators who went on to overexpose the asteroid story in media. Rather, *Rock Prophecy* is The Newest Testament, an interpretation of history which defines a faith in unexpected ways, with unprecedented connections.

So go ahead, be my guest, attribute the asteroid craze to any of many space rock stories reported prior to 1995. That's *exactly* what the dominator media has taken pains to persuade everyone of. They'll say the craze was caused by *anything* other than *Rock Prophecy*.

As Elaine Pagles said, "It's the winners who write history – *their* way." *RP* has been suppressed by the media elite, who have instead presented their own false version of what happened (they like to pedestalize the late great Eugene Shoemaker as the reigning "asteroid guru" – it's safer that way, he's dead.) But another version of history exists, and it's not a dominator "winners" delusion. It's the truth.

Rock Prophecy is the original trigger for an avalanche of asteroid stories in recent media. The *timing* is the key to consider, because *RP* appeared in that critical period of 1995 prior to the media blitz about space rocks. And with Paul Allen's involvement with the Hendrix lawsuit, why *wouldn't* his legal team monitor my stories, including *Rock Prophecy*? As this book's Introduction points out, I was the writer for the Hollywood company that was being sued.

For the historical record: we would have seen NO media overexposure of asteroid stories had not the Hendrix connection with this issue been seen in Washington D.C. in spring 1995. To claim otherwise is to subscribe to the dominators' version of history – a revisionist re-write, like the way Constantine's scribes reconstructed the story of Jesus long after the Crucifixion.

Today's media has ethnically cleansed Hendrix out of any mention of asteroids. However the fact remains that Jimi made his prediction three decades earlier, he was on the way to conveying it, and today's media elites became aware of it all in spring 1995, after *Rock Prophecy* was studied at the Library of Congress.

Tell your friends about *Rock Prophecy*, quickly. And please, contact First Century Press with names of newspapers and magazines that will advertise this book, or stores and shops that will distribute it. To fulfill our mission, we need your help.

Contents

ૐ

Dominator Introduction

ॐ

Our first intentions, we want to be respected after we're dead. Who doesn't want to be remembered in history? We want to be completely honest and bare-faced.   — Jimi[1]

Human beliefs are suited to maintaining elite privileges for a dominant group. A small fraction of our race enjoys unending pleasure while multitudes remain unable to free themselves from the designs of inequity.
                                                         – *A Touch of Hendrix* 1988[2]

Seattle's Experience Music Project was first notified by me about a certain world class collection of Jimi Hendrix material. In May 1992 I began a six month lobbying effort of phone calls and letter writing to the Seattle museum project to make possible their purchase of this historic Hendrix collection.

The museum, now known as the Experience Music Project (EMP), is the creation of billionaire Microsoft co-founder, and Hendrix fan, Paul Allen. In 1995 the *New York Times* reported, "The late Jimi Hendrix, a Seattle native, has had more influence on Mr. Allen than perhaps anyone except Mr. [Bill] Gates . . . More than 10,000 Hendrix artifacts will make up the bulk of the collection at the $60 million Experience Music Project, which Mr. Allen is building in the shadow of the Seattle Space Needle."[3]

My work and vision in 1992 resulted in the EMP's purchase of a collection of thousands of Hendrix items for nearly a half million dollars. Paul Allen was interested in acquiring ownership of rights to Jimi's music for his museum project.

Leo Branton began negotiations with some major players to license rights...among the bidders was Hendrix freak Paul Allen, billionaire co-founder of the computer software giant Microsoft. But even though he is thought to have put in a higher bid, the rights went to Matsushita in Japan who own MCA. Backed by a presumably miffed Paul Allen, [Jimi's father] hit Branton with a law suit claiming...conflict of interest...

                                                           – Harry Shapiro[4]

1. New England Scene 11/68.
2. Michael Fairchild, *A Touch of Hendrix*, unpublished manuscript (1988), p.4.
3. The New York Times 10/29/95, sec. 3, p.11.
4. Harry Shapiro, *Electric Gypsy*, (New York: St. Martins Press, 1995), p.491.

In 1993, Paul Allen made available a $5 million interest free loan to Jimi's father, Al Hendrix. The billionaire's money financed a lawsuit brought by Al and his attorneys against people who had bought and sold rights to Jimi's music many years earlier. In 1995, the lawsuit was settled out of court. As a result of the settlement, the Hendrix production company in Hollywood, Are You Experienced? Ltd., that had employed me as writer and consultant for seven years, was bought out and closed.

AYE? Ltd. was run by producer Alan Douglas. "Michael probably knows more about Jimi than anyone in the world," said Alan, the producer whom MTV describes as "a man who plays the role of Satan in many a Hendrix purist's fantasies."[5]

I was criticized for working with Alan. His work with the Hendrix legacy is controversial. "A lot of people are going to hate you because of me," he said. "You're one of the *bad guys*." But as the writer for AYE? Ltd. I achieved the most visibility of the world's Hendrix experts. My booklets included with 14 official Hendrix CDs are familiar to more than six million people.[6] Many of these people dislike Alan Douglas. "The collectors all hate me," Alan told me, "because I have control of the situation. They all want to have that, just like . . . I would like you to have it if I'm not around. OK?"[7]

I was in line to succeed Alan as Creative Director of AYE? Ltd. Then the lawsuit filed by Jimi's father, and financed by Paul Allen's money, toppled my opportunity. The job of Creative Director that I had been trained for was instead given to Al Hendrix's adopted daughter, a Japanese-American woman named Janie, who is no blood relative of Jimi's and barely knew him. I was left unemployed. And officials at Paul Allen's Experience Music Project informed me that I will not be compensated for all of the work I'd done to help build the Hendrix collection for Paul Allen's museum.

Then Janie, the Japanese-American woman who took my job, began taking all of my booklets included with Jimi's CDs off the market and substituting them with uninteresting junk. The irony is that I was the main conceptualist for the Hendrix company responsible for ideas that helped push new Jimi releases to the Top-10, and even the Top -5, on *Billboard* charts. **Hendrix fans bought those CDs for the music,** but I knew how to package and present Jimi's music in ways that drove those titles up the charts. We won't see that again. For the highest charting Hendrix releases in the 1990s, I suggested most of the songs used and programmed their order. They carried my booklet notes and many of those CDs were titled by me too.

The way I was treated by the Seattle dominators represents a microcosm of a much larger story at the heart of *Rock Prophecy.* My experience with Paul Allen's project, and the Hendrix family disaster, is cited here, not with malice or ill will, but as a prime example of what this book calls the *silencing of the seers* and the *retarding of history.* The EMP incident forms the basis for an interpretation of society explained later in this book.

---

5. Kurt Loder, MTV News, 4/95.
6. Alan Douglas interview, Guitar World, 7/95, p 181.
7. Discussion with Alan Douglas 12/94.

I aimed to help build the museum's collection. I offered my insights regarding Hendrix for employment with the Project. I expected compensation for the Hendrix contacts I made available. Proposals that I submitted to Paul Allen contained ideas that were acted upon by museum officials. For example, Jerry Goldstein is a producer who filmed Hendrix on tour in Europe in 1969. In 1992, I spoke with Jerry and suggested that he make his unreleased films of Jimi available to Paul Allen's museum. He expressed interest, so I contacted the museum and proposed a collaboration with Goldstein and told the EMP how to contact Jerry. Within weeks officials from the museum visited Jerry and began discussions.

On January 6, 1993, after I orchestrated the EMP's purchase of a major collection of Hendrix items, I wrote a letter to Paul Allen :

> *I'm pleased at your acquisition of the . . . collection. For over a year I had lobbied to find a home for this treasure... [Now it is] a cornerstone nucleus library for the museum . . . What I uniquely bring [to your project] is a detailed historical perspective sensitive to all issues and events which formed the hallmarks of Jimi's generation. As writer/historian/ researcher/performing artist . . . I am the most integrated advocate of Jimi's legacy. I possess a passion for retaining and recalling much of the most arcane and esoteric realms of Hendrixia, an ability which eclipses other researchers in this field. I am also the most intuitive when it comes to speculation about Jimi, and perception of conflicting data. I am an expert at psychological readings of Jimi and his original audience/times . . . and hold in active memory the multi-thousand points of details surrounding the entire Hendrix scene. It is not possible to teach this . . . I am able to develop the most integrated, entertaining, and informative exhibits ever seen.*

Through my efforts the museum found what is arguably the most extensive collection of magazines featuring Hendrix covers and articles about Jimi from around the world, thousands of rare magazines published during the late 1960s and 1970s, all in mint condition. Such a collection is very valuable as a museum database. An intense amount of obscure information, and rare interviews, are contained in these publications.

After the EMP purchased the magazines in early 1993, an equally amazing collection of Hendrix posters followed. These core collections of Hendrix items became cornerstones of Paul Allen's Hendrix database at the museum. And the posters were followed by a collection of thousands of rare and obscure Hendrix "bootleg" CDs and albums. Through me the EMP was steered into this stunning assemblage of mint pieces snagged for just under a half million dollars. Paul Allen must have been thrilled by the results.

Soon after I persuaded museum officials to investigate this collection in 1992, Paul Allen financed a loan to Al Hendrix, Jimi's father, for a lawsuit which, in 1995, resulted in closing Are You Experienced? Ltd., the Hendrix production company in Hollywood where I was employed. My job was gone. Two years earlier in 1993 Al Hendrix filed suit against his attorney, Leo Branton, and sought to regain control of the rights to Jimi's music and assets. In the 1970s, the rights had been sold to foreign investors through deals negotiated by Branton, who then set up AYE? Ltd., the Hendrix production company that hired me in 1989. Alan Douglas was the Creative Director of AYE? Ltd., he had worked for Jimi as a producer. Alan recognized that I had amassed unique research about Hendrix.

CORNERSTONES

In 1990, Alan asked me to select songs to be included on an official Hendrix album that I christened *Cornerstones*. I wrote the liner notes for this CD and when it was released it reached the Top-5 on *Billboard* charts. *Cornerstones* was the first and last Hendrix record in twenty years to break the Top-5 on the charts. It was a hit record, and I was paid $3000 for my consulting which helped make it the highest charting Hendrix release since 1971. But the producer, Alan Douglas, neglected to credit me on the packaging for my programming work!

Four years later I did receive a "programming consultant" credit for my work on the *Jimi Hendrix :Blues* CD, released by MCA in 1994. In addition to writing the critically acclaimed 28-page booklet included with that 1994 CD, I also selected several of the songs to be included (like the acoustic version of *Hear My Train A'Comin'* that opens the CD, and the electric version at the end). I also suggested the order for the tracks. *:Blues* reached the Top-10 on *Billboard* charts in May 1994, making it the third highest charting Hendrix release since 1971.

FAT SATURNS AND IMITATION FAIRCHILDS

But despite these and other successes, my career at the Hendrix company was ruined, and the job of Creative Director went to a Japanese-American woman, who is no blood relative of Hendrix, and she proceeded to replace my work with drastically bad substitutes. The amazing media attention given to Jimi Hendrix from 1990 through 1995, when I was making the decisions with Alan Douglas, has completely disappeared. It's as if the purpose, or result, of Paul Allen's "litigation money" has been to once again marginalize Hendrix outside of public awareness.

My job at the Hendrix company underpaid me for the decisions I made, but in order to get my ideas about Jimi through to a worldwide audience, it was necessary to work for Alan Douglas. At the same time, anyone connected with Alan became a target of intense resentment from a network of Hendrix collectors and researchers. Many of these people despised him. I took heat for working with Alan.

As a writer, I had achieved the most visibility of the Hendrix experts. My booklets, included with many officially released CDs, by the mid-1990s were distributed to well over six-million people. None of the dozens of books written about Jimi achieved such circulation. This is why I'm "the most widely read" Hendrix scholar. Since my exile from the Hendrix company, none of the junky subsequent releases, with deadly dull booklets, can scrape the bottom of the barrel on the charts.

Landing the job of writing the first booklets for Hendrix CDs during the early 1990s was like winning the Olympics of rock journalism. The competition was intense because the stakes were so high. No one had yet explained to the public how the issues and connections surrounding the life of Hendrix are the most explosive controversies at the center of our culture. All of society's hot button issues are triggered in unexpected ways, ways which are concealed from the public by media elites who obstruct any attempt to publish or air the real story.

I became the target of intense resentment from jealous writers and collectors. The contempt that they held for Alan was transferred on to me, because I'm the one Alan said he wanted to succeed him as Creative Director of the Hendrix company. It was my goal to climb the ladder of the "estate" and advance an interpretation of Jimi's legacy to a worldwide audience. After six years of amazing successes, running a non-stop, exhausting obstacle course, I had positioned myself for a job that I knew I could perform better than anyone.

But caught in the crossfire of the "Hendrix/Microsoft" lawsuit was me, the only one who understood the vision and the Prophecy that Jimi was fighting to communicate.

In the summer of 1995, while I was writing this book, a settlement was reached for the lawsuit, and Al Hendrix regained rights to Jimi's music. AYE? Ltd. was closed in Hollywood, and I was unemployed. The people I had worked for, making successes for the Hendrix company with my consulting and writing, received multi million dollar settlements. I didn't even get severance pay.

> *It's very small. It's just like animals fighting among each other – then the big animals will come and take it all away.*   – Jimi[8]

Officials at the Experience Music Project informed me that I was owed nothing for what I'd done to help build their Hendrix collection. I had worked for them believing in good faith that I'd be paid, but they instead cited our "lack of agreement" as reason to deny me compensation. "We are grateful to you for some of the ideas which you have given to us," a Project official wrote to me, "but for us to 'compensate' a party when we did not believe we were contractually obligated could, as a technical matter I'm told, jeopardize our non-profit status . . . The Experience Music Project does not have a paid position for you."[9]

---

8. San Diego Free Press 6/13/69.
9. Letter from the EMP 7/10/95.

A CONVERSATION WITH "BS"

In 1995 I spoke with "BS," who worked for the EMP in Seattle:

MF: The extent to which I've acted as an agent for the acquisition of many of the key core -

BS: Michael, that's old business, that's old news. I'm happy to give you credit for connecting to [the collections].

MF: We're going on three years now that I've done work and . . . there's not even any acknowledgement as to the work that I've done.

BS: You shouldn't expect . . . any acknowledgement that your work is moving this project forward . . . You've done nothing for the museum in particular . . . there was no quid pro quo, no understanding of any obligation of any sort.

MF: It was part of an application for a job. I had applied for a job there in 1992 . . . that's all documented . . . it can be demonstrated in any court of law.

BS: Look, you start talking about suing us, that's a dead end, you want to pull that stuff go ahead . . . There are ten thousand people each year that try to contact Paul Allen directly and you know how many do? Exactly zero . . . The executive director of the museum [Paul's sister] has the project completely under her control, she has had access to everything that you sent in and has not determined that there is any response necessary... We didn't have any agreement or understanding, certainly no signed agreement. . . Your materials are on file, we've destroyed nothing, there's a record of your correspondence.

MF: Including *A Touch Of Hendrix* [my unpublished 1988 manuscript].

BS: Yes.

MF: How that manuscript got there, through Leon Hendrix [Jimi's brother] who solicited that from me for his [publishing] company project. It was not intended to be for the museum.

BS: I never looked at it. No one has looked at it.

MF: How do I know that there hasn't been copies made that are still stashed at the museum? . . . There's a [lot] of knowledge.

BS: Well I can assure you no one else ever even looked at it. I had it at my house for two years, and I finally brought it in here because I needed to make room in my home. No one read it.

MF: It can be scanned in a matter of minutes.

BS: No one did, you can't scan text like that.

MF: [How does BS know what the text is like if "no one looked at it"?]
I find it hard to believe that Mr. Allen would begrudge me payment
for [my work] if it was brought to his attention. Is that his
decision or is it the museum's decision?

BS: It's the museum's decision and I can absolutely with one hundred
percent confidence assure you that that is absolutely consistent
with his feeling on it.

MF: I put that [collections deal] together. That's all documented,
there's no dispute about how [it] got there and what the
circumstances were.

BS: But that's irrelevant. We didn't agree to pay you anything . . .
Michael, believe me, if you mess with Paul Allen you'd be
squashed like a bug, with whatever it takes to squash you. You're
dealing with one of the most powerful people in the world, if you
mess with them, they'll mess with you. If you antagonize those
guys believe me you will never understand how big a mistake you
made. I would recommend that you be very careful with those
guys, because they're not particularly sophisticated, but they're
immensely powerful.

Be Careful Of Those For Whom You Do Good.

Jess Hansen, a friend of the Hendrix family in Seattle, phoned me in early November
1995 and described his visit to the offices of the Experience Music Project. "Somebody
at the museum brought the fact up that you were wanting money for providing phone
numbers to them," said Jess, "they were laughing about that, saying, 'oh, he gave us some
phone numbers and he wants money for this?!' It was a humorous matter to them.
They're brown nosing yuppies down over there, I tell ya."

The EMP could have helped me, and they chose not to. I needed help to publish
Jimi's Prophecy, but insights like those in this book are what dominators routinely seek
to obstruct and crush. As *Rock Prophecy* explains, Jimi predicted an asteroid due to
impact our planet. Had he lived to communicate this, or had I been helped by any of the
people who instead obstructed me, we would have survived. Our world would have been
saved. *Rock Prophecy* is the story of the end of life here, at the hands of Satanic trash,
agents of hate, face of Satan. In a word: *dominators*.

> *. . . you're in for trouble. You give God a tenth of the spices from your garden*
> *. . . Yet you neglect the more important matters of the Law, such as justice,*
> *mercy, and faithfulness . . . You strain out a small fly but swallow a camel!*
> *. . . you're in for trouble. You wash the outside of your cups and dishes,*
> *while inside there is nothing but greed and selfishness . . . You're like tombs*
> *that have been whitewashed. On the outside they are beautiful, but inside*

they are full of bones and filth. That's what you are like. Outside you look good, but inside you are evil and only pretend to be good . . . You build monuments for the prophets and decorate tombs of good people . . . But you prove that you really are the relatives of the ones who killed the prophets . . . you will be held guilty for the murder of every good person . . . people living today will be punished for all of these things! – Jesus (Matthew 23:23-36)

OBSESSED

Once Hendrix came along, everybody said, "Gee, if I turn up my amps, everybody will go berserk." But what they were really going berserk for was Jimi's pioneering musicianship and his art. No matter what kind of inspirational thing happens, somebody will latch on to one of the external details and call it that. It's called mistaking the finger for the moon: you point to the moon and somebody looks at the finger. It's inevitable.

– Peter Tork[10]

I'm not "obsessed" with Hendrix, but for years I was intrigued with the way Jimi's story ties together issues and insights presented in this book. I've sought a way to explain a Prophecy encoded in Jimi's words. But Hendrix is a threat to dominators. The media routinely distorts Jimi's personality and ideas. When I point out details of his Prophecy many people "mistake the finger" for what I'm pointing to and label me "obsessed," as if I'm studying "external details" devoid of meaning.

Men who control media try and persuade the public to ridicule and dismiss anything related to Hendrix. Consumers are trained to sneer at titles like *Hendrix scholar*. I am an expert on Hendrix, but it is not *Jimi* that this book is about. Rather, it is through Jimi that I point to the *Prophecy*.

The media trains people to accept scholars who devote their lives to the study of many different things. From Jane Goodall's study of chimpanzees to Carl Sagan's study of galaxies, such specialists are respected. We accept men who devote their lives to things like market research. We praise physicists whose days are filled with sub-atomic theories. Even people who specialize in details about JFK's assassination are considered legitimate. But to study Hendrix in depth is discouraged, as if Jimi is a subject unworthy of detailed investigation. "He'd dead, let it rest, forget the past," says the detractor.

. . . as you stare into the vacuum of his eyes . . . – Bob Dylan[11]

---

10. Bruce Pollock, *When the Music Mattered - Rock in the 1960s,* chapter: *The Big Rock Candy Mountain,* (1976) p.145.
11. Bob Dylan, "Like A Rolling Stone", Columbia Records 1965.

Objections to study of Hendrix often mask thinly veiled racism. But among those who do study Hendrix, I was the only one to recognize the full scope of Jimi's story. Hendrix is the centerpiece around which revolves the issues described in *Rock Prophecy*. For making the connections presented in this book, I endure persecution from people trained to hate what Hendrix represents. The connections are complex. The concepts remain unexplained outside of these pages. The unfree media will ignore this book, until the time comes when they will have to ridicule it and persuade the trained public that *Rock Prophecy* is a delusion of obsession that everyone must dismiss.

MUSIC VS. MYTHOLOGY

In terms of the written word, what is it about Jimi that is best conveyed on page? What ideas exist outside of the expected fixation on biographical data? What can be said to a disinterested public, besides recounting facts about his life and music, with lots of photos? To the worldwide network of collectors who pursue Hendrix items, recordings are a priority. The collector's world is one of sensory overload: aural and visual. The *sound* of Hendrix music speaks for itself in a universal language. The *sight* of Jimi ranks next in priority among collectors who bid for every shred of photographic, poster, and video evidence. Third in the chain of network concerns comes Jimi's interviews and handwritten remnants: collected pages of his poems, lyrics, and letters. A distant fourth concern to most collectors are the tens of thousands of published articles about Jimi.

Nowhere within the collectors' network is there much interest in conclusions drawn from this huge database. Interpretation of the information is usually dismissed by collectors. Dozens of "Hendrix books" reflect the problem. Unimaginative publishers insist on approaching Jimi from a tedious MENtality: the MAN, the MUSIC, the MEMORABILIA. They're all the same book and they miss the most interesting "M": *meaning.*

Ideas about the significance of the *story* never registers to most collectors. Connecting facts about Hendrix with historic social issues is a concept usually met with a chorus of ridicule and derision. "The MUSIC is what's important, man," is a standard reaction. The more any discussion strays from fixation on the music, or on recitals of facts about Jimi, the more it will be jeered or ignored by the network of collectors.

Because I'm interested in issues and conclusions drawn from Jimi's story, many people accuse me of being obsessed with Hendrix. But I study this subject in a scholarly way. While in college I studied music and used my training to explore Jimi's recordings. I learned to perform Hendrix improvisations with the same attention to detail that I use to play piano recitals of Chopin nocturnes. By the mid-1980s, I was able to recite 70 Hendrix compositions with this method. And through live performances of the music, I met collectors who together form a network of Hendrix researchers.

Throughout the 1980s, I amassed a world-class database of information about Jimi. But the music and the data were always fueling something else: a *story* that connects with ideas, insights, and attitudes about all of the laws and beliefs I'd been trained to obey, and disobey. I began to think of Jimi in another context. Biography and history became mythology. What I learned transformed my opinions and beliefs about many issues, and these ideas are explained in *Rock Prophecy*.

There exists tremendous resistance to portrayals of Hendrix as a centerpiece symbol for our culture. A brutal bondage of the mind forces us to fixate solely on the music as an end in itself. Any attempt to express insight into issues beyond the music is met with vicious derision from men obsessed with appearing non-obsessed about Hendrix. Passion in the attraction of many people to Jimi's music brings unreasonably extreme competition in a race to possess anything exclusive about him, even if it's just an exclusive *idea*. But collectors of memorabilia are usually concerned with just a narrow range of information. And the more well known anyone becomes for presenting *ideas* about Jimi, the more they resent it.

> *After Jimi died I resented people liking Hendrix, because I felt so possessive about him. It was like "You're talking about my mother and you know what color her underwear is."*   – Eric Clapton[12]

> *Michael Fairchild? Oh yeah, he can tell me what color underwear we wore!*
> – Noel Redding (Jimi's bassist)[13]

Men who control media keep the public unaware that a global subculture exists dedicated to exploring Hendrix. The media doesn't cover this culture of millions of people. Rather, the entire Hendrix-curious population is usually written off and dismissed as insignificant.

At the same time, the Hendrix network itself is a madhouse of acrimony, a seething snake-pit tornado of hate. Among the collectors there are more backstabbing divisions than there were under Constantine's schisms. Most of the researchers and writers resent the level of visibility my writings reached in media. It's like politics: those who become influential become targets for competing interests. Teams form and one side tries to put a negative spin on everything the opposing side does. The irony is that I'm one of the few who sought to work with everyone that researched Jimi; my goal was not to compete, but the Hendrix network is so fragmented – with so many people hating so many other people – my visibility made me a scapegoat for their frustrations. The attention that my writings received incited unnatural envy and unfair attacks from other researchers.

No one has yet succeeded in communicating the implications of Jimi's story to the masses who care little for the music of Hendrix. Of the dozens of biographies about Jimi *none* contain a clue about what he was trying to communicate. The vision is explained only in *Rock Prophecy*, and this book is not a "Hendrix book." It is not a biography. Those who denounce me for dwelling on *ideas* surrounding Hendrix insist that his music

---

12. Rolling Stone 12/29/94.
13. WBBR-FM, Ithaca, NY 11/10/90.

is the important thing. But I hear the music as an eternal draw to the *story*, like a parting of the sea, enabling the issues raised in *Rock Prophecy* to surface from beneath suppression.

I became known among moguls who resist any attempt to connect Hendrix with mainstream culture: "Keep this market confined to the guitar greaser crowd of music fixated people. Don't publish or air anything that links Hendrix with universal concerns." The objective of such selective editing censorship is to dismiss all Hendrix-curious people *as a class*.

Rock Prophecy breaks free from fixation on Jimi's music and biography. In the absence of this book, what he communicates remains unknown. Without *Rock Prophecy* no one will see the meaning of what happened.

We know Jimi's music is amazing, his look is engaging, his thoughts are strange – but all of this contributes to a story that is key to comprehending our beliefs. The issues raised give insight into the ways we behave. There are answers, explanations that relieve anxiety and clarify confusion. The *sound* is a separate issue. This book focuses on the *implications* of Jimi, on interpretations of his thoughts and the meaning of his message, the connected perceptions that form a Prophecy, an underlying context within which Hendrix conveys philosophy.

> *Our music is almost all philosophy.* – Jimi[14]

Jimi is the key with which we unravel the past. *Rock Prophecy* presents the extra-musical view: thoughts of Hendrix as symbol and myth. Music is the lure to this separate priority of *story*, a mythology that entertains with concepts, a silent music of the intellect, a morphing of attitudes for which Jimi is figurehead.

TOP FREE – TO DO WHAT I PLEASE

> *I think that too many people these days are hung up because they're covered up . . . The human body is the most beautiful thing, it shouldn't be kept covered.*   – Jimi[15]

Some of the sexual issues described in this book have preoccupied my research for a long time. In 1973, I was expelled from high school for "insubordination" after I trespassed into the men's faculty lounge. Male teachers at Marshall High had covered the lounge walls with erotic pictures of nude women, over which I hung a poster of a dead bird with the words: "Women Are Not Chicks." Then some feminist students circulated leaflets to the PTA describing how the male faculty, aroused after breaks in the porno lounge, returned to class to instruct daughters of PTA members. School officials held me

---

14. Interview with Nancy Carter, L.A. 6/15/69, *Hendrix Speaks*, 1990 Rhino Records.
15. Sun Mirror 2/9/69.

in contempt. They charged me with insubordination and expelled me from school.

A decade later, I resumed my attacks on sexism in a more effective way. The big thing on my mind in the early '80s was figuring out why men, and not women, are free to be bare chested in public on hot summer days. I began a habit of phoning radio opinion programs on stations WHAM and WBBF in my hometown, Rochester, New York. I taunted women for their compliance with laws that forbid females to be top free. I harangued and challenged local residents to do something about it. Thousands of people heard my radio tirades, and they didn't forget.

Two years later I was performing recitals of Hendrix music with my band, EXP, when the "Top Free 7" became national headlines. Seven local women began staging protests by strolling around in public naked from the waist up. A series of busts resulted in more demonstrations and arrests. The debate escalated in our city over the course of several summers, resulting in a celebrated courtroom showdown. The issue was taken all the way to the New York State Supreme Court. Finally in the summer of 1992, the Court issued a landmark ruling which lifted the ban on bare breasts and allowed women the same right as men to be top free!

My radio speeches had planted fruitful seeds. While the Top Free 7 were making headlines, I decided to chronicle what was happening to me in Rochester. I began keeping a diary for the first time. I knew that I could never *prove* that some women in town had listened to my radio harangues about the ban on bare breasts. I could not *prove* that the Top Free 7 protests resulted from my radio speeches heard by thousands of people during 1981 through '83. I could not *suggest* that I was responsible for motivating women to run around bare breasted in the streets, because doing so would fit the pattern of men claiming credit for everything. But I *know* what happened on those radio talk shows. The listeners were *riled*. I *intended* my words to disturb those who think *only* men should be allowed to take off their shirts on Main Street during a heatwave. How obscene it is for women to be forced to stay uncomfortable while men flaunt their freedom in everyone's face. I rubbed it in thick. Was I the catalyst behind the history that was made in New York State?

The diary describes the creation of my 1988 manuscript, *A Touch of Hendrix*, a work which remains the only comprehensive account of the Vietnam backdrop to Jimi's career. With pride we can report that more than 100 publishers of the anti-equality unfree media closed ranks to obstruct the publication of *A Touch of Hendrix*. But against this Goliath I won a little coup: in the 28-page booklets that I wrote for the official Hendrix CD series on MCA Records in 1993-'95, if you look at the credits page at the back of the booklets you'll see that *A Touch of Hendrix* is listed at the top of them all in the bibliography. Those CD booklets have been read by millions of people in many countries, and today *A Touch of Hendrix* is one of the world's most famous unpublished books.

Although that manuscript was blocked from publication, it has nonetheless been available since 1988 for anyone to read at the Library of Congress. Later on in the 1990s my writings about Jimi became well known to a subculture of millions of people, and several ideas in my 1988 manuscript began to appear in books by other writers, despite the fact that *A Touch of Hendrix* is still unpublished!

In 1989, a book by British writer Charles Murray was published. (In 1988, several British publishers requested to see *A Touch of Hendrix*, and I sent the manuscript to England.) My letters of inquiry to publishers for *A Touch of Hendrix* in 1988 describe the story as "Jimi's <u>transit</u> through landmark events of the 1960s . . . a <u>trajectory</u> of <u>intersections</u>."

Crosstown Traffic (!) became the title, eighteen months later, of Charles Murray's book about Jimi's music. This book was published by St. Martins Press. How do we account for the similarities between my book and that of Murray? Here are several sections from my 1988 manuscript juxtaposed with excerpts of Murray's later book:

<u>1988</u> – excerpt of *A Touch of Hendrix* by Michael Fairchild:

> White army officials were sending most of the black soldiers to the frontlines in Vietnam (the frontline was re-named "Soulville" because of its disproportionate numbers of black soldiers) to kill another non-white race . . . "Machine Gun" [Hendrix song] was testament to a rage that gave birth to the Black Panthers . . . Harlem was a cauldron of the sentiments that inspired "Machine Gun." Jimi intuitively channeled these feelings back into the ghetto . . . The racist draft system was a form of genocide against minority males. One fifth of U.S. combat troops in Vietnam were black. A staggering 50 percent of frontline infantry in Soulville was comprised of drafted blacks . . . Soldiers who fought and died in Vietnam were "had" in the worst way; fired up with slick, sentimental propaganda, they were sent off to battle for the salaries of business executives and crony politicians.[16]

<u>1989</u> – excerpt of *Crosstown Traffic* by Charles Murray:

> Hendrix knew the score as far as the position of the black GI was concerned; in 'Nam they represented 2 per cent of the officers and were assigned 28 per cent of the combat missions. When he dedicated "Machine Gun" to "all the soldiers fighting in Vietnam," he was neither jiving his audience nor indulging in cheap irony. Hendrix knew exactly who was paying the price of the politicians' games.[17]

<u>1988</u> – excerpt of *A Touch of Hendrix* by Michael Fairchild:

---

16. *A Touch of Hendrix*, unpublished manuscript, (1988), pp.52, 181, 417.
17. *Crosstown Traffic*, (New York: St. Martin's Press, 1989), p.23.

Americans . . . had no cause to interpret "freedom" as a euphemism.
For many Americans the meaning of freedom is the ability to maintain
wealth without interference. "Freedom" becomes license to take
advantage of others for one's own self interests, without requirement to
share with less lucky people. This "freedom" allows discrimination
against anyone who is unsuited to the priorities of the ruling classes.
Under capitalism, "freedom" has meant manipulated information in the
interests of profiteers. The interests of mankind and the environment
become non-priority. The establishment's "freedom" is the *freedom to*
exploit . . . people are discriminated against and forced into poverty by
"freedom" to withhold employment from certain groups . . . capitalists
wage war for the *freedom to* profit at the expense of others . . . Those
who prospered from the Vietnam war had to portray North Vietnam's
struggle for sovereignty and equality as a threat to "freedom." The real
freedom that the profiteers cared about was the *freedom to* concentrate
wealth among a privileged few at the expense of an impoverished
majority . . . Malcolm Tent [main character] championed freedom of
expression . . . he demanded *freedom from* inequality.[18]

<u>1989</u> – excerpt of *Crosstown Traffic* by Charles Murray:

"Freedom" is still treasured, but it is interpreted almost exclusively in
terms of freedom *to* as opposed to freedom *from*. P.J. O'Rourke, for
example, is perhaps the most articulate and vociferous spokesman for
the oldest of all Western freedoms: that of the well-off white male to do
just about anything he wants, anywhere in the world. The notion of
freedom from (poverty, racism, illness, pollution, homelessness,
unemployment, war) is once again suspect; after all, no one except a
fool or a troublemaker would question the essential rightness of a social
system under which they have personally profited. At their most
inspired, the political and theoretical branches of hippie transcended
the cliches of both left and right-wing political discourse by demanding
both freedom *from* and freedom *to*, but once the economic pressure
was on, the two freedoms proved distinctly unequal.[19]

The above excerpts of *Crosstown Traffic* come from Chapter 1 in that book, twenty
pages titled "The We Decade." How incongruous this chapter is with the rest of Murray's
book. It chronicles the Hendrix trajectory through historical intersections of the 1960s,

---

18. *A Touch of Hendrix*, unpublished manuscript, (1988), pp.232, 259, 196-7, 208.
19. *Crosstown Traffic*, p.26.

but reads like a section tacked onto the book as an afterthought, as if a publisher or editor decided to stick this up front, it'll *seem like* the *first* thing written for the book. What a *coincidence* that "The We Decade" reads like a condensed outline of *A Touch of Hendrix*.

Editors and publishers who saw *A Touch of Hendrix* in 1988 didn't forget what they'd run across.

I intended to write *Rock Prophecy* after I completed *A Touch of Hendrix* in 1988. On page 351 of *A Touch of Hendrix* I wrote: "There is so much more about Jimi [besides] the music . . . historical intersections of his activities with technology, LSD and cultural-political upheavals, and an as yet unmentioned prophecy." But then on January 9, 1989 Alan Douglas requested to see *A Touch of Hendrix*. I sent the manuscript to Are You Experienced? Ltd. in Hollywood and soon afterwards I was hired to work as a writer and consultant for the official Hendrix company.

One of the first things I did was to contact Jimi's brother, Leon. Leon was in the process of setting up a publishing group. I told him about my manuscript and in April 1989 I got a letter from Leon in which he wrote, "*A Touch of Hendrix* has piqued our curiosity and enthusiasm as we are considering the future production of such materials . . . I've requested reviewing the synopsis and full blown version . . . Do dash off the synopsis and manuscript . . . We will contact you soon."

So I sent *A Touch of Hendrix* to Leon and received a letter back from him in which he wrote, "I like the manuscript you sent . . . You will receive our International Newsletter Magazine for one year."

In autumn of that year, Leon's organization published three issues of their magazine called *Axis*, and then the organization folded. I lost touch with Leon in 1990, but sometime during that year he gave the copy of *A Touch Of Hendrix* that I'd sent him to Jess Hansen, a friend of the Hendrix family in Seattle.

By New Year 1990, I had completed five major assignments for the Hendrix company. I told Alan Douglas that I wanted to produce a project of my own. Alan said to me, "Propose a project that you can do and we will help you produce it." What I had in mind was a University Exhibition and lecture program in which I could present the concepts of *A Touch of Hendrix* and *Rock Prophecy* in a multi-media setting. On February 14, 1990, I sent my written proposal to Alan. He was impressed. He told me he liked the idea. "I like it a lot," he said.

During the spring and summer of 1990, I wrote outlines for the university tour project. In the first draft, I focused on musical concepts, with a few ideas from *A Touch of Hendrix* worked into the program. But I didn't reveal anything about *Rock Prophecy* yet. I was waiting to strike a deal for my proposal. I traveled to Los Angeles and met Alan on July 1, 1990. During lunch he said he was considering a "more well known name" than me to produce my project. But he had told me in February to "propose a project that you can do and we will help you produce it."

As we drove back to the office that day, I told Alan that I am the only person who is aware of Jimi's Prophecy. Alan asked me what the Prophecy is and I said, "I won't speak it to anyone. I'll write it out when the time is right." He smiled and changed the subject. For more than five years after that we never discussed the Prophecy again until after I'd written the first draft of this book and copyrighted it in spring 1995.

From 1989 through 1995, I was in a non-stop blur of deadlines for Hendrix projects. In my diary, I recorded hourly increments of everything that happened along the way as my writings for 14 official Hendrix CDs, several video box covers, and many magazine cover stories, were brought before an international audience of millions of people.

Meanwhile, in September 1991, Alan took my proposal for the exhibition tour to England and hired Adrian Boot of Exhibit-A to produce the project. I was outraged. I alone understood Jimi's Prophecy and now the vehicle I had conceived to present it was being hijacked away from me. Neil Storey was hired as chief editor on the Exhibition project. But Neil had a limited working knowledge about Jimi's life. His job was to work on captions for the various exhibits. I was assigned as a consultant for this work. But throughout those years, I kept dwelling on a way to present the Prophecy. I wrote a letter to Alan and warned him that "time is running out."

> *Whatever is hidden will be made manifest, whatever is covered up will be uncovered.*   — Jesus (Thomas:6)

Having my Exhibition project hijacked away from me was not the only reason why I kept silent about the Prophecy. By 1991, a pattern had set in for a story I call *Credit Theft – Discontents of a Hendrix Expert*. The incidents are too numerous to list in this book, but I must mention the autobiography of Jimi, a book titled *Room Full of Mirrors*.

JIMI'S AUTOBIOGRAPHY

In October 1989, Alan asked me to compile all known Hendrix quotes from all sources in my archives and begin to edit these into categories such as "childhood," "school," "family," "army," "songs," etc. The quotes were to form the basis of Jimi's life story told in his own words. In November, we negotiated an agreement for my work. My main concerns were for a percentage of the book profits and credit for my contributions. On Nov. 13, 1989, I spoke with Alan and then wrote in my diary, "He said I'd get a percentage and credits on the book and film – with a forward by me."

All of my editing work for Jimi's autobiography were submitted in written letters. The documents reveal that I contributed more than 1000 major edit ideas to the construction of Jimi's autobiography. A decade after work began on *Room Full of Mirrors*, the book remains unpublished, and half of my fee remains unpaid. I suspect that the present Hendrix production company will never release Jimi's autobiography, probably because my contract for work on that book entitles me to payment upon its publication.

The hatred of Alan Douglas by so many people in the Hendrix network was so unfairly transferred on to me. No one knew that I was the one who was fighting Alan behind the scenes, trying to dissuade him from making decisions that caused so many people to criticize the Hendrix company he ran. I warned Alan of the consequences of his actions, this was my job, and I kept detailed notes throughout the years. What I was witness to made me ill. But it was a matter of keeping silent or lose my job, and I had to keep that job to reach the millions of people who read my work. Someday, I figured, somehow I'd find a way to bring *Rock Prophecy* to the attention of my readers.

My other manuscript, *A Touch of Hendrix*, ended up in Paul Allen's museum without my knowledge or permission. Jimi's brother had given it to Jess Hansen and Jess gave it to Paul Allen's Hendrix Museum, the Experience Music Project. The manuscript was with the museum for a couple of years before I learned of it. When I informed the EMP that they were in possession of my work without my consent they returned it to me and said that no one there had copied or transferred the text. But, as we'll see later in this book, the museum has a history of *coincidence* with regards to ideas that I've written.

THE DEITY LEADS ME

> . . . *the seeker is beginning to find the seer, beginning to find that the one he's looking for is the one that is doing the looking, and as one encounters this aspect of oneself . . . the seeker begins to experience meaningful coincidence and synchronicity, begins to notice that intention spontaneously orchestrates space-time events in order to bring about the outcome that was intended . . . the seeker is beginning to understand, literally, the mechanics of creation . . . that brings about the world of the magical and the miraculous . . . the seer is the timeless factor in the midst of time bound experience, all experience is time bound: it has a beginning, a middle and an ending. The seer is ever the same, the same seer in the midst of different experiences. To carry the consciousness of the seer is to carry the consciousness of eternity in the field of time, it is to carry the consciousness of infinity in the field of matter and energy . . . this experience of the seer gives birth also to a transformation of magical thinking, meaningful coincidence, synchronicity . . . thinking now acquires this magical quality that whatever you intend begins to happen. When that accelerates, that process is part of the experience of what is called cosmic consciousness, because your awareness is local and non-local at the same time: the scenery, which is local, and the seer, which is unbounded, free, immortal, eternal, timeless, now here, and nowhere at the same time. Now the miracles begin to come, you begin to experience the miraculous, which is the acceleration of meaningful coincidences, it's the acceleration . . . of cosmic consciousness, which is the simultaneity of spirit, form, matter, information, energy, local,*

> *non-local, simultaneous . . . This is real power because it magnetizes things*
> *– events, people, circumstances – around your intention. It happens with the*
> *birth of the seer.*   – Deepak Chopra[20]

THESE EVENTS SET THE STAGE FOR ROCK PROPHECY

There have been stories about asteroids ever since Jules Verne wrote *Off On a Comet* in 1877. But Hollywood films about asteroids have been received by the public with little enthusiasm: *When Worlds Collide* (1951), *The Day the Sky Exploded* (1958), *On the Comet* (1970), *A Fire In the Sky* (1978), *Meteor* (1979), and *Night of the Comet* (1984). Audiences have always regarded asteroid stories as science fiction. Even the widely publicized impacts of comet fragments on Jupiter in July 1994 were a passing attraction. The media dropped the story by August. No one seemed interested in dwelling on rocks from outer space.

Then, 15 months after the 1994 asteroid impacts on Jupiter, everything changed. It was as if the men who control mass media had issued an edict: "Do up the asteroid story – Big Time!" Starting in autumn 1995, and throughout 1996, a rising tide of reports about rocks in space flooded the world's media. Growing hysteria climaxed in February 1997 when TV screens were overloaded with scenes of NBC's *ASTEROID* miniseries. And then another year of overblown reports fueled the 1998 Hollywood blockbusters *Deep Impact* and *Armageddon*.

But prior to 1995 the public was exposed only slightly to stories about possible asteroid disasters on Earth. Our mass media didn't really pick up this story in earnest until autumn 1995. It wasn't until well *after* the first draft of my *Rock Prophecy* manuscript arrived at the Library of Congress copyright office in June 1995 that the media began to churn out endless reports about asteroids. What was the catalyst that suddenly inspired corporate executives and financiers to decree a media field day on asteroid stories? The number of news reports started to skyrocket just a few months after *Rock Prophecy* arrived at the LOC in Washington D.C. Is it possible that the manuscript for this book was read by consultants for media executives? Did they learn what my research reveals and decide to warn the public about asteroids in a way that *excludes* the Hendrix connection? There are reasons why media moguls would monitor my unpublished writings at the Library of Congress. The lawsuit filed by Jimi's father against the Hendrix production company where I worked was funded by money from Microsoft's Paul Allen. Why wouldn't his legal team read my stories? I was the mouthpiece for the company they were suing.

The chronology below traces escalating incidents of asteroid reports in mass media during four years following the copyright of this book. When *Rock Prophecy* is read from beginning to end, come back to the chronology listed below. Read through the succession of major media reports and decide for yourself whether or not my

20. Deepak Chopra, *The Way of the Wizard*, PBS 12/95.

unpublished manuscript had an effect on wealthy behind-the-scenes string-pullers who set the agenda of issues covered by mass media.

Below I've listed reports mainly from major mass media, but for each of these entries, hundreds of other asteroid stories appeared in local newspapers, magazines, radio, and TV outlets. In other words, the following chronology is just the tip of the iceberg. (Anyone who can add asteroid reports to this list please contact First Century Press.)

TIMELINE
A FOUR-YEAR CHRONOLOGY

April 11, 1995: MCA Records' worldwide release of the Jimi Hendrix *Voodoo Soup* CD includes my 24-page booklet text about Jimi's vision of an explosion on the planet Jupiter. The *Voodoo Soup* booklet also pin-points the birth of Hendrix happening simultaneously with the Allies' 1942 breakthrough in deciphering the Nazi's "Ultra Secret" Enigma machine code. The tide of war then turned in favor of the Allies.

Also on April 11, 1995, the story of *Rock Prophecy* was copied onto disk and sealed in a dated envelope in my attorney's office. *Rock Prophecy* reveals for the first time Jimi's hidden prediction of an asteroid aimed to collide with Earth.

April 12, 1995: A giant triple rainbow over my home is the focus of local media. This rainbow is like an entrance gate into the *Rock Prophecy* period, which was kicked off by the events of yesterday described above. When the second draft of *Rock Prophecy* was completed in August 1997, the giant triple rainbow re-appeared over my home, like an exit gate leading out of the period that produced this book. These rainbows remind me of a quote I once gave to the local newspaper:

> *"I'm like Noah, and the flood is coming, and everyone is stoning me!"*
> – *Democrat & Chronicle*, Rochester, NY – May 5, 1994

June 1995: The Hendrix magazine named *Straight Ahead* publishes my article titled *GrinchRich – the D.C. Witch-hunt*. The article reports how a publishing house contacted me after discovering my 1988 manuscript, *A Touch of Hendrix*, at the Library of Congress, where the text is registered and stored for copyright protection. *GrinchRich – the D.C. Witch-hunt* explains why my unpublished stories on file at the LOC are "monitored." Was my 1988 manuscript, *A Touch of Hendrix*, studied by consultants for the men who control media? *A Touch of Hendrix* describes Jimi as a key figure in the battle to defeat the "elite" who oppose equality. In reaction to my 1988 manuscript, did consultants advise Republicans to co-opt the term "elitist" and start labeling liberal Democrats as the "elite"? In May 1992, Dan Quayle kicked off a media campaign designed to assign the term "cultural elite" to "liberals" who seek equality among people.

In *GrinchRich – the D.C. Witch-hunt,* I assert that all information about Jimi that arrives at the Library of Congress is scrutinized by men who realize a need for controlling the public's perception of Hendrix. Think tanks funded by men who control media devise strategies to shape public opinion about many issues. My *GrinchRich* article was written at the height of the Hendrix lawsuit, funded by Paul Allen. Why wouldn't investigators for that case examine my writings available at the LOC? I was the writer for the company they were fighting, and it's *legal* for anyone to read unpublished manuscripts filed at the LOC.

Was my 1988 manuscript, *A Touch of Hendrix,* studied by media think tanks? That text defines "elitists" as people who believe some of us *deserve* more money than others.

TERMS/USAGE

*"Elitist" means someone who **believes in** economic inequality.*

*"Dominator" means someone who **acts out** these beliefs by taking, or trying to take, for themselves or others, more money or valuables than anyone should have, more than anyone deserves. Such acts are crimes against Creation.*

Did Republicans jump to reverse the tables and label their enemies "the elite" after they saw how that term is used in *A Touch of Hendrix?* In *reaction* to my 1988 manuscript, did Republican think tanks formulate a policy to start calling "elitist" any Democrat who tries to use government to promote equality?

Since 1992, Republicans have repeatedly portrayed their opponents as the "cultural elite." Then, in 1995, when my new manuscript *Rock Prophecy* was sent to the Library of Congress for copyright registration, was it, like my 1988 book, "monitored" by the men who control media? In the months *after Rock Prophecy* arrived in Washington D.C. (as described ahead in this Timeline), the media began a massive campaign to influence public opinion about asteroids. Did the men who control media learn about *Rock Prophecy* and then order their writers and producers to churn out asteroid stories?

Teams of think-tank publicists figure out ways to use media to react to any effect that publication of the *real* story surrounding Hendrix might stir. The issues and connections surrounding Hendrix reveal how a wealthy class of anti-equality men have arranged a situation in which today's society is unable to raise a defense in time to stop the Rock that Jimi foresaw hurtling towards Earth. *Rock Prophecy* describes this. When my manuscript arrived at the Library of Congress, were plans implemented to deluge the public with an avalanche of asteroid reports from mass media?

Workers at the Library of Congress who object to what goes on there are silenced. They are often ordered to undergo Forced Psychiatric Testing. "You have to tell them everything about yourself, personal things about yourself and your family," said an LOC worker named "Lois" who was interviewed by CBS News "It goes on for hours, and then they tell you to come back for more. It's very degrading. I have been rendered unemployed. I've lost my home."[21]

For many decades, Forced Psychiatric Testing was a legal way to harass whistle blowers in government agencies. In 1996, CBS News reported that recently "Congress banned Forced Tests inside the government and later imposed tight restrictions on their use in the private sector. Businesses can still use them but only in extremely rare cases. But incredibly, Congress did not apply all of these restrictions to itself or its Library."[22]

"A number of people have had their lives destroyed by this," said David Moore, a union steward who witnessed Forced Psychiatric Testing done to LOC workers after they reported wrong doing in the Library. "It was a weapon and it was used the same as psychiatry was used in the former Soviet Union: designed to harass and intimidate and silence an employee."[23]

Donald Soulken, a psychiatric social worker who investigated Forced Testing, concludes, "This is a technique in which you can go inside of a person's head and pull out information that can be used against them. If it gets into your file and you can't get it expunged, you're finished."[24]

Another employee who witnessed foul play at the LOC was ordered to undergo Forced Psychiatric Testing: "I was shocked," he told CBS, "they turn you inside out. I use the word *rape* – I just felt like I was raped because they take you from your childhood through your personal life through anything that they can think of . . . They've destroyed a lot of peoples' lives."[25]

The Library of Congress acknowledges that in just the past few years 37 workers have undergone Forced Psychiatric Testing. Unofficial sources claim that the "tests" are much more widespread. What did these workers witness that made them targets for this *legal* harassment from the government? As growing numbers of employees leaked their stories to the free press, the LOC was forced to abandon Forced Psychiatric Testing, but why was this practice outlawed for most private businesses and government agencies *except* for the Library of Congress? Why did the ruling class retain the tactic of forced mental harassment specifically for the LOC? Why is it vital to control the minds of people who work at the LOC? What goes on there?

The Library of Congress houses the copyrighted works and writings of the nation's artists and thinkers. The public has access to works registered and kept at the LOC. My copyrighted manuscripts, although unpublished, are available for people to see at the LOC, all anyone has to do is pay a fee and sit at a desk and read. The public is not allowed to remove works from the building, but various forms of note taking are permitted.

Imagine workers at the LOC learning that my writings, or anyone else's, are being monitored by paid consultants who study unpublished manuscripts. What if LOC employees see ideas from certain stories "stolen" from the Library, transformed into a news story or film release, and then introduced to the public?

---

21. CBS Evening News 7/6/96.
22. Ibid.
23. Ibid.
24. Ibid.
25. Ibid.

What if a worker learns that the Library is being used as a front for easy access to any new idea or story sent there for copyright protection? Do agents for media moguls assess "hot" topics coming into the LOC and then re-package the concepts for presentation by their own companies? Moguls decide when and how certain issues are promoted and who gets credit for them. They also determine how to divert, co-opt, or redefine any topic that threatens the interests of the ruling class (for a quick introduction into how this is done, there are two essential video documentaries to get hold of: *Manufacturing Consent*, a 1992 film about Noam Chomsky, available at many libraries, and *Free Speech for Sale*, a 1999 film with Bill Moyers, available from Public Affairs Television, Inc., PO Box 2284, S. Burlington, VT 05407).

Did workers at the LOC see how the media co-opted and whitewashed the asteroid prediction that *Rock Prophecy* is based on? Were these workers forced to undergo Psychiatric Testing? Were their memories altered? Did their protests result in the CBS News investigation of Forced Psychiatric Testing?

Just months after my *Rock Prophecy* manuscript arrived at the LOC in June 1995, a media blitz of reports and stories about asteroids began bombarding the public.

June 5, 1995: The hardcopy manuscript of *Rock Prophecy* is registered for copyright at the Library of Congress in Washington, D.C. June 5 is also the 10,495th anniversary of the Carolina Meteorite impact on Earth, as calculated by the Mayan calendar, and rediscovered by Otto Muck.[26]

After *Rock Prophecy* arrived at the Library of Congress on June 5, it was as if an edict was decreed by the men who control media: "Flood the airwaves with asteroid stories! Over-expose this issue through all manner of communications!" Every form of media under mogul control seemed ordered to co-opt the central issue of Jimi's prediction.

Two things must be kept in mind:

   1) by the mid 1990s my readership exceeded 6 million people due to my published writings about Hendrix, and

   2) any media consultants, the "moles of the moguls," who saw my unpublished writings at the LOC learned how Hendrix is the central connection which most threatens dominators.

When my *Rock Prophecy* manuscript arrived at the LOC in June 1995, did the men who control media approve plans to redefine the whole issue of asteroids for the public? It was as if there was a deliberate attempt to make the mass audience tired of hearing about asteroids, an attempt to make us unreceptive to what *Rock Prophecy* reveals.

---

26. Otto Muck, *The Secret of Atlantis*, (New York: Times Books, 1978), p.252.

BEHOLD THE WAVE
A MEDIA BLITZ ASTEROID CRAZE INSTIGATED BY *ROCK PROPHECY*

Does the chronology of events listed below result from the arrival of my manuscript at the LOC in June 1995?:

<u>July 10, 1995</u>: Microsoft billionaire Paul Allen's Experience Music Project in Seattle (aka the Jimi Hendrix Museum) declines to compensate me for help I contributed to the project. A settlement had just been reached in the lawsuit filed by the Hendrix family against their Hollywood production company. The lawsuit was financed by a loan from Paul Allen. Settlement of this case resulted in closing the Hendrix production company that had employed me for seven years. On July 10, I learned that I could expect no help from Paul Allen, despite my contributions to his Hendrix museum in Seattle.

<u>August 1995</u>: *UniVibes*, the International Hendrix magazine, reports: "Michael Fairchild's *Rock Prophecy: Sex and Jimi Hendrix In World Religions* is about to be published by First Century Press."

<u>August 1995</u>: *Straight Ahead*, International Hendrix magazine, reports: "First Century Press will publish *Rock Prophecy* by Michael Fairchild."

<u>September 1995</u>: *Voodoo Child*, the Hendrix newsletter, reports: "Michael Fairchild's *Rock Prophecy: Sex and Jimi Hendrix In World Religions* will be released by First Century Press."

<u>September 18, 1995</u>: On the 25th anniversary of Jimi's death, Monika Dannemann's book, *The Inner World of Jimi Hendrix*, is published by St. Martins Press, and for the first time one of Jimi's friends reveals that he spoke about the destruction of Atlantis by a comet. Five and a half months before this book came out, I had corresponded with St. Martin's Press about "Jimi's Prophecy."

<u>October 29, 1995</u>: The New York Times reports Paul Allen's $500 million investment in DreamWorks Pictures, controlling 18% of the new movie studio. What type of films will Mr. Allen approve for production in the years ahead?

> *The way we're going to "take" [rivals] is by studying them, know what they know, do what they do, watch them, look for every angle, stay on their shoulders, clone them, take every one of **their** good ideas and make it one of **our** good ideas.* — Steve Ballmer, Microsoft Vice President – 1995[27]

---

27. PBS News Hour 4/14/97, rebroadcast of a 1995 speech by Steve Ballmer.

<u>October 31, 1995</u>: The PBS series *NOVA* airs a new episode titled *Doomsday Asteroid*. This program marks the start of a mass media blitz. For the next four years the public is overexposed to asteroid stories, while I search for a way to publish *Rock Prophecy*.

<u>November 1995</u>: *Enigma* by Robert Harris becomes a best seller in England. The story is about how the Allies turned the tide of war in their favor by deciphering the Nazi's "Ultra Secret" Enigma machine code. *Rock Prophecy* describes how the code was broken the moment Hendrix was born, and proclaims the start of the first century on November 27 (1942 Common Era) with the birth of Jimi and the simultaneous Enigma breakthrough, which meant a means of defeating the Nazis, the ultimate dominators. The Nazis climaxed 5000 years of "retarded history" which leaves Earth defenseless against asteroids. Modern years are counted, by much of the world, in relation to the birth of Christ. Historians used to designate time periods as "B.C." (Before Christ), or "A.D." (Ano Domino, Latin for Year of Our Lord). Modern scholars, however, have re-titled these periods as "C.E." (Common Era), which follows the birth of Jesus, and "B.C.E." (Before the Common Era). But it is important to realize that the Common Era is a period limited to just 1,942 years. In November of that one thousand nine hundred and forty-second year, our liberation from dominators began with Jimi's birth, a day from which we now count in Hendrix Correct terms: we are *not* in the "twenty-first" century, rather, we are in the *first* century of the Hendrix Millennium – the *Un*common Era. *Rock Prophecy* explains why this numerical shift is a critical necessity.

<u>December 12, 1995</u>: NBC News reports the approach of Hale-Bopp comet towards the Sun, due to pass Earth in spring 1997. That the media is giving this comet so much publicity 18 months in advance of its arrival indicates a policy shift for 1996: the men who control media seem determined to shove rocks from space down everyone's throat.

<u>January 30, 1996</u>: Comet Hyakutake is discovered by a Japanese astronomer. The comet's approach becomes a strangely over-reported mass media event.

<u>February 13, 1996</u>: The *Weekly World News* tabloid cover story reads: "Hubble Finds Doomsday Comet and It's Speeding Toward Earth!" The feature article describes how a space rock will "smash Earth into pieces, sending fragments reeling into the icy, airless vastness of space, killing us all."

<u>February 15, 1996</u>: The A&E cable TV channel airs an episode of *Ancient Mysteries* titled *Atlantis: Lost Civilization* in which the continent is destroyed by a comet. This is the first time that any television program has linked the destruction of Atlantis with a rock from outer space.

<u>March 21, 1996</u>: Republican presidential candidate Bob Dole unexpectedly proposes resurrection of "Star Wars," the laser satellite systems plan. In 1983 President Reagan proposed a program called the Strategic Defense Initiative, a space-based defense system

designed to protect the United States from attack by incoming missiles. Reagan's SDI plans included satellites equipped with orbiting lasers capable of destroying rockets launched at the U.S., but the plan was shelved in the 1980s. "We talk about Star Wars as if all we have to do is decide to go and we go," protested Senator John Glen, "but the physics haven't been invented yet to do Star Wars."[28]

In March 1996, less than a year after *Rock Prophecy* was sent to the Library of Congress, Bob Dole kicked off his campaign for the presidency by unveiling the "Defend America Act." Dole said, "When I ask most people what would you have the President do if there was an incoming ballistic missile? they say 'Shoot it down!' But we can't . . . If North Korea would launch a single missile at the United States, we could do nothing to stop its deadly flight toward an American city."[29]

In a post Cold War era, when the U.S. military is unchallenged in the world, Dole's fear of a *missile* attack didn't seem like an urgent concern to most people. After Dole made his announcement CBS News reported, "The CIA told Congress in February [1996] that a threat from rogue missiles is at least 15 years away . . . John Steinbruner [Brookings Institute defense expert] argues that 'the most realistic threat won't come from enemy missiles anyway.'"[30]

"Enemy missiles" are not the real concern of D.C. policy makers. Asteroids are. But any prediction of an asteroid disaster would be political suicide. A politician who makes the prediction is labeled "lunatic." Anti-asteroid technology is instead developed under the guise of something the public can approve of, like an "anti-missile" system. In 1996, the PBS News Hour reported that "former CIA Director R. James Woolsey called [missile attack] the most significant threat that faces us . . . The [Star Wars] system would expand over time to create a layered defense against larger and more sophisticated ballistic missile threats as they emerge. The Congressional Budget Office says that would bring the cost to between $31 and $60 billion. Those recent estimates gave some Republican deficit hawks sticker shock, forcing their defense minded colleagues to rework the plan."[31]

The need for laser satellites is a hard sell to voters. To suggest that the weapons be built because of asteroids will require evidence of a threat. Political leaders can't urge the public to support the expense of anti-asteroid technology unless an Earth-crossing rock has already been sighted. But by the time one is spotted, it will be too late to stop it.

<u>March 26, 1996</u>: Hyakutake comet makes its closest approach to Earth as ABC News concludes with a report about our unpreparedness for fending off a rock aimed at our planet. Astronomer Neil Tyson of the Hayden Planetarium sums up, "I know of no way that we can stop it."

28. PBS News Hour 6/4/96.
29. Bob Dole speech 3/21/95, broadcast on CBS Evening News 5/25/96.
30. CBS Evening News 5/25/96.
31. News Hour with Jim Lehrer, PBS 6/4/96.

Monika Dannemann commits suicide on Good Friday. Descriptions about Jimi and the comet that were inserted into her book from St. Martins Press, released five and a half months after I wrote to St. Martins about "Jimi's Prophecy," are explained in *Rock Prophecy*. Monika's death leaves unanswered the question of how paragraphs about Hendrix and the comet came to be added to her book.

April 8, 1996: Jesus is featured simultaneously on the magazine covers of *Time*, *Newsweek*, and *U.S. News & World Report*. The establishMENt uses its media to persuade the public that the appeal of Jesus is "life after death," rather than *equality for all* on Earth.

April 26, 1996: NBC Nightly News reports that scientists are monitoring the trajectory of a giant asteroid which is on a path to collide with Earth, but not for a million years.

April-May 1996: More than two hundred members of the anti-equality unfree elitist media close ranks to obstruct publication of *Rock Prophecy*. Even though several million people are familiar with my published stories, media gatekeepers weed out all calls for equality between people, which happens to be a subject of this book.

During 1996 and 1997, as the asteroid issue ignited by *Rock Prophecy* becomes overexposed throughout world media, hundreds of editors and publishers who obstructed publication of my book are all witness to the increase of interest in asteroids. Many editors and publishers remain *aware* that *Rock Prophecy* is the original prediction, they knew in the spring of 1996 that the manuscript was circulating, yet all remained silent. None will lift a finger for any story about equality.

> *There's the real mass media, the kinds that are aimed at the guys who get a six pack, the purpose of those media is just to dull people's minds. For 80% [of the public] the main thing for them is to **divert** them, to get them to watch national football and to worry about the motherless child with six heads, or whatever you pick up at the supermarket stands, or look at astrology, or get involved in fundamentalist stuff, or something – just **get them away from things that matter**, and for that it's important to reduce their capacity to think. . . Those who occupy managerial positions in the media, or gain status within them as commentators, belong to. . . **privileged elites**, and might be expected to share the perceptions, aspirations, and attitudes of their associates, **reflecting their own class interests** as well. Journalists entering the system are **unlikely to make their way unless they conform** to these ideological pressures, generally by **internalizing the values**. It is not easy to say one thing and believe another – and **those who fail to conform will tend to be weeded out by familiar mechanisms**.* — Noam Chomsky[32]

---

32. Noam Chomsky, *Necessary Illusions – Thought Control in Democratic Societies*, (South End Press, 1989), p.8, *Manufacturing Consent*, 1992, aired on PBS 9/95.

May 1, 1996: The PBS News Hour reports the discovery of an unknown manuscript by Louisa May Alcott. Jim Lehrer announces that the story will be published "so that people won't have to go to the Library of Congress to read it." Eleven months later the story is produced into a CBS television movie called *The Inheritance*. Manuscripts registered and stored at the Library of Congress, including *Rock Prophecy*, are available for *anyone* to read, including consultants for mass media.

Also on May 1st, CBS airs a prime time TV special titled *Mysteries of the Millennium*. A description in *TV Guide* reports that this is a show "examining visions of the future, from the prophetic predictions of Nostradamus to the psychic visions of American medium Edgar Cayce, as well as scientific forecasts of earthquakes." But instead of these topics, when the special came on TV at 8 p.m., it was all about an asteroid on course to collide with Earth! It's as if at the last minute the original show was replaced by another program. What appeared on TV is a *Mysteries of the Millennium* show that covers the following:

　　　1) 1994 comet impact on Jupiter
　　　2) Atlantis
　　　3) Maya Indian beliefs
　　　4) dinosaur extinction
　　　5) antichrist
　　　6) cellular metamorphosis
　　　7) Victor Clube
　　　8) lunar craters
　　　9) comments from Deepak Chopra

This CBS program reads like a blueprint for *Rock Prophecy*, minus the Hendrix connections (which, if used, would violate my copyright). There are two possibilities: 1) my writings are being monitored at the Library of Congress, or 2) coincidences beyond probability are occurring.

Mysteries of the Millennium reports that the "apocalypse prophecy" calls for the appearance of the antichrist who is present in the world (and the same age as me). Is the media setting the stage to label *Rock Prophecy* as work of the antichrist? Might a wealthy Hendrix enthusiast monitor the Library of Congress for unpublished manuscripts about Jimi and fashion programs for the media based on the contents?

May 19, 1996: Asteroid JA-1 passes within 279,000 miles of Earth. This is a near miss. The rock is a third of a mile in diameter. Scientist claim that a rock only a mile wide would wipe out our civilization. JA-1 was spotted by Arizona astronomer Tim Spahr just four days before it passed. "If it hit Earth it sure would mess things up," said Spahr.[33]

---

33. Associated Press 5/19/96.

"A fairly sizeable asteroid went across the sky in less than five days," reported an official at the Jet Propulsion Laboratory. "We would not have had time to do anything that would have diverted this object."[34]

<u>June 8, 1996</u>: NBC-TV, on the verge of announcing its partnership with Paul Allen's Microsoft to launch the cable TV network MSNBC, airs *Prophecies IV – The Final Visions.* This program reports a future "shift of the Earth's axis, a shift that will trigger a gravitational change." A psychic explains that "in the Bible, *Revelation* chapter eight, it says that something like a burning meteor hits the Earth and destroys a third of all mankind." Another psychic on the show foresees "a significant drop in population between now and the 22nd century." A professor is interviewed and explains that the drop may be caused by "an asteroid or another extra-planetary body coming into contact with the Earth, and that would cause weather and climate change, like a pole shift."[35]

In *The Final Visions,* an Indian seer predicts that near Seattle "Mount Rainier will erupt." Similarities with *Rock Prophecy* continue as the program explores beliefs of the Maya Indians.

The Final Visions is a program that makes any prediction about the future seem ridiculous, as if the producers were intent on persuading the audience that prophecy stories are of interest only to fools. A mystic featured in the show compares our modern world with the fall of Mayan civilization, of which he claims: "Their dogs talked to them, their turkeys talked to them and lectured them about what they'd been failing to do . . . If you've ever worried about all the things you've got plugged-in in your house . . . imagine all of them getting a mind of their own and deciding they don't like you. In the previous [Maya] disaster it was just tortilla griddles on the fire, now it will be your waffle iron that will fly in your face; you're putting stuff in your food processor and the next thing you know it's processing you . . . Cats and dogs, caged birds, all of these will turn against us, all of them will start talking to us, all of them will turn to attack us."[36]

<u>July 15, 1996</u>: MSNBC goes on the air. This cable-TV channel is a partnership between Paul Allen's Microsoft and the NBC network. NBC and Microsoft teamed up to broadcast news stories. Billionaire Paul Allen, the "third richest American,"[37] and founder of the Jimi Hendrix Museum, now has influence over the NBC-TV network. What's in store for NBC?

<u>July 28, 1996</u>: "The Asteroids Are Coming! The Asteroids Are Coming!" is the title of a *New York Times Magazine* article. The following excerpts from this article relate to my *Rock Prophecy* manuscript, which had been at the Library of Congress unpublished for over a year when this article appeared:

34. *Doomsday: What Can We Do?*, A Termite Art Production, Fox 2/14/97.
35. Hal Lindsey, Chet Snow, *Prophecies IV – The Final Visions,* NBC 6/8/96.
36. Dennis Tedlock, Ibid.
37. Forbes 10/13/97 p.154.

The New York Times:

1) "Very few people will ever have the chance to save humanity from instant doom. One who thinks he might is the asteroid hunter Tom Gehrels . . . searching for the single object that might end our view of them forever . . . 'We know there's at least a thousand of them, that any of these thousand may have our name on it. The dinosaurs were around for 200 million years and never became smart enough to build a Spacewatch system. We did it, but did we do it soon enough?'"

2) "From time to time [asteroids] are thrown off course by forces like Jupiter's gravity, and then their orbits can intersect those of the Earth."

3) "[an asteroid disaster] might do more to change humanity's outlook and behavior than any religion or congress of nations has ever managed to do."

4) ". . . one of the estimated thousand-plus giant near-earth objects (N.E.O.'s) is barreling down on us and only a year or so away . . . what could we do? Say good-bye to each other and regret that we didn't wake up to this sooner.'"

5) "The study of asteroid impact has what scientists like to call a high 'giggle factor.'"

6) "Gehrels pugnaciously deplores all the fighting and all the 'bandwagoneers' whose sudden interest in asteroids was excited by the smell of money and jobs."

<u>August 1996</u>: *Asteroid – Earth Destroyer or New Frontier?* by Patricia Barnes-Svarney is published by Plenum Books. The author warns, "All types of evidence keep popping up all over our planet, letting us know that we have not escaped (and will never escape) the attacks from impacting space objects."

<u>December 1996</u>: A feature article in *Reader's Digest* titled "On a Collision Course With Earth" reports, "Astronomers have discovered more than 300 objects that could cross Earth's orbit . . . If an object some 1600 feet wide hit land, the impact would create a three-mile-wide crater and destroy almost 4000 square miles of property . . . A meteorite about one mile across could trigger a catastrophe in which more than one-quarter of the human population would die . . . we could face a surprise encounter with a large, previously undetected object . . . it could be tomorrow."

<u>December 25, 1996</u>: The Talking Phone Book, a free telephone recording service in New York State, includes this Christmas Day message for callers to listen to:

> *No fewer than six of the world's great religions agree . . . that Earth will undergo swift and cataclysmic changes beginning in 1997, followed by the end of the world on Jan. 16th in the year 2000 . . . Immediately after mankind is wiped out by twin meteorites . . . and a doomsday comet, God will establish heaven on Earth . . . That's the word from religion scholar Dr. Marian Derlet, who reached her conclusions on the heels of a 25-year study of apocalyptic prophecies dating back to the year 3500 B.C. The expert now says that 1997 is in fact the beginning of the end and every event that occurs at this critical juncture in history is just another rung on the ladder we are descending on a perilous and dizzying journey to the end. "This isn't the fantasy of some doomsday cult," she continues, "it's a vision that's shared by no fewer than six of the worlds great spiritual traditions, including Christianity, Judaism, Islam, Hinduism and throughout the Egyptian and Maya belief systems. Earthquakes of unprecedented magnitude, the drifting of entire continents, the shifting of the Earth's poles, terrifying extremes of weather, epidemics, and global war – these are just a few of the prophecies that religions foretold as far back as 3500 B.C. The similarities of the prophecies are uncanny," said the expert . . . "Looking back at my research, comparing the prophecies, it's clear that humanity really has only one religious outlook: in the final analysis, virtually all cultures and traditions have foreseen the same stark vision of mankind's future. I can only believe that all people everywhere throughout history have had an innate understanding of a very definite cycle: a clearly defined beginning and end to all that was, is, and will be."* – The Talking Phone Book

<u>December 29, 1996</u>: NBC-TV, the network that recently collaborated with Paul Allen's Microsoft to establish the MSNBC cable-TV channel, begins a mammoth six week media blitz to advertise a new blockbuster TV miniseries titled *ASTEROID*, scheduled to air on NBC in mid-February 1997.

<u>January 16, 1997</u>: The Seattle Human Rights Department files a discrimination complaint against Paul Allen's Experience Music Project and begins to investigate my involvement with the Microsoft billionaire's EMP, aka the Jimi Hendrix Museum.

<u>February 2, 1997</u>: PBS Masterpiece Theater broadcasts *Breaking the Code*, a film about Alan Turing, the man who spearheaded efforts to break the Ultra Secret Nazi Enigma machine codes. Turing's brainpower was largely responsible for winning the war for the Allies and saving civilization from a new Dark Age. But instead of being rewarded for his contributions, Turing was arrested and persecuted in England for being homosexual.

February 7, 1997: *Dateline NBC*, the network TV news show, reports, "We've been hearing a lot about asteroids lately . . . We may be the third rock from the sun but there's plenty of others." *Dateline* covers the asteroid story with by now familiar mass-audience cliches: "the number of scientists scanning the sky for trouble is less than the staff of a McDonald's restaurant." This 20-minute *Dateline* NBC segment includes interviews with Eugene Shoemaker and David Levey, who repeat asteroid facts now heard in a dozen other asteroid documentaries that today saturate the airwaves. Corporate executives who control media have by this time shoved the whole space rock issue down everyone's throat. NBC, the network in partnership with Paul Allen's Microsoft, is especially hot on the topic of asteroids. Paul Allen founded Seattle's Jimi Hendrix Museum. If Mr. Allen were to become interested in asteroids it wouldn't take much for him to initiate media projects on the subject. I'm not saying that all of the entries listed in this Timeline were caused directly by Paul Allen. They wouldn't all *have to be*. Certain media organizations begin waving the asteroid banner and a *trickle down effect* sets hundreds of other media outlets following the lead. And soon no one recalls where it all started or when we first began to hear loads of reports about asteroids. But, as this book explains, I had a reason to keep track.

Most of *Dateline's* televised reports are available on video cassettes for the public to purchase ($24 per cassette). Strangely, this Feb. 7th asteroid report is not for sale from NBC.[38]

February 14, 1997: The FOX TV network broadcasts an hour long prime time special titled *Doomsday: What Can We Do?* The second half of the show is focused on the ancient asteroid that wiped out the dinosaurs. The narrator asks, "Could history repeat itself? The odds are it could. The only question is when. And if an asteroid was on a final collision course, there would be nothing we could do." An official from NORAD explains "we have no weapon capable of going into space to intercept this particular object." A Disaster Psychologist acknowledges that nothing humans do will prevent an asteroid disaster: "There's going to be a lot of feeling of helplessness and powerlessness and people are going to have to deal with the fact that they're not going to be able to do anything to prevent it." The program concludes that "the threat of doomsday should unite mankind as never before, but we should not have to wait until the threat becomes reality."

February 14, 1997: An episode of *Unsolved Mysteries* on CBS-TV covers asteroid impacts on Earth. Robert Stack's examination of the rock that wiped out the dinosaurs includes comments from Eugene Shoemaker in which Shoemaker repeats his warning about the inevitability of a future impact.

February 15, 1997: A feature story about asteroids in *TV Guide* reports "cosmic collisions are the subject of two TV documentaries and three movies hurtling towards your local multiplex."

---

38. If you have a video copy of this Dateline NBC report, please contact First Century Press.

February 16-17, 1997: The men who control media climax their blitz with NBC-TV's flashy, super-hyped miniseries *ASTEROID*. The establishment's policy on impact disasters is mouthed through the story's patriarch grandfather who concludes, "Nobody is to blame. We just got in each other's way."

ASTEROID was made for TV by NBC. NBC and Microsoft are partners in major media projects like the MSNBC cable-TV network. Paul Allen is co-founder of Microsoft and the financier of Seattle's Jimi Hendrix Museum. My manuscript about Hendrix and asteroids has been on file and available at the Library of Congress since June 1995. Is it possible that people who are aware of my unpublished writings about asteroids, and Hendrix, issued instructions in 1995 to media producers?: "Do the asteroid story as big as you can!"

"This subject was presented as: 1) a giant asteroid hits the Earth, and 2) the biggest thing to hit television ever," said Sam Nicholson, whose Stargate Films produced the special effects for NBC's *ASTEROID* miniseries. "The effect of the miniseries is informative as well as being just exciting from the word go," said Nicholson, "and keeping the pedal to the metal through the excitement and pushing the envelope with all of the kind of thing that you find in multi-million dollar features."[39] A huge amount of money produced and advertised *ASTEROID* for NBC, the Network that is partners with Microsoft. Sam Nicholson's *Stargate* Films was "pushing the envelope with all of the kind of thing that you find in multi-million dollar features."

"Paul Allen wants to do cool stuff that pushes the envelope of technology," said Mike Slade,[40] president of Paul Allen's *Starwave* company. Paul Allen is the son of two *librarians*, and he invested $500 million into DreamWorks SKG, the movie studio headed by Steven Spielberg, David Geffen, and Jeffrey Katzenberg. "They may use me as a sounding board for some of the new multi-media areas," said billionaire Paul. "All of a sudden you've got pretty incredible assets giving you ability to do a lot of things."[41]

Twenty months earlier my *Rock Prophecy* manuscript was sent to the Library of Congress. Is it possible that the NBC-Microsoft-Hendrix connection described in *Rock Prophecy* is a factor in NBC's sudden and extreme interest in asteroids?

February 17, 1997: NBC Nightly News reports that an undersea expedition has unearthed the first scientific evidence for a massive asteroid that destroyed the dinosaurs 65 million years ago. Simultaneously CBS Evening News reports, "drilling deep into the ocean floor off the Florida coast, scientists have found the story written in layers of sand, including a two-inch layer of gray clay, indicating life was nearly wiped off this planet for nearly five thousand years after the asteroid hit."

"Will such an asteroid strike again in our lifetime?" asks NBC. "The odds are about the same as winning the lottery."

---

39. News 10-NBC WHEC TV, Rochester, NY 2/16/97.
40. The New York Times 10/29/95 section 3, Money & Business p.1.
41. Ibid.

February 17, 1997: The PBS News Hour airs a report titled *Ground Zero* on the theme of an asteroid striking mid-West America.

February 18, 1997: ABC-TV's *Hard Copy* reports "Scientists are right now tracking a new near-Earth asteroid hurtling through space at 50,000 miles-per-hour. It crossed the Earth's orbit last month and experts say it just missed us . . . the reality might be a lot scarier than anything you'll see on TV." This *Hard Copy* TV segment features interviews with Eugene and Carolyn Shoemaker and an official of the Jet Propulsion Laboratory who reveals, "We find between one hundred and two hundred asteroids a night. Some of them are new, some of them are known."

February 26, 1997: Microsoft sponsors NBC's *National Geographic* prime time TV special titled *Asteroids: Deadly Impact*. This hour long documentary deals in large part with the career of Eugene Shoemaker, who warns, "These things have hit the Earth in the past, they will hit the Earth in the future. It's a catastrophe that exceeds all other known disasters by a large measure." The main focus of this NBC special seems to be to convince the public that the over-reporting of asteroid stories during 1996-1997 was triggered by comet fragments that struck Jupiter in July 1994. But by August 1994, the public and the media had lost interest in the Jupiter story. The 1994 impacts on Jupiter are *NOT* what caused the 1996-1999 media blitz about asteroids.

If the Jupiter impacts had inspired the men who control media to saturate the airwaves with asteroid stories, *we would have seen a mass media blitz during autumn 1994 and into spring-summer of 1995. But during that period there were no media reports about asteroids, especially in comparison with what the media reported later on in 1996 through 1999. Interest in the asteroid issue remained low until the end of 1995.* There was no renewed public interest in the six Hollywood movies about asteroids made from 1951 through 1984. But long after the 1994 impacts on Jupiter were over, something else happened that pushed the asteroid issue to top priority among men who control media.

For anyone who follows the order of reports about asteroids, the "trigger" point is very clear: the media picked up this story in earnest in late October 1995, *five months following* the arrival of *Rock Prophecy* for copyright registration at the Library of Congress in Washington, D.C. Are the contents of *Rock Prophecy* what compelled the men who control media to initiate an asteroid craze during 1996 and 1997?

> *It is the winners who write history – **their way**.*   – Elaine Pagels[42]

The intent of NBC's *Asteroids: Deadly Impact* seems to be to shift the cause of the 1996-1997 media blitz away from *Rock Prophecy* and blur the timeline of media reports on asteroids. The program makes it appear as though there has been continuous media

---

42. Elaine Pagels, *The Gnostic Gospels,* (New York: Random House, 1979), p.142.

interest in asteroids ever since 1994. But the blitz began in October 1995, after *Rock Prophecy* was copyrighted. Who might be interested in undermining the impact of *Rock Prophecy* by saturating the airwaves with asteroid stories and minimizing any Hendrix connection with asteroids?

In February 1997, NBC's *Asteroids: Deadly Impact*, sponsored by Microsoft, reports that, "Shoemaker was one of the very first to find out if there are bullets out there that might strike the Earth in the future . . . Before Eugene Shoemaker few people gave impacts much thought, one of the most powerful forces in the making of our planet, and perhaps the deadliest hazard we face."

The writers of *Asteroids: Deadly Impact* pedestalize Shoemaker as the person who discovered that craters on Earth are the result of asteroids. Only in a quick aside does the program mention Daniel Moreau Barringer. Nearly a hundred years ago Barringer's study of Meteor Crater in Arizona was a major catalyst in the push towards acceptance of the concept of impact cratering on Earth. By comparison, Shoemaker's research in the 1950s and 60s was simply "accepted" by a scientific community that took a half century to catch up to Barringer.

But besides Barringer and Shoemaker, it is Jimi Hendrix who is one of the "few people who gave impacts much thought." Anyone who read *Rock Prophecy* at the LOC in 1995 learned that Hendrix infused his music and poems with elaborate visions and lyrics about asteroid impacts on the Earth, moon, and planets. Suddenly it became *important* for the men who control media to saturate the airwaves with asteroid reports. It's as if orders were issued to writers and producers: inform the public that Shoemaker (not Hendrix) gets credit for alerting us to the asteroid threat. Was this the purpose of NBC's *Asteroids: Deadly Impact?*, sponsored by Microsoft.

Rock Prophecy was read at the LOC in 1995. Were writers and consultants for the men who control media instructed to pump out "treatments" of the asteroid story? Were they paid to frame Shoemaker and the 1994 impacts on Jupiter as the reason of the asteroid craze that began in late 1995?

NBC's *Asteroids: Deadly Impact* reports that in the search for rocks in outer space "the US Airforce has contributed technology and expertise. Big science has taken up the hunt for asteroids...[and] awaits with all of us the next messenger from the stars. The question is not if, but when . . . Only a fraction of large Earth-crossing asteroids have been located, this may prove to be the greatest oversight in human history."

Rock Prophecy describes how our vulnerability to collision is no "oversight." Jimi Hendrix was the messenger seer who had foresight of the disaster. He tried to warn us, and there were other visionaries who understood the threat and knew what our race was supposed to do. They too tried to warn us, and were silenced. I tried to warn, and was obstructed. The fact that today we have no defense against asteroids is not an "oversight." Hendrix mentioned deliberate delays in allocating funds to develop a technology that can defend Earth. The battle over this issue unfolds like cosmic drama and mythic religion.

Rock Prophecy explains the specific prediction of Jimi Hendrix that is the real catalyst for late-20th century asteroid hysteria. This book is the original trigger for the media blitz which is now a familiar story to us all. *Rock Prophecy* is a story that's been suppressed since 1995. That this book remains unread is *important* to men who control media. It is so *important* to them that no one knows the Prophecy.

Following the broadcast of *Asteroids: Deadly Impact* on February 26, NBC's *Dateline* continues the theme of catastrophe with an hour of "Nature's Wrath" stories about volcanoes, hurricanes and earthquakes.

March 6, 1997: Seattle's Department of Human Rights informs me that, although Paul Allen's Jimi Hendrix Museum is being built in the city of Seattle, the museum offices are currently outside city limits, in Bellevue. Therefore, the Human Rights Dept. has no jurisdiction over my dispute with Paul Allen's project. And a dozen attorneys have by now declined to represent my request for justice against Mr. Allen's Hendrix museum.

March 13, 1997: CBS Evening News reports the passing of Hale-Bopp comet. An observer comments, "It looks like a fuzzy ball coming at you."

March 21, 1997: ABC World News reports, "Most ancient civilizations watched the skies, where they believed their gods lived, and used celestial objects as symbols marking events, like the birth of Jesus. Comets were often a source of terror because they are rare, even now they stir up concern, will one strike the Earth?"

March 22, 1997: *Astronomy* magazine's cover story is headlined "Comet Hale-Bopp Takes Center Stage." Alan Hale co-discovered this space rock, which is three times the size of an average comet. Writing for *Astronomy* Hale notes, "On March 22, 1997 Comet Hale-Bopp will be in conjunction with the Sun . . . It will also be nearest the Earth on this date . . . a total solar eclipse will be visible across Mongolia." Hale notes that the appearance of a comet during an eclipse is "extremely rare; less than half a dozen 'eclipse comets' have been seen throughout recorded history."

March 23, 1997: *TBS*, the cable-TV channel, airs *Fire In the Sky*. This hour long show presents "facts from scientists and astronomers that explain why fire from the sky could become tomorrow's news." Shoemaker and Levey are interviewed yet again as *Fire In the Sky* aims to persuade viewers that "it was a massive impact into Jupiter in 1994 that revealed the magnitude of the threat to Earth." Instead of the Prophecy of Hendrix, we instead hear David Levey's blunt prediction, "Someday the Earth will get hit by a comet and an asteroid. It'll happen, there's no way out of it. It has happened in the past, it will happen again . . . The chances that we'll die in a comet collision are about the same as the chances that we'll die in an airplane crash, and just think of how much money the U.S. spends on improving aircraft safety."

Like *Rock Prophecy*, *TBS*'s asteroid documentary points out that "we are the first species to recognize this threat from space and only by dealing with it can we ensure our future on planet Earth . . . Despite our growing awareness of this potential threat, funding is being cut worldwide for space watch programs."

Fire In the Sky intensifies the alarmist tone with which the media has come to report asteroid stories during the two years following the copyright of *Rock Prophecy*. *TBS* concludes with Eugene Shoemaker's bleak warning, "If we fail to respond to the technical challenge of preventing these catastrophes, sooner or later there will be an object, an asteroid or a comet, that will hit the Earth and cause devastation."

<u>March 24, 1997</u>: *Newsweek* magazine's cover story is "The Great Comet." "These days," says the owner of the Psychic Eye in Los Angeles, "I've been seeing comets come into my readings about 90 percent of the time."

A feature article in this issue of *Newsweek* is titled "Attention: Incoming Object – How to defend Earth against collisions." *Newsweek* explains, "At the moment Earth is defenseless against a large comet or asteroid headed for the planet. Scientists and other star warriors are exploring a variety of defensive schemes . . . It's Ronald Reagan's Star Wars program, with a vengeance . . . For more than a decade, U.S. and Russian nuclear strategists have talked about their common enemies from space. The United Nations has sponsored conferences, too. 'During the cold war, I was always hoping we could find an incoming threat,' says Tom Gehrels of Spacewatch. 'Then we could all go after a common enemy.'"

<u>March 28, 1997</u>: An NBC Nightly News story about comets reports, "Through history they've inspired and terrified. Often believed to herald the birth of a leader: Moses, Christ, Buddha. More often regarded . . . as an omen of doom . . . Scientists do believe a comet did wipe out one species here on Earth, the dinosaur, 65 million years ago. And now as we get closer to the year 2000 and the end of the millennium, more and more fringe groups are spreading doomsday predictions of the end of the human species."

<u>April 1997</u>: The splashy cover story of *Popular Mechanics* features "Killer Asteroids." The magazine article predicts, "In October 2005 an asteroid nearly 1 mile wide is seen hurtling through space . . . headed straight for Earth. There isn't enough time to . . . deflect or destroy it . . . the very survival of mankind is threatened . . . As sure as there are stars in the sky, it will happen . . . a 7 ft. object can produce a . . . blast the equivalent of igniting 1000 tons of high explosives . . . scientists estimate there are . . . 2000 Earth-crossers out there, and any one of them could be the doomsday rock . . . If one of them were on a collision course with Earth, we wouldn't get more than a few months warning."

<u>May 28, 1997</u>: CBS News reports, "Astronomers assured people that the possibility of a comet actually striking the Earth was rare indeed. But today scientists reported the Earth is virtually under attack by comets, thousands of comets smash into the Earth's atmosphere every day. Dr. Louis Frank discovered the comet bombardment . . . the comets were photographed for the first time by cameras aboard a new NASA satellite . . . The new pictures confirm a theory that Dr. Frank has held for more than 15 years, but that no one else accepted."

<u>June 1, 1997</u>: PBS[43] airs an episode of *Astronomy* titled *Cosmic Travelers: Comets and Asteroids*. The program asks, "What would happen if a comet collided with the Earth?"

<u>June 12, 1997</u>: News-10 NBC reports, "Last week a 53 pound boulder fell from the sky near Moscow into a garden. The apparent meteorite caused no injuries."

<u>Summer 1997</u>: *Reese's* airs a TV commercial in which a flying peanutbutter cup saves the world from an incoming flaming asteroid.

<u>July 18, 1997</u>: Eugene Shoemaker, age 69, dies in a car crash in Australia.

<u>July 20, 1997</u>: ABC World News reports, "Washington was the scene of another disaster today . . . the shooting of a movie about a meteor that collides with Earth. At least it has a clear cut storyline. The Republican drama is murkier, a whodunit, or tried to vote Newt Gingrich out of his job." Gingrich, and his "cultural elite" comments, are subjects of my article "GrinchRich – the D.C. Witch-hunt," which kicked off this Timeline more than two years earlier.

<u>July 26, 1997</u>: The Learning Channel cable TV network begins a week long spectacle called *Solar Empire*: "Crashing out of control . . . killer asteroids . . . one smash hit after another . . . and we're stuck in the middle of it."

<u>July 30, 1997</u>: FOX-TV's prime time special *Prophecies of the Millennium* features a mystic who advises us to, "Watch for something falling from the skies." A Hopi guru predicts, "I see it descending from the skies in the form of . . . a colliding comet or asteroid."

The narrator reports, "Experts warn that space based weapons would have to be perfected if we hope to defend against a heavenly body on a predicted collision course with Earth." Oliver North appears on screen and warns, "I would suggest to those who think that we could survive the impact of a massive asteroid striking this country, need to think again."

"What if mankind's ultimate challenge," concludes *Prophecies of the Millennium*, "is coping with the knowledge that, like other species who've come before us, we're here for only a given period of history. What if the prophets are right, and our time is almost up?"

<u>August 11, 1997</u>: A huge double rainbow over my home is the focus of local media this evening, as meteor showers light up tonight's sky, and the second draft of *Rock Prophecy* is in the process of being printed out. The April 12, 1995 rainbow was a gateway entrance into the period of *Rock Prophecy*. This August 1997 rainbow return coincides with the completion of this book, like an exit gateway arching through the sky.

---

43. Broadcast on WCNY in Syracuse, NY.

<u>August 12, 1997</u>: Draft #2 of *Rock Prophecy* is sent to the Library of Congress for copyright registration.

<u>August 24, 1997</u>: Cable TV's Family Channel begins airing the movie *Doomsday Rock* starring Connie Sellecca and William DeVane. This is the asteroid issue dressed down to its lowest common denominator, for grandma and the kids. *Doomsday Rock* similarities with *Rock Prophecy* are amazing. DeVane plays the seer who writes a book which decodes, not Hendrix, nor Maya Indian, predictions, but "*Aborigine* inscriptions"! The plot boils down to a possessed shaman (William DeVane) vs. the dominators (the U.S. military seeks to silence the seer). A Pentagon official scoffs at how DeVane's book "accompanied a warning of an asteroid that is supposed to hit the Earth. We consider it lunacy . . . there's a lot of orbit calculations [in the book] and pages and pages of cave paintings from some aboriginal tribe in Australia."

It's as if the writers of *Doomsday Rock* were instructed to replace the written prophecy of Hendrix with: "some ancient prophecy by Australian aboriginals . . . The aborigines have very powerful spirituality. [We] found this huge cave filled with the most amazing paintings . . . they had all been done by one single artist. This man had been taken over by what they call the dream spirit. The spirit was so strong it could see into the future. There had been a **timeline** etched into the wall."

Whereas *Rock Prophecy* explains Jimi's prediction of the 1994 comet impacts on Jupiter, *Doomsday Rock* explains how historical "events fit into the paintings and the **timeline**" of the aboriginal prophet, leading to "the demon rock hitting the Earth and destroying it." In other words, the *Rock Prophecy* concept, of a shaman [Jimi] appearing at just the right time in history to predict the Rock, is used in this movie called *Doomsday Rock*.

And instead of *Rock Prophecy's* description of Maya Indian observations about how the orbits of Venus and the Moon direct asteroids towards Earth, *Doomsday Rock* reworks the chain reaction formula into a scenario in which a comet "splits, part of it . . . connects directly with the asteroid . . . this impact will alter its orbit, sending it towards Earth."

"We are the only ones who believe," laments Sellecca.

"The prophecy is true," DeVane tells her. "Study my book. If they kill me the Earth is doomed . . . True genius is the gift of being able to find what's always been there waiting to be found."

<u>September 1997</u>: On tour the *Rolling Stones* start their shows with giant multi-media enactment's of an asteroid flaming into the stadium.

<u>October 15, 1997</u>: A front page story in *USA Today* reports President Clinton's *veto* of a proposed $30 million research project to plan a "space-based system to intercept an asteroid that might threaten Earth."

<u>October 20, 1997</u>: Two months after draft #2 of *Rock Prophecy* arrived at the Library of Congress for copyright registration, NBC Nightly News begins a series of reports on "War Between the Sexes."

<u>December 30, 1997</u>: The *Weekly World News* cover headlines proclaim "Lost Prophecies From the New Testament Found!" The report predicts that "a massive comet will strike somewhere in Asia, killing millions immediately and spreading choking fallout that will kill millions more over the following weeks . . . a new land mass will rise from the sea."

On this night, the PBS News Hour airs a TV report about Paul Allen's impact in Jimi's hometown of Seattle. Allen is shown playing Hendrix-style guitar music with a rock band.

The following night, New Year's Eve, *Asteroids:Deadly Impact*, which was sponsored by Microsoft, is re-broadcast on NBC-TV and dedicated to the recently deceased Eugene Shoemaker.

<u>January 15, 1998</u>: PBS airs a TV segment of *Science Odyssey* titled "Origins" which reports, "Earlier in the century most scientists did not believe that the Earth had ever been struck by large meteors. Craters . . . were thought by geologists to be made by volcanic action . . . When the tide shifted in the late 1950s and '60s toward the belief that indeed almost all of these features were a result of meteorite impact, it brought a phenomenal new understanding to the activity in the solar system . . . Manned exploration of the Moon in 1969 confirmed that moon craters were not the result of volcanoes, as had been largely believed since the time of Galileo, but the result of frequent, often massive asteroid impacts. But if the Moon had been a target, why not the Earth? . . . Imagine the impact of a typical nuclear warhead multiplied a hundred million times."

<u>January 22, 1998</u>: At a peak of global hysteria over the sex life of President Bill Clinton, PBS TV airs a show called *Eyewitness* which warns, "Beyond Mars lies the asteroid belt . . . fragments are sometimes dislodged from their orbit, traveling as far as the Earth . . . in 1972 a huge meteorite grazed the atmosphere. Had this fireball hit the Earth it would have exploded with the force of five atomic bombs."

<u>January 1998</u>: The National Cattlemen's Beef Association sponsors a prime time TV commercial depicting a backyard astronomer who spots an incoming asteroid. In the remaining moments before the end of the world, the astronomer decides to grill himself a thick, juicy steak.

<u>February 1998</u>: A prime time TV commercial for American Express features Jerry Seinfeld urging Superman to save the Earth from an approaching asteroid.

In early February, the first page of the *Rock Prophecy* website appears on the Internet.

All through the winter of 1998, the movie *Titanic* remains a global obsession. In a subconscious way, mankind senses an impending disaster and sublimates this feeling with fixation on Titanic, relating to the ship as a metaphor for civilization, on a course for collision with a floating mountain. Disaster could have been avoided if everyone were aware of certain details. *Rock Prophecy* is about these details.

<u>March 3, 1998</u>: The third draft of *Rock Prophecy*, printed out on February 24, 1998, is registered for copyright at the Library of Congress.

<u>March 11, 1998</u>: From 9 a.m. until noon, I write the following letter and mail copies to five people:

> The complete hardcopy manuscript of *Rock Prophecy* – *the Hendrix/asteroid/Microsoft connection* – was recently printed out.
>
> A timely prophecy remains hidden within the writings of Jimi Hendrix. In 1993, while working for Harper Collins on the book, *Cherokee Mist – the Lost Writings of Jimi Hendrix*, I grasped the vision that this shaman seer was racing to communicate at the time of his death in 1970. In the spring of 1995, I sent a hardcopy draft of the story to the Library of Congress for copyright. The manuscript is titled *Rock Prophecy*, it is the original trigger for an avalanche of asteroid stories in recent media.
>
> Microsoft co-founder Paul Allen, the third wealthiest American, was seeking to acquire rights to the Hendrix legacy for his $60 million Hendrix Museum in Seattle. In 1993, Mr. Allen loaned the Hendrix family $5 million to finance a lawsuit that resulted in the closing of the Hendrix production company in Hollywood. For seven years, I had been employed by Jimi's production company as their writer and consultant. My unusual stories, which are included as booklets in 14 official Hendrix CDs published by MCA, Warner Bros., and Polydor, are well known to an international audience of several million people. I am the author of many other non-Hendrix publications, including Atlantic Record's 1994 *Woodstock Diary* CD booklet, and a dozen cover stories in national magazines.
>
> I was responsible for initiating and developing projects and products which became some of the most celebrated successes of the Hendrix legacy, and I was in line to become the next Creative Director of the Hendrix production company in Hollywood. My position allowed me to

orchestrate, for Paul Allen's Hendrix museum in Seattle, the purchase of several of the world's most excellent collections of Hendrix items. Nearly a half million dollars was paid by Mr. Allen's museum for this material. The collections now comprise the core database about Jimi that resides at Paul Allen's "Hendrix museum" in Seattle.

But then the lawsuit from the Hendrix family against officials at their Hollywood production company, a lawsuit financed by Paul Allen, resulted in closing the Hollywood company. My job was gone, and my opportunity to be Creative Director of Jimi's estate was toppled. I was left unemployed, there was no severance pay, and Paul Allen's Seattle museum refused to compensate me for my efforts which connected his museum up with a world class Hendrix collection.

I had done only unusual good for all of these people, yet from their actions my seven year career of incredible successes was destroyed. And all the while I was the only one who understood the Prophecy.

At the height of the highly publicized lawsuit proceedings in 1995, I wrote the story of Jimi's prediction of an asteroid on course to impact Earth. At the same time, one of my articles appeared in a magazine for Hendrix fans and it describes why my unpublished writings, registered and stored at the Library of Congress, are being monitored by interested parties. Did representatives from Paul Allen's Hendrix museum or legal team see *Rock Prophecy* at the LOC in the spring of 1995? Within five months after the manuscript arrived there for copyright, the media began churning out dramatic asteroid stories. An escalating frenzy of reports, in all major media throughout 1996, climaxed in 1997 with several feature films, documentaries, and an NBC-TV mini-series.

In July 1996, NBC teamed up with Paul Allen's Microsoft to launch MSNBC. Subsequently NBC became particularly hot on the topic of rocks from space, as if mogul orders had decreed, "Do up the asteroid story – Big Time!"

The Microsoft connection is, however, but a sliver within *Rock Prophecy*, just a small part. And the full story cannot be described as a "Hendrix book." Analysis of Jimi's prediction is but a third of the manuscript. Hendrix is presented as an authentic Afro-American Cherokee seer, a shaman who glimpsed the trajectory of extraterrestrial events already in place during his lifetime. He was racing to communicate his vision in a screenplay he composed titled *Moondust*.

Rock Prophecy is the story of how the dominators have silenced the seers throughout the ages and "retarded history" by impeding humanity's advance towards anti-asteroid technology. We are today at a technological state which should have been realized several millennia ago. The slim window (in geologic time) which exists between major impacts is due to close. *Rock Prophecy* will remain as the explanation of what happened. And like the suppressed Gnostic gospels, this text will surface during a future civilization on the other side of the coming dark ages of a Hendrix Millennium, to be dug out from under the rubble of an (avoidably) smashed planet, like a new Nag Hammadi library. This is the book which today's dominators are most concerned to obstruct and crush.

Rock Prophecy explains the biological base of our human tragedy, the struggle of one sex to dominate the other, a conflict which thwarted the collective effort necessary for our civilization's survival. The Prophecy centers on sexual tensions behind world religions, a collision of myths for which Hendrix is figurehead. The origins and function of homosexuality are finally revealed – nature's "avert-a-birth" herd thinners.

Rock Prophecy proclaims the start of the first century of the *Un*common Era when, simultaneously, the Ultra Secret Enigma code of the Nazis was broken at the moment Jimi was born. The tide of war turned in favor of the Allies. Dominator culture shriveled in the presence of Hendrix and then reasserted itself in the circumstances of his death. Thirty years later it is up to me to leave behind the persecuted manuscript, like a reenactment of the writings of Paul three decades after the Crucifixion. There are two crucial differences: 1) dozens of my stories are familiar to millions of people who own the MCA, Warner Bros. and Polydor publications, and 2) the Internet.

It is critical to Paul Allen that Microsoft controls the Internet. *Rock Prophecy* draws parallels between the Seattle billionaire and the Emperor Constantine. Like the Roman dominator, Mr. Allen seeks to co-opt and re-write a theology, complete with gaudy cathedrals in the prophet's hometown. Whereas the ancient Gnostics buried their texts in the desert, I've dug out a website to eject *Rock Prophecy* into cyberspace. The struggle between good and evil today comes down to whether or not the U.S. Department of Justice can prevent Microsoft dominators from controlling the Internet and obstructing the circulation of *Rock Prophecy*.

You are requested to intervene in this cosmic drama. Help *Rock Prophecy* reach its readers.   – Michael Fairchild

This letter was copied and mailed to five people at noon on March 11, 1998. Six hours and 53 minutes later, at 6:53 pm, e.s.t. ABC World News was the first media to report that scientist had just discovered a mile wide asteroid, named 1997XF11, due to come within 30,000 miles of Earth in thirty years time. Amazingly, "thirty years" is the key Hendrix quote from *Rock Prophecy* contained in Jimi's prediction of an impact "in about thirty years."

On March 11, 1998, the letter that I mailed at noon was literally written at the moment when the asteroid's path was discovered. I didn't know this while I wrote the letter, I could *not* have known it. During the afternoon of March 11th, no one knew about the asteroid's discovery except for a few scientists at the Central Bureau for Astronomical Telegrams. Dr. Brian Marsden, Director of CBAT, later explained, "There's an automatic program and when we were running it on Wednesday morning [March 11, 1998] the program suddenly stopped. We investigated why and found that it had stopped because something [in the solar system] went very close to something else."[44]

On Wednesday afternoon CBAT confirmed their calculations of the asteroid's path. The results were reported to media late in the day on Wednesday. I can *prove* that my letter about the asteroid prediction was written and mailed on Wednesday *before* the media knew that an asteroid is coming, because one of the letters that I mailed on March 11 was incorrectly addressed and therefore returned to me *unopened!* Today, my letter remains inside an envelope that was sealed and dated by the United States Post Office on March 11, 1998. The envelope has "PM" stamped on its outside, meaning it was mailed BEFORE 5:00 p.m. (when the Post Office closed) and BEFORE the asteroid story broke over the airwaves at 6:53 p.m. Thus, I can prove that I was writing my letter at the same moment that the asteroid's path was discovered at CBAT.

The first reports about the asteroid aired on the Evening News and a rising tide of anxiety consumed all world media. Humanity awoke to a black Thursday on March 12 and stared at blaring headlines: "Asteroid Heads Towards Earth!" For the next several days everyone everywhere was abuzz with the news.

And still the anti-equality unfree elitist media obstructs publication of *Rock Prophecy*.

March 13, 1998: An official at *Rolling Stone* magazine is contacted about *Rock Prophecy* and refers me to the managing editor. I fax a letter describing the Hendrix/asteroid/Microsoft incident, while world media is still consumed with yesterday's news about asteroid 1997XF11. To see the reaction of *Rolling Stone*, skip ahead one year to FOOLS day – April 1, 1999.

March 15, 1998: NBC's *Dateline* produces a second major TV report about asteroids. And ABC's *Entertainment Tonight* covers the coincidence of the discovery of asteroid 1997XF11 coming just as two major Hollywood films about rocks from space are being prepared for premiers in theaters worldwide.

---

44. Brain Marsden interview, Dateline NBC, 3/15/98.

<u>March 29, 1998</u>: The elaborate NBC miniseries, *ASTEROID*, is again broadcast on primetime network TV on a Sunday evening.

<u>March-April 1998</u>: Throughout the spring of 1998, at a time when literally thousands of reports about asteroids are appearing in local media around the globe, several hundred members of the anti-equality elitist media again close ranks to obstruct publication of *Rock Prophecy*. Each of them is aware of my manuscript's role in the unfolding asteroid phenomenon, yet the gatekeepers are trained to "reject" texts that call for equality.

<u>April 6-7, 1998</u>: *From Jesus To Christ*, a four part TV series, is broadcast on PBS. "Separating Jesus from Christ" is the title of a chapter in *Rock Prophecy*. Incredibly, many of the scholars quoted in *Rock Prophecy* became the main talking heads interviewed for the new PBS series. But whereas *Rock Prophecy* reveals the twisted history of Constantine and Irenaeus, *From Jesus To Christ* portrays these dominators as "heroes." And the producers of *From Jesus To Christ* fixate on Jesus' "class," offering weak evidence to suggest that some early Christians were middle class, and not poor. The program ignores how Jesus appeals to people who are attracted to equality, *no matter what class such people might be in or from.* There are many people who have wealth and yet still believe that everyone should somehow be equal. And Jesus, a symbol for equality, appeals to them. But the elitist media consistently portrays Jesus instead as figurehead for life after death, rather than as a preacher of equality.

<u>April 10, 1998</u>: The PBS McLaughlin Group debates Vice President Gore's proposal for an orbiting satellite named Triana that will transmit round-the-clock live video images of Earth for cable TV and the Internet. John McLaughlin speculates that the camera's real purpose is "to spot asteroids coming towards Earth." This issue is close to a scene in *Rock Prophecy* about "globally televised live extinction, broadcast on MSNBC."[45]

<u>April 17, 1998</u>: TV commercials begin for the asteroid movie *Deep Impact*, starring MSNBC. Paul Allen is a major invested partner in DreamWorks Pictures, the company that produced *Deep Impact*. Like NBC's fixation on asteroids after Paul Allen's Microsoft teamed up with MSNBC, now DreamWorks, another Paul Allen partnership, picks up the asteroid banner too. Is it possible that my manuscript, stored at the Library of Congress three years ago during the Hendrix family lawsuit (financed by a loan from Paul Allen), is the inspiration for all of these asteroid stories? Did media moguls become aware of *Rock Prophecy* in the mid-1990s and then order their companies to beat the asteroid story to a pulp?

<u>May 1998</u>: Several times during May, cable TV's Showtime channel airs the 1979 Sean Connery movie *Meteor*, starring Henry Fonda, Natalie Wood, Brian Keith, Karl Malden and Martin Landau. Despite its cast, this flick is plagued with bad acting and embarrassing dialogue. In between the film's scenarios of valuable information injected

into the script by JPL and NASA consultants, dreary characters dreamed up by Hollywood screen writers put viewers to sleep.

<u>May 1, 1998</u>: A program titled *Killer Asteroids* on cable TV's Discovery Channel reports, "A mile wide asteroid hitting the Atlantic . . . would pretty much kill everyone in New England immediately, but the global effects would be more devastating – famines, crop failure and climate changes that would probably kill about a quarter of the population of the planet . . . Asteroids that are the size of a room hit us a couple times a year . . . The Earth is part of a cosmic shooting gallery. You need only look at our own pock marked Moon to see how often asteroids and comets are pulled from their orbits and turned our way . . . Mass extinctions that have happened at other times in the last 500 million years might be due to asteroid and comet impacts."

<u>May 1, 1998</u>: An episode of *Unsolved Mysteries,* broadcast on the Lifetime cable TV channel, covers asteroid impacts on Earth. Robert Stack's examination of the rock that wiped out the dinosaurs includes one of Eugene Shoemaker's last interviews, in which he repeats his warning about the inevitability of future impacts.

<u>May 2, 1998</u>: ABC-TV's *Access Hollywood* program sets a standard for pre-processed "asteroid reports." All of the standard media cliches are assembly-line compressed into formulas according to what wealthy moguls want to say, and *Rock Prophecy* is not included. "The most likely warning we would have for the impact of an asteroid," notes *Access Hollywood*, "is just the same as the warning the dinosaurs had – zero!"

<u>May 4, 1998</u>: Cable TV's Discovery Channel runs a three hour asteroid extravaganza titled *Impact: Could It Happen.* This show encourages viewers to think of today's asteroid craze as being triggered by the July 1994 comet impacts on Jupiter. The men who control media want everyone to believe that the 1994 impacts on Jupiter are what, years later, inspired today's asteroid craze. But their version of history is written in response to *Rock Prophecy*.

People who believe the asteroid craze started with comet Shoemaker/Levey 9 subscribe to a spin on history spun by the ruling class and aimed to dismiss this book. This Timeline list sets events straight as they happened. Media moguls had their writers delete any mention of the Hendrix connection with the issue of asteroids. And then, in the late '90s, a campaign was waged to persuade the public that the craze for asteroids results not from *Rock Prophecy,* but from a comet that hit Jupiter years earlier. The three hour May 4th Discovery Channel extravaganza is designed to establish this interpretation for a mass audience. *Impact: Could It Happen* is an example of the so-called "winners" – the *dominators* – writing history **their way**, in *their* interests, and *excluding* the Hendrix connections described in this book.

<u>May 7, 1998</u>: ABC World News reports, "Two hundred and fourteen million years ago, 80 percent of life on Earth may have been wiped out by asteroids . . . there may have been

five events that may have occurred within as brief a period of time as four hours . . . [scientists] studied impact craters that seemed unrelated on a modern map, but when you turn back the clock 200 million years to where the continents were before they drifted to their current positions, the craters are almost in a straight line . . . indicating that the body that collided with Earth came in in chunks – bang, bang, bang . . . To scan the sky for danger, NASA is doubling its budget to $3 million. But of course the comet movie that opens tomorrow cost $75 million."

<u>May 8, 1998</u>: Paul Allen's DreamWorks Pictures' production of the space rock flick *Deep Impact* premiers in theaters throughout America.

> *The way we're going to "take" [rivals] is by studying them, know what they know, do what they do, watch them, look for every angle, stay on their shoulders, clone them, take every one of **their** good ideas and make it one of **our** good ideas.*   – Steve Ballmer, Microsoft Vice President – 1995[46]

Deep Impact, the film, is filled with images of MSNBC. Paul Allen's Microsoft TV Network, MSNBC, is actually a central character in *Deep Impact*, a space rock movie produced by Paul Allen's DreamWorks Pictures. In *Rock Prophecy*, there is a scene about "globally televised live extinction, broadcast on MSNBC."[47] *Deep Impact*, with its scenes of broadcast news shown as MSNBC TV reports, seems to portray this vision from my book.

Advertisements for *Deep Impact* show a mountain-high tidal wave sweeping over Manhattan. The image is a visual depiction of what Hendrix called "Valleys of Neptune – Arising." Jimi wrote this song about great sloping valleys of a tidal wave rising up over the continental shelf following impact. "*Look out East Coast,*" he sings, "*you're gonna have a neighbor.*"[48]

Rock Prophecy contains a chapter on the concept of "Messiah" and "Messiah" is the name of the ship that saves the world in *Deep Impact*, a film that's more like a *shallow scratch* of what everyone expects from an asteroid movie from Paul Allen's company and NBC connections. By contrast, *Rock Prophecy* conveys the *unexpected* Hendrix connections that started it all.

<u>May 9, 1998</u>: *How'd They Do That?*, a TV show on The Learning Channel, reports, "The 1997 NBC miniseries *ASTEROID* was seen by more than 70 million viewers. It featured the most expensive and elaborate special effects ever created for television . . . For NBC's $19 million blockbuster miniseries, *ASTEROID*, with its scenes of urban destruction unprecedented on television, the network . . . wanted to create a show that was nothing short of a television event . . . The day after the miniseries ended, government officials

---

46. News Hour with Jim Lehrer, PBS 4/14/98.
47. *Rock Prophecy* p.E – 32.
48. "Valleys of Neptune", *Lifelines – The Jimi Hendrix Story*, Warner Records, 1990, disk III.

received more than ten thousand phone calls from people inquiring if [an impact] could really happen. We're gonna give you the answer – the answer is NO!!"

<u>May 9, 1998</u>: The Discovery Channel airs an hour segment of a three-hour asteroid special titled *Three Minutes To Impact – Our Number's Up*.

<u>May 14, 1998</u>: The Associated Press and CNN report, "If professional stargazers catch sight of an asteroid that might be on a crash course for Earth, **the government wants them to keep quiet about it** – for at least 72 hours. The new procedures aim to avoid panic . . . astronomers whose work is funded by NASA have agreed for now to **keep asteroid and comet discoveries to themselves** . . . Some scientists question the new push from NASA. 'I don't think one should be secret about these things,' said Brian Marsden, director of the International Astronomical Union . . . Usually, new observations are immediately reported to the Minor Planet Center, where it is posted on a Website." But government officials are gearing up for even tighter restrictions against free speech when it comes to asteroids. A meeting is scheduled to discuss the issue in California on June 6th. What they intend to do is use that "72 hours" to **creatively re-calculate** any threatening asteroid's orbit and disclaim it as a threat before any news is reported to the public.

<u>May 16, 1998</u>: Cable TV's Family Channel re-broadcasts the 1997 asteroid movie *Doomsday Rock*.

<u>May 18, 1998</u>: "The United States Justice Department and twenty states accuse Microsoft of conducting a campaign to suffocate competitors," reports NBC Nightly News. "Lawyers for the States say Microsoft improperly muscled the market, stifling new ideas." The Justice Department files a lawsuit against Paul Allen's company, charging Microsoft with exerting a "chokehold" over other businesses and accusing the company of threatening to "cut off the air supply" of software manufacturers. "They have enormous power over a bottleneck," said the Assistant Attorney General, "which they can leverage and hurt competition and hurt consumers, and really can dry up innovation, because people are not going to invest the money it takes if they think along can come Microsoft, put a heavy thumb on the scales, and make it impossible to compete."[49]

"They try to turn around and strangle innovation and strangle their competitors," said the New York State Attorney General.[50]

"The company that can control Internet commerce ultimately can control commerce itself in industry, business, news and entertainment," pointed out the Connecticut Attorney General, who warns Microsoft: "Stop your eight hundred pound gorilla from blocking access to the Internet Information Superhighway."[51]

---

49. Joel Klein, Assistant Attorney General, News Hour with Jim Lehrer, PBS 5/18/98.
50. Dennis Vaco, New York Attorney General, NBC Nightly News 5/18/98.
51. Richard Blumenthal, Connecticut Attorney General, CBS Evening News 5/18/98.

What if 90 percent of America's television sets were controlled by a single company, and those TVs were rigged to steer consumers to a handful of channels that same company owned? The government says that is the world Microsoft has been trying to create . . . The Internet [is] a market that's too important, the government says, for one company to act as gatekeeper.
— ABC News[52]

Meanwhile, gatekeepers obstruct publication of *Rock Prophecy.*

May 24, 1998: On The Learning Channel a show called *Solar Empire* depicts an asteroid disaster and explores how humans may be transported to another planet traveling inside "a huge hollowed-out asteroid, a space ark. Inside, four thousand families and a traveling zoo of species leave our solar system forever." Also, on this day the Cinemax cable-TV channel airs the 1984 film *Night of the Comet.*

May 29, 1998: *Unsolved Mysteries,* on the Lifetime cable TV channel, re-broadcasts an episode about asteroid impacts.

June 3, 1998: USA cable network premiers *Meteorites!,* a made-for-TV movie starring Tom Wopat. This film takes the cake as the flakiest asteroid flick to date, something like the *Dukes of Hazard* vs. *Jaws.* The plot includes an annual Miss UFO Festival in a town suddenly bombarded by rocks from space. With its *Jaws*-like formula for small town disaster scripts, the mayor of *Meteorites!* asks, "So something fell out of the sky, how does that concern me?. . . I'll have [investigators] come in after the festival is over . . . What do you want me to tell people? – 'We don't know what it was, but you folks better put your hard hats on just in case?' . . . I suggest we put the whole situation on the back burner until after the festival . . . it's the major source of revenue for this town." The ensuing scenes of mayhem are indistinguishable from explosions in a half dozen other asteroid flicks produced within the past two years.

June 6 1998: The Associated Press reports that in Irvine, California the National Research Council convenes a meeting of astronomers and experts in risk assessment and hazard management to "plan methods for asteroid warnings that won't trigger mass panic." The NRC's Committee on Planetary and Lunar Exploration stresses that just a few discovered asteroids turn out to be headed towards Earth "**once scientists refine orbital calculations.**" The Committee proposes a code of conduct under which "astronomers would **seek verification**" before reporting news of a sighting. In other words, a bit of refined *creative calculations* is all it takes to silence the seers. The government thus further tightens its control over what, if any, news about asteroids the public will hear in the future, and when...

---

52. ABC World News 5/18/98.

<u>June 20, 1998</u>: Summer kicks off with a TV blitz advertising the upcoming premier of the movie *Armageddon*. Even McDonalds plasters the airwaves with asteroid ads.

<u>June 29, 1998</u>: The Learning Channel cable TV network airs another new hour-long documentary titled *Doomsday Asteroid*. This is one of the better space rock documentaries and it covers many key issues. It is also the first to portray the March 11, 1998 global scare over news of asteroid 1997XF11's rendezvous with Earth in the year 2028. The program reports how "as astronomers and government agencies scrambled for more data, the public began to grapple with the possibility that the human race was a mere thirty years from extinction." "Thirty years" is the time period that Hendrix predicted for the coming disaster.

"There's about 1500 similar large asteroids that we have yet to discover," reports *Doomsday Asteroid*, "and all it takes is one, to end life on Earth as we know it . . . The threshold for causing a global catastrophe on the Earth is a [rock] about a half mile wide . . . experts estimate that there are as many as half a million Earth crossing asteroids and comets that have yet to be discovered . . . Current surveillance techniques discover an average of twelve new potentially threatening Near Earth Objects per year. But with an estimated two thousand NEOs uncharted, the chances of one entering our orbit undetected are extremely high . . . It is not a matter of *if* it will happen, but *when*."

Rock Prophecy reveals that human life was evolved by Earth specifically for the purpose of developing flight/explosives/speed capability that can protect the planet from impacts. All planets that support life anywhere in the universe evolve the same capability: life forms that can build flight/explosives technology. *Rock Prophecy* maintains that this process is the *main thing* that planets are concerned to do. And *Doomsday Asteroid* speculates that "at long last a species has evolved which is smart enough and has the technology to actually intercede. . . Unlike earthquakes and unlike hurricanes, cosmic impacts are the one natural disaster that we *can* do something about if we make up our minds to do so."

But as Steve Ostro explains, "The key question is whether there are any threatening large asteroids or comets on a collision course with the Earth during the next century."

It always was *a matter of time*. How long did civilization have to fathom our purpose and rise to the occasion before it's too late? *Rock Prophecy* describes the phenomenon of "retarded history" by which humanity's advance towards anti-asteroid technology has been impeded. It is "dominator culture," resources hoarded by a wealthy few at the expense of everyone, which has set efforts back. *Doomsday Asteroid* points out that "the longer you wait to think through what you ought to do, and the longer you wait to put together some sort of a response, the greater the chances are that you will be hit . . . But even if we can detect an Earth-bound object months or years before impact, what can be done to avert a deadly collision? . . . Many of the leading researchers and scientists in the field fear that without additional funding, current projects may be too little too late."

USAF Col. Mike Bodenheimer of NORAD explains that the notion of using nuclear weapons to protect Earth is a fantasy: "Most people have a misconception of our capability to shoot down an incoming asteroid. We can track it through space and we'll know where it's going to land, but we have no weapon capable of going into space to intercept this particular object and try to destroy it or veer it off course. That capability simply doesn't exist at this stage."

In his interview for *Doomsday Asteroid*, filmmaker Paul Almond warns us to, "Pray to be right in the path of that asteroid, because if you are on the other side of the world, then you're going to die slowly. You're going to starve to death. The crops will wither, the days will be like twilight, and there you'll be, trying to protect your one liter of water and your one can of beans from these marauding gangs of bandits, savage and starving, who will stop at nothing to keep themselves alive and take your food and your shelter."

JPL scientist Steve Ostro comments, "We're due to have some contact with [asteroids] . . . We do live in a swarm. Ultimately objects like these will come to us and they'll terminate our civilization . . . So in the long term, these objects represent WINDOWS into our destiny."

Doomsday Asteroid was followed on TLC by a program called *Nature's Fury* which features a "Seattle Doomsday Scenario" depicting the eruption of Mt. Rainier and an earthquake along the Cascadia faultline off the coast of Washington State.

June/July 1998: Cable TV's The Learning Channel rotates repeated broadcasts of the 1996 show *Prophecies – The Final Visions*, and the 1997 program *Prophecies of the Millennium*, both with asteroid segments.

July 1, 1998: The Bruce Willis asteroid movie, *Armageddon*, premiers in theaters worldwide. This film is produced by Jerry Bruckheimer, who also produced the 1996 movie *The Rock*. What's next, a Bruckheimer film titled *And the Prophecy*? It's as if there was a communication between movie producers and financiers sometime in the mid 1990s. A decision was made to cover the asteroid story from several perspectives: from a McDonalds' TV commercial and *The Simpsons Show* to National Geographic and The New York Times. All genre of media began mobilizing for the great "brain train," the conditioning of the public by the media elite to think about asteroids.

When it came to Hollywood films designed for this cause, it was as if Paul Allen's and Steven Speilberg's DreamWorks took the assignment to produce a more "high brow" script, which became the film *Deep Impact*. At the same time, it's as if Bruckheimer accepted the task of creating a "low brow" gut-bucket treatment, a movie for Joe six-pack and the rock and roll crowd. *Armageddon* is the more effective of the two films.

Like *Rock Prophecy, Armageddon* is about a six hundred mile wide asteroid. In the film, the president's "Armageddon speech" is even closer to *Rock Prophecy* when we hear descriptions of civilization as a process of evolution towards anti-asteroid technology.

July 2, 1998: Cable TV's TNT network broadcasts the 1978 feature film *A Fire In the Sky*, about a rock from space slamming into Phoenix, Arizona. Unlike *Meteor*, produced a year later in 1979, *A Fire In The Sky* is at least well written.

July 6, 1998: Jay Leno's monologue on NBC's *Tonight Show* includes jokes about "everybody and his brother making asteroid movies these days."

July 7, 1998: Cable TV's Encore and Movie-Plex channels broadcast the 1979 Sean Connery flick *Meteor.* If you watch back-to-back the 1951 film *When Worlds Collide*, the 1979 film *Meteor*, and the 1998 film *Armageddon,* you see the evolution in human awareness of the asteroid issue over the past half century.

July 8, 1998: There is a segment on ABC-TV's *Good Morning America* on the difference between asteroids and comets, and discussion of scientific facts behind current Hollywood films about space rocks.

July 8, 1998: ABC-TV airs yet another prime time asteroid documentary, titled *Armageddon: Target Earth*, hosted by Leonard Nimoy. "Asteroids have been front page lately," notes Mr. Spock. This ABC special reports that "Earth has a better chance of a fatal collision in orbit than you do on the highway. Swarms of unidentified asteroids are lurking throughout the solar system. The most likely warning is zero." *Target Earth* is the 10th asteroid documentary to bemoan the fact that "there are more people working in your average McDonalds than there are astronomers patrolling the heavens." (And all of the documentaries use almost the exact same wording for this phrase that was first used in the October 1995 *NOVA* documentary titled *Doomsday Asteroid.*)

Space Policy Analyst Joan Johnson Freese appears in *Target Earth* and warns, "If today we were to discover an asteroid, about all we could do is try and launch a nuclear warhead on currently existing launch technology. We have no operational capability to deal with an incoming object at this time. If you're assuming that, if there's an incoming object, somebody's going to get a call and say 'Don't worry, we'll take care of it,' you're assuming that that somebody is in the government, and there's nobody there to answer the phone."

July 9, 1998: The *Rock Prophecy* Timeline appears on the internet.

July 11, 1998: Cable TV's Sci-Fi channel airs yet another new hour-long asteroid documentary titled *On A Collision Course With Earth.* Also today, the TNT network broadcasts the 1978 film *A Fire In the Sky.*

July 12, 1998: The Discovery Channel's *Science of the Impossible* program broadcasts another new segment about the asteroid threat, featuring insightful interviews with Steve Ostro and David Morrison.

Throughout July 1998, hundreds of media reports focus on the #1 box office movie in America: *Armageddon.*

Aug. 5, 1998: NASA reports that scientists "have discovered two real asteroids heading in Earth's direction . . . The two asteroids, each of them at least one mile across, have been classified as 'potentially hazardous objects' by the NASA Jet Propulsion Laboratory in Pasadena, California, because they are large enough to cause global effects if they hit Earth."[53]

This is the first "controlled" report about asteroids headed towards Earth after the National Research Council agreed on June 5 to have **all reports censored by the government**. This report claims only that the asteroids are due to arrive "*in a few decades*," but the discovery should have caused more of a stir than the March 11, 1998 reports about asteroid 1997XF11. The difference is **a crack down ban** on space rock stories, ordered by the government in May 1998.

From now on the government, and the unjust monied men who control government, dictate what the public will hear, and not hear, about asteroids.

Informing the public that we need to build "Star Wars" weapons as protection against asteroids is impractical. Panic reactions would accompany denial, disbelief, and ridicule. The most effective action government today can take is to convince us that we need Star Wars lasers to fend off missiles from rogue nations. Much of the public is conditioned to listen to this logic. And that's exactly what's happening at millennium's end, we are mounting a half-hearted, feeble, and SECRET attempt to build anti-asteroid technology, and the government is telling the public that these expenditures are for "anti missile systems."

December 1, 1998: PBS airs *Toutatis,* produced by the National Film Board of Canada. This is the last of the *great awakening* asteroid documentaries. All of the familiar faces featured in previous treatments reappear for a final warning in this chic new age production. An astronomer from Spacewatch explains how each night, "In about an hour and a half, we take three pictures of the sky, each about as big as my finger held out at arm's length, over six or seven hours we might cover an area of sky about as big as my whole hand. It's interesting to think of how little area we actually cover of the sky, compared to the whole sky that's up there, and yet we're able still to find many hundreds of asteroids each night."

March 17, 1999: "Closely following Senate approval of a missile-defense bill," reports the Associated Press, "the House passed its own version of a system to protect…against a limited ballistic missile attack."

The chief sponsor of the legislation told colleagues, "It's a national priority that this Congress needs to address." The bill would commit the Pentagon to building the system. The House voted 317-102 to approve it. President Clinton vetoed a similar measure in 1995. The House bill states that "it is the official policy of the United States to deploy a national missile defense." The chairman of the House intelligence committee said the legislation of only 15 words "is **a deceptively simple bill, but it speaks volumes to the entire planet.**" The House measure envisions a scaled-back version of the Strategic

53. CNN Internet News 8/6/98.

Defense Initiative proposed by then-President Ronald Reagan – and derided by Democrats as "Star Wars."

April 1, 1999: *Rolling Stone* pulls an April Fool's joke in mid March. Exactly one year after learning about *Rock Prophecy*, editors at *Rolling Stone* put Hendrix on the worst cover in the magazine's history. Dated April 1st, this foolish issue features inane interviews with guitar greaser musicians discussing Jimi's "monster technique." And as if to drive home the point that *Rock Prophecy* is *alien* to *Stone* age sensibilities, this Fool's Day rag contains hyped up tripe about cyber brat Joe Firmage's super superficial claims of visitation by "Lost In Space" extraterrestrials.

A common ASSumption is that interest in asteroid impacts on Earth is similar to interest in UFO's, outer space, and even space people. Many people ASSociate asteroids with the occult. Which is ironic because this is one case where scientists think the opposite! *Any* geologist or planetary scientist will attest to, not only the *real* existing threat of asteroid disaster, but also to the *inevitability* of it.

May 20, 1999: On the day when the fourth sequel to the *Star Wars* movie premiers worldwide, ABC World News reports, "On a mountain top in New Mexico stands the once Top Secret Starfire Optical Range. Here physicists developed a laser that military planners hoped to take into space as part of the $32 billion Star Wars project, to use space-based laser weapons... Now the Air Force dream has fallen from deep space to 40,000 feet, to a 747 [airplane] armed with a laser...It's a $1.6 billion gamble. If it works, the military wants $11 billion to equip seven 747s with lasers...The Pentagon worries that it may not work...A defense department assessment warned that **the lasers effectiveness might be reduced by atmospheric turbulance...and the laser can only fire so far**...The Air Force has scheduled more tests, but the head of the program does not believe there should be any further delays. '**We don't have time to wait around,**' said Col. Mike Booen, '**We need to hurry.**' But it's the Air Force's need to hurry that worries Congress and many in the Pentagon. The airborne laser program is experimental, rush it, they say, and you risk, like Star Wars, wasting billions of dollars on something that may never work."

June 4, 1999: The PBS News Hour airs a segment titled "Rocket Science" which reports, "In 1983 Ronald Reagan...envisioned space based lasers that would shoot down incoming missiles....Sixteen years and more than $50 billion after President Reagan's announcement, the Clinton administration is developing a more modest ground based national missile defense system...The system would be designed to knock down enemy missiles above the atmosphere... but critics question whether it will ever work...Joseph Cirincione of the Carnegie Endowment for International Peace says **the challenges may be insurmountable**: "Since 1962 **America has spent $120 billion trying to create a missile defense system**...Since the Star Wars program began in 1983, we've spent almost $55 billion just on this latest rush. **It's not for lack of money, it's not for lack of effort, that we don't have a missile defense system.**"

> *We talk about Star Wars as if all we have to do is decide to go and we go, but*
> *the physics haven't been invented yet to do Star Wars.*   – John Glen

<u>July 31, 1999</u>: The ashes of Eugene Shoemaker are encapsulated in a satellite and crashed onto the lunar surface by NASA.

<u>August 8, 1999</u>: Cable's Sci-Fi Channel begins "The Sky Is Falling" week, and airs a parade of space rock flicks depicted in this Timeline.

<u>August 26, 1999</u>: ABC's Nightline In Primetime considers the issue of mass extinctions in this hour long TV special.

<u>November, 1999</u>: Against monumental odds, *Rock Prophecy* is finally published by First Century Press in time to proclaim the Unmillennium.

In 2002 NASA plans to land a rover machine on an asteroid.

The asteroid story can't be taken any further by media. A similar thing happened with the Hendrix story. Several dozen "Hendrix books" have been published, and in a sense they're all the same book, because they all follow a narrow menu range of concepts about Hendrix, ideas that the media elite approve of and permit/finance. Statements about Hendrix that don't fit into this narrow litmus test list of concepts are weeded out, left unpublished.

We are in a period where the same thing has happened to the "asteroid story." The media elite have defined the "dozen high concepts" that published reports about asteroids follow. Ideas like those expressed in *Rock Prophecy* are excluded. But the blitz of asteroid stories and reports listed in the Timeline above, and triggered by *Rock Prophecy,* now set the stage for a text of revolutionary context surrounding the asteroid issue. *Rock Prophecy* is a philosophical horror story – what the anti-equality, unfree media is most concerned to obstruct and crush.

When *Rock Prophecy* is read from beginning to end, come back to the Timeline listings above and gauge for yourself whether or not my unpublished manuscript influenced wealthy string-pullers who set an agenda for asteroid issues in mass media. Was my manuscript studied at the LOC by paid consultants? In response to the contents of *Rock Prophecy,* were strategies devised to use media to influence the public's attitude about asteroids?

Overexposing the asteroid story in mass media achieves the effect of distancing this issue away from Hendrix. The *purpose* of overexposing asteroid reports is to dilute the whole topic, it is a tactic designed to deny Jimi's prediction. Left out of all media reports about asteroids are the implications that Jimi's *Prophecy* holds for world history and religions. Those implications are explained in this book.

Because stories about asteroids were relentlessly reported during 1996 and 1997 and 1998 and 1999, this book has been made to appear like an example of what *The New York Times* calls "bandwagoneers whose sudden interest in asteroids was excited by the smell of money."[54] But the June 5, 1995 copyright date for my manuscript proves that the opposite is true: *Rock Prophecy* was *not* inspired by stories in the media, rather, were the men who control media inspired by my research? What the ruling class seeks is this: as the asteroid approaches Earth, the men who control media can now say, "This is *not* a Hendrix Prophecy! Many people were predicting an asteroid disaster and reporting the possibility, if Hendrix was on to this too, it's just a meaningless coincidence."

Keep in mind the following:

1) No one anywhere understood Jimi's Prophecy until I deciphered his writings and copyrighted the explanation on June 5, 1995.

2) More than three decades ago Hendrix envisioned an asteroid disaster. He was not just *aware* of the possibility, he *predicted* in 1969 that "in about thirty years" we'll see what he means.

3) The escalation of asteroid stories that appeared in the media, starting in October 1995, five months *after Rock Prophecy* arrived at the Library of Congress, suggests that my writings are being monitored at the LOC.

4) A third of this book explains Jimi's prediction. The rest explains how and why men have designed world religions to control women and maximize access to sex. Throughout history it's been these beliefs and customs that have impeded our advance and left us vulnerable to impacts. Hendrix is central to our understanding of this, in ways previously unseen.

The ruling class of dominators will arrange to confiscate all copies of *Rock Prophecy*. They aim to erase every trace of this book. As the asteroid approaches and civilization nears its end, the dominators intend that during our final years, the unjust monied, so-called "rich," will enjoy access to undeserved pleasures in unlimited amounts. *Rock Prophecy* reveals what Hendrix intended to communicate: dominators have enslaved humanity and left us prone to a catastrophe that need not have been.

EstablishMENt think tanks have monitored the world's network of Hendrix researchers since before Jimi's death in September 1970. When the connections in *Rock Prophecy* are made available to the public, men who control media will condemn this book and obstruct publicity about it. Resist by spreading word of the Prophecy. Anyone who can help, please contact First Century Press.

---

54. The New York Times Magazine 7/28/96, p.18.

A BLEND OF REJECTIONS

In my efforts to publish this book, of the people I contacted, everyone who was rich, or in a position to help publish, chose instead to obstruct the Prophecy, but their victims – people who are persecuted and discriminated against – were eager to read it. This book therefore is the dividing line between the unjust monied, so-called "rich," and the masses of enslaved workers. *Rock Prophecy* is the dividing line between good and evil during the final days of our race.

> *This Child is destined...to be a sign that will be opposed so that the inner thoughts of many will be revealed.*   – Luke 2:34-35

Men said, "It's a feminist story;" women said, "Hendrix is a male icon."

Whites said, "It's a black culture book;" blacks said, "Hendrix appeals to whites."

Heterosexuals said, "It's a gay book;" homosexuals said, "Hendrix has nothing to do with gay liberation."

Theologians said, "This is antichrist heresy;" atheists said, "It's too religious."

Hendrix fans said, "But Jimi is just a fraction of your story;" Hendrix haters said, "There's too much Jimi."

Optimists said, "It's a pessimistic plot;" pessimists said, "If we're doomed, who cares?"

Science buffs said, "There's too much mysticism;" spiritualists said, "it's space age sci-fi."

Young people said, "Forget about the past;" old people said, "The future won't concern us."

Academics said, "It's a humorous story;" comedians said, "It's a serious book."

Jewish people said, "You're unsympathetic to Semitic culture;" skinheads said, "You're an apologist for Hebrew myths."

Employers said, "You're fired for the thoughts in your head;" the welfare board said, "New laws make you ineligible for help."

> My supporters said, "Everyone is persecuting you;" my persecutors said, "We'll take you to court with lots of money and use laws written by and for rich men to obstruct this book and you'll be out of work and ineligible for welfare and left to vie among criminals in the street where we'll make your murder look like an act of random violence . . ."

They would not be warned about Jimi's prediction, they were conditioned not to listen.

The unfree elitist media will ignore *Rock Prophecy*. Reviewers who are compelled to mention it will dismiss the story and deny what it explains. But my interpretations of Jimi's words can then legitimately be considered *deconstructions*. Chris Baldick explains, "The dominant Western tradition of thought has attempted to establish grounds of certainty and truth by repressing the limitless instability of language. The differential nature of meanings in language ceaselessly defers or postpones any determinate meaning: language is an endless chain or 'play of difference' which logocentric discourses try vainly to fix to some original or final term that can never be reached. Deconstructive readings track down within a text the . . . internal contradiction that undermines its claims to coherent meaning; or they reveal how texts can be seen to deconstruct themselves . . . to think the 'unthinkable,' often by recourse to strange . . . wordplay . . . to place literary problems of figurative language and interpretation above philosophers' and historians' claims to truth . . . [Deconstruction] opens up limitless possibilities of interpretations . . . tending to challenge the status of the author's intention or of the external world as a source of meaning in texts."[55]

> *I just call it raw, spiritual music, and it's up to the person himself to make what he wants of it.* — Jimi[56]

One more thought about deconstruction:

> *Writing provides the logical model for the working of all language (including speech), with its . . . present meaning beyond the author's power to control or even know. Thus, there can be no question of "this person [guaranteeing] the authenticity of what he says by presiding over it as a controlling consciousness" . . . the effort [is] not to dissolve or annihilate the text but to defamiliarize it, to refresh perception of it by redirecting attention to a process of signification that, however basic, had been overlooked or forgotten or repressed in previous critical practice . . . The endless deferral of definitive meaning that writing reveals and speech conceals but cannot prevent or stop, had been too easily or wishfully short-*

55. Chris Baldick, *The Concise Oxford Dictionary of Literary Terms*, (Oxford Univ. Press, 1990), pp.51-3.
56. David Henderson, *Jimi Hendrix – Voodoo Child of the Aquarian Age*, (New York: Doubleday, 1978), p.257.

circuited by a . . . tradition predisposed to seize, fix, and foreclose meaning
(or the illusion of meaning) through the surreptitious return of writing to
speech . . . The text is only accessible, only exists through interpretation,
and must thus always already hold the potential insight that enables
recognition of the blindness of any of its constructions. Deconstruction, as
the term suggests, is the shadow-side, the dark alter ego, the spectral
conscience of construction. Hence its predisposition toward authors and
texts of a critical, theoretical, or philosophical nature . . . because it leaves
all constituent parts undamaged, enables their reassembly on the more
abstract plane of its own commentary, in the form of an "aftertext" that
survives the blast.   – Howard Felperin[57]

Jimi's Prophecy was known only to me during the seven years that I was writer and consultant for the Hendrix production company. When that company closed, I wrote this book. In the tradition of deconstruction, I reconstruct the Hendrix legacy as an interpretation of world history and religions. I believe these things to be true.

When the asteroid lands, *Rock Prophecy* is intended to be "an aftertext that survives the blast."

About the Format for Quoted Passages:

Rock Prophecy is the *Newest* Testament. "Mini gospels" are interspersed throughout it in the form of quoted passages from the new prophets: Campbell, Chomsky, Chopra, Cohen, Crossan, Daly, McKenna, Muck, Nader, Pagels, Robbins, Romer, Ryan, Tannahill, Ventura, and the rest.

Statements in this book are the opinion of the author, usage of attributed sources is in no way meant to express an endorsement by that person of the work.

If the Bible can be written by a deity in the "third person," with lots of "books" by a supporting cast of writers, then critics should not consider my style unorthodox. Once more the prophets speak for themselves, this time within my edits, arrangements, orderings, and transitions.

                                          – St. Michael – Archangel of Heaven
                    First Century Year 56 of the Uncommon Era (6/6/99 C.E.)

57. Howard Felperin, *Beyond Deconstruction – the Uses and Abuses of Literary Theory*, (Oxford, Clarendon Press, 1985), pp.117-9.

ROCK PROPHECY

Sex & Jimi Hendrix in World Religions
The Original Asteroid Prediction & Microsoft Connection

Chapter 1: Electric Love

ॐ

Everybody has a right to their own releases or their own beliefs,
if they want to believe that a star is purple, or whatever . . .

— Jimi[1]

As a child, Jimi Hendrix liked to draw pictures of outer space. His father recalls times when Jimi would be stargazing and asking questions about where the universe ended. "I wanted to be an actor or a painter," Jimi recalled of those days. "I particularly liked to paint scenes of other planets, *Summer Afternoon on Venus*, and stuff like that. At school the teacher used to say, 'Paint three scenes' and I'd do abstract stuff like *Martian Sunset*. The idea of space travel excited me more than anything . . . Pictures have always fascinated me. I still sketch a lot, but now I've got to learn to paint pictures with my music. That's what the future is about, to paint pictures of Earth and everything."[2]

When he was 23, Jimi was an unknown living in New York and writing songs about the solar system. As his Village friend, Paul Caruso, recalls, "We would talk seriously about trans-cultural phenomena and people from different galaxies, a cultural exchange program."[3] Another friend, Emeretta Marks, remembers, "We would sit there and talk about UFOs and we were *serious*. Nobody wanted to talk about stuff like that, but Jimi would talk about it. He wasn't stupid, I mean, he was so *in tune* with what's out there."[4]

"I want to write mythology stories set to music," Hendrix said, "based on a planetary thing and my imagination in general. It wouldn't be similar to classical music, but I'd use strings and harps, with extreme and opposite musical textures. Like Holst's Planets? No, even greater contrasts."[5]

Science fiction fantasies about outer space and the future are natural companions to Jimi's life and music. His appearance and sound on stage introduced a new era. Nothing like it had been seen nor heard before. No one knew how such noise was made. It was *futuristic*. Like the ancient apes confronting the mysterious monolith in *2001: A Space Odyssey*, rock crowds cowered in awe before Jimi's dramatic amplifier stacks. King Kong screaming through speakers as big as the U.N. building couldn't have been any louder, it seemed. The

1. Douglas Kent Hall and Sue Clark, *The Superstars – In Their Own Words*, (New York: Music Sales Corporation, 1970), p.134.
2. Sunday Observer 3/12/67, Melody Maker 9/26/70.
3. UniVibes #10, 5/93, p.49.
4. Interview with author 11/27/94.
5. Melody Maker 12/23/67.

sound of Hendrix signaled a quantum leap into the future. Not since cave people discovered fire had imaginations been driven to such overload.

> *I was playin' the radio all the time. Thank you very much for lettin' me play the radio. You think I'm jivin', don't you?*
>
> – Jimi on stage[6]

To audiences in 1966, the initial sight of Marshall amp stacks resembled big transistor radios. Hendrix plugged in and waved his guitar-antenna like a conductor's baton, receiving and transmitting extraterrestrial frequencies via Celestion speakers.[7]

> *O Transistor-feeder can you hear me thank you?*
> *The time has come for us to be on the watch,*
> *to know the scent, to recognize,*
> *to stand and visualize, stand and realize.* – Jimi[8]

Hendrix stands as the eternal guitar archetype. Nearly all of that instrument's electronic effects are derivative of him. At the moment when baby boomer audiences became fixated on guitar gurus, Jimi seemed to pop out of Aladdin's lamp and bewitch the whole scene. He was in the ultimate position from which to deliver a Prophecy.

> *You'd think I'd found the lost chord! . . . What we're saying is not protesting, but giving answers. Our next two albums will be toward that scene, giving some kind of solutions for people to grasp.*
>
> – Jimi[9]

Early in 1969, he arrived in London and announced a new vision for a New Year: "The *Electric Ladyland* album was good for the time when we did it, but now we're on to other things. We're going to release another album. It'll be called *First Ray of the New Rising Sun*. I'm trying to use my power. If you give deeper thoughts in your music then the masses will buy them. *First Ray of the New Rising Sun* will be about what we have seen."[10]

---

6. Recording from Worcester, MA, Clark University, Atwood Hall 3/15/68.

7. "Celestion" is a brand of speakers inside Marshall amplifiers.

8. *Cherokee Mist – The Lost Writings of Jimi Hendrix*, with Introduction by M. Fairchild, (New York: Harper Collins, 1993), p.117, *Terra Revolution and Venus*.

9. Tony Brown, *Jimi Hendrix – In His Own Words* (New York: Omnibus Press, 1994), p.81, from an interview in London 1/7/69, and Record Mirror, *King Jimi Holds Court – Plans Mammoth Album*, interview with John King, 1/69.

10. Top Pops, *The First Ray of the New Rising Sun*, 1/69 interview with Tony Norman, p.9, Melody Maker 1/11/69.

FIRST RAY

Jimi's vision of a New Rising Sun was literal and influenced by science fiction books he liked to read. Specifically, in Arthur Clarke's 1952 story, *The Sands of Mars*, scientists detonate one of the Martian moons and transform it into a miniature star. The star warms the surface of the planet, making Mars hospitable for human life. "Project Dawn" climaxes when

> *... the eastern sky was aglow with **the first light of the rising sun**... spilling over the horizon now **the first rays** were touching the hills.* [11]

Similarly, when Hendrix recorded the song "First Ray of the New Rising Sun" in 1970, he envisioned a planet that becomes a star: he sang about "*the Jupiter Sun.*"[12]

BY JOVE!

A dozen years later, the 1982 film of Arthur Clarke's story, *2010, Odyssey 2*, climaxes with an explosion of Jupiter into a star. Clarke borrowed his own Project Dawn concept, from *The Sand of Mars,* of a moon igniting into a star. He adapted the idea to *2010, Odyssey 2* so that, instead of an exploding moon, it is the planet Jupiter that ignites. Clarke's idea of a Jupiter Sun in this 1982 movie is the same vision that Jimi sang about back in 1970 after he read Clarke's book *The Sands of Mars*. Hendrix and Clarke, independently of each other, both envisioned Jupiter becoming a second sun for our solar system, a new sun to light up the night side of Earth and ensure inexhaustible energy as both hemispheres bathe in perpetual daylight. Nighttime becomes a thing of the past. *First Ray of the New Rising Sun* is Jimi's Utopian metaphor for a future world drenched in the energy of multiple-sun plenty: civilization without want, people without need.

> *The Sun is going to give you anything and everything you want.*
> — Jimi[13]

The Sands of Mars was not the only sci-fi story to ignite Jimi's interest in "light." His lyrics for "Purple Haze" are an inspired re-working of Phillip Jose Farmer's 1957 story *Night of Light*, in which violent sunspot activity bathes an alien planet in a recurring "purplish haze," driving the inhabitants to sleep, or to madness.

> *The sky was clear but the stars seemed far away, blobs straining to pierce the purplish haze ... the moon shone golden-purple in the center and silver-*

---

11. Arthur C. Clark, *The Sands of Mars*, (New York: Harcourt Brace, 1952), p.195.
12. Hey Baby (Land of the New Rising Sun)", *Rainbow Bridge* album, Reprise Records 10/71, recorded at Electric Lady Studio on July 1, 1970.
13. Hall and Clark, *The Superstars – In Their Own Words*, p.26.

purple around the edges. So huge was it, it seemed to be falling, and this
apparent down-hurtling was strengthened by the slight shifting of hue in the
purple haze.   – Phillip Jose Farmer[14]

"Purple Haze" by the Jimi Hendrix Experience was introduced to Americans during the summer of 1967. In August Jimi's band was filmed in Los Angeles at the Rudolf Valentino mansion. There they hung out in a room filled with mirrors from floor to ceiling.

Sometime after this trip, Hendrix sang about the mirror room in a demo tape he made of a traditional Mississippi Delta standard called "Catfish Blues."[15] Jimi abandoned the song's usual verses and began singing new lyrics he'd written. Playing the "Catfish" riff on guitar, he sings about himself as a *Voodoo Chile:*

My arrows are made of desire
*from far away as **Jupiter's** sulfur mines,*
down by the methane sea,
my room is made of mirrors . . .[16]

This Hendrix demo tape reveals three things:

1) "Voodoo Chile" is a Hendrix song evolved directly out of "Catfish Blues,"
   an early traditional blues standard;
2) The original lyrics for "Voodoo Chile" include Jimi's earliest known
   reference to a room of mirrors; and
3) "Voodoo Chile" lyrics link the room of mirrors with Jupiter's "sulfur
   mine/methane sea."

"Voodoo Chile" and the mirror room are lyrics that Jimi spun off from "Catfish Blues," the Delta staple made famous by Muddy Waters. Jimi added lyrics about Jupiter's "sulfur mine/methane sea," a cauldron that Hendrix sensed to be volatile. Out of this primordial soup of murky blues emerged the First Ray of his premonition about Jupiter

---

14. Phillip Jose Farmer, *Night of Light*, 1957, published 6/66 by Berkeley Medallion Books, pp.47-8.
15. This song's origins go back to field hollers pre-dating blues recordings. A recorded evolution of "Catfish Blues" *floating versus* and riffs traces the course of Delta performers: "Rollin' and Tumblin' Blues" by Hambone Willie Newburn (1929), "If I had Possession Over Judgement Day" by Robert Johnson (1936), "Catfish Blues" by Robert Petway (1940), "Deep Sea Blues" by Tommy McLennan (1942), "Rolling Stone" by Muddy Waters (1950), "Still a Fool" by Muddy Waters (1951), and "Oh Yeah" by Bo Diddley (1958). In this blues collage Jimi included riffs from "Cat's Squirrel" by Dr. Ross (1959) and "All I Want is a Spoonful" by Papa Charlie Jackson (1925), later adapted as "Spoonful" by Willie Dixon (1960) for Howlin' Wolf. Often Jimi would also throw in some verses of "Rollin' and Tumblin'" by Muddy Waters (1950).
16. "Voodoo Chile/Cherokee Mist" 1968, released on *Jimi By Himself – The Home Recordings* CD included with the book *Voodoo Child – The Illustrated Legend of Jimi Hendrix*, produced by Martin Green, (Berkshire Studios, 1995).

as a sun, as if its light had broken through Jimi's subconscious and surfaced into awareness while he was under a Voodoo spell.

> *You have to go down into a really bad scene before you can come up with*
> *light again.* — Jimi[17]

"Sulfur mines" and "methane seas" are the explosive mix on Jupiter that Jimi saw igniting the giant gas ball planet into a blinding star. It's a vision that came to him in the room full of mirrors, a place of insight and reflection. But this crystal ball of inner visions became an imprisoning state of agitation. Jimi wrote about it in the song "Room Full of Mirrors." "That's more of a mental disarrangement that a person might be thinking," he said. "It says something about broken glass used to be all in my brain."[18]

Jimi introduced the mirror room as a lyric aside when he sang "Voodoo Chile". "Room Full of Mirrors" and "Voodoo Chile" are songs with a shared theme of transformed perceptions and expanded human powers. The mirror room first appears in Jimi's pages of lyrics for the song "Voodoo Chile." He writes about losing sight of himself in the looking glass: *"I see you but Lord knows I can't see me."*[19] Both of these songs address the issue of involuntary *possession*, as if Jimi's body and mind were seized as vehicles through which some inhabitant addresses us. As an artist, Hendrix was evolving, or *being directed*, to introduce our senses to new mediums of communication.

He spoke of constructing a special room for the purpose of transmitting his vision: "This little room can be like a total audio-visual environment type of thing. Like you can go in there and you just lay back and the whole thing just blossoms out with this color and sound type of scene. It's like a reflection room where you go in . . . and just jingle out your nerves."[20]

His own nerves were tormented by "mental disarrangement," as he put it – states of involuntary possession, trans-medium channeling and spontaneous astral travel. He called it the mirror room because he felt trapped in visions of self-reflection, seen through the eyes of a shaman transfixed with extrasensory perceptions. Staring back at him through the looking glass was the person he named *Voodoo Child*.

> *The mirrors are beating the hell out of my mind. I feel like my mind is hung*
> *up on a clothes rack . . . I can't see my own reflection . . . Scream out the*
> *reflection of your friends, and you know I'm gonna scream. There are a*

17. Circus 3/69, p.40.
18. Tony Brown, *Hendrix – The Final Days* (London: Rogan House, 1997), p.91, from an interview with Keith Altham, London, 9/11/70.
19. "Voodoo Chile/Cherokee Mist" 1968, released on *Jimi By Himself – The Home Recordings* CD included with the book *Voodoo Child – The Illustrated Legend of Jimi Hendrix*.
20. Brown, *Hendrix – The Final Days*, p.93, from an interview with Keith Altham, London, 9/11/70.

million lions trapped in the Grand Canyon. Scream out – Friend; God, tell
this idiot to get the hell out of me, and to get me the hell out of this dammed
mirror room!   – Jimi[21]

In 1968, Jimi conceived of "Room Full of Mirrors" and "The New Rising Sun" near the end of a creative streak that produced his third album, *Electric Ladyland*. The three descending chords of the song "The New Rising Sun" are reversed into three ascending chords in "Room Full of Mirrors," representing a rise to perceptual breakthrough. In "Room Full of Mirrors" he emphasizes the uplifting progression with octave-heightened tonal effects and slides up the guitar frets. Endless echo conveys infinite reflections – *"See nothing but sunshine, all around"* – he sings of Earth surrounded by light, each turn of the axis seeing a Sun over horizons of perpetual day. This is what Jimi called the *Valleys of Sunrise.*[22]

<u>BOTH SUNS</u>

Hendrix unveiled "Room Full of Mirrors" at Record Plant Studios in August 1968. Two weeks later, during a week of police riots at Chicago's Democratic Convention, he scripted a *Letter to the Room Full of Mirrors* in which he wrote, *"the sky cracked wide open . . . 'That's law and order,' said the Border guard . . . splitting **both suns** apart . . ."*

In September, he rented a house in L.A. and recorded "Room Full of Mirrors" at TTG Studios. A year had passed since his trip to the mirror room in the Valentino mansion. At TTG, Paul Caruso played harp for Jimi's new song. "Room Full of Mirrors" is about inner visions of light. He sang about Jupiter and the mirror room when he wrote "Voodoo Chile." "Jimi was very *Jovian* you know," said Paul.[23] In astrology, Jupiter rules Sagittarius, Jimi's birth sign. Jupiter is the planet of Law, an ignitable sulfur mine that Hendrix saw becoming one in a pair of *"both suns."*

While he recorded "Room Full of Mirrors," millions of miles away a strange thing was happening in outer space. A comet had entered our solar system. It was heading for Jupiter.

> *For eons the comet must have drifted inwards, picking up speed. In the early*
> *1970s it was nabbed by Jupiter's strong gravity and eventually torn apart. At*
> *that point a head on collision was inevitable.*
>
>   – Michael Guillen[24]

---

21. Jimi Hendrix, *Room Full of Mirrors* rap, late 1960s, a portion of this rap is published in *Electric Gypsy by* Harry Shapiro (London: Heinemann, 1990) p.356, the complete transcript is published in *Jimi Hendrix – The Studio Log* (Jimpress, 12/96), pp.48-9.
22. *Valleys Of Neptune – Arising,* Air France stationary 6/7/69, published in *Cherokee Mist – The Lost Writings of Jimi Hendrix,* p.70.
23. UniVibes #10 5/93 p.49.
24. ABC News Nightline 7/22/94.

Jupiter is the solar system's vacuum cleaner. If Jupiter weren't there those comets would still be running around, smashing into all of the inner planets, including the Earth...and we wouldn't be here, we couldn't live on an Earth that was being smashed by a comet every thousand years.

— David Levey[25]

Hendrix's premonition was to sense a flash on Jupiter. In a visionary state he foresaw an immense Jovian explosion which he interpreted as the gasball planet's detonation, as if a bullet had pierced a huge balloon. Like the Sun, Jupiter is composed of gas. The planet is in fact so much like the Sun that many astronomers consider it to be a fallen star. "Some people call Jupiter a failed star," notes John Spencer of the Lowell Observatory. "If Jupiter was maybe thirty times more massive, the heat in the center would be so intense that nuclear reaction could start and it would be like a second Sun in the solar system."[26]

Planetary geologist, the late Eugene Shoemaker, and his wife Carolyn, both of the Lowell Observatory, specialized in asteroids and comets. They discovered more comets in space than anyone in history, and they knew that collisions play a key role in our evolving solar system. In March 1993, the Shoemakers and astronomer David Levey spotted the comet that had been drawn into Jupiter's gravitational field back when Jimi was alive. The ball of rock and ice had been torn apart by the planet's gravity. When spotted by astronomers on Earth, the Shoemaker-Levey 9 comet existed as a row of twenty-six glowing fragments. It was christened the "String-of-Pearls."

In July 1994, on the 25th anniversary of Neil Armstrong's first walk on the Moon, each of the 26 pieces of Shoemaker-Levey 9 individually bombarded the surface of Jupiter. One of the rocks was nearly two miles wide. When it struck the Jovian atmosphere, it produced an explosion that rose up thousands of miles into space. The impact gave the planet a massive black eye, a ring of destruction wider in diameter than the entire Earth. "Imagine one Hiroshima-strength bomb being exploded every second for several years," said David Levey, "that was the energy released by Shoemaker-Levey 9. It left a cloud larger than the Earth that lasted on Jupiter for almost a year . . . What if it hit us? . . . After comet Shoemaker-Levey 9 nobody was laughing."[27]

Prior to the comet's impact, scientists worldwide had debated the possibility of it detonating the Jovian globe and producing a monster flare. But Eugene Shoemaker concluded that the mass of the largest comet fragment was "not strong enough to ignite Jupiter." Carolyn Shoemaker explained, "In order to really ignite, you need oxygen also, and we don't have that in those bands of atmosphere that are being impacted."[28]

---

25. *On Jupiter*, Discovery Channel 12/95.
26. Ibid.
27. *Fire In The Sky*, TBS 3/23/97.
28. McNeil/Lehrer News Hour, PBS 7/22/94.

However, after the impact data were studied, it was revealed that *water*, which contains oxygen, is present. As a result of the massive 1994 explosions, scientists made several other striking discoveries. Vicki Meadows of the JPL/Anglo-Australian-Observatory explains, "The infrared spectrum we were taking, in that wavelength range, in all those colors, we were able to pick up many, many molecules that are visible in comets and in Jupiter. So we were able to see, initially, material from Jupiter come up; things like methane and ammonia we saw first, and after that we saw something which was very amazing to us, which was a lot of carbon monoxide and water."[29]

In December 1995, the Galileo Space Probe became the first man-made object to penetrate Jupiter's thick brownish clouds. Galileo project manager Bill O'Neil announced, "There is ammonia, there is *methane*, and there is *sulfur*."[30] More than a quarter century prior to this discovery Hendrix sang of *"Jupiter's sulfur mines, down by the methane sea."* How did Jimi know that Jupiter's environment was full of sulfur and methane?

The 1995 Galileo probe revealed that Jupiter's surface is not warmed by the Sun, but rather from an internal heat source. On Earth, two miles beneath the ocean surface, animals of the deep-sea beds survive on sulfur and heat rather than sunlight and plants. Scientists theorize that similar conditions exist on one of Jupiter's moons: Europa. John Spencer of the Lowell Observatory concludes, "If there's anywhere in the solar system where there might be physical life other than the Earth, Europa would be close to that."[31]

Monika Dannemann, Hendrix's last girlfriend, has reported how "Jimi said that he comes from the planet Jupiter."[32] Might she have interpreted a statement from him expressing premonitions and visions that *come* from Jupiter as being *about* Jupiter?

> *In all your strength and splendor. . . I come running home to you Jupiter.*
> — Jimi[33]

GYPSY SUN

After his *Electric Ladyland* album was released, including the "Voodoo Chile" lyrics about Jupiter's sulfur mines and methane seas, Hendrix started to speak frequently about "First Ray of the New Rising Sun." In 1969, as the String-of-Pearls were getting sucked into Jupiter's gravity, Jimi formed a new band he called Gypsy Sun & Rainbows. When this group debuted at Woodstock, Hendrix announced on stage, "This is the First Ray." The band featured new songs named "Steppingstone" and "Message To Love," titles that are explained later.

---

29. *On Jupiter*, Discovery Channel 12/95.
30. Ibid.
31. Ibid.
32. Monika Dannemann, (unpublished manuscript, edited by Richard Levey, 1971), p.95.
33. Monika Dannemann, *The Inner World of Jimi Hendrix*, (New York: St. Martin's Press, 1995), p.104.

"Gypsy Sun" is Jimi's name for the new star. His new group was named for this. The point is that Hendrix sensed an immense light coming from Jupiter, and he sensed it at a time when a comet was captured by Jupiter's gravity, destined to impact that planet a quarter century later as Shoemaker-Levey-9. Those blinding impacts flashing from Jupiter in 1994 represent Jimi's premonition, an intense glare predestined in the trajectory of the comet while Jimi was alive, when it was nabbed by Jupiter's gravity.

What Jimi saw was a remote view of a process actually happening in the solar system while he lived. In a sense, Hendrix was sensing messages from the system of planets, as if Jupiter were emitting signals to somehow "communicate" that its gravity had captured a rock and was pulling it to impact (it would take 25 more years to arrive). Is it so inconceivable that planets might "signal" in this way, like great whales squealing to each other from across oceans? Was Hendrix sensitive to, or somehow *viewing* events out in space?

Impact on the giant gas planet Jupiter meant intense upset to the asteroid belt. This chain of rocks is kept in orbit by the shepherd-like presence of Jovian gravity. When a comet hits Jupiter, vibrating disturbances scatter asteroids like ricochet, raining down on the inner planets.

Whether Jupiter explodes into a star, or is impacted by a comet, Jimi refers to the resulting flash as "the Jupiter Sun" and "the Gypsy Sun." The impact explosions in July '94 are what these titles predict. Hendrix sensed that this event dislodges the Rock and catapults its path into Earth. In his lyrics for "Voodoo Chile," he warns of the threat. He recapitulates this song at the end of the *Electric Ladyland* album, and sings about chopping down a mountain into pieces.

> *If I don't see you no more in this world,*
> *I'll meet you in the next one, don't be late...*
>
> *— Jimi[34]*

As soon as that album was released, Jimi turned his attention to developing and recording "The New Rising Sun" and "Room Full of Mirrors." He now sang about *smashing* the mirrors. He was laying in place the foundation of a *Prophecy*.

THIRTY YEARS

Electric Ladyland hit the top of the charts while *Billboard* and *Rolling Stone* magazines voted the Jimi Hendrix Experience as Group of the Year. It was then that Jimi started dropping hints to the media about an event due to happen in thirty years' time:

---

34. "Voodoo Child (slight return)", *Electric Ladyland*, Reprise Records 10/68.

We're not here to collect awards. We're here to turn people on to the right way, because there's some really strange scenes coming up through . . . There's other moves I have to make now. Some of the vibrations people claim they're getting now, it's true considering the fact that the Earth is going through a physical change soon. Since the people are part of Earth, they are going to feel it too. In many ways they are a lot of the reason for causing it . . . **The solar system is going through a change soon and it's going to affect the Earth itself in about thirty years**. *This room is just a crumb from the crust of the pie, and there's no moving from any one land to another to save yourself in that respect.*
                                                                              – Jimi[35]

Sometimes there's a lot of things that add up in your head...so I just unmasked appearances.   – Jimi [36]

Jimi started to tell me about being from an asteroid belt off the coast of Mars.
                                                                              – Chuck Wein[37]

The asteroid belt orbiting between Mars and Jupiter in our solar system is a zone of rocks and boulders tumbling around the Sun. Occasionally these mountains collide, break up, and scatter piecemeal among the planets. One category is known as the "chaotic group"; these wander in and out of the orbits of the planets, often moving in wildly strange ways. Another group of unusual asteroids is called the "Trojans," because they chaperone the planet Jupiter. Some of the rocks lead the giant planet in its orbit, while others follow.

Victor Clube of Oxford University explains, "Essentially, there are two catastrophic machines in the solar system which are directing missiles at us. One of them is the . . . Oort Cloud [surrounding the outer solar system] which is perturbed by the galactic environment. And the other one is the . . . asteroid belt, which is regularly perturbed by Jupiter in its orbit close to the asteroid belt."[38]

The story of the asteroid belt in our solar system is explained.   – Jimi[39]

---

35. L.A. Free Press 1969.

36. Henderson, *Jimi Hendrix – Voodoo Child of the Aquarian Age*, p.400, from an interview with John Burks, NYC 2/4/70.

37. Rolling Stone, *Live From the Asteroid Belt*, 10/26/72, p.12.

38. Nova, *Doomsday Asteroid*, PBS 10/31/95.

39. *Moondust* 30 page screenplay by Jimi Hendrix. 27 handwritten pages of the 30 page script were published in *Cherokee Mist – The Lost Writings of Jimi Hendrix* (Harper Collins 1993), pp.32-45, the 28th page of *Moondust* was published as exhibit #479 in the catalogue for Sothebys sale 6258 *Animation Art and Rock 'n' Roll Memorabilia Dec. 14 and 17, 1991*. The remaining two pages, 29 and 30, appeared with the entire 30 page manuscript on public display at Sothebys in New York during the week prior to the auction on December 14. 1991. While on public display, the final two pages of *Moondust* were read and noted by Charles Blass, including the last page in which Jimi reveals that his screenplay is a set up for "*the story of the asteroid belt in our solar system.*"

> *Jupiter became the controlling body in the outer solar system, which included keeping the asteroid belt in its place . . . What if there is some quirk of fate – the perturbation of an orbit because of a passing star or the push of a shock wave from a supernova – that throws more asteroids in our direction for us to dodge?* — Patricia Barnes-Svarney[40]

Jimi saw a blinding flash on Jupiter, an explosion which generates massive shock waves through space and disrupts millions of asteroids out of their solar orbits and out of the Oort Cloud (named after its discoverer: *J. Hendrik* Oort). Shockwaves from the 1994 Jupiter blast dislodged countless rocks from the asteroid belt and catapulted them like projectiles in towards the Sun and towards Earth.

COMETS, METEORS, ASTEROIDS

Asteroid and comet collisions with Earth are not uncommon. Geologists have identified nearly 200 impact craters around the world. Eugene and Carolyn Shoemaker chronicled the pockmarked history of our globe and discovered more impact sites than anyone else. "The swarm of small bodies which we call planetesimals continues to buzz around the planets," explained Eugene. "Long after the planets were formed, there was still an intense bombardment. Somewhat less than 10 percent [of the rocks] remain today in a huge cloud surrounding the Sun and if passing stars go near this cloud they perturb a few of them which fall down towards the Sun to the neighborhood of the Earth and we see them as comets."[41]

Comets are iced-over rocks. "They sometimes come very near to the Earth," notes physicist Otto Muck. "These encounters are usually harmless because there is only a minute amount of substance in these 'shooting stars.' The core of a comet, sometimes called its 'head,' is very insubstantial and often breaks up into several parts. So does the 'tail,' which consists of the mass of gases following the comet's head. Most comets end up as showers."[42]

More dangerous than comets are meteorites, such as the Taiga meteorite which smashed to the ground near the Tunguska River in Siberia on June 30, 1908. Meteorites enter the Earth's atmosphere with extreme velocity. Traveling at the rate of several miles per second, their front surface becomes extremely hot. "The meteor can be seen as a dim, gaseous ball," writes Muck, "its brightness increasing toward the center, which is usually reddish or greenish in color. Occasionally it trails a gaseous tail like that of a comet, and the very large specimens are sometimes brighter than the Sun. The tremendous heat expansion sets up high tensile stresses in the body of the meteorite,

---

40. Patricia Barnes-Svarney, *Asteroid – Earth Destroyer or New Frontier?* (New York: Plenum Press, 1996), pp.46, 222.
41. Nova, *The Outer Planets,* PBS 1990.
42. Otto Muck, *The Secret of Atlantis,* p.159.

usually strong enough to explode it, often with a thunderous bang . . . fireballs of various sizes may rain from the sky. But, the vast majority of meteorites, for all their amazing brilliance, are minute substance. Only a few weigh more than three and a half ounces. They become vaporized and are extinguished long before they reach the ground . . . Not all meteorites are harmless, however, as the enormous hole of the Arizona Crater shows."[43]

An even larger hole was discovered in the Atlantic Ocean. American anthropologist Alan Kelso de Montigny was the first to assert that a giant asteroid had smashed into the Caribbean Sea near the arc of the Lesser Antilles. Otto Muck researched the geological evidence for what is known as the Carolina Meteorite. Muck concurs that a huge rock crashed into the Atlantic eleven thousand years ago near what is now Charleston, North Carolina. In a radius of several hundred miles around the impact site, on the ocean floor, are the remains of the rim of a half-submerged giant crater. Within a wider radius, which encompasses parts of America's eastern seaboard, the pockmarked surface of a crater field remains.

"The crater field could not have been formed by either a burst comet head or by a very large shower of meteorites," theorizes Muck. "A comet head is much too small and too deficient in mass. Its explosion might have caused an impressive display of celestial fireworks . . . but these illuminations high up in the atmosphere would have had no consequences on Earth . . . It would have been much larger than a meteor, as defined by astronomers . . . [for] the Carolina Meteorite . . . the weight of the solid core of the celestial body will be in excess of 10^{12} tonnes . . . which corresponds to a sphere about 6 1/4 miles in diameter . . . a diameter of several miles before it exploded . . . The Carolina Meteorite . . . must in fact have been something greater than a meteorite or a comet. It was much too big to be included in this category of small, or very small, celestial vagrants. It must have been an asteroid."[44]

Asteroids, or minor planets, were first discovered by Italian astronomer Giuseppe Piazzi on New Year's Day, 1801. By 1905, five hundred of them had been located. Fifty years later more than two thousand were mapped. Muck notes that "at the perihelion they come very close to the Sun inside the orbits of Mars, of Earth, and even of Venus. The only other bodies that have such extreme orbital conditions are periodical comets and meteor showers."[45]

"There are classes of them," explains Dr. James Garvin of the Goddard Spaceflight Center. "Some are perturbed from the asteroid belt to cross the orbits of the Earth . . . Meteors are rocks that are under a mile across. Once you get to the size of an asteroid, a mile or larger, the potential for mass destruction becomes more of a certainty."[46]

43. Ibid. p.160.
44. Ibid. pp.157-8, 164.
45. Ibid. p.165.
46. Practical Guide to the Universe, The Learning Channel 2/95.

In February 1936, a large asteroid named Adonis passed within 186,000 miles of Earth, so close that it was nearly captured by our planet's gravity. Had it fallen it would have wrought destruction equal to several nuclear explosions.[47] A year later, three small asteroids exploded in tremendous fireballs a mile above the jungle floor of Brazil, igniting a ground fire that destroyed over 800 square miles of rain forest.[48] In 1994, another asteroid hit over the Pacific Ocean near Micronesia. It blew up in the atmosphere with a force five times the size of the bomb dropped on Hiroshima.

"There are potentially thousands to millions of these Earth crossing asteroids that are ready to shove in the right direction to collide with our Earth," warns Dr. Garvin, "and they're going to, there is no question."[49]

> *One thing that makes the comet and asteroid impact hazard so important relative to other hazards is that it is the one hazard that is capable of killing billions of people, of putting at risk our entire civilization. We could have any number of storms or earthquakes or volcanoes and they can do terrible damage locally but they do not put the entire planet at risk the way an impact does.* — David Morrison[50]

"If you have two hundred objects with diameters of a kilometer or more with orbits that cross the Earth's orbit," estimates physicist Ed Tagliaferri, "a significant fraction of those are going to hit the Earth. It's not if, it's when."[51]

> *The solar system is going through a change soon and it's going to affect the Earth itself in about thirty years.* — Jimi [52]

> *The people were forewarned...We must prepare for the amazement in how the truth shall be presented. Nature shows more than anything, and it does get pretty amazing.* — Jimi[53]

In 1994, Earth was witness to the amazing String-of-Pearls impact explosions on Jupiter. Blinding lights from the blasts flashed as a warning to our planet. The explosions triggered massive shock waves, perturbing the asteroid belt's chain of rocks, held in place by Jupiter's gravity and the Sun's magnetic field.

---

47. Muck, *The Secret of Atlantis*, p.166.
48. *Fire In The Sky*, TBS 3/23/97.
49. *Practical Guide to the Universe*, The Learning Channel 2/95.
50. *Asteroids: Deadly Impact*, NBC National Geographic 2/26/97
51. *Fire In The Sky*, TBS 3/23/97.
52. San Diego Free Press 6/13/69
53. *Cherokee Mist – The Lost Writings of Jimi Hendrix*, pp.115, 117, *Terra Revolution and Venus*.

> *. . . reasons for the change to the chain of the space rocks . . . the Sun*
> *reacted and the magnet, upset, destroyed the world.*   — Jimi[54]

Like a shot of cosmic billiards, a chain reaction domino effect from the Jupiter explosions has dislodged a Rock and set it on a collision course with Earth. Back in 1969, Hendrix prophesied that our planet will be affected "in about thirty years." His prediction is non-specific; it is an approximation based on his vision of events set in motion around our solar system while he was alive. In terms of geologic time, "about thirty years" could be any time during the next decade.

In addition, "about thirty years" after Jimi made his prediction came the discovery in 1998 of asteroid 1997XF11, which is due to rendezvous with Earth in "about thirty years," 2028. It could be that asteroid 1997XF11 is the Rock that Jimi predicted will hit us.

The point is that the asteroid's trajectory had been set at a time when Hendrix could sense its impending impact and warn us. He described the coming upheaval in a song called "Valleys of Neptune Arising," with lyrics about mountain-size tidal waves and erupting volcanoes as the Earth is shaken from end to end. He sings, *"This ain't bad news, good news or any news, it's just the truth, better save your souls while you can."*[55]

> **There's a physical change coming soon. It's neither bad nor good. It's just true. The world's gonna go like topsy-turvy soon.**
>   — Jimi[56]

Astronomer Jim Scotti predicts, "Objects bigger than a kilometer, which we think are the ones that we should really most be worried about, that can do the most damage, given enough time, sooner or later one of them will hit us. There are something like fifteen hundred to two thousand of those objects on Earth-crossing orbits."[57]

"If we get to a really big event," estimates Eugene Shoemaker, "say a ten kilometer crater, which is still small compared to the biggest, that's equal to the energy of all of the nuclear weapons in the world if you heap them up in a pile and set them off. Ten thousand megatons makes a ten kilometer crater."[58]

A rock ten kilometers wide would unleash a billion-megaton blast. Such a catastrophe devastated the Earth 65 million years ago. The tip of what is now Mexico's Yucatan peninsula is the site where scientists discovered that an asteroid five miles in diameter plunged to Earth and wiped out the dinosaurs. "You would have seen an enormous bright flash in the sky," said Shoemaker, "in fact it would have been a flash like looking at a nuclear explosion."[59]

---

54. Ibid. pp.115-6.
55. Ibid. p.70 *Valleys of Neptune-Arising.*
56. Brown, *Jimi Hendrix — In His Own Words*, p.65, from an interview in Beverly Hills, CA 6/69.
57. *On Jupiter*, Discovery Channel 12/95.
58. Nova, *Doomsday Asteroid*, PBS 10/31/95.
59. CBS Evening News 6/30?/91.

> *At a height of about 248 miles, it began to be surrounded by the red glow of the*
> *hydrogen light. The hotter the asteroid became, the whiter and more brilliant*
> *was the light it emitted. Its gaseous tail became immense. This lethal*
> *thunderbolt must have struck more violently than any comet could possibly*
> *have done, and in a blaze of light that made the Sun pale. Eyes that saw it would*
> *have been permanently blinded. The temperature of its front surface . . . would*
> *exceed 36,032° F. Its luminosity would be 20-100 times that of the Sun's disk.*
> *The gases hurled backward would have increased the fantastic appearance of*
> *this flaming giant . . . The core broke in two immediately above the ground, with*
> *a thunderclap that ruptured every eardrum . . . It must have appeared as a*
> *parabola rising into the sky in the northwest from the horizon and spanning*
> *about 500-620 miles. Brilliant fragments would have dropped from this silently*
> *approaching mass, which would give the appearance of disintegrating in the*
> *sky. Barely two minutes can have elapsed between the moment when it first*
> *flared up on the horizon and the thunder of the impact of the core. It was no*
> *doubt heard in every part of the Earth except by those who lived in the explosion*
> *strip. They would be dead before the sound could reach them.*
>
> – Otto Muck[60]

Our world's atmosphere turned a hellfire red and black. Prolonged impact winter set in. Most living creatures perished. As the planet recovered over the ensuing centuries, out of the rubble emerged smaller mammals, including the ancestors of man. The asteroid that brought extinction for the dinosaurs also opened the door for human evolution. A curse for one species became a blessing for another. This is why Jimi regarded these solar events as being "neither bad nor good."

> *Good and evil lay side by side,*
> *while Electric Love penetrates the sky.*
>
> – Jimi[61]

ELECTRIC LOVE – A CRUMB FROM THE CRUST

Electric Love is the name Jimi gave to the Rock that is hurtling through space, on course to penetrate our atmosphere. "*Invent a word called Love,*" he wrote. Hendrix was no stranger to wordplay.

> *There are some people running around with long hair preaching the word*
> *"love" and they don't know what they're talking about because there's no*
> *such thing as Love until truth and understanding come about . . . I'm tired*

---

60. Muck, *The Secret of Atlantis*, pp.167-8.
61. "Have You Ever Been (to Electric Ladyland)", released on *Electric Ladyland*, Reprise Records 10/68.

of people using the word "Love" so much, though. You can mess up a good
theme like that. I don't know, we can go on and on. What is perfect?
Perfect is death. It's a physical death. Termination.   – Jimi[62]

Jimi used many metaphors with hidden meanings: "Third Stone" was his term for
Earth. "Confetti bits of tape" was what he called crummy edits of his recordings. In his
diary he used the letters "O.K." to indicate times when he experienced good acid trips.
In response to a journalist who asked if he had "outgrown dope?" Jimi laughed back, "At
least stop it from *growing*."[63] Replying to another reporter who asked if his songs
marked the start of psychedelic music, he remarked, "Psychedelic? I don't even know
what that word means, really. What is it, like you say one thing then mean another, or you
can get three different meanings out of one thing?"[64]

For Jimi, his lyrics often had a very personal meaning. The same went for
certain expressions, names and symbols. Many of these were derived from
visions...he was fully aware that most others did not see the things he saw:
namely, visions and astral experiences . . . listeners, readers and critics
interpret Jimi's art through their own minds, but they must be aware that
he most definitely saw different meanings behind his symbolisms from
those they saw.   – Monika Dannemann[65]

"Electric Love" is the most arcane Hendrix expression and his most esoteric
metaphor. It is found only once, in his lyrics for "Have You Ever Been (To Electric
Ladyland)": *Good and evil lay side by side, while Electric Love penetrates the sky*.

Electric Love is one in a series of his "Electric" phrases: Electric Ladyland (an
album), Electric Lady (a studio), Electric Church (a concert hall), Electric Religion (his
music), Electric Temple (a studio), Electric Stagehand (his alter ego), Electric Circus (a
bad gig), Electric Hair (an Afro), Electric Lobster (a sunburned journalist), and Electric
Kool-Aid (LSD in a drink). They were all offshoots of the catch phrase of his career:
Electric Guitar.

As the world's foremost innovator of electronic music, Hendrix thought a lot about
the nature of electricity and its effect on the world. He once referred to himself as "the
reincarnation of Thomas Edison."[66]

---

62. Hall and Clark, *The Superstars – In Their Own Words*, p.26, L.A. Free Press 1969.
63. Henderson, *Jimi Hendrix – Voodoo Child of the Aquarian Age*, from an interview with John Burks, New
York 2/4/70.
64. Brown, *Hendrix – The Final Days*, p.91, from an interview with Keith Altham, London 9/11/70.
65. Dannemann, *The Inner World of Jimi Hendrix*, p.88.
66. *See My Music Talking*, produced by John Marshall 12/67.

We do use electric guitars. Everything is electrified nowadays. So therefore the belief comes in through electricity to the people.   — Jimi[67]

Possibly Edison's discovery of the lightbulb crossed Jimi's mind when he christened the asteroid "Electric Love." Maybe he was thinking of the old blues term *lovelight*.

Turn on your lovelight, baby. . .
— Bobby Blue Bland, 1962

Electric Love is a hybrid of Electric light/Lovelight, because the appearance of the Rock, when it comes streaking into our atmosphere, will light up the sky like a giant bulb. This is the vision that partly explains Jimi's name for the Rock.

A great star fell from heaven, burning like a torch.
— Revelation 8:10

The Rock will be the most powerful force humans have ever seen and, as such, Jimi fittingly christened it Love. "Love can change your whole world," he said, "it's that powerful, that bold. People kill themselves for Love."[68] Hendrix mythologized this word to reflect his vision.

You have . . . Greek gods and all that mythology, well, you can have your **own** *mythology.*   — Jimi[69]

A century ago, in 1898, German and French astronomers Gustav Witt and A. Chalois discovered one of the largest known asteroids (21 miles wide) near Earth and named it *Eros*. "Eros" is defined in the Random House Dictionary as the Greek word for "Love." Eros is the "god of Love, son of Aphrodite, identified by the Romans with Cupid . . . a winged figure . . . representing the power of love . . . physical love and sexual desire."

It is Eros that inspired the title of Electric Love. Hendrix kept a statue of Cupid in his apartment. Part of the figure's wing was missing. "That's the groovy thing about him," said Jimi, "he can fly with a broken arm."[70]

In the song "Electric Ladyland" Jimi sings, "*Look up ahead, I see the Love land. Do you understand?*" His wordplay changes "land" from noun to verb: he sees Electric Love *land* on our planet.

---

67. The Dick Cavett Show, ABC 8/69.
68. *Bold As Love* magazine 2/68.
69. Meatball Fulton interview 12/67, released on *Hendrix Speaks* CD, Rhino Records 1990.
70. New Musical Express, 9/9/67.

BEHIND THE SUN

> *If a comet should appear from behind the Sun, we might only have a one or*
> *two year warning.*   — Carolyn Shoemaker[71]

> *In 1989 we had an asteroid pass us at only 690,000 miles away, a little over*
> *twice the distance between us and the Moon. And in 1991 the Earth came*
> *perilously close to yet another encounter with an asteroid. This asteroid*
> *passed the Earth at a distance of only 106,000 miles, which is less than half*
> *the distance to the Moon. These asteroids just barely missed us. Had they*
> *been at just a slightly different path, or been traveling at just a tiny different*
> *speed, the human race and much of the life on our planet would be gone*
> *now...These two most recent close passes by asteroids were discovered only*
> *a couple of months before they would have hit.*
>   — Practical Guide to the Universe[72]

"Imagine for a moment," said Steve Ostro of the Jet Propulsion Laboratory, "instead of these objects being tiny and not visible to the naked eye, they were suddenly made visible. Suppose that there was a button you could push and you could light up all the Earth-crossing asteroids larger than ten meters. There would be over a hundred million of these objects in the sky and you'd go outside at night and instead of being able to see a few thousand bright stars, the sky would be filled with millions of these objects, all of which are capable of colliding with the Earth."[73]

The fate of civilization is predestined in the orbit of our world through this cosmic obstacle course. Hendrix realized that, as a society, all of our actions must be tempered with the knowledge that it is only a matter of time before a Rock intersects our path. These encounters are natural and must be accepted. "*People must never be afraid of paths chosen by God,*" wrote Jimi. "*Love is being tested here.*"[74] Whether or not our civilization can influence an asteroid in our path depends upon our collective effort in mobilizing a defense.

> *An asteroid about the size of a house comes between the orbit of the Earth*
> *and moon about once each day. An asteroid about the size of a football field*
> *comes between the Earth and moon about once each month.*
>   — William Bottke[75]

---

71. McNeil/Lehrer News Hour, PBS 7/23?/94.
72. Practical Guide to the Universe, The Learning Channel 2/95.
73. Nova, *Doomsday Asteroid*, PBS 10/31/95.
74. *Cherokee Mist – The Lost Writings of Jimi Hendrix*, p.117, *Terra Revolution and Venus*.
75. *Fire In The Sky*, TBS 3/23/97.

> *Recently declassified information has revealed some worrying statistics. On average our atmosphere is hit by an icy object from space, maybe 30 feet across, once a month. The information used to be secret, so similar were the impacts to high altitude explosions. Indeed, Earth-space is abuzz with debris. There are more chunks of asteroids and comets in our vicinity than scientists have ever suspected. It would take just one the size of an office building to make it to the ground for a catastrophe.*
>
> – Wonders of the Universe[76]

"These smaller objects . . . nevertheless cause widespread devastation," notes Duncan Steel of the Anglo-Australian Observatory. "We certainly should be expecting at least one of those to occur over the next fifty or one hundred years."[77]

A decade-long study by the U.S. military revealed 250 detonations in the atmosphere over ten years. That averages 25 detonations a year, or one nuclear-type explosion every two weeks.[78] "Society is only beginning to realize that there is a threat from the skies," warns Clark Chapman. "It really could have immense, horrible, terrible consequences, even the end of civilization, and the risk on a strict numerical odds is the same as the risk of dying from an airplane crash for a typical American."[79]

In 1991, the U.S. Congress requested a Spaceguard Survey. NASA conducted a study that recommended building a global network of telescopes to search for asteroids. Scientists calculated that our chances of dying from an incoming object are about the same as being killed by a tornado. "Fears of a killer asteroid were once dismissed as scientific paranoia," reported CBS News, "but recent events have turned the paranoia into prudence."[80] Plans were drawn up for telescopes to patrol the skies thoroughly enough to give plenty of advance warning before any asteroid began a deadly approach. Today two programs in the United States watch for asteroids: Spacewatch, in Arizona, and Near-Earth Asteroid Tracking (NEAT) in Maui. These telescopes cover less than 10 percent of the sky each month. To properly expand this network and maintain it would cost $10 million a year, ten times the current budget for asteroid detection. Congress got bogged down in debates over the degree of urgency for such expenditures. The debate ended after elections in 1994 put Republican conservatives in control of Congress. NASA's budget was cut and plans for Spaceguard were scrapped.

> *How do we get rid of the giggle factor? You go to Congress and you say a comet could hit the Earth someday and everyone laughs.*
>
> – David Levey[81]

76. The Learning Channel 5/95.
77. Nova, *Doomsday Asteroid*, PBS 10/31/95.
78. *Fire In The Sky*, TBS 3/23/97.
79. Nova, *Doomsday Asteroid*, PBS 10/31/95.
80. CBS Evening News 6/30?/91.
81. *Fire In The Sky*, TBS 3/23/97.

The chance of such a civilization threatening collision in the next century is one in a thousand. Now, one in a thousand is pretty high, you probably wouldn't travel on a commercial airline if the chance of dying was one in a thousand.   – Carl Sagan[82]

82. ABC News Nightline 7/23?/94.

Chapter 2: Riddle of the Dead Seer Scrolls

ॐ

Why did Hendrix express his vision couched in riddles and metaphors? Why not explain it in straightforward language?

> . . . *people came in from the now-asteroid belt . . . reasons for the change to the chain of the space rocks . . . it was then believed that Love itself did not exist.*
>
> — Jimi[1]

To understand why he encoded the Prophecy in metaphors requires some historical background. During Jimi's lifetime, scientists dismissed as paranoia any theory about the Earth being prone to mass destruction from recurring asteroid impacts. Well into the 20th century, giant asteroid collisions were banished to the realm of science fiction. Fireballs in the sky did not become a subject for modern science until the 1950s, when Eugene Shoemaker examined the mile-wide crater in Arizona. Scientists had long thought the crater to be an extinct volcano. But, Shoemaker recognized the giant hole to be the impact site of a huge meteorite. He recalls, "Almost nobody was working on it in the mid-1950s when I first came here to Meteor Crater and started to study this crater in very great detail. So once you've studied this kind of a thing your next question is, well, what are the bullets out there that make these things and how often do they hit?[2] ...At the speed these things travel even a small object is dangerous. The asteroid that crashed at Meteor Crater was no bigger than a 747 [airplane]."[3]

From the time that Isaac Newton discovered how gravity keeps the planets revolving in predictable orbits around the Sun, all bodies in the galaxy were believed to be fixed along permanent, predictable trajectories. Scientists therefore argued that the Earth's landscape was formed over billions of years by gradual processes, like wind and rain. "It was science with catastrophism written out of it," states Victor Clube. "The picture that emerged was clearly the one that Newton himself was picturing where the solar system was seen as a giant clockwork machine and the image was that this clockwork would function forever."[4]

---

1. *Cherokee Mist — The Lost Writings of Jimi Hendrix*, p.114, *Terra Revolution and Venus.*
2. *Fire In The Sky*, TBS 3/23/97.
3. *On Jupiter*, Discovery Channel 12/95.
4. Nova, *Doomsday Asteroid*, PBS 10/31/95.

Only in the last 50 years have we begun to accept the fact that the Earth is a
potential target, even though the evidence was hanging right in front of us. Our
Moon bears the scars of over 30,000 impacts, but for centuries we believed Earth
was somehow spared these bombardments. In the last 20 years we have
identified 180 impact craters on Earth. If you could strip away Earth's jungles
and oceans, scientists believe we would find another 2000 craters.

– Mark Mitchell[5]

Throughout the lifetime of Hendrix, no one in mainstream science believed that the Earth was prone to disastrous impacts. When Shoemaker began to assert that such impacts had indeed occurred, he had to present proof. "Maybe it looks obvious now that the craters on the Moon were formed by impact," said Shoemaker in 1995, "but in fact the vast majority of scientists who studied the Moon, astronomers in particular, at the time that I began this work, thought that these craters on the Moon were probably formed by volcanoes. That had been the prevailing idea for a century before[6]...As an undergraduate student I didn't learn anything about impacts. It wasn't part of geology at that time. Geologists are the kind of folks that like to say 'I'd like to see what the process is, I'd like to see it happen, then I'll believe that it's happened in the past.'"[7]

Impact cratering . . . on the planets and our Moon, was not accepted by the
majority of the scientific community before the early 1900s. Even as far
back as 1803, after several scientists mentioned the idea that objects could
actually fall from our sky, the majority scoffed publicly at such theories. The
majority believed that the impact craters were produced from processes of
ancient, and now inactive, volcanoes . . . Such ideas endured in the
geological world until about 1880, when British astronomer Richard Proctor
suggested that the Moon's craters were from the impact of meteoric origins.
Even then, the skeptics held on to the volcanism story.

– Patricia Barnes-Svarney[8]

On May 24, 1969, while Apollo 10 circled the Moon to prepare for the first manned lunar landing, and just five months after the first Apollo mission returned from lunar orbit, Hendrix said, "They found *memorandums* on the Moon, no telling when they're going to get there, but when they do, they are going to find memorandums."[9] When Apollo 17 astronauts later explored the lunar surface in 1972, their tests revealed that the moon's craters have the same geological structure as craters from meteor collisions. These were no volcano holes—they are "memorandums" of past impacts.

---

5. *Fire In The Sky*, TBS 3/23/97.
6. Nova, *Doomsday Asteroid*, PBS 10/31/95.
7. *Asteroids: Deadly Impact*, NBC National Geographic 2/26/97.
8. Barnes-Svarney, *Asteroid – Earth Destroyer or New Frontier?*, p.155.
9. San Diego Free Press 6/13/69.

"We understood that there were big craters made on the Earth," recalls Shoemaker, "and that meant [for] those big craters we saw on the Moon, which I was also pretty sure were of impact origin, we now had a way of saying yes, it's happened on the Earth, the proof is here, but they are also on the Moon."[10]

In 1969, Hendrix comprehended that Moon craters are *mementos* reminding us of what has happened before and will happen again. This is what he referred to in the lyric *"singing about ancient…Moon trips."*[11]

> *I see miracles every day now. I used to be aware of them maybe once or twice a week, but some are so drastic that I couldn't explain them to a person or I'd probably be locked up by this time…There are a few chosen people that are here to help get these people out of this certain sleepiness that they are in. You may not necessarily be one of the chosen few ones to help. Everybody can't or else there would be nothing but every single person having his own different religion, and pretty soon they would wind up fighting and we'd go right back to the same thing again. I'm not better than you in this sense. It's just that maybe I'm not going to say it until a wider range of people see it. It's a universal thought.*
>
> – Jimi[12]

While Jimi carried his vision, unspoken to anyone, he planned when and how to convey a warning that people will believe. "You've got to gentle people along for a while until they are clued in on the scene," he said.[13] He realized that a warning from him would be ridiculed and unheeded. He feared that if he described his vision he'd be "locked up" by psychiatrists. So instead he created images with his songs to "gentle people along" until the time arrived when a "wider range of people see it."

> *To be said aloud, to be accepted or followed, to be believed, it must go through actual hell.*   – Jimi[14]

"Jimi had a lot of thoughts about who he was in relation to the universe," states Hendrix friend and bassist Billy Cox. "He briefly touched the surface in some of his songs. That's probably the way you have to do it, not go any deeper, because people brand things that they don't understand or are afraid of. So he didn't really go into depth about that."[15]

---

10. *Asteroids: Deadly Impact,* NBC National Geographic 2/26/97.

11. *Cherokee Mist – The Lost Writings of Jimi Hendrix,* p.70, *Valleys of Neptune Arising.*

12. San Diego Free Press 6/13/69, (from 5/24/69 San Diego interview).

13. New Musical Express 4/15/67 p.4.

14. *Cherokee Mist – The Lost Writings of Jimi Hendrix,* p.116 *Terra Revolution and Venus.*

15. Guitar World 9/85 p.83.

It's like a spaceship. If a spaceship came down and you know nothin' about it, the first thing you're going to think about is shooting it. In other words, you get negative in the first place, which is not really the natural way of thinking. It's like shooting at a flying saucer as it tries to land without giving the occupants a chance to identify themselves. — Jimi[16]

Hendrix knew he'd be ridiculed and dismissed if he began issuing warnings about an asteroid due to hit in thirty years time, although he did come close to explicitly saying this on at least two occasions. But it didn't matter, he was ignored. Scientists would not believe him. They *could* not believe him.

It took until the 1960s for scientists to recognize fully the first impact craters on Earth. Before then many scientists still insisted that most of the circular or boxlike craters were remnants from ancient volcanic explosions.
— Patricia Barnes-Svarney[17]

If he spoke out he'd invite trouble. He instead spread his message indirectly in song lyrics and metaphors. "Everything was very calculated with him," recalls Paul Caruso, "he was very introspective about the moves he made. You could tell even when he met a person. There was an inner dialogue with himself about timing and what to say. He was being very careful, because he was damn sure he was going to be a rock and roll star. And so he used his humility, his 'aw, shucks' humility. It opened doors for him everywhere. It was so natural to him. It would have been laughable on anyone else."[18]

In public Jimi played humble pie and stayed silent about the Rock. But he imbedded its image in his songs, couched in lyrics that no one understood, until now. He referred to the Prophecy indirectly, which often gave a mysterious quality to his thoughts.

To someone who didn't understand the way his mind worked, it must have looked peculiar, which made some people give Jimi a reputation for being "spaced out." — Monika Dannemann[19]

But occasionally his temper flared in frustration at being surrounded by people who didn't understand, who *could not* understand what he was trying to accomplish with his music.

16. Hall and Clark, *The Superstars – In Their Own Words*, p.24, Hit Parader 1/70.
17. Barnes-Svarney, *Asteroid – Earth Destroyer or New Frontier?* pp.156-7.
18. UniVibes #10 5/93 p.46.
19. Dannemann, *The Inner World of Jimi Hendrix*, p.88.

The music is better now, and people just don't even know, it's right in their faces and they don't even know how to accept it because it's just so much better. And they have to have gimmicks and imagery to go by. If they don't have these things in the way then they don't know nothin' about music. That's the way some people think, which is a big fat drag, sometimes.

Loneliness is such a drag . . .

I've never had anyone I could pour myself out to and tell everything. I'd like that. I'm here to communicate, that's my reason for being around, that's what it's all about. I want to turn people on and let them know what's happening.
— Jimi[20]

David Morrison, director of space at NASA Ames Research Center and author of *Impacts on the Earth by Asteroids and Comets—Assessing the Hazard*, concludes that society is not prepared to deal with the aftermath of a major impact. "Only a few astronomers are engaged in the search for potentially threatening comets and asteroids," complains Morrison, "in fact the total number of people working on this problem is less than the staff of one McDonalds."[21]

*The thing about the Shoemakers is they are one of the three or four little groups of astronomers who more or less on their own are finding these near-Earth asteroids. But we need a significant program, this is a **serious** issue.*
— Carl Sagan[22]

I hate the thought of us behaving like ostriches and stuffing our heads in the ground pretending that there are no potential dangers around the corner. The reality is that these fireball increases will happen fairly suddenly when they happen. We have no means at the moment of predicting them; they may happen tomorrow, they may happen a hundred years hence. The fact is that we do not as a world society have the means of handling this situation at the moment.
— Victor Clube[23]

IGNORED WARNINGS

Jimi explained to me that when he was experiencing astral travel he had seen the auras of the planets which he described...He explained that while a

20. Brown, *Jimi Hendrix – In His Own Words*, p.79, from interview in Vancouver 9/7/68. "Burning of the Midnight Lamp" released on *Electric Ladyland*, Reprise Records 10/68, Sun Mirror 9/20/70, Music Now 9/12/70.
21. Nova, *Doomsday Asteroid*, PBS 10/31/95.
22. ABC News Nightline 7/23?/94.
23. Nova, *Doomsday Asteroid*, PBS 10/31/95.

*person is living on Earth his or her spirit could actually leave the body for a
period of time...we can behold visions from the past, present and future...He
said that this power is called clairvoyance.*   — Monika Dannemann[24]

In 1974, a psychic working for the CIA drew sketches of the inside of a Soviet top-secret
testing facility. The psychic had never been to the facility but he accurately described objects
inside, descriptions that were confirmed by people who had been inside the facility. This
incident convinced officials of the U.S. Government to begin a $20 million Top Secret
program. For more than two decades, a psychic espionage program was directed by the CIA
and the Defense Intelligence Agency. Hundreds of psychics were hired to describe people,
places and things that they had never seen before from hundreds and thousands of miles
away.[25] Government scientists refer to this phenomenon as "Remote Viewing." Elsewhere it's
known as Extra Sensory Perception, or ESP.

By 1996, psychic spying had been used in about 500 government cases. It was used to
locate U.S. Brigadier General James Doizier who was kidnapped by Italian militants in 1982.
For five years physicist Dale Graft directed the DIA's Remote Viewing program, code named
Project Stargate. "Early on, as a physicist," recalls Graft, "I really wasn't sure if there was
anything to this phenomenon. But if you go out in the field and you work with it over and
over and you see some of these very interesting cases, it can't all be written off by chance."[26]

Nuclear physicist Edwin May performed 1500 experiments for the government
between 1975 and 1995 to test the scientific validity of Remote Viewing. "My main role
in this was the guy doing the research," states May. "While I'm interested in applications,
perhaps even intelligence applications, my main focus was to figure out how it works and
what we can confirm in the laboratory, and to that extent we've had dramatic cases in the
laboratory, both statistically important as well as visually compelling...About fifteen
percent of our data, over fifteen hundred separate Remote Viewing trials, are of such a
quality that you might think they were staged. But they were done in very tight protocols,
the best that modern science, physics, physiology, and psychology could bring to bear on
the issue. The remaining data is somewhat statistical so it's really hard to look at the data
and say 'that's real,' but fifteen percent of it is extremely compelling. It's kind of like a
native talent; those people who can do it, do it; those people who can't, can't."[27]

Jessica Ucts, a University of California at Davis statistics professor, examined the
evidence and reported, "Remote Viewing has been demonstrated over the twenty years of
work that's been sponsored by the government. What it proves to me is that we don't quite
understand either the nature of the mind or perhaps the nature of time and space. But
there is some mystery out there that we need to solve."[28]

---

24. Dannemann, *The Inner World of Jimi Hendrix,* pp.102, 84, 92.
25. ABC News Nightline 11/28/95.
26. Ibid.
27. Ibid.
28. Ibid.

Remote Viewing was a native talent in Jimi. Hendrix possessed perceptions that represent an evolutionary leap for our species. Juxtaposed quotes below from Dr. Deepak Chopra, Director for the Institute of Mind Body Medicine, and Jimi, form a dialogue on the power of the mind:

DECONSTRUCTED CONVERSATIONS WITH JIMI AND DEEPAK CHOPRA[29]

DC: Ninety-nine percent of the human body is mostly empty space, and the .001% that you experience as material is actually also empty space. In other words, this whole thing is made out of nothing. Go beyond the facade of molecules and you enter a subatomic cloud, go beyond the cloud and you end up with a handful of nothing, and then the question is, what is this nothingness from where we come?

JH: Forget of my name...my name is distraction. It all comes from God.[30]

DC: The animating force of life is non-local, not trapped in space and time. The body's nervous system is the instrument that gives this space/time experience, but the real you is non-local . . . We learn how to perceive as a result of our cultural indoctrination, our social indoctrination, our evolutionary history, etc. In reality, impulses of intelligence create our body in new forms every second. Impulses of intelligence are impulses of information and energy. They are our thoughts and feelings and emotions and desires. But although each of us seems to be separate and independent, all of us are connected to patterns of intelligence that govern the whole cosmos. There are no well defined edges to the quantum mechanical body. We are localized bundles of information and energy in a universe of information and energy . . . this is an intelligent universe and we are conscious beings in a conscious universe and the human nervous system is that privileged organ of nature through which the universe itself is becoming conscious of itself.

Perhaps from the small beginnings of the universe the greatest force has emerged just in the last 50,000 years. It is the force of the human mind and imagination.   – Practical Guide to the Universe[31]

---

29. *Body, Mind & Soul – The Mystery and the Magic*, PBS 8/95.
30. *Cherokee Mist – The Lost Writings of Jimi Hendrix*, p.116, Honolulu Star Bulletin 5/31/69.
31. *Science*, Practical Guide to the Universe, TLC 7/95.

DC: If we have to survive as a species on our planet and we have to ensure the survival of the planet itself, we need a new kind of evolution, distinct from so-called Darwinian evolution...we are over with physical evolution, but in a new phase of our evolution, the evolution of consciousness . . . Johnas Salk coined the term "survival of the wisest" instead of survival of the fittest. In order to have that new evolutionary phase unfold . . . it is important to understand what is consciousness. What is mind? What is matter? And what's the connection between these three? Possibly there's no "connection," they are all inseparably one.

JH: See, evolution of man is changing the brain, so quite naturally you're gonna have hang-ups, here and there, of thought. But still, the whole past is going towards a higher way of thinking, towards a clearer way of thinking.[32]

DC: Perhaps what we call everyday reality is nothing more than a socially programmed hypnosis, an induced fiction in which we have collectively agreed to participate.

JH: But there are still some hard-heads, just like you're talkin' about, that think this way because they don't give themselves a chance to develop in the brain or let the soul develop or the emotions, you know?[33]

DC: And once in a while somebody breaks out of that hypnosis of social conditioning, it's an interesting and motley group of sages and psychotics and geniuses.

JH: Reality is nothing but each individual's own way of thinking.[34]

DC: Our whole experience of everyday reality comes about as a result of the interpretation of sensory experience. That's how we experience the world, after all, through our senses . . . The picture of the world is not *the look of* it, it's *our way of looking* at it. And we have learned how to look at it in a certain way. We have looked at it, until now, through the superstition of materialism, which holds that this is a material world and we are material entities in a

32. Interview with Nancy Carter, L.A., 6/15/69, *Hendrix Speaks*, 1990 Rhino Records.
33. Ibid.
34. Brown, *Hendrix – The Final Days*, p.90, from an interview with Keith Altham, London 9/11/70.

physical world. It says trust your senses even when common sense informs us that if anything our senses are the least reliable test of reality. After all, our senses tell us that the Earth is flat.

JH: What's happening is we have all these different senses; we've got eyes, nose, hearing, taste, and feeling and so forth. Well, there's a sixth sense that's coming in. Everybody has their own name for it, but I call it Free Soul, and that's more into a mental kind of thing. That's why everything is beyond the eyes now. The eyes only carry you so far out. You have to know how to develop other things that will carry you further and more clear.[35]

DC: The physical world is made up of information and energy that we experience through our sensors. Our sensors are just transducers that convert information and energy into taste and texture and form and color. You and I give form and texture and color and taste and smell to that field, which is a radically ambiguous and ceaselessly flowing quantum soup of information and energy. And we experience that same information and energy here as the physical body, and we experience the same information and energy in our mind as our thoughts and feelings and emotions and desires, so it's all the same in different disguises.

JH: At the moment people use only a minute part of their mind and there's so much more scope. If only people wouldn't concentrate on the superficial things, they might find the real meaning and true happiness. Things like witchcraft, which is a form of exploration, and imagination, have been banned by the establishment and called evil. It's because people are frightened to find out the full power of the mind.[36]

DC: It has been known now for almost 15-20 years that there are bio chemical substrata to the thinking process; that emotions and feelings and desires and instincts and drives and memories, they transform themselves into biochemical events.

JH: Scientists have apparently found a way to harness some thought-impulses. They got people to switch channels on a television set...a

35. Hall and Clark, *The Superstars – In Their Own Words*, p.22.
36. Record Mirror 3/69.

certain impulse created by the thought process worked the set. There are so many possibilities to be derived from this kind of thing.[37]

DC: If we want to get to a new understanding of the human body-mind and of human potential, we have to discard our old notions about reality, which are based on the superstition of materialism. We have to forget thinking of the human body as a frozen anatomical structure . . . The essential stuff of the universe is non-stuff . . . *thinking* non-stuff. If you say, "If I'm not in this body, where am I?" The answer is, it's the wrong question, because as soon as you say "where?" you imply a location to something in space that doesn't occupy space, and you imply moments in time to something that's timeless, and yet [that something is] you.

JH: I like to consider myself timeless, after all, it's not how long you've been around or how old you are that matters; it's how many miles you've traveled . . . A person's not actually old in numbers of years, but how many miles he's traveled, you know, how he keeps his mind active and creative.[38]

DC: The way we can access this realm of our own awareness, the thinker of the thought, is through the silent spaces between thoughts. Between every thought is a space where we manufacture the thought...the thinker of the thought has two characteristics to it: 1) it is silent . . . 2) it's a field of infinite possibilities, infinite potentiality . . . the possibility of any thought.

JH: What's the fastest speed you can think of? They say the speed of light is the fastest thing – that's the eyes – but then there's the speed of

---

37. Ibid. In November 1995, a quarter century after Jimi made this statement, ABC World News reported: "At a laboratory in Dayton, Ohio, the Air Force is running an experiment...the man in the simulator is controlling its movements using thought, thoughts that trigger certain patterns of brain waves that a computer receives via wires from his body, and translates into left turns and right turns...using thought in this way represents a breakthrough...this is the real frontier of brain research...scientists have learned more about how the brain works in the last 20 years than in all of the time before that... thought is biology...some of what science has learned is about to hit the marketplace. This winter the MindDrive will appear in computer stores, a $200 device worn on the finger that reads brainwaves and translates them into signals that control movements on a computer screen...the first of many such applications in the future as science races ahead in understanding what really goes on in the head on our shoulders." (John Donvan.)

38. Interview with Nancy Carter, L.A., 6/15/69, *Hendrix Speaks*, 1990 Rhino Records, Rochester, NY, Democrat & Chronicle 9/14/69.

thought, which is beyond that. You can get on the other side of this theme in a matter of thinking about it, for instance.[39]

DC: Is it possible that nature goes to exactly the same place to create a galaxy of stars or a cluster of nebulas or a rain forest or a human body as it goes to create a thought? Have you ever wondered what a thought is? Have you ever wondered where it comes from? . . . a thought is a quantum event. A quantum is defined by a physicist as the smallest indivisible unit in which waves of information and energy are either emitted or absorbed...labels for defining units of energy and information. In fact, a quantum is fleeting, it's unpredictable, it's invisible. A thought is also a unit of information and energy...Thoughts, being quantum events, transform themselves into space-time events that we call matter...A good understanding of this inseparability between mind and matter, not only in our own physiology, but in the physiology of nature, is really crucial for our survival, not only as a species, but for the survival of our planet...Awareness is the source of biological information and energy in everything that's alive...In order to get to that awareness you have to learn to slip in the spaces between thoughts. When we do that we eavesdrop on the software that runs the machinery of the universe.

JH: I'd like to write symphonies that take you somewhere, sight and sound together creating an entire new sense...and with this music we will paint pictures of Earth and space, so that the listener can be taken somewhere. It's going to be something that will open up a new sense in peoples' minds. They are getting their minds ready now.[40]

LAUGHING SAM'S DICE

[Venus], *the second stone from our star has been very busy getting ready for the time to communicate with Earth, to try and warn the people of Earth of potential self destruction which is completely against the will and grace of living.*   – Jimi[41]

"Stars That Play with Laughing Sam's Dice," or STP/LSD, is the title of Jimi's song about perceptual breakthroughs inspired by psychoactive plants. Although consumption

39. Hall and Clark, *The Superstars – In Their Own Words*, p.22.
40. Record Mirror 9/19/70, Rolling Stone 10/1/70.
41. *Cherokee Mist – The Lost Writings of Jimi Hendrix*, p.116 *Terra Revolution and Venus.*

of "magic" mushrooms, cactus, seeds, bark and leaves has been the inheritance, the birthright, of our species, dominators persecute people who use hallucinogens. Despite evidence that these plants have been catalysts for advances and leaps in cognitive development, their benefits are today denied and derided beneath a media blitzkrieg of rabid propaganda. Jimi realized that punishing those who seek perceptual enhancements is "*completely against the will and grace of living.*" That we have become a society so closed-minded against expanded perceptions now results in our "*potential self-destruction.*"

> *Before LSD there were visions of eternities, so many blisters unmedicated,*
> *unraped by humane eyes as today on all across this Earth.*
>   – Jimi[42]

Crater scars from past impacts form "*blisters...all across this Earth.*" Prior to the first LSD experiments, staged just a few months after Jimi was born, it was rare for humans to see what Hendrix called "*visions of eternities,*" perceptions outside of our everyday senses. "*Unmedicated*" eyes see the Moon and never register the *meaning* of craters. Craters were there before humans existed. By the time people saw them through telescopes, society had outlawed use of plant enhancements that can inspire comprehension. When Hendrix looked at the lunar landscape through *medicated* eyes, he saw "memorandums" of asteroids. Jimi understood that hallucinogenic stimulation of our senses is necessary to access awareness of what otherwise goes unnoticed. A certain *type* of remote viewing is made possible with the aid of our planet's plants.

> *You know all Indians have different ways of stimulants, their own steps*
> *towards God, spiritual forms, or whatever, which it should be kept as,*
> *nothing but a step, mind you.*   – Jimi[43]

During his last interview a journalist told Hendrix, "It has been said that you invented psychedelic music."

"Psychedelic?" replied Jimi, "I don't even know what that word means, really."

"To most people it has connotations with LSD."

"Oh, you mean strictly LSD? You mean with that type of consciousness? Right, yeah, well you have to give them a little bit of it to dream on, so they can hear it over again, because they might be in a different mood. Dreams come from different moods, you know."[44]

> *Myths and dreams come from the same place. They come from realizations*
> *of some kind that have then to find expression in symbolic form. The only*

---

42. Ibid. p.117.

43. International Times 3/28/69 - London interview with Jane de Mendelssohn.

44. Henderson, *Jimi Hendrix – Voodoo Child of the Aquarian Age*, pp.482-3, from an interview with Keith Altham, London, 9/11/70.

*myth that's going to be worth thinking about in the immediate future is one
that's talking about the planet. Not this city, not these people – but the
planet and everybody on it.*   – Joseph Campbell[45]

Hendrix knew that for us to obstruct and outlaw "that type of consciousness,"
inspired by hallucinogens, limits our options and awareness in a way that is *potential
self-destruction.*" As Terrence McKenna points out, psychoactive plants can be thought
of as "our umbilicus to the feminine mind of the planet."

*Mutation-causing, psychoactive chemical compounds in the early human diet
directly influenced the rapid reorganization of the brain's information-
processing capacities. Alkaloids in plants, specifically the hallucinogenic
compounds...catalyzed the emergence of human self-reflection...hallucinogens
acted as catalysts in the development of imagination, fueling the creation of
internal stratagems and hopes that may well have synergized the emergence of
language and religion.*   – Terrence McKenna[46]

Through the human nervous system, our planet becomes aware of itself. Earth
nourishes human perceptual development by providing specialized food for our brains.
McKenna suggests that the biosphere may be "an organism whose interconnected
components act upon and communicate with one another through the release of
chemical signals [plant hallucinogens] into the environment . . . The hallucinogens
function as interspecies chemical messengers."[47]

By ingesting psychoactive plants, ancient shamans mapped constellations out of
patterns among stars in the sky. Our ancestors imagined ever more complex leaps in
comprehension of all phenomena. Hendrix expressed our reception of altered mental
states generated by Earth's plants—the planet as plant. It's as if the biosphere itself is
aware of a deadly threat from asteroids and has spawned humans as its evolutionary
defense. Plant hallucinogens are the "chemical messengers" meant to propel us towards
sensing the greatest threat that the planet has known: the Rock. Our species' aggressive
fascination with explosives is meant to be channeled into an effective defense of our
globe. Awareness of this may be invisible to us without use of hallucinogens. With the aid
of psychoactive plants, we imagine into being the plans for systems that will influence
Rocks. This mission is the ultimate "religion" of our species.

*Use of hallucinogenic mushrooms on the grasslands of Africa gave us the
model for all religions to follow.*   – Terrence McKenna[48]

---

45. The Power of Myth, *The Hero's Adventure*, 1987 interview with Bill Moyers, PBS 3/88.
46. Terrance McKenna, *Food of the Gods*, (New York: Bantam Books, 1992), p 24.
47. Ibid. p.41.
48. Ibid. p.39.

There have been some very interesting researches made in the plants associated with these cults and barley is very closely associated. There's a barley drink that is consumed by the people who are going to go through the great ceremony before attending the rites. One of the important hallucinogens is ergot, which is a parasite on barley, and it is believed now by many that the barley broth contains a bit of the ergot. There was a family that for many, many centuries had been in charge of the rites. There is a really fine study called ["The Road To Eleusis – Unveiling the Secrets of the Mysteries" 49] written by Albert Hoffman, who is the man who invented LSD, and Gordon Wasson and [Carl Ruck] a classical scholar...This book deals with the whole ritual of Eleusis in detail as a ceremony associated with a matching of the state of rapture of the people who have taken the drink, and the theatrical performance that is rendered in the way of an Epiphany, so that there is an inward readiness and an outward fulfillment that works. Socrates himself is reported to have spoken about the importance, to him, of the experience at Eleusis. There's something in the way of a revelation actually experienced there.   – Joseph Campbell[50]

Of the early vegetation religions Tom Robbins writes, "Fertility was of prime concern to those folks, and most of their magic and ritual consisted of trying to induce lust and promote fecundity in human, beast and vegetable."

Through art, dance, song and elaborate outdoor fucking, humans tried to entice God and Mother Earth to get it on. In an effort to gain more influence over God's passions, the ancients attempted to find links with him on Earth...the mushroom was fraught with sexual allusions...[it] filled one with the divine spirit...The rites of the toadstool cults were closely guarded secrets...[Ancient tribes on shrooms] take immediate solace in the knowledge that the spirit world is not closed to them...perhaps when they give up their earthly bodies, their souls will go to dwell forever in that world, that Happy Hunting Ground, Nirvana, Heaven...So they build crude altars in gratitude. As they grow in numbers and sophistication, they replace the altars with temples...The temples become cathedrals...Empires are built...the little scarlet toadstool that started it is long since forgotten... the Amanita muscaria [mushroom] is not likely to regain its rightful place in the hierarchy of human development. We simply have too much invested in..."civilization" to revamp our historical and theological traditions to conform with the notion of a holy plant, however valid, however true.   – Tom Robbins[51]

---

49. Albert Hoffmann, Gordon Wasson and Carl AP Ruck, *The Road To Eleusis - Unveiling the Secrets of the Mysteries,* (New York: Harcourt Brace Jovanovich, 1978).
50. Joseph Campbell , *Mythos - the Mystical Life,* PBS 12/1/96.
51. High Times 12/76, pp.94, 130.

Ancient shamans set up temples in homage to their hallucinogen-induced awareness. In today's age, Jimi's albums form the temples and altars which house our precious new perceptions. With his recordings Hendrix erected pillars of modern consciousness. LSD was first synthesized three years prior to his birth and then tested on humans soon after he was born. Acid became the sensory breakthrough to a new age that later thrust Hendrix to the outer limits of perception. Like an ancient shaman of the great mushroom religions, Jimi sought to convey vision to a society which restricts awareness.

> *These lost souls did not know and still do not fully realize that we are not here alone, that there is God besides the temples...Why is my soul...going fast as the speed of thought, the fastest and longest far reaching thing we know. Long ago, sleepless nights would drift in with their bags and books of wonderments and self-debates, not of my self but of stars, music, Saturn's rings, astro-notions. Before LSD there were visions of eternities . . .*
>
> — Jimi[52]

"The psychedelic issue is a civil rights and civil liberties issue," states McKenna. "It is an issue concerned with the most basic of human freedom: religious practice and the privacy of the individual mind...History is the story of these plant relationships ...discussion of human sexuality was repressed until the work of Freud and others brought it into the light...[Society must] examine the basic human need for chemical dependency and then find and sanction avenues for expression of this need. We are discovering that human beings are creatures of chemical habit with the same horrified disbelief as when the Victorians discovered that humans are creatures of sexual fantasy and obsession. This problem of facing ourselves as a species is a necessary precondition to the creation of a more humane social and natural order...the adventure of self-understanding can begin only when we take note of our innate and legitimate need for an environment rich in mental states that are induced through an act of will."[53]

Prohibition against psychoactive plants seems ludicrous when we realize that drug sales, with an annual take worldwide of approximately $400 billion, are today greater than car sales globally. Drug sales comprise approximately eight percent of world commerce.[54]

In the song "Stars That Play with Laughing Sam's Dice," Jimi likens our chance of destroying the Rock to a crapshoot because a majority of humans will choose not to heed the Prophecy. Societal restrictions on hallucinogens prevent perception. Anti-drug laws, written by unjust monied industrialists who crave a zombie workforce greased for aggression, have created a culture blind to insights made possible from use of the planet's plants.

52. *Cherokee Mist – The Lost Writings of Jimi Hendrix*, pp.115, 117 *Terra Revolution & Venus.*
53. McKenna, *Food of the Gods*, pp.255-6.
54. NBC Nightly News 7/22/97.

*They forgot, did not believe, or just snuffed the feelings or thoughts off to
continue with their crazy soul.*   – Jimi[55]

Hendrix could only warn and watch us roll the dice as we gamble that the Rock
won't tumble our way. We play with fate. Laughing Sam's Dice *"makes us feel that's why
the world's for us."* But sooner or later our world is smashed from above when *"the
Zodiac glass gleams through the sky, it could happen soon . . ."*[56]

*In their hearts they see the path so much more clearly and truthfully than ever
the eyes...Today I burn under my brain's consciousness of what propels me out
of trouble at times into time itself, outside into the space of it all. My body
cannot breathe there, what is my mind doing there? Why is my soul surpassing
curious egos security, etc., going fast as the speed of thought, the fastest and
longest far reaching thing we know.*   – Jimi[57]

"They call me Astro Man," wrote Hendrix, *"if you signal, I'll give you a hand...to
blow out what I can...in the rest of your mind."*[58] It's a song about astral travel –
awareness that spans the galaxy – the most remote viewing, free of space/time
enclosures, receptive of *signals*. Jimi's perceptions were like an antenna for Earth; he
was an authentic astral traveler viewing remote developments in our solar system and
picking up signals from planets about asteroids. The Earth itself had directed his
attention to its greatest threat and made Jimi aware of the Rock. Whatever terror Hendrix
felt over knowledge of the coming impact, he was obliged to keep silent and wait for a
chance to "unmask appearances," as he put it.

*It's not a hazy thing out of frustration or bitterness that I'm trying to build up.
It's out of what's directing me, what I was here in the first place to do. It does
mean I am going to strip myself from my identity, because this isn't my only
identity. I was foolish to cut my hair, but that was part of the step of me learning
what I was really here for. Really, I'm just an actor. The only difference between
me and those cats in Hollywood is that I write my own script. My initial success
was a step in the right direction, but it was only a step. Now I plan to get into
many other things...Everybody should play their own parts. Everybody should be
actors in their own sins, as where they write their own scripts. All of the script
is coming from God. It's up to them to play out their parts.*   – Jimi[59]

55. *Cherokee Mist – The Lost Writings of Jimi Hendrix*, p.115 *Terra Revolution and Venus.*
56. "Stars That Play with Laughing Sam's Dice", released on *Loose Ends*, Barclay Records, 3/74.
57. *Cherokee Mist – The Lost Writings of Jimi Hendrix,* p.117 *Terra Revolution and Venus.*
58. Ibid. p.106.
59. L.A. Free Press 1969, Rochester, NY, Democrat & Chronicle 9/14/69, Brown, *Jimi Hendrix – In His Own
Words*, p.65, from interview in Beverly Hills 6/69.

Hendrix wrote a film script and planned to produce a movie that would warn us of the Rock. In the meantime, he kept the Prophecy to himself. His first reference to it in music was in 1966 with the first original tune he recorded, titled "Stone Free." And during a summer heatwave in New York that year he wrote "Third Stone From the Sun," a song about the Earth being "blown up." From the summer of '66 onwards, Jimi wrote about the Rock. He wouldn't discuss it with anyone, but he left a trail of references in his songs and interviews.

> *In the earlier songs he frequently used symbols to express himself and one*
> *needed to know these to fully understand his lyrics. At the beginning of his*
> *career he had felt that he should conceal some of the things he wanted to*
> *convey, because the time was not right for him to speak openly.*
> — Monika Dannemann[60]

MOONDUST AND STAR WARS

When Jimi got to England and recorded "Third Stone From the Sun," everyone heard for the first time the sound of Rock colliding with Earth. In *rock* music Hendrix etched aural impressions of the asteroid impact. His recordings are rife with sounds of gigantic explosions. Jimi was America's authentic musical shaman whose mission it was to find a way to communicate a warning. He had to catch the attention of humans dulled by "sleepiness" in their perceptions. He waited for the right time to introduce the Prophecy.

> *I'm not going to say it until a wider range of people see it.* — Jimi[61]

He titled his screenplay *Moondust*. Particles of Earth matter, pulverized by the impact, will billow into outer space, collecting around and settling on the lunar surface. The Moon will be coated with debris. Moondust. Remnants of us. In his script Jimi writes, *"the story of the asteroid belt in our solar system is explained..."* [62]

> *The sky opens up after sounds of rumbling, swaying-cracking effect*
> *happens... a beam of light comes through [the] opening as flying saucers in*

---

60. Dannemann, *The Inner World of Jimi Hendrix*, p.165.

61. San Diego Free Press 6/13/69.

62. *Moondust* 30 page screenplay by Jimi Hendrix. 27 handwritten pages of the 30 page script were published in *Cherokee Mist – The Lost Writings of Jimi Hendrix* (Harper Collins 1993), pp.32-45, the 28th page of *Moondust* was published as exhibit #479 in the catalogue for Sothebys sale 6258 *Animation Art and Rock 'n' Roll Memorabilia Dec. 14 and 17, 1991*. The remaining two pages, 29 and 30, appeared with the entire 30 page manuscript on public display at Sothebys in New York during the week prior to the auction on December 14. 1991. While on public display, the final two pages of *Moondust* were read and noted by Charles Blass, including the last page in which Jimi reveals that his screenplay is a set up for *"the story of the asteroid belt in our solar system."*

formation appear on each side...the trembling ground...the catastrophe is still happening.   — Jimi[63]

The Moon...was possibly born of catastrophe; the product of a cosmic collision...the Earth is struck by an object the size of Mars, in the maelstrom that follows, the Moon condenses, it forms from material blasted into space from the impact.

— Wonders of the Universe[64]

Impacts produce Moondust. And satellite technology is the answer that Hendrix championed for asteroids. Thirteen years after Jimi's death, President Reagan proposed a program called the Strategic Defense Initiative (SDI) which involves building satellites armed with interceptor rockets that would orbit the Earth with the capability of tracking down and destroying incoming enemy missiles. Physicist Ed Tagliaferri points out, "The Ballistic Missile Defense organization, originally called the Strategic Defense Initiative, actually developed the technologies which allow us to deal with these threats. All of the things that you need to do to intercept a ballistic missile are the same sorts of things that you need to do to intercept and deploy an asteroid."[65] The proposal, dubbed Star Wars, was eventually shelved when the Cold War ended in the 1980s. But more than a decade before Reagan proposed Star Wars, and years before scientists regarded such technology as even possible, Hendrix was using the media in 1969 to advocate a need to develop laser-carrying satellites:

Do you realize that they have a laser beam that you could put in satellites that'll circle the world and it'll stop any rockets from being let off anywhere in the world?. . . Do you realize they have inventions now that make it so you don't have to think about defense problems now, forever?. . . They have a plan where they have a laser-beam and a chain of satellites around the world and any rocket released, this will automatically blow it up, anywhere in the world, through a certain chart plan. All this is true . . . This is so much of a better idea to spend all that money on . . . But no, they don't want to hear about these new ideas, they want to hear about the old ones, like spend up all this money and get a big missile system. That's just one of the things that I'm gonna try to put through songs.

— Jimi[66]

63. Ibid. From the 28th page of *Moondust*, published as exhibit #479 in the catalogue for Sothebys sale 6258 *Animation Art and Rock 'n' Roll Memorabilia Dec. 14 and 17, 1991.*
64. Wonders of the Universe, The Learning Channel 3/28/95.
65. *Fire In The Sky*, TBS 3/23/97.
66. Tony Brown, *Jimi Hendrix – In His Own Words*, p.89 (from Beverly Hills, CA interview 6/69), and interview with Nancy Carter, L.A., 6/15/69, *Hendrix Speaks.*

What prevents any defense from being developed to handle asteroids is a perceived absence of imminent threat. There is only Jimi's prediction. Science requires *hard* evidence of a certain impact, or resources won't go into anti-asteroid efforts until a collision is expected. In October 1997, President Clinton vetoed a bill to fund research into such technology. Jimi's vision is dismissed. But what if Hendrix sensed this event in a way that is outside of scientific inquiry? He sings of watching *"the sunrise from the bottom of the sea...let me prove it to you"* as if to say that he'll be proved right when we see the blinding parabola streaking up over the horizon, as if from beneath the sea.

Earth is a sitting duck, defenseless in a cosmic shooting gallery, prone to collision with projectiles whizzing past us at 50,000 miles per hour. "They're missiles and they're bombs," warns Steven Ostro. "When they hit they will produce explosions that are enormous compared to anything that we have at our disposal today."[67]

The untimely death of Hendrix, and our inability to comprehend his message, has meant that today we remain vulnerable, warnings are long over-due. Laser technology is no where near powerful enough to affect a massive Rock. It will be many decades before we can even begin to protect Earth from impact. Had Jimi lived and communicated his vision, satellite laser technology would have evolved during the short number of years our civilization has left. But today we remain armed only with ineffective nuclear warheads. In 1992, NASA issued a report to Congress that spelled out our options for dealing with an asteroid aimed at Earth. The report concluded that our best hope today is "a small arsenal of nuclear weapons hurriedly launched to blow up these vagrant little worlds while they are still many thousands of miles out in space."[68]

"A typical thermonuclear weapon would have the energy required to move the asteroid," claims Clark Chapman, "but exactly how to use those weapons...these details have not been worked out...Perhaps the worst thing that could happen is if we...blast a bomb and the thing comes apart in several pieces that we can't control and several pieces rain down on our planet...You wouldn't be able to predict where the pieces would go, it might rain down on the planet like buckshot and create more damage than if it were just to strike as one single piece."[69]

Hendrix realized that the priorities of society must shift radically and accelerate the pace of research. "Scientists are being respected only to keep test tubes clean," he complained, "that's wrong. Anyway, all this comes out through music. We're musicians."[70] Rather than call a press conference where he'd be misunderstood, or stumble through an interview where writers could filter his vision, Jimi made plans for a film that would communicate what had to be said.

I've got to learn to paint pictures with my music. That's what the future is about, to paint pictures of Earth and everything. I'm going to show a film

---

67. CBS Evening News 6/30?/91.

68. The New York Times Magazine 7/28/96, p.18.

69. Nova, *Doomsday Asteroid*, PBS 10/31/95, *Doomsday: What Can We Do?*, Fox 2/14/97.

70. Brown, *Jimi Hendrix – In His Own Words*, p.89, from Beverly Hills, CA interview 6/69.

*with my music so there's no mistaking what I'm playing about . . . What it's
all about is new ideas and old laws. In some ways it's getting like Pompeii.
There are more dreams but I won't discuss them at the moment . . . I'm
going to develop the sound and then put a film out with it. It's going to be
an audio-visual thing that you sit down and plug into and really take in
through your ears and eyes . . . I want to create new sounds, try to transmit
my dreams to the audience. I'm always having visions and I know that it's
building up to something really major. I'm working on my own religion and
it's simply life. I had very strange feelings that I was here for something and
I was going to get a chance to be heard. I got the guitar together because that
was all I had.*   *– Jimi*[71]

Until he could produce *Moondust*, Hendrix spoke in riddles about the Rock and in
metaphors about his role. He created a character for himself called Astro Man who's
concern is "living in peace of mind," said Jimi, adding, "Astro Man will leave you in
pieces." Astro Man means *cat*ASTRO*phe* Man. Only through the efforts of Hendrix would
we avert a shattered world.

Catastrophe, you always are a part of me . . .
                                    – Jimi sings Frankie Laine song[72]

*I'd try to use my music as a machine to move these people to get changes
done, because if people go too long, when they get older, they'll realize, or
they'll get mediocre and fall right into that dead scene.*
                                                                    – Jimi[73]

The death of Hendrix sealed the fate of our race, as if the consciousness of the Earth
had fallen to sleep.

*I could go to sleep and write fifteen symphonies. Before I can remember anything
I can remember music and stars and planets.*
                                                                    – Jimi[74]

71. Melody Maker 9/26/70, Melody Maker 3/8/69, Rochester, NY, Democrat & Chronicle 9/14/69, Expressen
    1/6/68, Life 10/3/69.
72. "Catastrophe" release on *War Heroes* album, Reprise Records 2/72.
73. New England Scene 11/68.
74. Life 10/3/69.

Chapter 3: Terrestrial Revolutions

ॐ

Was Hendrix possessed with telepathy? Extraterrestrial visions inspired his writing.

What I like to do is write a lot of mythical scenes. I'd like to write a story for the stage and compose the music for it. For example, take Greek mythology, or old stories about the Vikings – I'd like to present that on stage with light and lots of sound. Doing songs about the Milky Way, the stars and the planets and space people, people who come here from out there. Or perhaps a space war between Neptune and Uranus, like the history of the wars on Neptune, and the reason why the rings are there...This whole thing's gonna blow wide open soon.

– Jimi[1]

Uranus and its neighboring planet, Neptune, are similar in size and appearance. Both Neptune and Uranus are encircled by rings resembling the rings of Saturn, but much smaller. Jimi understood that "the reason why the rings are there" around any planet is the same reason why a person gets a black eye: from impacts. He saw rings as remnants of shattered debris after planets collide with asteroids.

Phobos . . . orbiting . . . above [Mars] . . . is a moon that appears to be ready one day to crash into its gravitationally attractive master planet, but it will probably break into a ring of debris long before that occurs.

– Patricia Barnes-Svarney[2]

In the mid-1980s, when the Voyager space probe approached Uranus, scientists were amazed to discover magnetic poles located near the planet's equator: Uranus is tipped on its side, with magnetic poles tilted 60 degrees away from its rotational axis. The planet's magnetic field is offset from its center. Whereas Earth spins more or less straight up and down, with sunlight falling on the equator rather than on the poles, Uranus is spinning on its side so that sunlight falls directly over the poles. The whole Uranian system of moons and rings is flipped over on its side like a spinning bull's-eye.

An ancient collision with a huge comet or asteroid left Uranus knocked for a loop. A

---

1. Expressen 1/6/68, Meatball Fulton interview 12/67, *Hendrix Speaks* CD, Rhino Records 1990.
2. Barnes-Svarney, *Asteroid – Earth Destroyer or New Frontier?*, p.111.

cloud of smashed debris settled into a ring of material orbiting above the planet's newly positioned equator. How Hendrix knew that Uranus has rings is a mystery. The ten faint bands are just a few miles wide and invisible from Earth telescopes. They were discovered by researchers onboard the Kuiper Airborne Observatory in 1977, seven years after Jimi died. In addition to knowledge of the rings, Hendrix was also aware of asteroid bombardment of the outer planets. He referred to it as "the wars on Neptune." His screenplay (or stage play) would have explained the cause of the rings around Uranus. He pointed to these worlds as examples of what's in store for Earth: an impact with a Rock called "Love" will leave us knocked lopsided off our axis, with rings of debris.

BOWLED OVER

> *Love can change your whole world. It can turn it upside-down, like the Axis of the Earth. The Axis of the Earth turns around and changes the face of the Earth and it only takes about a quarter of a day. A completely different age comes about.*
> — Jimi[3]

> *Plato's contention that [Atlantis sank] "in a single dreadful day and in a single dreadful night" is what the critics found hard to accept.*
> — Otto Muck[4]

In the song "Up From the Skies," Jimi wrote of our world burned by "*a change of climate*." He sings of seeing "*the stars misplaced*" and describes Earth after the Rock knocks our globe sideways off its axis. Such a cataclysmic event is described in detail by Otto Muck: "The world's axis, which ends in the Pole Star, is the pivot around which the heavens revolve. A glance at the night sky, particularly in the polar regions, will show that the fixed stars move around the celestial pole in recognizably circular orbits . . . But the celestial pole exists only in our imagination. It is the point of junction between an infinitely extended Earth's axis of rotation and the imaginary dome of the sky. If this celestial pole, this imaginary point, seems to be displaced, it is really the Earth's pole of rotation that has shifted . . . the gyroscopic movement of the Earth would be affected. Imagine the Earth as a slowly rotating, spinning top and the asteroid as a small pebble that suddenly hits the top obliquely from above. What happens to the top when it is hit in this manner? It will react in the same way as a stabilizer. It will begin to wobble, in scientific terms, to precess. As its axis begins to wobble, it no longer remains in a vertical position on its base but executes a gyratory movement . . . If we should feel this stable Earth of ours receive a tremendous shock – much greater than an earthquake – we will not, oriented as we are, have the impression that the Earth is wobbling and tumbling. The disturbance will seem to be in the sky, that great dome above us with its innumerable

---

3. Rolling Stone 3/9/68.
4. Muck, *The Secret of Atlantis*, p.189.

flickering stars. If it seems to the observer that the Sun is tumbling across the sky this is, in fact, the course of the terrestrial disturbance. The observer sees it as a shift in the Sun's orbit."[5]

> *The Sun shone on stone battlements from the south,*
> *The ground turned green with verdant leek.*
> *From the south the Sun, the Moon's companion,*
> *Touched the edge of the heavens.*
> *The Sun did not know his halls.*
> *The Moon did not know her might.*
> *The stars did not know their places . . .*
>
>   – the Voluspa

According to Muck, the *Voluspa,* an ancient epic of the gods which dates back far beyond pre-Germanic times and was still sung in Iceland in the Middle Ages, is the story of the eleven-thousand-year-old Carolina Meteorite.

The *Voluspa,* says Muck, describes "the phenomenon of the celestial pole shift. It is not the celestial axis that wobbles until it has established a new equilibrium; it is the Earth's axis . . . The Sun is suddenly hurled from his position high in the sky to the 'edge of the horizon' . . . In the warm light of the Sun, which rises in the south, the ground that has been freed from ice becomes covered with green growing things [verdant leek] . . . the wobbling, rising, and trembling of the Earth has been transposed to the sky. The Sun, Moon, and stars wander aimlessly, not knowing their places. Apparently they have left their geocentric orbits and entered new ones. When the Earth trembles, it is, for those who live on Earth, as if the universe with all its stars is trembling."[6]

> *What shall be the sign of thy coming and of the end of the world? And Jesus answered . . . the coming of the Son of Man will be like lightning that can be seen from east to west...after the tribulations of those days shall the Sun be darkened, and the Moon shall not give her light, and the stars shall fall from heaven, and the powers of the heavens shall be shaken. And then shall appear the sign of the Son of man in heaven . . . and they shall see the Son of man coming in the clouds of heaven with power and great glory...At the sound of a loud trumpet, he will send his angels . .*
>
>   – Matthew 24:3-4, 27-30

> *Trumpets and violins I can hear in the distance, I think they're calling our names...*
>
>   – Jimi[7]

5. Ibid. pp.175, 172.

6. Ibid. p.177.

7. "Are You Experienced" from the album of the same title, Reprise Records 9/67.

> *Jimi explained that the "distant trumpets and violins" symbolize the message*
> *. . . Trumpets stand for prophecies, while violins represent music . . . The*
> *trumpet, he explained, heralds something new appearing on the horizon.*
> — Monika Dannemann[8]

Hendrix sang of "*the stars misplaced*"[9] and foresaw "Valleys of Neptune Arising" over the continental shelf. Mountainous tidal waves well up in response to the rock's Deep Impact into the sea.

> *Look out East Coast, you're gonna have a neighbor . . . a rebirth land . . .*
> *getting ready for the new tides . . . the New Valleys of Sunrise . . . on the*
> *burning edge horizon.*   — Jimi[10]

> *If it hit on the West Coast, the East Coast would go down in an earthquake;*
> *all your buildings in New York would collapse.*   — Tom Gehrels[11]

> *I taste the honey from a flower named Blue, way down in California, and*
> *New York drowns as we held hands.*   — Jimi.[12]

The face of the Earth will change radically after the impact of Electric Love, *"Just ask the Axis,"* Jimi warns in the title song for his album *Axis:Bold As Love*.

> *The Axis of the Earth, if it changes, well it changes the whole face of the Earth,*
> *like every few thousand years, so that new civilizations come every time it*
> *changes. And it's like Love that a human being has, if he really falls in Love deep*
> *enough it will change him, might change his whole life, so both of them can*
> *really go together. The Axis of the Earth turns around and changes the face of*
> *the Earth and it only takes about a quarter of a day. A completely different age*
> *comes about. The same with Love. Love can change your whole world. It can*
> *turn it upside-down, like the Axis of the Earth. It's that powerful, that bold.*
> *People kill themselves for Love, but when you have it for somebody or*
> *something, an idea maybe, it can beat anger any time and even move the sea*
> *and the mountains. That's what I'm trying to say: Axis:Bold as Love – 1-2-3*
> *Rock Around the Clock . . . Third Stone From the Sun is Earth, you know, they*
> *have Mercury, Venus, and the Earth.*   — Jimi[13]

---

8. Dannemann, *The Inner World of Jimi Hendrix*, p.82.
9. "Up from the Skies", released on *Axis: Bold As Love*, Track Records 12/67.
10. *Cherokee Mist – The Lost Writings of Jimi Hendrix*, p.70 *Valleys of Neptune Arising*.
11. New York Times Magazine 7/28/96, p.18.
12. "Voodoo Chile" released on *Electric Ladyland*, Reprise Records 10/68.
13. Interview for Stockholm Radio 1/8/68, Rolling Stone 3/9/68, Bold As Love magazine 2/68.

Mercury, Venus, Earth. 1-2-3, Third Stone. Rock Around the Clock. Jimi's sundial game of cosmic billiards, *"Paths chosen by God."* Axis:Bold as Love is a warning that bold action is required if humans are to escape disaster. *"Your questionable timid compromises,"* notes Jimi, *"which I intend to erase,"* or else the human race will face extinction – *"Soon you may almost forget the smell of your family"*[14] – after Electric Love knocks our planet's axis sideways.

AXIS: BOWLED (OVER BY) LOVE

> *Love is being tested here. Love for our WHOLE world. Not just our families.*
> — Jimi[15]

> *I am only a messenger – And you a sheep in process of evolution. Almost at death with yourself, and on the staircase of birth…* — Jimi[16]

"Nobody knows, really, where Jimi is at," observed bassist Noel Redding, "somewhere between enlightenment and paranoid." While he lived, Hendrix couldn't state his warning about the asteroid in a direct way. No one was ready to hear it. He would've been ineffective and he knew it. A journalist once tried to pin him down to explain his message and Jimi flashed back in frustration, "I can't say it right now because I'm thinking about it. What we're saying is not protesting, but giving the answers, some kind of solution, instead of going towards the negative scene."[17]

> *You might tell them something kinda hard but you don't want to be a completely hard character in their minds and be known for all that because there's other sides of you and sometimes they leak on to the records too. That's when the fantasy songs come in, like "1983 (a merman I should turn to be)," that's something to keep your mind off what's happening today, but not necessarily completely hiding away from it.* — Jimi[18]

URANUS AND ATLANTIS

In the song "1983 (a merman I should turn to be)," Jimi depicts a world submerged beneath the sea. He sings about people squandering resources on war: *"The machines that we built would never save us"*[19] – save us from a fate like that which destroyed Atlantis. The

---

14. *Cherokee Mist – The Lost Writings of Jimi Hendrix*, p.128
15. Ibid. p.117 *Terra Revolution and Venus*.
16. Ibid. p.128, *Forget of My Name*.
17. Brown, *Jimi Hendrix – In His Own Words*, p.81, from an interview in London 1/7/69.
18. International Times 3/28/69 - London interview with Jane de Mendelssohn.
19. "1983 (a merman I should turn to be)" released on *Electric Ladyland*, Reprise Records 10/68.

sonata-form musical movements of "1983" culminate in a coda titled "Moon Turn the Tides." This music's image of global deluge presided over by lunar movement is similar with a prophecy about the planet Uranus and the year of Jimi's birth: 1942. Hendrix was born under the Zodiac sign of Sagittarius, the Sage, or seer.

At the time of Jimi's birth in 1942, Uranus was positioned in an orbit aligned with the Sun, Earth and Saturn. This alignment, which occurs every 45-46 years, is known as the Saturn-Uranus Conjunction (see pages 220-223). When Jimi was born, the conjunction took place under his sign of Sagittarius. The conjunction's relevance to the song "1983," Jimi's music about Atlantis, is described next:

> *The combined effect of the Saturn-Uranus conjunction will definitely implement a turning point in Mankind's world view – be that view literal, psychological, or both. The sign of this conjunction's placement, Sagittarius, governs religious beliefs . . . a prophecy concerning Uranus' very own instability, giving rise to its leaving its orbit entirely and plunging in towards the Sun. As it passes the Earth, so the prophecy goes, Uranus will rip our Moon from its orbit, creating the gigantic cataclysm that shall bring Atlantis back once more.* — Lyn Birkbeck[20]

"1983" and "Moon Turn the Tides" are songs that predict a global disturbance which leaves people trapped in the underwater refuge of Atlantis. In 1968 Hendrix composed "1983," a song to mythologize the coming upheaval. 1968 is also the year for which psychic Edgar Casey had predicted discovery of the lost continent of Atlantis.

> *In 1939 Casey predicted that proof of Atlantis would be found in the waters off the coast of Bimini near Bermuda, not only that, he predicted the exact year of its discovery: 1968. Precisely 29 years later, as prophesied, scientists flying over the shallow coastal waters of Bimini observed a massive submerged shape beneath the surface. Divers dispatched to the scene confirmed its existence. Almost 2000 feet long, the object uncannily appeared to look like a wide wall or elevated roadway, it's one end curving mysteriously into the shape of a gigantic "J".* — Joshua Hamig[21]

Ancient stone slabs used for this wall had been cut with exceptional precision and aligned in geometric patterns by an unknown civilization. The slabs are similar to other megalithic sites, like Palenque in Mexico, Stonehenge in England, and Machu Picchu in Peru.

---

20. Lyn Birkbeck, *The Saturn-Uranus Conjunction – Its Spiritual and Historical Significance*, (Horoscope, 2/88), p.20.
21. *Atlantis: Lost Civilization*, A&E 2/15/96.

> *Some archaeologists are convinced their purpose was . . . an attempt to predict impending celestial collisions.*
>
> — Joshua Hamig[22]

The submerged "J" wall from Atlantis was found in 1968 while Jimi was writing the song "1983," about Atlantis. "1983" is music intended for the years when civilization was supposed to build a defense against the Rock. 1983 was the year when world media was abuzz with reports about American plans to build orbiting laser satellites. Jimi's song "1983" is an anthem meant to guide and uplift us towards such an achievement. "Better save your souls while you can," he warned.[23] "My goal is to erase all boundaries from the world. You have to set some heavy goals to keep yourself going. As long as I know there are people out there who aren't fully together I can't withdraw to lesser goals. If I quit making money I would still want to change the world . . . The walls are crumbling and the establishment doesn't want to let go. We're trying to save the kids, to create a buffer between young and old. Our music is shock therapy to help them realize a little more of what their goals should be. Almost anyone who has the power to keep their minds open listens to our music."[24]

"1983" is a song that uses Atlantis as a metaphor, a parable meant to prepare us for global change as we scramble to direct resources towards anti-asteroid technology. Hendrix said, "1983" is music to "keep your mind off what's happening" while "not hiding away from it."

> *Jimi saw a time of destruction like a global deluge approaching for our world . . . He told me that he felt that if mankind continued to follow its path of destruction, it would lead to global disaster . . . Jimi told me that he thought his lyrics could make an important contribution to solving mankind's problems, trying to give answers . . . He pointed out that certain spirits, guardian angels, were guiding people here on Earth . . . and in dangerous situations can send us important ideas, or can even rescue us.*
>
> — Monika Dannemann[25]

A SEQUENCE OF FACTS

Monika Dannemann spent several days with Hendrix and wrote a manuscript about her experience. "The idea of writing a book about Jimi's message first came to me soon after his death in 1970," she claims. "I put aside the idea of publishing a book . . . after

---

22. Ibid.
23. *Cherokee Mist – The Lost Writings of Jimi Hendrix* p.70, *Valleys of Neptune Arising*.
24. Henderson, *Jimi Hendrix – Voodoo Child of the Aquarian Age*, pp.256-7, Village Voice 1968.
25. Dannemann, *The Inner World of Jimi Hendrix*, pp.128, 123, 88, 82.

not having thought about a book for many years, a new way forward began to appear, and this time it felt right. So eventually the book was completed in a very short period of time . . . a lot of it is based directly on my first original manuscript, written back in 1970."[26]

In 1995, a revised draft of Monika's quarter-century-old manuscript was finally published by St. Martin's Press. Her new book contains many alterations of the old version. In her 1970 draft, she describes Jimi's song, "1983 (a merman I should turn to be)", and makes no mention of Atlantis, nor any mention of a comet. Instead, the old manuscript paraphrases a conversation with Jimi about the song "1983" in which he speaks of his attraction to the peace and harmony of the ocean, and his distaste for human violence in cities.

But then in September 1995, when St. Martin's Press published Monika's new book, passages about Atlantis and a *comet* were now included with her description of the song "1983." This new book came out five and a half months *after* I had contacted St. Martin's Press about "Jimi's Prophecy." The following is what transpired.

In autumn 1993, I began contacting several publishers about a book I was writing with Kathy Etchingham, Jimi's British girlfriend. Kathy and Jimi were living together before Hendrix was famous, and they remained close for the rest of his life. My letter to the publishers contained a proposal for *The Hendrix/Etchingham Story*:

> *A female Hendrix perspective remains conspicuously absent from the existing biographies about Jimi. To the outside world, Kathy's experience is the one affair that offers fascinating and comprehensive insight into Jimi's personality, habits and psychology.*[27]

Camille Cline, an editor in New York, asked to see samples of the story, which I forwarded. In January 1995, she phoned me to say she was taking the story to St. Martin's Press to see about getting it published. So I wrote to her contact at St. Martin's and forwarded an additional 17-pages titled "The Electric Church Introduction." On February 16, 1995, St. Martin's rejected *The Hendrix/Etchingham Story* as not being "the right next big Hendrix story." The editor for that publisher wrote, "However, I am interested in any other ideas you may have . . . please keep me posted on other potential Jimi Hendrix projects you have on tap."

I did. In April 1995, I sent this editor an article I was about to have published titled "GrinchRich – The D.C. Witch-hunt." This story is about my unpublished manuscripts sent to the Library of Congress in Washington for copyright registration, only to be accessed by people who pirate concepts and publish similar ideas as their own work. I sent this "Witch-hunt" article, detailing my texts at the Library of Congress, to St. Martin's on April 3, 1995. Along with it was my letter saying, "Today I'm trying to finish a new

---

26. Ibid. p.8.
27. From letter sent to 100 editors and publishers 11/15/93.

version of the 'Electric Church Introduction' . . . The new draft reveals Jimi's Prophecies
. . . Part of these Prophecies will be published next week with MCA's *Voodoo Soup* CD
package [which contains my booklet story about Jimi's vision of an explosion on Jupiter]
. . . I'm the only one who's figured out Jimi's Prophecies."

The "Electric Church Introduction," written in March 1995, was re-named *Rock
Prophecy*, the story of Jimi's asteroid prediction. On June 5, 1995, the new text arrived
at the Library of Congress for copyright registration. That draft contains the following
sequence about Hendrix, Atlantis, and a Rock from space:

> . . . there has been a fatal delay in implementing Star Wars laser
> technology to pulverize Electric Love when it appears.

> *The Machines that we built would never save us, that's what they say.*
> — Jimi "1983"

> "We'll play anywhere where we know it's gonna make some kind of
> penetration or some kind of impact," said Jimi. "Keep the Axis turning
> so that Love follows music as the Night the Day. We'll be on a truth kick.
> There's a lot of things we might be saying that people might want to
> escape the truth of. Like you might tell them something kinda hard but
> you don't want to be a completely hard character in their minds and be
> known for all that because there's other sides of you and sometimes they
> leak on to the records too. That's when the fantasy songs come in, like
> '1983 (a merman I should turn to be).'" [28]

In my manuscript sent to the LOC, the passage shown above is followed by Jimi's lyrics
for "1983," his song about Atlantis. And after that I placed his quotes about asteroids:

> *Once earlier there was a small passing thought that people came in from the
> now-asteroid belt (then a planet the approximate size of Earth). Reasons
> for the change to the chain of the space rocks as they are today were of men
> and other life . . .*   — Jimi[29]

The point is that I had already made the connection between Jimi, Atlantis, and
asteroids. I copyrighted the story in spring 1995 and notified St. Martin's Press that I was
writing about "Jimi's Prophecy." *Rock Prophecy* was available at the Library of Congress
for anyone to read. And then five and a half months later, in autumn 1995, St. Martin's
Press — the company I had approached with my concept for the first *"female Hendrix*

28. Hall and Clark, *The Superstars – In Their Own Words*, p.26, Disc 12/30/67, Brown, *Jimi Hendrix – In
His Own Words*, p.26, International Times 3/28/69.
29. *Cherokee Mist – The Lost Writings of Jimi Hendrix,* p.114 *Terra Revolution and Venus.*

perspective . . . offer[ing] . . . insights into Jimi's personality, habits and psychology" –
and the company which rejected my manuscript for *The Hendrix/Etchingham Story*,
instead published Monika Dannemann's memories of Jimi. But unlike her 1970 manuscript,
Monika's new book from St. Martins now contains "Jimi's Prophecy."[30] Whereas her
previous manuscript made no mention about Atlantis in connection with Jimi's song "1983,"
her new version now contains text about a ***rock*** striking Atlantis. Monika's revised book, in
describing the song "1983," includes the following passage:

> *Jimi told me the story of the final destruction of Atlantis. It was not an atomic*
> *bomb, but a force from outer space that brought about its demise . . . In the end*
> *a comet hit Atlantis and its islands. Within a single day the whole archipelago*
> *had sunk to the depths of the sea . . . Jimi told me that in his view today's world*
> *is in a similar situation to the time of Atlantis. But it still may not be too late*
> *to avert the disaster which will inevitably follow if mankind continues to*
> *pursue its present egotistical path.*
>
> – Monika Dannemann[31]

Monika does not say that Hendrix was *predicting* an asteroid or comet impact of
the Earth. Whereas in *Rock Prophecy* I detail for the first time Jimi's prediction of an
asteroid impact, Monika, in her book, instead concludes that Jimi's Prophecy predicts
the arrival of aliens on Earth:

> *He was convinced that, in the near future, Galacticans from outer space,*
> *from another galaxy of great positive power, would come to our planet to*
> *help mankind in its struggle against evil.*
>
> – Monika Dannemann[32]

Monika's book includes these descriptions of Atlantis, the comet, and the "Galacticans,"
in a chapter titled "Jimi's Prophecy."

> *[My] new text reveals Jimi's Prophecy...I'm the only one who's figured out*
> *Jimi's Prophecy.*
>
> – Fairchild letter to St. Martin's, April 3, 1995

Monika acknowledged that her 1995 book "was completed in a very short period
of time."[33] It was published five and a half months ***after*** I'd written to St. Martin's about
"Jimi's Prophecy."

---

30. Dannemann, *The Inner World of Jimi Hendrix,* p.133.
31 Ibid. p.131.
32. Ibid. p.133.
33. Ibid. p.8.

> *When Monika finally accepted an offer to publish a book on Hendrix, it was*
> *to be a coffee table art book. But, according to Dannemann, as the project*
> *moved along, the publisher asked her for a 30,000-word manuscript . . . It*
> *was not meant to be a biography.*   — Ken Voss[34]

If Jimi spoke to Monika about the song "1983" and said that a comet destroyed
Atlantis, why didn't she include this critical information in her 1970 manuscript, in the
section about the song "1983"? If Hendrix did speak to her about a comet, it is evidence
that my interpretation of his lyrics and hidden message is correct, he *was* writing about
disaster from space. And if he told Monika of the Atlantis comet, it is evidence that his
message remained hidden even from her, because she did not claim that he was
predicting a Rock heading towards Earth. Instead, Jimi's comments to Monika about
Atlantis are consistent with what he intended "fantasy songs" like "1983" to accomplish:
"*tell them something kinda hard, but you don't want to be a completely hard
character in their minds.*"[35] He therefore used Atlantis as a "softer" metaphor for his
warning, *without* actually *predicting* to Monika that, like Atlantis, our world is destined
for disaster from outer space. In this way he avoided appearing to her as a "hard
character." He instead told her a parable about Atlantis meant to prepare her (and us)
for his real Prophecy about the Rock.

A more sinister interpretation of the similarities between her September 1995
book and my June 1995 manuscript about Atlantis and the Rock, is a scenario where
someone read my unpublished text at the Library of Congress and introduced my
research into Monika's book then being prepared at St. Martins for publication
several months later.

Furthermore, regarding the section of Monika's book about Atlantis being
struck by a comet, this concept is not Jimi's insight anyway. The "Atlantis comet" was
described by Plato himself in the earliest written account of the lost continent, as can
be seen in three different translations from Plato's *Timaeus and Critias* text about
the comet:

Translation 1:

> *Your [Greek] story of how Phaethon, child of the sun, harnessed his father's*
> *chariot, but was unable to guide it along his father's course and so burnt up*
> *things on the Earth and was himself destroyed by a thunderbolt, is a*
> *mythical version of the truth that there is at long intervals a variation in the*
> *course of the heavenly bodies and a consequent widespread destruction by*
> *fire of things on the Earth.*   — Desmond Lee translation[36]

34. Voodoo Child newsletter # 39, Winter 95-Spring 96, p.2.
35. International Times 3/28/69 - London interview with Jane de Mendelssohn.
36. *Timaeus and Critias*, translated by Desmond Lee, (Penguin Books, 1965), p.35.

Translation 2:

> *There is a story, which even you [Greeks] have preserved, that once upon a time Phaethon, the son of Helios, having yoked the steeds in his father's chariot, because he was not able to drive them in the path of his father, burnt up all that was upon the Earth, and was himself destroyed by a thunderbolt. Now this has the form of a myth, but really signifies a declination of the bodies moving in the heavens around the Earth, and a great conflagration of things upon the Earth, which recurs after long intervals.*   *– J.V. Luce translation[37]*

Translation 3:

> *The story has the fashion of a legend, but the truth of it lies in the occurrence of a shifting of the bodies in the heavens which move round the Earth .*
>   *– Joshua Hamig translation[38]*

Plato's description of the legend of Phaethon is analyzed in the 1966 book *The Secret of Atlantis*, by German scientist Otto Muck. Muck interprets the legend to be a story about the eleven-thousand-year-old Carolina Meteorite:

> "Phaethon, son of Helios, could not control the Sun chariot and caused a terrible conflagration on Earth," notes Muck. "Struck by Zeus's thunderbolt, he fell into the Eridanus river; the tears wept by his sister were turned into amber; possibly a folk memory of a West European people of the fall of the celestial body that unleashed the [destruction of Atlantis] . . . The story of Phaethon . . . forms an important part of this collective memory. It is only in the later versions that Phaethon is actually called the son of Helios, the Sun god. In Homer and the earlier poets 'Phaethon the Radiant' is another name for Helios himself. In the myth, the Sun-chariot leaves its prescribed track across the sky, comes too close to the Earth, and scorches half of it. The charioteer, struck by Zeus's thunderbolt, glowed like the meteor that is implicit in his name as he plunged into the waters of the Eridanus, the mythical river in the west. Suppose we regard this not as a mythical description, but as a poetic view of a real cosmic event . . . The tumbling of the Sun's chariot . . . became merged in popular memory with the fall of the meteorite . . . The two images combined result in the myth of Phaethon struck by a thunderbolt and tumbling from the Sun's chariot."[39]

37. J.V. Luce, *Lost Atlantis – New Light on an Old Legend*, (New York: McGraw-Hill, 1969),   p.208.
38. *Atlantis: Lost Civilization*, A&E 2/15/96.
39. Muck, *The Secret of Atlantis*, pp.262, 175.

*Phaethon was the son of Merops; and...the people who inhabited Atlantis
were the Meropes, the people of Meron . . . The Egyptians claim that their
ancestors came from the Island of Mero . . . where in deep caves, and from
the seas, receding under the great heat, the human race, crying out for
mercy, with uplifted and blistered hands, survived the cataclysm.*

— Ignatius Donnelly[40]

In his 1883 book titled *Ragnarok: The Age of Fire and Gravel*, Ignatius Donnelly
described more than a century ago the destruction of Atlantis after a comet crosses the
Earth's path. Donnelly's first book, *Atlantis: The Antediluvian World*, was published a
year earlier by Harper's, in 1882. According to E.F. Bleiler the book "became the
standard account of Atlantis, and set the pattern for all later work in this area. It was
probably the most influential pseudo-scientific work of the later nineteenth century."[41]

A year after his groundbreaking book on Atlantis was released, Donnelly published
Ragnarok, which was later retitled *The Destruction of Atlantis*. Basing his arguments
on geology and comparative mythology, Donnelly proposed that comets are responsible
for creating ancient upheavals on Earth, upheavals such as those described in various
myths and folklore, including Bible stories such as the flood. He claims that the comet
that destroyed Atlantis is named Ragnarok:

*In the Hindu legend of the battle between Rama (the sun) and Ravana (the
comet) the scene is laid on the Island of Lanka . . . wherever any of these
legends refer to the locality where the disaster came and where man
survived, the scene is placed upon an island, in the ocean, in the midst of
the waters . . . the conclusion is irresistible that here was Atlantis; here was
Lanka . . . This island was Atlantis. Ovid says it was the land of Neptune,
Poseidon. It is Neptune who cries out for mercy. And it is associated with
Atlas, the king or god of Atlantis . . . And Ovid informs us that this land,
"with a mighty trembling, sank down a little" in the ocean, and the Gothic
and Briton (Druid) legends tell us of a prolongation of Western Europe
which went down at the same time . . . And here it is that Ragnarok comes.*

— Ignatius Donnelly[42]

The point is that — from Plato, to Donnelly, to Muck, to Hendrix — the theory that
Atlantis was destroyed by a comet has a long history. But, as noted earlier, there is no
mention of Atlantis, nor of a comet, in Monika Dannemann's 1970 manuscript about
Hendrix. Then in 1995, when her new book was prepared for publication, an Atlantis
comet is described with her memory of what Jimi said about the song "1983."

40. Ignatius Donnelly, *Ragnarok*, 1883, (Rudolph Steiner Publications, 1971), p.370.
41. Donnelly, *Atlantis – The Antediluvian World*, (New York: Dover Press, 1976), p.ix.
42. Donnelly, *Ragnarok*, pp.374-5, 370-1.

The interesting twist is that Monika met Jimi in Dusseldorf, Germany, where she was born and raised. Atlantis scholar Otto Muck was also a German resident of Dusseldorf. Muck died in 1966 before his book, *The Secret of Atlantis*, was published. The book details Muck's theory that an asteroid destroyed Atlantis. Muck's manuscript was posthumously copyrighted in Dusseldorf by Econ Verlag in 1976. The book was then published two years later in German and French. Muck's research is impressive and his book is extraordinary. In Dusseldorf, *The Secret of Atlantis* must have become quite a subject of discussion in the late 1970s. Could Monika have learned of the Atlantis comet, not from Jimi in 1970, but as a result of Otto Muck's book in the late 1970s? This would explain why the comet story was not included in her 1970 manuscript.

The discrepancy between her 1970 and 1995 texts raises questions as to whether Hendrix really spoke to her about a comet striking Atlantis. Or, did she become aware of the Atlantis comet after reading Otto Muck's book in 1978 (or later) and subsequently insert the idea into her own 1995 book, claiming it as Jimi's belief?

Could she have inserted the comet scene at the behest of someone who had read my unpublished *Rock Prophecy* manuscript in the Library of Congress? Certainly there were people at St. Martin's Press in the spring of 1995 who were preparing to release Monika's book at the same time my proposal arrived at St. Martin's for a book about "Jimi's Prophecy." Did the editors simply lift out of my writings the entire concept of Jimi predicting an impact and insert the idea into Monika's text several months prior to her book's publication by St. Marti(a)ns?

MESSAGE TO LOVE

Around the time he died, Jimi was getting ready to warn us about the Rock.. His final tour in the summer of 1970 was a string of seven concerts book-ended by two huge Sunday festivals: the Isle of Wight "Festival of Love" on Sunday August 31 and the Isle of Fehmarn "Love and Peace Festival" on Sunday September 6. In between these festivals, he played auditoriums on successive nights. The only music common to all seven of these final concerts is a medley of his songs "New Rising Sun" and "Message To Love." Songs about the asteroid became the centerpiece of his shows. And then he died twelve days later without having directly communicated his vision.

Nearly a quarter-century later comet Shoemaker-Levey 9 was seen igniting the surface of Jupiter.

> *We must prepare for the amazement in how the truth shall be presented. Nature shows more than anything, and it does get pretty amazing. What's sometimes more amazing is how people miss the warnings of tidal waves, volcanoes, earth-quakes, etc. I know inside they pretend to miss the message.*   – Jimi[43]

---

43. *Cherokee Mist – The Lost Writings of Jimi Hendrix*, p.117, *Terra Revolution and Venus*.

Jimi's Message to *Love* is a warning about the Rock. He was gone before he found a way to convey it, but he left the Prophecy encoded in words and lyrics, using popular phrases of the day: *Peace* and *Love*.

> *Going through the battles of carrying any belief leads to painting disguising or masquerading...therefore symbols, signs, non-arguments, clownery, today's techniques must be used.*   — Jimi[44]

Hendrix was a messenger, an astral traveler shaman who offered us "peace of mind" with his insights about the asteroid. He called himself Astro Man, a superhero upon whom our survival depends, because without his efforts our world is left shattered.

> *We have this [song] called "Astro Man"...talkin' about living in peace of mind, well Astro Man will leave you in pieces.*   — Jimi[45]

Jimi's prediction would've alerted us in time to prevent the Earth from being smashed to pieces. But he died, after one last concert at a Love & Peace Festival. He played "New Rising Sun/Message To Love" — a medley for his message about the Rock and a Gypsy Sun — for a Love & Peace Festival, i.e. *Electric Love & Pieces.*

> *It'll take somebody like us to get it together. Regardless of whether it's gonna be us, ourselves...If I die tomorrow, the feeling is there . . . You know my song "I Don't Live Today"? That's where it's at . . . There ain't no life nowhere.*
> — Jimi[46]

A number of clues about the Prophecy are strewn throughout Jimi's lyrics. He knew that if he "dies tomorrow" someone would be drawn to the songs with enough interest to see his hidden vision. If he didn't live to communicate it, to "get it together" with his film, then "somebody like us" would eventually interpret his lyrics for what they really mean. If he'd lived, the Prophecy would've become *Moondust*, a film meant to function as "a machine to move these people" into action against asteroids. His music has the power to carry that message against anyone's attempted obstruction.

> *The establishment is...trying to blow us all up and give us awards so that they can just dust away.*   — Jimi[47]

---

44. Ibid. p.116.
45. Brown, *Hendrix – The Final Days,* p.91, from an interview with Keith Altham, London, 9/11/70.
46. Jerry Hopkins, *Hit & Run,* (New York: Perigee Books, 1983), p.208, Distant Drummer 4/17/69, p.8.
47. L.A. Free Press 1969.

So he infused his songs with the Prophecy, a message imbedded within stirring sounds. Hendrix music is meant to charge us up to feel that we *can* beat the clock and stop the Rock coming at us.

> *I can explain everything better through music. You hypnotize people to where they go right back to their natural state which is pure positive – like in childhood when you got natural highs. And when you get people at that weakest point, you can preach into their subconscious what we want to say . . . it releases a certain thing inside a person's head so you can say what you want right into that little gap. It's something to ride with. I always like to take people on trips. That's why music is magic. Already this idea of living today is magic. There's a lot of sacrifices to make. I'm working on music to be completely, utterly a magic science, where it's all pure positive. It can't work if it's not positive. The more doubts and negatives you knock out of anything, the heavier it gets and the clearer it gets, and the deeper it gets into whoever's around it. It gets contagious.*   — Jimi [48]

It's as if civilization had a chance to organize a defense in time to ward off disaster, but that chance depended on whether or not we comprehend Hendrix.

> *As my tears drop on my crystal ball, magnifies the reflections of Christ. As I blink, his angels take him away . . . Is this the way all heroes go, carrying the first necklace of death. His preaching the belief of eternal happiness to rest, or were his angels just UFOs . . .*   — Jimi[49]

> *. . . angel, a word that translates the Hebrew term for messenger (*mal'ak) *into Greek (*angelos).   — Elaine Pagels[50]

In a climactic scene from *Moondust*, Hendrix writes about the "*catastrophe*" as the "*sky opens up...a beam of light comes through* [the] *opening as flying saucers in formation appear on each side.*"[51]

> *"There really are other people in the solar system,"* claimed Jimi, *"and they have the same feelings too, not necessarily bad feelings, but see, [humanity] upsets their way of living, and they're a whole lot heavier than we are. It's no war game. They keep the same place*[52] *. . . In one sense we might be*

48. Life 10/3/69, Hall and Clark, *The Superstars – In Their Own Words*, p.23.
49. *Cherokee Mist – The Lost Writings of Jimi Hendrix*, p.75.
50. Pagels, *The Origin of Satan*, p.39.
51. *Moondust*, p.28, published as exhibit #479 in the catalogue for Sothebys sale 6258 *Animation Art and Rock 'n' Roll Memorabilia Dec. 14 and 17, 1991.*
52. L.A. Free Press 1969.

nothin' but little ants to them, they might not even want to bother us. They might be on their way to somewhere else. You wouldn't go about two miles out of your way just to step on an ant hill . . . It's very abstract. I really get into a dream about getting into something and going off, away to somewhere else." [53]

The song "Third Stone From the Sun" mocks an Earth not worth saving. Jimi said that "Third Stone" is about "these guys coming from another planet, they observe Earth for a while and they think that the smartest animal on the whole Earth is chickens, you know, hens, and there's nothing else here to offer, they don't like the people too much, so they just blow it up at the end."[54]

In another song titled "Somewhere," he again warns of extraterrestrial visitors amused by human chaos: *"Up in the sky I can imagine UFOs chuckling to themselves, laughing, they're saying, 'Those people so uptight, they sure know how to make a mess.'"* [55]

A REVOLUTION OF THE TERRAIN AND VENUS

I'd just like to have a ringside seat, I want to know about the New Mother Earth . . .   — Jimi [56]

Otto Muck analyzed the elaborate calendar of ancient Mayan Indians and established that its purpose is to commemorate the date and time of impact of the asteroid that crashed into the Atlantic more than ten thousand years ago. Muck's research concludes that the impact coincided with a conjunction of the Sun, Moon, and Venus. This triple conjunction enables a calculation of orbits to find the exact moment of impact: 20:00 hours local time on June 5, 8498 B.C.E.[57] From this cataclysmic moment 10,500 years ago, marked by a triple conjunction, ancient Mayans counted the days and years of their calendar.

"The continuous day count, the baktun count," wrote Muck, "and the periodicity of the years and the calendar cycle were checked, first by a continuous count of 260-day periods . . . based on the rhythm of the Moon. The second astronomical correction was based on the changes in aspect of the planet Venus. Venus, because of its proximity to the Sun, exhibits a change of phases like the Moon . . . [The Mayans] also had an amazingly detailed knowledge about the period of revolution of the giant planet Jupiter. This is about 12 years, and it would provide them with a further practical correction standard amenable to simple astronomical checks . . . The continuous day count on which the

---

53. *See My Music Talking*, produced by John Marshall 12/67.
54. Stockholm Radio interview 5/25/67.
55. "Somewhere", released on *Crash Landing*, Reprise Records 3/95.
56. "Up From the Skies", released on *Axis:Bold As Love*, Track Records 2/67.
57. June 5 is also the day on which *Rock Prophecy* was copyrighted in 1995.

baktun periodicity is based, began . . . on the critical date, June 5, 8498 B.C. Gregorian calendar. This, as Henseling emphasizes, coincided with a conjunction of the three brightest celestial bodies, the Sun, the Moon, and Venus. We would say, at new Moon and new Venus. This means that the correction cycle of Venus also began on the same day. Even Henseling says, 'It is impossible to regard this combination of facts as a coincidence' . . . the Mayans selected this day and no other for their Zero Day A. Henseling inclines to the view that the triple conjunction of Sun, Moon, and Venus was the reason for choosing this particular day . . . There is everything to suggest that Zero Day A is identical with the terrible day on which the great bang set off the catastrophe in the Atlantic . . . the conclusion must be inescapable."[58]

Muck asserts that the fall of the asteroid and the triple conjunction of Sun, Moon and Venus are linked events: "Venus and Earth revolve in circular orbits around the Sun. The Moon, in a smaller circle, revolves around Earth. From a geocentric viewpoint, Venus and the Moon are near the Sun. Heliocentrically, this corresponds to an Earth, Moon, and Venus conjunction. This was the conjunction on the day the Earth captured Asteroid A. The eccentric elliptical orbit of the asteroid...[as it] approached from its perihelion, that is, *from the direction of the Sun past Venus.* [emphasis added] The effect of the triple conjunction was that the asteroid was influenced not only by Earth, but shortly before it had been influenced also by Venus and by the Moon in such a way that its orbit was deflected even closer to the Earth's position. Owing to their conjunction with the Sun . . . Venus and the Moon together brought about the fall of the asteroid into the Atlantic . . . The destruction of a world, the triggering of the greatest catastrophe in the history of mankind, was predestined in the orbits of the planets and of the asteroid."[59] In other words, as Jimi said, *"paths chosen by God."*[60]

It is a fact that Venus is the one planet in our solar system which rotates in reverse direction from all other planets. This is because Venus has in the past been hit by a massive asteroid that sent it spinning backwards. Jimi tried to alert us to the warning:

> [Venus], *the second stone from our star has been very busy getting ready for the time to communicate with Earth, to try and warn people of Earth...*
> — Jimi[61]

> *Scientist Immanuel Velikovsky turned the scientific world upside-down in the 1950s when he wrote that the planet Venus had nearly collided with Earth several times in ancient history. Venus passed so close to Earth that the Earth shook on its axis. The seasons were thrown out of sequence. There*

58. Muck, *The Secret of Atlantis*, p.253.
59. Ibid. p.253.
60. *Cherokee Mist – The Lost Writings of Jimi Hendrix*, p.117 *Terra Revolution and Venus.*
61. Ibid.

> *were periods of great darkness. There were great changes on the surface of*
> *the planet and beneath it. Deep cracks were even created in the tectonic*
> *plates beneath the continents.*   – Wendy Stein[62]

"There cannot be much doubt that the starting date of the Maya calendar is identical with the catastrophic onset of the Quinternary Age," concludes Muck. "There was a drastic change in the whole surface of the Earth . . . The geological evidence here is of the utmost importance. It provides incontrovertible proof of the existence of terrestrial revolutions . . . Plato's Atlantis became submerged at the end of the Quaternary Age in the course of a terrestrial revolution."[63]

A terrestrial revolution precipitated by Venus.

"Terra Revolution and Venus" is the title of Jimi's 9-page handwritten description of the Prophecy. This amazing Hendrix text is discussed below. Otto Muck died in 1966, leaving his research unpublished and untranslated into English. His book was published posthumously in 1978, eight years after Hendrix died. And Jimi's insights about Venus and asteroids don't mention Muck. So, as with the Arthur Clarke coincidence, where Clarke and Hendrix, independently of each other, saw the vision of a Jupiter Sun, Hendrix and Muck, also independently of each other, became aware of the Venus connection with asteroids.

The title for Jimi's description of this connection, "Terra Revolution and Venus," refers to the surface *terrain* of Earth *revolutionized* by a Rock ("terrestrial revolution") influenced by *Venus*. This is a reason why he called the asteroid Love, in honor of Venus, goddess of Love – Electric Lady/Electric Love.

> *These people of Venus are of a younger group from this asteroid womb of*
> *humans. Love is with them, as they are closer to the Sun. Closer to the Sun*
> *is the mission of today but in order for something to be realized we break*
> *things down into personal opinions which then have to be beat upon,*
> *stoned, tarred and feathered. Anything and everything it must go through to*
> *even stay abreast with the faith keeping it in light.*   – Jimi[64]

Venus is closer to the Sun than is the Earth, and from behind the Sun the Rock emerges.

> *If a comet should appear from behind the Sun, we might only have a one or*
> *two year warning.*   – Carolyn Shoemaker[65]

62. Wendy Stein, *Great Mysteries – Atlantis – Opposing Viewpoints*, (San Diego: Greenhaven Press, 1989), p.99.
63. Muck, *The Secret of Atlantis*, p.257, 140.
64. *Cherokee Mist – The Lost Writings of Jimi Hendrix*, p.116 *Terra Revolution and Venus*.
65. McNeil/Lehrer News Hour, PBS 7/22/94.

Hendrix realized that his warnings would be ignored: "*It was then believed that Love itself did not exist,*" he wrote, "*until the meeting of the races, or should I say 'worlds'.*" He then refers to a "*passing thought that people came in from the now-asteroid belt (then a planet the approximate size of Earth). Reasons for the change to the chain of the space rocks as they are today were of men and other life.*"[66] This part of "Terra Revolution and Venus" explains that the asteroid belt itself is comprised of smashed fragments from what once was a planet nearly the size of Earth. That planet was shattered, and its millions of scattered pieces remain today in orbit around the Sun between Mars and Jupiter.

> *The gap between Mars and Jupiter looks like a perfect place for another planet to have formed. But instead there is a wide zone of rocks and dust called the asteroid belt...It's really only a ring of dust, sand, boulders and mountain size chunks spread out in bands much like the rings around Saturn.*
> – Practical Guide to the Universe[67]

> *Astronomer Kiyotsugu Hirayama in 1918 . . . showed that three groups of known asteroids have similar orbital characteristics and believed that they were all members of a single body that experienced massive collisions in the past.*   – Patricia Barnes-Svarney[68]

Jimi realized that before the planet was destroyed it was inhabited by intelligent beings. "*The race of people from this planet played with God,*" he wrote. "*They built rockets the size of Maine on the so-called eastern side of the planet. They tried moving or altering the whole orbit of their life umbilical cord.*"[69]

Gigantic rocket engines were erected on the surface of their world to try and jettison it away from incoming asteroids. But the sudden movements of the planet in its orbit triggered massive shock waves, a domino effect: "*The Sun reacted and the magnet, upset, destroyed the world known as its normal state,*" notes Jimi, adding, "*At least it has been thought that the people were forewarned and left. Few of them went to Mars, eventually tampered with the natural working motion there . . . soon to be as the cold dead servant Moon.*"[70]

With their world smashed into asteroids, the aliens sought to colonize Mars. Their efforts transformed the red planet into a desert wasteland. But Jimi envisioned that these "*people came in from the now-asteroid belt,*" they came to Earth. They are our original ancestors.

66. *Cherokee Mist – The Lost Writings of Jimi Hendrix*, p.114 *Terra Revolution and Venus*.
67. Practical Guide to the Universe, The Learning Channel 2/95.
68. Barnes-Svarney, *Asteroid – Earth Destroyer or New Frontier?* pp.95-6.
69. *Cherokee Mist – The Lost Writings of Jimi Hendrix*, p.114 *Terra Revolution and Venus*.
70. Ibid. p.115.

Gods and goddesses being mentioned too much pulls the awareness and bizarreness in clash with actual honest communicating to whoever or whatever, unless the point of the whole subject itself is completely understood or <u>proved</u>. . . or some sort of evidence dropped into the package.

— Jimi[71]

1996 was a banner year for evidence of extraterrestrials that once inhabited Mars. The first revelation came from British researcher David Percy. After studying NASA photographs of Mars for twenty years, he announced his discovery of structures on the Martian surface that mirror geological formations around Avebury, England. "The earthen ramparts and ditch at Avebury is a copy of a crater on Mars," said Percy. "There's a crater with a little tetrahedral pyramid on the rim, and [to the south] a spiral mound. At Avebury, the earthen ramparts and ditch represent the crater, and to the south we have a spiral mound called Silbury Hill."[72]

Silbury Hill is the largest prehistoric sculpture in the world. For 4000 years it has stood as a monument to the Earth Goddess. In a 30-mile radius around the mound are found the great ceremonial circles at Avebury and Stonehendge. Percy took transparent overlays of the structures at Avebury and superimposed them on to NASA's photos of Mars. "When we bring the picture behind it we can see very clearly that the correspondence is stunning," he claims. "We have structures on Mars that have been put there by intelligent life, and [humans] didn't do it."[73]

On the heels of Percy's announcement came discovery of "Martians." Using new technology and high resolution electron microscopes, a team of scientists from Stanford University and the NASA-Johnson Space Center placed a Martian meteorite in a vacuum chamber and bombarded it with laser beams. Imprinted within the rock they located the fossilized remains of microbes. These single-cell structures represent Martian microfossils of organic molecules commonly found when microorganisms die. The finding was the first chemical evidence of extraterrestrial biological activity. In other words, life on Mars.

The fossilized remains resemble bacterial molecules called hydrocarbons, the building blocks of life: egg-shaped tubular particles called magnetites are arranged in the Mars rock in conjunctions similar with those produced by bacteria on Earth. Such hydrocarbons would have been formed in the presence of water. Mars, with its landscape of dried up river beds, flooded plains and polar ice caps, shows evidence of once having been covered with water. This was the original oasis for the refugees from the planet that was smashed into what is now the asteroid belt. But the aliens *"tampered with the natural working motion"* on Mars and their experiments left the red planet *"as the cold dead servant Moon"*[74] – useless for supporting life.

---

71. Ibid. p.117.

72. Hard Copy, ABC 7/13/96.

73. Ibid.

74. *Cherokee Mist – The Lost Writings of Jimi Hendrix*, p.115 *Terra Revolution and Venus*.

Jimi realized these things about our solar system's history. More than a quarter century after his death, the meteorite from Mars, like a space age Rosetta Stone bearing chemical hieroglyphics, was deciphered. The inscriptions tell us what Hendrix knew all along: "We are not alone," announced Dr. Richard Zare of Stanford University. "The evidence is strongly suggestive. Is it possible that we are all Martians? That life actually first started on Mars and came from Mars to Earth via a meteorite?"[75]

> *If a rock can go from planet to planet could it carry something inside? Suppose there is a tiny speck of life in the rock . . . when a giant meteor crashed . . . and sends this rock soaring into deep space carrying a tiny bacteria. Is it possible that that bacteria could in effect hitch-hike from here all the way to there and land and get out and start a whole new life? . . . Can any creature live that long? . . . [Yes] it is possible to hibernate for millions of years . . . Could it be that the very first life forms in the whole solar system did not begin life on Earth? They may have started life on Mars or Venus and then somehow be bounced to Earth.*
>
> — Robert Krulwich[76]

Jimi wrote about an inhabited planet that was shattered. He described how "*people came in from the now-asteroid belt.*" They came to Earth and now we, their descendents, face the same fate: a pulverized world.

> *on the Moon . . .so many traces*
> *on Mars . . .so many places*
> *on Venus . . .so many races*
> *on Earth . . .so many faces*
>
> — Jimi[77]

"*The second stone from our star has been very busy getting ready for the time to communicate with Earth,*" wrote Jimi, "*to try and warn the people of Earth of potential self destruction.*"[78] He refers to the orbits of Earth and Venus relative to the Sun and Moon. Their positions, when aligned, orchestrate a gravitational channeling of the Rock, from the direction of the Sun, into our world. By the time Electric Love emerges into view outside of the solar glare, a few months will be all that remains before impact. The "warning" is in the orbits, Venus is the key. Preparing defensive technology in a ring of satellites around the Earth is our only hope.

75. ABC News Nightline 8/6/96.
76. ABC World News, 7/11/97.
77. *Cherokee Mist – The Lost Writings of Jimi Hendrix*, p.117 *Terra Revolution and Venus*.
78. Ibid. p.116.

The truth shall be known to all. The will to accept the truth must be fed, never suspiciously bled. It's just that we must prepare for the amazement in how the truth shall be presented.

— Jimi[79]

Hendrix said that people *"are going to feel"* the physical change of Earth, *"in many ways they are a lot of the reason for causing it."*[80] How are humans to blame for the impact? Hendrix presents a picture of disaster resulting from our *inability* to mobilize world resources in time to affect the Rock coming at us. The chapters ahead describe historical sources for this shortfall to explain our dilemma.

The most complicated kind of knowledge you can relate to an audience involves not just knowing something, but knowing what that something signifies. — Judith Applebaum[81]

We really could not care for our children . . . The time has come for us to be on the watch, to know the scent, to recognize, to stand and visualize, stand and realize.

— Jimi[82]

79. Ibid. p.117.
80. San Diego Free Press 6/13/69.
81. Judith Applebaum, *How to Get Happily Published* (New York: Harper Collins, 1978), p.62.
82. *Cherokee Mist — The Lost Writings of Jimi Hendrix*, p.117 *Terra Revolution and Venus*.

Chapter 4: Classic Lineage

ى

Pretend your mind is a big muddy bowl and the silt is very slowly
settling down – but remember your mind is still muddy and you can't
possibly grasp all I'm saying.   – Jimi[1]

"Jimi Hendrix in Britain" is an image filled with symbolism. A bluesman of African decent, Hendrix was also of Cherokee and Irish lineage. It is his *Irish* ancestry that links Jimi uniquely to the history of blues and positions him as a seminal point of reference. This is because the British Isles are key to a chain of blues history leading back through the music's Voodoo origins in the American South and even further back to the African slave trade in the West Indies.

When Hendrix arrived in London to spearhead the 1966 British blues boom, he was performing for a hippie culture patterned after *Diggers*. The Diggers of 17th century Cromwellian England were self-determined rebels who formed rural communes at the height of the witch hunts. Diggers dropped out of society at a time when thousands of Irish Celtic pagans were being persecuted for practicing the old pagan religions.

"The major studies don't mention that Africans were not the only slaves in the West Indies," notes Michael Ventura, "they were not even the only slaves who had a . . . 'pre-Christian' cosmology. In the 1650s, after Oliver Cromwell had conquered Ireland in a series of massacres, he left his brother, Henry, as the island's governor. In the next decade, Henry sold thousands of Irish people, mostly women and children, as slaves to the West Indies. Estimates range between 30,000 and 80,000 . . . Henry was trying to sell off as many pagans as he could. This was at the height of the English witch craze, which was a pogrom against those who still adhered to the Celtic religions. Ireland was the stronghold for the old beliefs. This explains the mercilessness of Cromwell's massacres . . . in Ireland the old ways were more a way of life than anywhere else . . . [In the West Indies] the Irish slaves, most of them women, were mated with the Africans. . . Virtually every account of Voodoo notes, at some point, how similar are its sorcery practices to the practices of European witchcraft . . . practicing pagans from Ireland infused their beliefs with the Africans, mingling in Voodoo two great streams of non-Christianist metaphysics."[2]

---

1. Life 10/3/69.
2. Michael Ventura, *Hear That Long Snake Moan*, Whole Earth Review, Spring 1987, pp.35-6.

The Hendrix family tree has roots in Africa and Georgia. Jimi's lineage is also Cherokee and Irish, and Irish/African lore is at the core of blues and Voodoo history. This Afro-Irish cauldron, within an American Cherokee melting pot, constitutes Jimi's classic lineage of the blues, "classic" because blues music itself is encoded with images and rhythms from Afro-Celtic Voodoo.

At the heart of rock 'n' roll is the beat of rhythm 'n' blues. R&B is a slicked-up, citified version of the old rural blues. Before being imported to the American South, the "blues beat" in Africa and the Caribbean was a focal point for native dance rites of *possession*. Animism is a belief system in which animals and natural objects are thought to possess spirits and souls. African *animist* beliefs feature intermediary spiritual messengers that act like bridges between man and God. These spirits are called *Loas*. Loas are the sub-deity messenger-gods invited during Voodoo rituals to possess tribal dancers. Loas are invisible energies that connect us with the ways of nature. The ancestors of rock 'n' roll used hypnotic rhythms from their sacred drums to enter a dance trance and *commune* with Loas. Being the multiple expressions of God, Loas are invoked to *flow through* a dancer caught up in physical-spiritual rapture. This fusion between people and deity produces ecstatic effects in the possessed.

DUALITY

But biblical influence over our thinking in the West imposes a *duality* between body and mind. World religions consider the physical body and the spiritual mind as polarized realms, separate and opposed. This notion of duality was developed in ancient Greece. "The Greek philosophers were into dualism," explains Rev. Michael Taylor, "and Christianity rapidly came under their spell. That dualism had two strands; one of which was saying that the body wasn't quite as important as the soul, so you get bits in Greek philosophy, [like] the body is the cloak, the garment, the clothes that the soul wears, [and the soul is] the real person. But then [the body] goes from secondary importance to really something that's bad: it's part of the material world, and there is a whole strain of Greek religion, the object of which is to rise above the material world, which is the arena of evil."[3]

The notion that the body is less important than the soul sets the stage for the Bible's tradition against sex. Spirit and flesh were written about as being *different* from each other. The human body-mind thinks of itself as being split in two, a view of life that is *dual*—spirit and flesh *duel* like swordsmen against each other. This philosophical battle has shaped all Western attitudes: sex and flesh are covered in shame, secrecy, guilt and rejection. Snickers and giggles attend their mention. Spirit, on the other hand, solemn in its sacred humorlessness, is exalted. Spirit is the language of God. Sex is the tongue of the Devil.

---

3. *The Power of Dance*, produced by Ellen Hovde and Muffie Meyer, MiddleMarch Files, PBS 5/93.

> *Although many pagans had come to believe that all the powers of the*
> *universe are ultimately one, only Jews and Christians worshipped a single*
> *God and denounced all others as evil demons. Only Christians divided the*
> *supernatural world into two opposing camps, the one true God against*
> *swarms of demons, and none but Christians preached – and practiced – the*
> *great majority of Christian teachings, based...on the conviction that God's*
> *spirit constantly contends against Satan.*   – Elaine Pagels[4]

This split between body and mind attained lasting impact when the authors of the Bible enshrined dualism in scripture.

> *That the righteousness of the law might be filled in us, who walk not after*
> *the flesh, but after the Spirit. . . For the carnally minded is death; but to be*
> *spiritually minded is life and peace. Because the carnal mind is enmity*
> *against God.*   – Paul: Romans 8:4-7

We in the West have been trained to associate lust with shame. We've been taught that the human spirit must transcend desires of the flesh. This is a central tenant of biblical thinking: spiritual realms *oppose* physical life. Only in the Garden of Eden are there no opposites, explains the Hebrew Bible; time is non-existent in the eternal now of Paradise. Past and future are unknown in Eden. Man and woman are indistinguishably *one* with God. It is written that this bliss was shattered when Adam ate forbidden fruit. Mortal life *begins* with the disobedience of Eve. From Eden's Tree of Knowledge they gained awareness of opposites. For this offense God cast mankind out of Eden and into mortality, into the illusional realm of *time*: past and present, then and now, life and death.

> *When you make the two one, and when you make the inside like the outside*
> *and the outside like the inside, and the above like the below, and when you*
> *make the male and the female one and the same . . . then you will enter*
> *[Paradise] . . . Damn the flesh that depends on the soul. Damn the soul that*
> *depends on the flesh . . . When you make the two into one you will become*
> *children of Adam.*   – Jesus (Thomas:22, 106, 112)

Outside the Garden, separated from God, alienated against nature, Adam and Eve were transfixed by their differences and covered themselves in *shame*. Their *fall* from Paradise was the result of indulging their senses: they hungered, they desired to taste the fruit, they ate. In satisfying the cravings of their *bodies,* Adam and Eve disobeyed God. The whole human race, it is written, is therefore punished by exile from Paradise, unable to enter heaven unless this human sin, originating with Adam and Eve, is *redeemed* from

4. Pagels, *The Origin of Satan,* p 130.

our soul. Redemption symbolically and formally condemns human flesh for its urges and temptations which trigger disobedient sin. This belief is called the *Fall of Nature* and it explains why, in Western culture, all impulsive acts, all behaviors that are inspired by nature, have been for centuries regarded as sin.

"That's the biblical condemnation of nature," explains Joseph Campbell, "[to say] God is *not* in nature, God is *separate* from nature and nature is not God. This distinction between God and the world is not to be found in basic Hinduism or Buddhism . . . this is a religious system that belongs to the near East following Zarathustra's time. It's in the biblical tradition all the way in Christianity and Islam as well – this business of *not* being with nature. We speak with derogation of 'the *nature* religions.' You see, with that Fall in the Garden nature was regarded as corrupt; here's a myth for you that corrupts the whole world for us! And every spontaneous act is sinful because nature is corrupt and has to be corrected and must not be yielded to . . . [this is] a refusal to affirm life. Life is evil in this view. Every natural impulse is sinful unless you've been baptized or circumcised in this tradition that we've inherited. For heaven's sake! . . . You get a totally different civilization, a totally different way of living according to your myth as to whether nature has fallen or whether nature is itself a manifestation of divinity, and the spirit being the revelation of the divinity that's inherent in nature."[5]

"We have functioned on the idea that one survives through control and domination over nature," agrees Susan Griffin, "and underneath is a subconscious belief that somehow we're going to be immortal through that. Our theologies talk about a heaven which we achieve through mastery of sensual life here on Earth, and if we're not sexually sinful, or sensually sinful, then we can achieve this immortality and we'll live forever."[6]

> *We have a concept of human nature that's epitomized by the story of Adam and Eve, banished from Paradise because of indulging in pleasure for which one has to suffer penance. The ideal of human nature is splitting the mind and the body, and the mind is superior to the body, and unless you control the body with your mind, your body is likely to erupt in chaos, you'll succumb to its impulses and once you succumb to those impulses heaven knows where it will end.* — Margaret MacKenzie[7]

> *Let not sin therefore reign in your mortal body, that ye should obey it in the lusts thereof.* — Paul: Romans 6:12

> *Because the carnal mind is enmity against God: for it is not subject to the law of God, neither indeed can be.* — Paul: Romans 8:7

---

5. The Power of Myth, *Message of the Myth*, 1987 interviews with Bill Moyers, PBS 3/88.
6. *The Famine Within – A Film by Katherine Gilday*, Direct Cinema Limited, 1990.
7. Ibid.

"It was Augustine who epitomized a general feeling among the Church Fathers that the act of intercourse was fundamentally disgusting," notes Reay Tannahill. "Arnobius called it filthy and degrading. Methodius unseemly, Jerome unclean, Tertullian shameful, Ambrose a defilement . . . Augustine . . . concluded that the fault lay not with God but with Adam and Eve. According to [Augustine's] reconstruction . . . sex in the Garden of Eden, if it had ever taken place, would have been cool and rarefied, with no eroticism, no uncontrollable responses, certainly no ecstasy . . . But when Adam and Eve fell into sin they became conscious of new and selfish impulses . . . over which they had no control. The immediate effect of their lapse from grace was that they became aware and ashamed of their nakedness, and Augustine interpreted this as meaning that their own disobedience to the Creator was reflected in sudden and willful activity on the part of their genitals . . . Lust and sex were integral to the doctrine of original sin, and every act of coitus performed by humanity subsequent to the Fall was necessarily evil, just as every child born of it was born into sin . . . Augustine had set out to validate the Church Fathers' revulsion against sex . . . The body was no more than a flawed vessel for the mind and spirit, and it was now up to the Church to propagate Christian morality in these terms."[8]

According to the Bible, the desires of the flesh and the urges of nature must be resisted. Physical cravings are to be suppressed because flesh is the *enemy* of heaven, sexual members are prone to be seized with *involuntary* pumping convulsions, chaotic erotic expressions of possession by wild demonic selfishness. In other words, *orgasm = disobedience.* Codified in these beliefs of Western societies is this struggle to control and pacify *earthly* urges.

> *For I delight in the law of God after the inward man, but I see another law in my members, warring against the law of my mind, and bringing me into captivity to the law of sin which is in my members. O wretched man that I am! who shall deliver me from the body of this death?...with the mind I myself serve the law of God; but with the flesh the law of sin.*
>
> — Paul: Romans 7:22-25

In exile from Eden, the mind of man wages war with his body. All of our attitudes have been colored by the belief that, born with original sin into God's disfavor, we are "fallen" and must *atone* for worldly want.

> *We are stardust, we are golden, we are caught in the Devil's bargain, and we've got to get ourselves back to the Garden.*
>
> — Joni Mitchell[9]

---

8. Reay Tannahill, *Sex In History,* (New York: Stein & Day, 1980), pp.141-142.
9. "Woodstock" by Joni Mitchell, 1969.

But such biblical myths were alien to the African forefathers of rock. Their possession dance rhythms inspire a vision of nature *as* divinity. To be filled with the rapture of Loas implies union of flesh with spirit. Through the trance of dance we can *inhabit* the deity and *be inhabited by* the deity. In bodily abandon to the sacred drums, induced by music of hypnotic rhythms, ecstatic dancers *become* God. The beat of blues, and of rock, originated in such rites. *Possession* is the message of the music, a message that celebrates sensual feeling.

> *The content of the old blues was singing about sex, problems with their old*
> *ladies, and booze.* — Jimi[10]

A COLLISION OF MYTHS

When African slaves were introduced to Christianity in America, they established their own churches. "A doctrine that denied the body, preached by a [Voodoo] practice that excited the body, would eventually drive the body into fulfilling itself elsewhere," notes Michael Ventura.[11] In black churches, the sanctified choirs exhort the congregations into trance-like excitement, led by an impassioned preacher who *feels the spirit* upon him. The process that the preacher goes through is the same as possession. "The worshipper would long for the mind/body unity felt when the church was 'rocking,'" explains Ventura. "The object of the Voodoo ceremony is possession by a god. Possession by the Holy Ghost is as much a formal goal of the religion in Holiness and Pentecostal churches as possession is in Voodoo. Speaking in tongues (in Haiti called 'talking with Africa') was evidence to many that the speaker was possessed by the Holy Spirit."[12]

Despite biblical prohibitions against the flesh, and in spite of Papal demands for abstinence as the price of salvation, the old ways survived in the black church.

> *The careless soul who goes to balls*
> *and seeks for pleasures there,*
> *With sinful conduct says to all*
> *"In Heaven I have no share."*
> *Remember those and those alone*
> *who spurn the dancing floor,*
> *Shall dwell with God upon his throne*
> *and live forevermore.*
> — 19th Century Baptist minister[13]

---

10. Henderson, *Jimi Hendrix – Voodoo Child of the Aquarian Age,* p.258.
11. Ventura, *Hear That Long Snake Moan,* Whole Earth Review, Spring 1987, p.42.
12. Ibid. p.43
13. *The Power of Dance,* produced by Ellen Hovde and Muffie Meyer, MiddleMarch Files, PBS 5/93.

When Celtic customs mingled with Voodoo ways in the Caribbean and in South America, both belief systems had to adapt to Catholic rule. Voodoo and pagan practices were subordinate to a Catholic establishment in the Americas. It is this Afro-Irish mixture of rituals and religions that forms the Voodoo religion which was imported to the southern United States. "It is no accident that what most closely resembles an old New Orleans funeral is an Irish wake," writes Ventura, "these are the two modern cultures most in touch with their non-Christianist roots . . . In Abomey Africa...deities that speak through humans are called 'vodun.' The word means 'mysteries.' From their 'vodun' comes our Voodoo . . . Voodoo consistently emphasizes that the holy and the earthly are supposed to meld in the body itself, and that to split the mind from the body is to do evil."[14]

Robert Moore, the great-grandfather of Jimi Hendrix, was an Irishman, and Irish lore is central to Voodoo and blues history. Jimi's ancestry links him to these Voodoo cultures at the root of blues. His Afro-Irish blend combines with his part-Cherokee heritage to produce a classic lineage of the blues, because it was in America, home of the Cherokees, that Afro-Celtic Voodoo rites blossomed into a new music called blues.

> *I'm a Voodoo Child, Lord knows I'm a Voodoo Child...*
> — Jimi

As the living embodiment of this lineage, Jimi played a shaman's Pied Piper role in leading hippies of the 1960s to convene in a manner alien to the prevailing ways of Western civilization. The behavior of rock culture teens was at odds with the conduct of their parents because the *message* transmitted through rock is at odds with Judeo-Christian myths. Rock was new during Jimi's career and it carried a message of *possession*, shaking to the beat in sexually expressive ways. Rhythm and movement excite our senses and incite arousal of *physical* feeling. Throughout history Indian seers and African shamans have transform themselves through these dances.

> *To dance is to meditate because the universe dances. And because the universe dances "he who does not dance does not know what happens." This is literally the body & soul of Voodoo.* — Michael Ventura[15]

Mushroom hallucinogens and other psychoactive plants enhance the perceptual skills of the shaman. Being the tribal seers, their peers rely on shamans to interpret urges and translate behavior. Their heightened intuitions enable them to sense intentions hidden by social customs. "At its fullest," notes Terrence McKenna, "shamanism is not simply religion, it is a dynamic connection into the totality of life on the planet."[16]

---

14. Michael Ventura, *Hear That Long Snake Moan*, Whole Earth Review, Summer 1987, p.82, Whole Earth Review, Spring 1987, pp.32, 35
15. Ventura, *Hear That Long Snake Moan*, Whole Earth Review, Spring 1987, p.35, Ventura is quoting from the Acts of John 95:17 *New Testament Apocrypha*, (Philadelphia: The Westminister Press, 1964), p.229.
16. McKenna, *Food of the Gods*, p 61.

Describing a typical shaman transformation, Joseph Campbell explains, "A boy becomes sick, psychologically sick . . . the child begins to tremble and is immobilized and the family is terribly concerned about it and they send for a shaman, who has had the experience in his own youth, to come as a psychoanalyst, you might say, and pull the youngster out of it. But instead of relieving him of the deities, he is *adapting* [the boy] to the deities and the deities to himself. It's a different problem from that of psychoanalysis. I think it was Nietzsche who said 'be careful lest in casting out your devil you cast out the best thing that's in you.' Here, the 'deities who have been encountered of the powers,' let's call them, are retained, the connection is retained, it's not broken, and these men then become the spiritual advisers and gift-givers of their people . . . The shaman is the person who has in his late childhood/early youth, could be male or female, had an overwhelming psychological experience that turns them totally inward, the whole unconscious has opened up and they've fallen into it. It's been described many, many times and it occurs [worldwide] all the way from Siberia right through the Americas right down to Tierra del Fuego. It's a kind of schizophrenic crack up, the shaman experience: dying and resurrecting, being on the brink of death and coming back, to actually experience the death experience; people who have very deep dreams – dream is a great source of the spirit – or people who, in the woods, have had mystical encounters."[17]

> *Human beings die too easily, you know. Like you might see an animal or something like that, and all the sudden you might have a very funny feeling go through you for a second. Like one time I seen this deer, I see a lot of deer around where I used to be from, and I said, "Wait!" Something went through me for one second, like I seen him before, like I had some real close connection with that deer for one split second, and then it just went away . . . Have you ever laid in bed and you was in this complete state where you couldn't move or nothing? You're like that and you feel like you're going deeper and deeper into something, not sleep, but it's something else. And every time I go into that then I say, "Oh hell, I'm scared as hell," so you try to say, "Help! Help!" You can't move, you can't scream, and you say "Help!" and you finally get out of there, because you just can't move. It's a very funny feeling. But one time while that feeling was coming through me I said, "Oh, here we go, this time I'm just gonna let it happen and see where I go, see what happens." So I was getting really scared in there. I was goin' ZZzzzZZZzz – like that. I said, "I'm not even asleep!" I said this is really strange, and somebody knocked on the door. I said, "Aw!" Because I wanted to find out.*
>
> – Jimi[18]

17. The Power of Myth, *The First Storytellers*, 1987 interviews with Bill Moyers, PBS 3/88.
18. Interview with Meatball Fulton 12/67, *Hendrix Speaks* CD, Rhino Records 1990.

"Shamans play the role that the priesthood plays in our eyes," notes Joseph Campbell. "There's a major difference, as I see it, between a shaman and a priest: a priest is a functionary of a social sort, the society worships certain deities in a certain way and the priest becomes ordained as a functionary to carry on that ritual, and the deity to whom he is devoted is a deity that was there before he came along. The shaman's powers are symbolized in familiars; deities of his own personal experience, and his authority comes out of a psychological experience, not a social ordination. He would become the interpreter of the heritage of mythological life . . .The myth makers in earlier days were the counterparts of our artists . . . The poetry of the traditional culture, and the ideas, come out of . . . an elite experience: the experience of people particularly gifted, whose ears are open to the song of the universe, and they speak *to* the folk, and there is an answer from the folk which is then received. There's an interaction, but the *first* impulse comes from *above*, not from below, in the shape of your folk tradition."[19]

> *The muses, the inspirations of poetry – which is to say, of religion, of mythology – are moved by the radiance of God.*   – Joseph Campbell[20]

Tribal customs imported to America with African slaves preserved the ancient rites of possession. Pagans appeared on the Mississippi Delta and showed Christians how to unite spirit with flesh. Government authorities abhorred the practice and decreed a ban on native drums. The Loa dance was outlawed in New Orleans in 1875. Jim Crow laws forbid blacks to gather in public parks. Dance ceremonials among American Indians were likewise prohibited by the United States government in 1904. The ban stayed in effect for thirty years.

To compensate for this silencing of sacred drums, and stilling of the possession dance, slaves created blues. Blues vented an overflowing animist instinct that had been stifled by Puritan prohibition laws. "The blues was everything African that had been lost, distilled into a sound where it could be found again," observes Ventura. ". . . One man could play the blues, so it was a form that allowed one man to preserve, add to, and pass on what in its native form had taken a tribe. Its beat was so implicit that the African for the first time didn't need a drum. The holy drum, the drum that is always silent, lived in the blues. One man with a guitar could play the blues and his entire tradition would be alive in his playing."[21]

Blues is music about the *beat*, the beat that inspires *dance*. So in place of tribal Voodoo jigs, communion with Loas was instead achieved through performance of *blues*. *Possession* survived. Blues remains America's most original and influential art form. In its improvised rhythmic interplay, ecstatic *abandon* lives on and dancers ride the Loas as dancers always have.

---

19. The Power of Myth, *The First Storytellers*, PBS 3/88.
20. Joseph Campbell, *Mythos - the Mystical Life*, PBS, 12/1/96.
21. Ventura, *Hear That Long Snake Moan*, Whole Earth Review, Summer 1987, p.82.

> *I play and move as I feel, it's no act. Perhaps it's sexy, but what music with a big beat isn't? The world revolves around sex . . . and it's behind a lot of music too . . . Music should be matched with human emotions and if you can tell me a more human one than sex then, man, you've got me fooled.*   — Jimi[22]

ELVIS CHANNELS AFRICA

When drum rhythms from the possession dance were used as backbeats for rock 'n' roll, the stage was set for a collision of myths. In 1956, mass markets in the West channeled Africa through Elvis. Presley's popularity introduced a mass audience of teens to the intoxicating effects of jungle drums. A spell had been cast as a frenzy of Loas inhabited the heartland. With more force than ever before, natural human impulses collided with biblical prohibitions against sensuality and sex. Our Western emphasis on spirit over matter collapsed into carnal snake dance. Body-music blues urged clergy to boogie. "Africa" battled the Vatican.

> *If they can't get release and respect from the older people then they go into these other things and their music gets louder and it gets rebellious because it's starting to form a religion, because you're not gonna find it in Church. A lot of kids don't find nothing in Church . . . It's nothin' but an institution, so they're not gonna find nothing there. So then it moves on to trying to find yourself.*
> — Jimi[23]

> *Those who have . . . been abandoned by institutional religion . . . have often retained a fundamentally spiritual insight, although in many cases they would be reluctant and even hostile to the idea of calling it "religious." At any rate, there is a remarkable radicalization of consciousness among these spiritual exiles.*   — Mary Daly[24]

> *I don't like the name 'church' because it sounds too funky, too sweaty. You think of a person prayin' between his legs on the ground. So until we find something better, we'll have to use that.*   — Jimi [25]

> *Popular music is antithetical to orthodox Church music. Celibate monks chant in order to subdue congregations into sexless, passive obedience, all*

---

22. Sunday Mirror 5/21/67 and 2/9/67, Beat Instrumental 6/3/69.
23. Interview with Nancy Carter, L.A. 6/15/69, *Hendrix Speaks*, 1990 Rhino Records.
24. Mary Daly, *Beyond God the Father*, (Boston: Beacon Press, 1973), p.153.
25. Shapiro, *Electric Gypsy*, pp.366-7, from June 8, 1969 interview with Jerry Hopkins in L.A.

> *the better to be controlled by Church and state. Popular music enlivens audiences and lures us beyond controls of Church and state by encouraging sexual pleasure, not to mention protest and revolution.*
> — Caroline Coon[26]

Puritan establishments were reviled by the pelvic paganisms of Elvis and his tribe. Rock 'n' roll made the young get funky. Jungle drums rekindled the frenzy of possession. Like pre-Christian heathens in dance-trance abandon, American youth of the 1950s became living cathedrals receptive of intoxicating spirits. After centuries of pious abstinence, the tribes were naturemen again.

> *Elvis' dance was the dance that everybody forgot. His dance was so strong that it took an entire civilization to forget it. And ten seconds on the Ed Sullivan Show to remember.*   — Michael Ventura[27]

> *Music and life, the flow goes together so closely, it's sort of like a parallel. Music is a form of life itself and people don't know it, but still music enters their lives in ways they don't even know, as where they feel they're acting because of some artificial means . . . When there are vast changes in the way the world goes it's usually something like art and music that changes it. Music is going to change the world next time.*   — Jimi[28]

"Rock 'n' roll is the healing music," said Little Richard, "the music that makes the blind see; it makes the lame, deaf, and dumb — hear, walk, and talk."[29] Songs encoded with Africa's rhythmic metaphysic act as subliminal relief for sexually uptight Westerners. It's as if in a drumbeat our original sin is forgiven. Sons and daughters of Victorian rigidity couldn't get enough. In the decade following their first dose of Elvis, a rock 'n' roll tidal wave climaxed in communal orgies that recalled the long lost pagan practice of *sabbats* and witchcraft. "They shared with pagan religions of pre-Christian Europe the conviction that religious worship is a bodily celebration," writes Ventura, "a dance of entire community, or as it was called in Europe when such belief had been driven underground, a 'sabbat' . . . In Cromwell's time sabbats are well documented throughout the continent."[30]

By the 1960s, after centuries of biblical taboos, pagans again danced en masse.

---

26. Adrian Boot & Chris Salewicz, *The Ultimate Experience*, (London: Boxtree, 1995), p.154.

27. Ventura, *Hear That Long Snake Moan*, Whole Earth Review, Summer 1987, p.91.

28. Henderson, *Jimi Hendrix — Voodoo Child of the Aquarian Age*, p.137 (from winter 1967 recorded interview with Jimi), Rolling Stone 10/1/70.

29. Robert Spitz, *Barefoot In Babylon*, (New York: W.W. Norton, 1979), p.25.

30. Ventura, *Hear That Long Snake Moan*, Whole Earth Review, Spring 1987, pp.31, 36.

YOUTH BOOM

> *The establishment has set up the Ten Commandments for us saying don't,*
> *don't, don't.*   — Jimi[31]

The boom in birthrates in the wake of World War II produced in the 1950s a population of teens that was bursting at the seams. This first generation weaned on rock 'n' roll ripened into a culture connected with antiquity. Like Paleolithic shamans who talked to the animals, Western youths were tuned in to an underground lineage of poets, seers, singers, healers, witches and sorcerers. In the '60s these boomer teens ingested hallucinogens and fixated on the beat. Dormant instincts, suppressed through the Dark Ages, suddenly turned on. Festivities kicked off in the ballrooms of Haight-Ashbury in San Francisco.

Since Gold Rush days in the 1840s, the Barbary Coast of California maintained a permissive history. Tolerance for alternative lifestyles drew westward the refugees from a repressive biblical culture. San Francisco – home to the beatniks in the 1950s and neighbor to Berkeley's Free Speech Movement in the 1960s – reigned as the cradle of American counterculture. Conditions in the Bay Area were ideal for people to come together in acts of theatrical protest. Rallying around music-magic, dropouts from Western ways explored Hindu, Voodoo and Zen Buddhist beliefs. Back-to-the-land animism of Native Americans was received like fresh air in a mausoleum.

This first generation of white rockers found common ground with cultures of color. Kids who had boogied to the beat all of their young lives were ripe to transfer allegiance to non-Western ways; they felt betrayed by their parents' legacy of befouling nature. As their ranks came of age, a majority abhorred war, especially Vietnam selective service – a racially lopsided draft had black men shooting yellow men to enrich white men on land looted from red men. The establishment traveled in patterns of fear and greed. It was up to the young to lead lost elders back to the *healing* ways of Nature.

> *The young are overtaking. I mean "young" as in today – natural thoughts –*
> *just letting them flow freely. When natural feelings conflict against laws that*
> *were made hundreds of years ago, that's when you get the hang ups. Those*
> *old laws and ideas really do hurt people mentally. I'm scared of some of*
> *those people because they have such a tight grip on those obsolete laws, rules*
> *and regulations. As long as you're not harming another human being what*
> *does it matter what you do?*   — Jimi[32]

31. East Village Other 1968, cited in *Hit & Run – The Jimi Hendrix Story* by Jerry Hopkins, p.171, and Henderson, *Jimi Hendrix – Voodoo Child of the Aquarian Age,* p.256.
32. Hall and Clark, *The Superstars – In Their Own Words*, p.26, Melody Maker 3/8/69, New England Scene 11/68, Sounds 10/10/70.

An energetic burst triggered by rock sparked environmental concerns among the young. In a short span of years, the new counterculture understood that it was up to them to save the Earth from the ravages of industry. Everything seemed possible within the virtual reality of an expanded mind.

In a teeth-gnashing sea of globe-trashing self-interest, San Francisco's Haight oasis was formed for the flowering of humanity. By 1966, this culture which countered competitive Puritanism had coalesced in perpetual *Festival*. The term made a New Year debut with the *Trips Festival* at Longshoreman Hall. Rock 'n' roll bands laid down the beat as flashing strobes danced on writhing freaks. Possessed trippers rode Loas and saw God. This winter '66 Trips Festival marks ten years of Elvis. At the end of that decade, in the wake of original mainstream rock, a generation's inner transformation boiled to a head. The spell of rhythm 'n' blues produced a new breed of teen. Their underground subculture mushroomed and mutated. They believed in people sharing everything for free, so they called themselves *freek*s.

TRIBAL TIES

During ten thousand years of recorded human history, nearly 495 of the last 500 generations have lived *tribally*.[33] In small villages or in roaming clusters of extended families, survival was dependent upon one's relationship with the group. But change came quickly with the Industrial Revolution. As tribal ties died in the age of the individual, so too did a feeling of connection with the web of cycles that supports us. A state of alienation reached World War proportions as we raced to waste the planet of its capacity for sustaining life. After centuries of indifferent dominion over the land, the human tide had grown large enough to disrupt our planet's eco-systems. Carbon dioxide in the atmosphere was first measured in 1958 while rock 'n' roll fueled forces that were reshaping our ties with nature. For the first time we realized that the environment was deteriorating at an accelerated rate. In the nick of time, native drums reawakened our instinct for *inter*dependence. The combination of rock music and hallucinogens produced revolutionary insights. Tribal life, lost during our pursuit of industry, reappeared through mass media, especially rock albums.

> *The only answer they can find is through music now . . . Music is in a state*
> *now where it's getting rid of all the rubbish.*   – Jimi[34]

The '66 spring equinox inspired the freeks of Frisco to bring their celebrations outdoors to the Free Fairs: open-air, free-admission expansions of the Trips Festival. Baby-boomer crowds grew larger and larger until consciousness blossomed in Golden Gate Park during the Great Human Be-In of January 14, 1967. On Sunday afternoon,

---

33. Utne Reader, *Tribal Community*, July/Aug. 1992, p.67.
34. San Diego Free Press 6/13/69.

twenty thousand heads reached bliss as they collectively gave birth to the *rock festival*.

Rock festivals loomed like initiation rites for a generation's defection from the way things were. These back-to-the-land mass-gathering rituals enacted the virtues of group living: cooperation, compassion, kindness, generosity, patience, tolerance – all were ideals enshrined at the Be-In, and each festival that followed was expected to adhere to these new tribal ways.

When the Summer of Love dawned in June '67, sprawling mass-gatherings, with back-to-back rock bands, became the new standard for youth entertainment. Ceremonies commenced at the three-day Monterey Pop Festival, just south of the Bay Area. With a ritual act of sacrificing his axe in flames, Hendrix stole the show and ascended to centerpiece status. Mass-gatherings set the stage for the Hendrix concert years, and Jimi's music set the tone for these tribal rites. Hendrix was the central event at the heaviest festivals, where his space-age Voodoo blues made him the Golden Calf idol of the tribes.

But soon after Monterey these vast networks of flying circuses came undone by their own size. Gates couldn't contain all who came, and walls couldn't keep out crowds that wouldn't pay. Rock festivals were forced to be free. With music and dance the acid-dosed masses raced to reclaim their ancient inheritance: they discovered anew that Eden, like Woodstock, has no gates.

Chapter 5: Spiritual Blues

ی

The history of America is (as much as anything), the history of the American body as it sought to unite with its spirit, with its consciousness, to heal itself and to stand against the enormous forces that work to destroy our relationship with our own flesh.

— Michael Ventura[1]

The background of our music is a Spiritual Blues thing.

— Jimi[2]

Spiritual Blues describes a view of human history, an explanation of the battle waged by Western civilization to gain unity of body with mind. *Spiritual* is the realm of mind and consciousness. *Blues* is the beat of the body, a dance-based physical art. Spiritual Blues describes our drive to unify spirit with flesh and *feel* God as physical bliss. Heaven and hell reconcile their lover's quarrel and make peace. Spiritual Blues represents a time in history when sexual energy is again expressed without shame or guilt. This change of orientation in the West is represented by the presence of Hendrix. Jimi, by way of his music and lineage, is the figurehead of Spiritual Blues.

An unnatural philosophical split between spirit and flesh had built up centuries of tension. Hendrix vented this pressure through his music – a clashing sound fueled by conflicting myths. Spiritual Blues is a story of liberation, an explanation of issues, an understanding of what happened.

*Lots of young people now feel they're not getting a fair deal, so they revert to something loud and harsh, almost verging on violence; if they didn't go to a concert they might be going to a riot. Our music is shock therapy to help them realize a little more of what their goals should be . . . We're making our music into electric church music; a new kind of Bible, not like in a hotel, but a Bible you carry in your hearts, one that will give you a **physical feeling**.*

— Jimi[3]

1. Ventura, *Hear That Long Snake Moan*, Whole Earth Review, Summer 1987, p.91.
2. Interview with Paul Zimmerman, New York 5/69.
3. Newsweek 5/26/69, Village Voice 1968.

Sam Phillips, the original producer for Elvis in Memphis, spoke of Presley's charm and appeal. "You don't want to put your finger on anything as great as what Elvis Presley could communicate," warned Phillips. "If you could figure it out it would be like wanting to know the future, and you don't *really* want to know the future. You want those surprises, along with whatever else comes. That's life."[4]

But what if the future is bringing an asteroid aimed at us? What if "putting your finger on what Elvis communicates" explains why we are prevented from defending ourselves? To comprehend Hendrix and the issues raised by his life is to "put your finger" on the meaning of Elvis, and rock and roll, and the biggest mystery of all.

The issues around Jimi and blues direct our attention to attitudes about sensuality throughout history. With these connections and events we can analyze past patterns of human traditions and see *reasons* for our fate. We will see why the asteroid disaster didn't have to be one of "those surprises, along with whatever else comes."

BLUEPRINTS

> *The Bible is the blueprint right now, it says what's going to happen in the future, but it doesn't have to be the only blueprint, they could make another blueprint, because people got a right to set their own destiny . . . They've been taught the wrong way . . . they think they're free, that's what the trouble is . . . You got the churches saying one thing, the status quo and governments saying certain things . . . The only way we can know something is to use equations and go back before pre-existence and find out what happened . . . You got to find out everything now, because that's the only way you're going to survive. You got to know everything.*
>
> – Sun Ra[5]

Beliefs about damnation awaiting those who pursue lust are recurrent themes throughout literature and films. One recent example is Brian Moore's 1985 novel *Blackrobe*. The story traces 16th century Jesuit missionaries who experience the naturism of Huron and Iroquois Indians. A young squaw sees a robed priest and asks her mate "why he feared to let the Blackrobe see him fuck, he said it was because of his god, who was also the Blackrobe's god. He said his god would be angry with him. Why would he be angry, she asked. What is wrong with fucking? . . . Blackrobes did not fuck and did not want others to fuck."

The Jesuit sees the couple make love and confesses to the girl's lover, "I too have committed a sin of the flesh . . . A sin of intent. Here. With that girl . . . We have sinned equally in the sight of God. Perhaps my sin is greater because I am a priest. Now we must ask His forgiveness and promise to amend our lives. I want you to kneel with me and say

---

4. *The Life and Times of Elvis*, The Discovery Channel 1/8/95.
5. Sun Ra, the late jazz great, from interview with Charles Blass, New York 10/24/91.

an act of contrition. And promise that we will avoid further temptation . . . the devil rules this land. Belial rules here; he rules the hearts and minds of these poor [Indian] people. Through them he seeks to wound Our Savior. Through them, and through our weakness. Through that girl, for instance . . . The devil infects their minds, making them resist the truth of our teachings . . . the Evil One has distracted you and filled you with a lust so strong that it drives out the fear you should feel now. The fear of losing your immortal soul. If you die tonight, in your state of mortal sin, you will find out that there *is* a hell. A hell for all eternity . . . What is more important than your immortal soul? . . . What could you do now that would be more important than going down on your knees and asking God's forgiveness? . . . let us pray together, for your sin and for mine . . . Merciful God, our Savior, we implore Your Pardon."[6]

The story of *Blackrobe* explores the split between mind (the Jesuits) and body (the Indians). This central conflict, spirit vs. flesh, shaped the history of settlers in the West. The Indians celebrated nature and sensuality and were therefore condemned by settlers.

A more curious taboo is the subject of Umberto Eco's 1980 novel *The Name of the Rose*. This 12th century monastery murder mystery centers on an aged and cantankerous monk who poisons younger members of the order. The old man murders those who read Aristotle's second book of Poetics, which is dedicated to comedy. "Only a fool lifts up his voice in laughter...Christ never laughed," barks the monk. "Our Lord did not have to employ such foolish things to point out the strait and narrow path to us. Nothing in his parables arouses laughter. . . Providence did not want futile things glorified...Laughter is a devilish wind, which deforms the ligaments of the face and makes men look like monkeys... laughter is weakness, corruption, the foolishness of our flesh. That laughter is proper to man is a sign of our limitation, sinners that we are . . . The prudence of the plebeians, the license of the plebeians must be restrained and humiliated, and intimidated by sternness. And the plebeians have no weapons for refining their laughter until they have made it an instrument against the seriousness of the spiritual shepherds who must lead them to eternal life and rescue them from the seductions of belly, pudenda, food, their sordid desires . . . if one day someone could say, 'I laugh at the Incarnation,' then we would have no weapons to combat that blasphemy, because it would summon the dark powers of corporal matter, those that are affirmed in the fart and the belch, and the fart and the belch would claim the right that is only of the spirit . . . laughter is something very close to death and to corruption of the body."[7]

Absence of humor is the key to sacredness. Unnatural seriousness pervades world religions with an attitude conducive to violence against irreverent dissenters. Sacred taboos look foolish when humor is used as a tool of persuasion. Laughter, like all sensuality, has been cast as an evil pleasure of the flesh.

---

6. Brian Moore, *Blackrobe*, (New York: Fawcett Crest Books, 1986), pp.85-6, 88, and from the film screenplay.

7. Umberto Eco, *The Name of the Rose*, (New York: Warner Books, 1984), pp.90, 576-7, 580, 108, and from the film screenplay.

Babette's Feast by Isak Dinesen is another novel to spotlight biblical prohibition against indulgence. The plot concerns a cook who possesses "the ability to turn a dinner . . . into a kind of love affair – into a love affair . . . in which one no longer distinguishes between bodily appetite and spiritual appetite."[8] When a group of 19th century Danish fundamentalists are cajoled into participating in Babette's culinary meal on the 100th birthday of their deceased Minister, they gather in prayer to reaffirm their faith and vow to refrain from enjoying Babette's feast. "They promised one another that...they would, on the great day, be silent upon all matters of food and drink. Nothing that might be set before them, be it even frogs or snails, should wring a word from their lips . . . the tongue is a little member and boasteth great things. The tongue can no man tame; it is an unruly evil, full of deadly poison. On the day of our master we will cleanse our tongues of all taste and purify them of all delight or disgust of the senses, keeping and preserving them for the higher things of praise and thanksgiving . . . At the word of 'food' the guests, with their old heads bent over their folded hands, remembered how they had vowed not to utter a word about the subject, and in their hearts they reinforced the vow: they would not even give it a thought! . . . It will be as if we never had the sense of taste."[9]

> *May the bread nourish my body*
> *May my body do my soul's bidding*
> *May my soul rise up to serve God eternally. Amen.*
> — Danish Prayer[10]

> *Food refusal by women dates back to medieval Europe where it was an*
> *expression of Christian faith and piety.*   — Katherine Gilday[11]

Sex, laughter and feasting are just three fleshly pleasures turned to sin by biblical decree. Dance is another forbidden activity. Such bans on bodily delights are key aspects of blues history, and Jimi Hendrix, with his Afro-Irish Voodoo roots, is a seminal symbol of blues. In the West, Hendrix represents everything that Church Fathers condemn.

Jimi became the first black male sex symbol for the mass white audience. Other black male celebrities preceded him, but stars like Nat King Cole, Harry Belafonte, Sidney Poitier or even James Brown and Little Richard were not overt "sex symbols" to a global white audience in the way that Hendrix was. None of these earlier artists succeeded in making blatant sexuality such a centerpiece of their acts, as Jimi did.

"A rhapsodic outpouring of sexuality is integral to Hendrix's popular appeal," writes Caroline Coon. "Hendrix knew that people threatened by sex would use his sexuality out of its musicianship context to trivialize him . . . Hendrix himself blurred the divide

---

8. Isak Dinesen, *Babette's Feast* (New York: Random House 1958, Vintage Books 1974), pp.50-1.
9. Ibid. pp.41,48, and from the film screenplay.
10. Ibid. p.48, and from the film screenplay.
11. *The Famine Within – A Film by Katherine Gilday*, Direct Cinema Limited, 1990.

between masculine and feminine. On stage Hendrix confounded our expectations of what it was to be manly...Blithely showing both how strong and delicate he could be . . . Hendrix's onstage shift to hermaphrodite mode was the first inkling many of us had of how far sexual liberation could go . . . [becoming] a succinct expression of the sixties' peace and love desire for destructive polarities between the sexes to vanish, a prophetic indication of what was to come, a vivid lesson in adjustment to the future. Chip technology, space travel, science fact, sexual revolution, gender dissolve: the twenty-first-century living experiment began. We struggled to free ourselves from war, heavy industry, pollution, class, race, sexual discrimination – and Hendrix was there creating the soundtrack . . . no sooner had musicians like Hendrix begun the sexual revolution than something horrible happened. Men in general discovered what women and homosexuals already knew. Blurring gender lines causes hysterical panic. More than anything else, the sexual revolution rather than any anti-Vietnam marches provoked the police."[12]

SEX DENIGRATE—THE CORE ISSUE

Our attitudes about our bodies arise from society's image of itself. So if we can learn how a person understands the workings of that complex system called the body, its organization, its spatial arrangement, and its priorities of needs, then we can guess much about the total pattern of self-understanding of the society, such as its perception of its own workings, its organization, its power structure, and its cosmology.
— Sheldon Isenberg & Dennis Owen[13]

The spiritual traditions have traditionally denigrated the passions of the body and denied its needs and actually pretended that sensuousness and sensuality . . . are sinful. They created this whole millennium of guilt and sorrow.
— Deepak Chopra[14]

Study of Hendrix reveals how our past and present lead to the central issue at the heart of blues: Sex Denigrate – condemning pleasures of the flesh (including blues, the "Devil's music"). For what purposes have major world religions "rejected" the human body? Why has so much of the human world been trained to denigrate sex?

The other half of a man is a woman. – Jimi[15]

12. Boot & Salewicz, *The Ultimate Experience*, pp.154-5, 158.
13. John Dominic Crossan, *Historical Jesus – The Life of a Mediterranean Jewish Peasant*, (New York: Harper Collins, 1991), p.313.
14. *Higher Self*, audio lecture tape.
15. At Woodstock 8/18/69, *Jimi Hendrix:Woodstock*, MCA Records 8/94. (Booklet text by Michael Fairchild).

Ancient healers who observed how a human body dies from loss of blood came to believe that blood drawn back into dead veins can restore life; thus were born Vampire legends. Vampires are the "living dead," restored to life by their daily intake of fresh blood. Ancient men observed bodily processes and devised other explanations and beliefs, especially regarding female anatomy and childbirth. In ancient times no one knew what caused an infant to grow inside of its mother. No one yet realized that a father's sperm is needed to fertilize the mother's egg. But everyone could see that *all* life enters into the world through women. Mothers are analogous to the Earth; they "grow" things – Mother Earth.

Discussing female deities, mythologist Joseph Campbell said, "The 'Goddess' comes in primarily with agriculture and the agricultural societies. It has to do with the Earth: the human woman does give birth as the Earth gives birth to the plants, she gives nourishment, as the plants do. So woman magic and Earth magic are the same, they are related, and the personification, then, of this energy which gives birth to forms, and nourishes forms, is properly female. And so it is in the agricultural world of ancient Mesopotamia, the Egyptian Nile, but also in the earlier planting culture systems, that the goddess is the mythic form that is dominant . . . When you have a goddess as the Creator it is her own very *body* that is the universe. She is identical with the universe . . . In Egypt you have the Mother Heavens, the Goddess Nuit, who is represented as the whole heavenly sphere . . . It is the female as the giver of forms . . . Man doesn't enter life except by woman, and so it is woman who brings us into the world of polarity and pairs of opposites and suffering and all."[16]

MOTHER = OTHER

"In primitive societies having a baby is the most impressive thing anybody can do," said Margaret Mead. "And when you get to modern societies, and you look at men who built the Empire State Building or the Bay Bridge, men get very impressive. But in primitive societies where the biggest thing a man makes is a canoe, making a baby, which they can all see [growing inside the mother], especially in the tropics, is a very impressive thing. And little boys grow up reasonably envious of women."[17]

The birth process itself is the central event associated with physical life, and it is exclusive to women. This fact makes men appear more removed from nature than women, according to the thinking of ancient men who wrote biblical myth, especially during prehistoric times when the male's role in procreation was still unknown. Men are less connected with creating physical life than are women. A female in labor is an obvious vessel for life. Males could therefore point to childbirth and proclaim how relatively *unphysical* men are by comparison. Among ancient people, whereas the physical body

16. The Power of Myth, *Love and the Goddess*, and *Message of the Myth*, 1987 interviews with Bill Moyers, PBS 3/88.

17. Mike Douglas Show 1972, featured in *Margaret Mead: An Observer Observed*, PBS 5/25/97.

appeared to be the creation of women exclusively, men claimed the *spirituality* of the mind as the province of males. The battle between the sexes thus produced to a mythology of physiology.

> *A woman is a vehicle of life. Life has overtaken her. Woman is what it's all about, the giving of birth and the giving of nourishment, she's identical with the goddess in her powers and she's got to realize that about herself. The boy does not have a happening of that kind. He has to be turned into a man, and voluntarily become a servant of something greater than himself. The woman becomes the vehicle of nature. The man becomes the vehicle of the society and the social order and the social purpose.* — Joseph Campbell [18]

Cultural anthropologist Margaret MacKenzie points out, "The body is closer to nature and the body and nature are both to be controlled. And who represents the body but women? Women are closer to nature, women should be controlled. They are dangerous, in our historical tradition, in the way that they can distract men from the higher preoccupations of study and scholarship and art."[19]

> *Thomas Aquinas argued that women should be subject to men because "in men the discretion of reason predominates."*
>
> — Mary Daly[20]

> *Spiritual freedom, intellectual freedom . . . these are appropriate only to men . . . For [woman] to presume upon the territory of transcendence is horrifying, unthinkable, polluting the high, pure realms of the will and spirit, where we rise **above** the flesh.* — Dana Densmore[21]

What happens when people believe that physical life is sinful and inferior to spiritual life? How are relations between men and women affected when religion convinces us that the body is "bad"?

> *. . . what the law could not do, in that it was weak through the flesh, God sending his own Son in the likeness of sinful flesh, and for sin, condemned sin in the flesh. That the righteousness of the law might be filled in us, who walk not after the flesh, but after the Spirit. For they that are after the flesh do mind the things of the flesh, but they that are after the Spirit the things*

---

18. The Power of Myth, *The First Storytellers*, PBS 3/88.
19. *The Famine Within – A Film by Katherine Gilday*, Direct Cinema Limited, 1990.
20. Daly, *Beyond God the Father*, p.101.
21. Dana Densmore, *Independence from the Sexual Revolution*, Notes from the Third Year: Women's Liberation, p.58.

of the Spirit. For the carnally minded is death, but to be spiritually minded is life and peace . . . So then they that are in the flesh cannot please God. But you are not in the flesh, but in the Spirit, if so be that the Spirit of God dwell in you. Now if any man have not the Spirit of Christ, he is none of his. And if Christ be in you, the body is dead because of sin, but the Spirit is life because of righteousness. — Paul: Romans 8:3-10

When the body and its urges are believed to be sinful, then all females, as potential sources of bodies (babies), are likewise sources of sin. Throughout the history of civilization in the West, the extent to which a woman is associated with sensuality is the extent to which she is wicked.

Gnosticism . . . held that what was of the flesh was inherently evil . . . Symbolically and socially, women have been identified with matter, sex, and evil. — Reay Tannahill[22]

Ascetic celibacy . . . denigrated the human body in general and the female body in particular. — John Crossan[23]

The denigration of sex has been ingrained in children ever since the Greeks decreed the human body to be the opposite of spirituality and therefore bad. Philosophers devised a logic of dualism and set the stage for condemning flesh and controlling the makers of flesh: women.

History books call it the dawn of Western civilization: the Golden age of Greece. For the man it was the beginning, for the woman it was the end. The Greeks announced that history would now begin and proceeded to obliterate or pervert the 25,000 years that had gone before. Athena was redefined: once the goddess of wisdom and love, she became the goddess of war. The violent and the erotic became linked as they never had before. Man, said men, had always been the natural masters of the Earth. He was now also the procreator. Athena sprang fully armed from the brow of Zeus. Eve was born from Adam's rib. Female inferiority forever was proclaimed by the book of Genesis. — Goddess Remembered[24]

Men cannot gestate babies and carry them into the world. Males are not the vessels for life nor the nurturers upon whose bodies infants suckle and feed. In fact, when a culture condemns flesh, a man who *destroys* life, such as a war hero, is more valued than a woman who *delivers* life. "To the Church, sexual pleasure was a sin," notes Tannahill.

22. Tannahill, *Sex In History,* p.139.
23. Crossan, *Historical Jesus,* p.298.
24. *Goddess Remembered,* National Film Board of Canada, PBS 8/96.

"Sin had come to play a more important . . . role in Christian morality even than redemption. And of all the sins encompassed by this morality, none had such wide application as the sins of sex . . . men and women with normal sexual appetites became obsessed by guilt. Sex might be their only sin, but in the eyes of the Church it was the greatest . . . the Christian sense of sin, which might have been a force for good, was diverted from areas where it could have been more usefully employed. By some mysterious alchemy, sexual purity came to neutralize other sins, so that even the moral oppression and physical barbarity that became characteristic of the Christian Church in later medieval and Renaissance times scarcely appeared as sins at all in comparison with the sins of sex and heresy."[25]

> *A Christian Church . . . found itself . . . increasingly tempted to treat sexuality . . . rather than greed and greed's dark shadow in a world of limited resources and famine, as the most abiding and disquieting symptom of the frailty of the human condition.*   – Peter Brown[26]

> *If sexuality was sin, then the woman was the greatest sinner of all.*
> – Burning Times[27]

> *The establishment is so uptight about sex that all it wants to do is make the groupies look bad.*   – Jimi[28]

"A woman's body, in this whole scheme of things," notes Susan Griffin, "becomes a symbol for mortality itself, for decay, for aging. For a woman who is aging, it's much less acceptable than a man who is aging, because a man represents the immortal principle, you know, he's going to live forever through his ideas and his systems of power and his institutions. And a woman is flesh, her aging reminds everyone of the reality of our human condition."[29] Most male-created religions demean whatever is associated primarily with women. This includes life itself because, as the "portholes" through which we enter the world, women, more so than men, are deemed nurturers of life.

> *I think it's a really childish attitude to say no to life with all its pain, to say this is something that should not have been.*

> – Joseph Campbell[30]

---

25. Tannahill, *Sex In History,* p.161.
26. Crossan, *Historical Jesus,* p.367.
27. *Burning Times*, National Film Board of Canada, PBS 8/96.
28. Henderson, *Jimi Hendrix – Voodoo Child of the Aquarian Age,* p.257.
29. *The Famine Within – A Film by Katherine Gilday*, Direct Cinema Limited, 1990.
30. The Power of Myth, *The Message of the Myth*, PBS 3/88.

When people believe that their bodies are sinful, males gain an advantage because men can point to female birth-nurture biology and say, "I may be physical, but I'm not *that* physical." Body = sin is a formula that has helped men to achieve power over women and dominate sexual customs. How and why such denigration of sex spread through society, and what it has to do with Jimi Hendrix and asteroids, is the subject of this book.

To set the big picture in relief, upcoming chapters six through ten digress away from Jimi specifically, in order to amplify underlying issues and context. Hendrix connections return at the end of chapter eleven.

Chapter 6: A Brief History of Sex

ॐ

*In history, as in faith, real truth, real insight, is never to be found in
bits of information – scientific facts – but in the order and in the
pattern that we choose to make with them.*   – John Romer[1]

The major religions proclaim our physical world to be less important than the
spiritual realm. A central concern of these creeds is for us to resist satisfying the urges
of our bodies. Behaviors associated with pleasure and sex – i.e. laughter, dance,
massage and feasting – have at one time or another been discouraged by religious
institutions. In traditional Muslim cultures, dance is shunned by men, except for rare
ceremonies among Sufi priests. Dance is a sensual expression of the body, like birth
and nurture. "In traditional society, dance is considered womanly, not manly,"
explains Koranic scholar Sidi Lagharissi. "It is part of a women's education to learn
to dance, for men it is not, it is not important for men to learn that."[2]

But Muslim customs forbid women to dance in the presence of men. The Koran
teaches that women must conceal or suppress whatever might arouse men sexually. In
India there are many folk tales and expressions about how a woman's beauty can drive
a man mad. That a man might have the same effect on women is not an issue because
women are stereotyped to begin with as being inherently obsessed with sex.

> *Indians (like most other peoples) regarded girls as naturally libidinous
> and certain to lose their virginity at the merest whisper of an
> opportunity.*   – Reay Tannahill[3]

Irrational double standards prevail. "A Muslim can enjoy sex for pleasure," explains
sociologist Fatima Mernissi, "but the problem Islam has is: once you accept sexuality,
how then are you going to manage it? That's the little hinge where the women have to pay,
because how it's organized is that it's made women the *explosive sexual beings* that you
have to control."[4] For centuries women have had this stigma of "explosive sexual beings"
projected onto them by men.

---

1. John Romer, *Testament*, *"Gospel Truth?"*, PBS 10/91.
2. The Power of Dance, Part 3 *Sex and Social Dance*, produced by Ellen Hovde and Muffie Meyer,
   MiddleMarch Files, PBS 5/93.
3. Tannahill, *Sex In History*, p.212.
4. The Power of Dance, Part 3 *Sex and Social Dance*, PBS 5/93.

All witchcraft comes from carnal lust, which is in women insatiable.
                                                            – Sprenger and Kramer[5]

I don't think you can understand patriarchy unless you look at the fact that fear is at the core, fear that female sexuality will somehow become this chaotic force and nature will become this chaotic force overtaking us. So we have to have everything very tightly controlled and hierarchically ordered.
                                                            – Sharleen Spretnek [6]

Through exaggerations of female sexuality, men erect a premise upon which control of "lecherous ladies" appears essential for everyone's survival. *Control* is the whole issue that males are concerned with because, from the beginning, females have always been the more natural *regulators* of sex.

FEMALES – BIOLOGICAL DOMINATORS

Some ladies are like Church to us.
                                                            – Jimi[7]

By studying various primates, anthropologists find clues to human evolution. For example, whereas the promiscuous female chimpanzee will mate with a series of males and bond with none of them, a female gibbon monkey bonds exclusively with one mate for many years. This may be because, like a human female, the gibbon lacks an estrus cycle, the reproductive cycle that drives most other female primates (like the chimpanzee) to seek intercourse during peak days of ovulation. Estrus cycles inspire promiscuity, because most female primates avoid sex when they are not ovulating, so male primates are in constant pursuit of any mate who is at the receptive stage of her cycle and ready for sex.

But since the female gibbon, like a human female, lacks an estrus cycle – and is therefore receptive during more days of her monthly menstrual cycle – a male can form a lasting bond because sex is accessible to him more often with this single mate. This is the theory behind monogamous mating, but it doesn't explain why a human female, even when receptive for sex throughout her menstrual cycle, often chooses to court several partners anyway, rather than bond with just one male. In fact, during the five thousand years of recorded history, most people have mated in a *promiscuous* way.

"If, in the early days, humanity bore a strong family resemblance to the chimpanzee," explains Tannahill, "at least one major biological change must subsequently have taken place . . . the human female's menstrual cycle must gradually

---

5. The "Malleus Maleficarum" of Heinrich Kramer and James Sprenger, Dover Publication 1971, p.47 [Originally published in 1928].

6. *Burning Times, Goddess Remembered* segment. National Film Board of Canada, PBS 8/96.

7. Brown, *Jimi Hendrix – In His Own Words*, p.63, from interview in London 1/7/69. p.88.

have replaced the estrus cycle of the primates, a modification with long-term results in the case of the female's own sexuality, and long-term repercussions on the relationship between men and women."[8]

Anthropologists theorize that the menstrual cycle of human females is what encourages one-partner mating, but geneticists point to other factors that encourage promiscuity. For example, in environments where food and safety are plentiful, women can raise children without help from men. Instead of bonding with one woman to procreate, it is more effective for men to have sex with as many mates as possible. Through widespread distribution of his genes, a male increases chances that his progeny will survive. "The female of the species had no such biological *carte blanche*," claims Tannahill. "Her genes could be propagated only in the children born of her own body; the result, regardless of climatic conditions, was a powerful genetic urge toward protectiveness."[9] Natural selection favored women who were strong nurturers of healthy children.

Both monogamy and polygamy have flourished among humans at differing times throughout pre-history. Such mating behaviors are adapted to the changing environment. With our needs shaped by a variety of unstable forces, flexibility in our response increases our chance for survival. "Perhaps the most reasonable hypothesis is that the human race originally resembled its chimpanzee relatives in being promiscuous," concludes Tannahill. "As living conditions fluctuated from good to indifferent to bad during the long ice-scarred millennia of mans early history, there may have been a slow pendulum swing from near-promiscuity to near-monogamy, and back again. And it may have been the women, not the men, who were promiscuous – for it was they who were in the minority."[10] Males of pre-history outnumbered females by three to two, and men, on average, outlived women by eight years.[11] This larger population of males, men who lived longer and were more aggressive than females, created a situation where males were able to force upon weaker members of society the beliefs and customs designed to *restrict* sexual options for women.

In species like birds, where infants need constant care, the bonding together of parent couples is common. Pair bonding among humans also likely results from infant dependency because children require adult supervision for many years. But such monogamy is rare among mammals: just three percent of mammals mate with a single spouse for a lifetime. Human beings are an exception, to a degree. Psychology professor Kim Wallen studied sexual behavior for more than twenty years and reported, "Male interest in the pair bond wavers after some period of time . . . this probably reflects a fundamental difference between males and females in the way they approach sexual behavior. It is characteristic of males that they have been selected to

8. Tannahill, *Sex In History,* p.20.
9. Ibid. p.21.
10. Ibid. p.22.
11. Ibid. p.30.

be interested in sex on a relatively continuous basis. Females on the other hand have been selected to be interested in sex on an intermittent basis. When females are interested in sex, they are as intensely interested in sex as males are, it's just that it's not as frequent as the case for males. So I think this tendency for pair bonds to split up after some period of time really reflects this tension between the male approach to sex and the female approach to sex."[12]

Compared with humans, the mating habits of most other primates are influenced more by hormones. Whereas most primates are usually *capable* of mating at any time, hormone levels typically trigger fertility *periodically* in females and thus determine *when* mating actually occurs. For example, Wallen has found that in the 28-day mating cycle of Rhesus monkeys, sexual desire is greatest in females during their three-day period of fertility. During the days furthest from ovulation, there is no sexual interest or activity. Wallen explains, "Male [Rhesus] spend their lives living in essentially a female dominated social structure: the females indicate when they want to engage in sex and who they want to engage in sex with and they are very persistent about that. It's clear in monkey groups that the female *regulates* the sexual interaction, and the female *chooses* which male she's going to interact with and *when* she's going to mate."

Wallen theorizes that the ancestors of modern man maintained a similar social structure: "I suspect that sexual activity of early hominids was probably quite different than what we see in modern society. First, females were probably much more sexually assertive than is the case today, and secondly, female relations were probably much more crucial to the social structure of early hominid groups. I think that the characteristic pattern of males to be interested in sex rather continuously was probably the same then as it is today. But *it was females that regulated the sexual activity by initiating sex with males when they were interested in this and not engaging in sex when they weren't.*"[13]

Under such conditions, where females regulate sex, and men maintained continual interest in sex, it would make sense that males would seek a means to undermine such control over them from their female mates. Men wanted open access to sex on *male terms*. They learned that the way to achieve this is all in the mind.

Through the concepts, stories, and myths of religion men built connections step-by-step that wrested from women the ability to regulate sex. By way of greater strength a father could force mother and child to learn stories and suffer consequences for disobedience to *rules*. Thus the myths of religion were erected by men for the purpose of *undermining* a woman's ability to refuse sex. "All in the mind" means that *belief* is all it takes to subvert the urges of biology.

A female's more intermittent interest in sex, as opposed to the typical male's ongoing lust, frustrated the men of pre-history, leaving them with a choice of abstinence,

12. *Understanding Sex*, The Learning Channel, 1/95.
13. Ibid. [emphasis added]

masturbation, or rape. Then everything changed when men learned to use beliefs about hell and damnation to weaken a woman's ability to refuse her mate's advances. "Laws of God" were invoked to undermine her *right* to abstain from sex. Men achieved this power through stories about the sinfulness of the body. By claiming that God condemns flesh, the religions of men proclaim that males are closer to God than females, because woman *produce* flesh. While this belief deems sex/sensuality as bad, it also demeans women, the makers of flesh, and thus sanctions supremacy for men.

For these unnatural attitudes society daily pays a price of violence and excessive aggression. Some anthropologists find a lesson for humans in the example of Bonobos Chimpanzees, our closest living relatives. Bonobos are closer to humans than they are to gorillas, for example, they communicate through complex vocalization, they form permanent close friendships, they divide themselves up into cliques and they are capable of jealous rivalries. The Mangutu tribe of Zaire believes that these chimps once coexisted with ancient humans as a single family. Many primate specialists theorize that the Bonobos closely resemble the common ancestors of humans and apes.

A unique trait of these chimps, however, is the way they've eliminated violence from their lives by practicing sex as a basic form of communication. Bonobos are the only primates besides humans that mate in the intimate face-to-face position. Expressions of sex and affection are observed in every aspect of their society. Every member of the troop is available to rub genitals with every other member, including males with males and females with females. From infancy, the baby chimps are trained to participate in an ongoing bisexual orgy. The result is a society in which violence is unknown. Free sex keeps the peace.

MY SON

> *There is nothing to suggest that man was even remotely aware of his own physical role in the production of children. That knowledge seems not to have come until the early days of farming, some time after 10,000 B.C., and it had a tonic effect on his ego. It also crystalized his sense of possessiveness, for the concept of "my son" required the child's mother to be tied to one man only.*
> — Reay Tannahill[14]

Among hunting tribes of pre-history, survival depended on the animals killed and on the men who hunted. Therefore the needs of male hunters were primary concerns for females. It was then believed that females were the sole child-makers, they created the children and it was their responsibility to raise and care for them. Ancient people equated a baby growing inside of its mother with a seed sprouting in the soil.

14. Tannahill, *Sex In History*, p.13.

Therefore, cultivation of land and gathering of food from it was considered work mainly for women. In later ages, when hunters became herders and women farmed the land, wives tending to the needs of their husbands was a custom that remained unchanged, a carryover from the hunting age, when tribes learned to worship aggressive male gods. Only rarely did female fertility stories form the basis for worship of a Supreme Goddess.

"In the earliest form of the Sumerian resurrection myth," notes Tannahill, "the goddess Inanna departs from the Earth for a temporary sojourn in the underworld. Until she returns the soil remains barren. But with this single exception all the fertility deities who figure in the surviving literature are male. Nowhere in the mythology of the Near East – Sumerian, Babylonian, Egyptian, Ugaritic, Hittite, or Hebrew – is there any goddess whose power is supreme . . . all are subsidiary to husbands or brothers . . . Only the Chinese come near the concept of a pre-eminent goddess, with their view of early woman as the Great Mother . . . There is a common misapprehension that, in Classical times at least, there were goddesses who reigned supreme . . . But the general concept of the Great Goddess owes as much to the Victorian imagination as to historical truth."[15]

> *For 25,000 years our ancestors found power in union and cooperation . . . but then the male asserted his total domination and so it has been for 3500 years . . . [Warfare] was by 2000 B.C. just about everywhere, except Crete, which is why the Minoan civilization is one where the goddess tradition survived intact the longest . . . By 1500 B.C. volcanoes, earthquakes, and armed invasions had buried the last great goddess culture.* — Goddess Remembered[16]

"It is possible that in India, before the advent of the nomadic Indo-Europeans, there may have been a Mother Goddess," admits Tannahill. "The south, to which the earlier peoples are believed to have fled after the invasion, has certainly always had a place for goddesses and female spirits."[17]

Some prehistoric societies may have worshipped a supreme female deity during the Neolithic age, at a time when women were regarded as the sole child-makers. But when man finally realized that his own seed was needed to make babies, everything changed. "The discovery hardened his attitude toward menstruation," notes Tannahill. "If his semen was the mystical catalyst of the process that ended in childbirth, then menstruation, which demonstrated women's failure to conceive, must have appeared as an insult and a rejection, a blood-letting that brutally denied his new role as child-maker."[18]

When men realized the connection between conception and semen, witch hunts began. Menstruation was deemed unclean by men who now viewed women as mere

15. Ibid. p.54.
16. *Goddess Remembered*, National Film Board of Canada, PBS 8/96.
17. Tannahill, *Sex In History*, p.53.
18. Ibid. p.46.

receptacles for the father's seed. Edicts against bleeding were issued first, becoming intentional weapons with which to keep women on the defensive.

> *Because of her sexual nature, woman was taboo as far as holy things were concerned. Jewish law prohibited sexual intercourse during menstruation or any other discharge of blood from the vagina, and for a period of seven days after the cessation of the flow of blood (Leviticus 18:19). Until the women became ritually purified from her "uncleanness" it was decreed that everything she would lie or sit upon would be unclean and whoever touched her bed or whatever she sat upon would be unclean. Such was the terrifying belief in the contamination that would result from blood.*
>
> — Nicholas Carter[19]

Those who menstruate were persecuted and punished. Men had finally erected a system of beliefs that undermined not only a female's regulation of sex, but transformed her very anatomy into a battleground of good against evil. Thus were the Creation myths of religion inspired: the key to male domination now lay in the deification and worship of "my son."

> *The men who emerged from the Neolithic into the period of recorded history had the kind of assurance, arrogance, and authority that spring not from useful toil, not from knowledge of a good job well done, but from the kind of blinding revelation – beyond argument, beyond questioning – that was later to be experienced by the prophets of the Old Testament and the saints of the New. Was it that, discovering their own crucial role in an area [reproduction] where mans potency had always been denied, they had (very humanly) overreacted? . . . it was now possible for a man to look at a child and call him 'my son'; to feel the need to call a woman 'my wife.' Whatever the marital customs before that time – monogamy, polygamy, polyandry – after it, women's sexual freedom began to be seriously curtailed.*
>
> — Reay Tannahill[20]

Pastoral societies roamed in tribes that were dependent on herds and flocks. It was the males among them who, during long hours spent watching over grazing animals, had the time to construct philosophy and dream up stories, explanations and myths. The movements of these tribes across the plains brought them into conflict with outsiders who sought to control territories. These male-oriented societies were the ancestors of Hebrew nomads and Indo-European pastoralists. From India westward they laid the foundation for paternal customs. Their male-dominated civilizations took root around the river valleys of the Near East. The few agricultural societies that still remained were

---

19. Nicholas Carter, *Routine Circumcision – the Tragic Myth* (London: Londinium Press, 1979), p.14.
20. Tannahill, *Sex In History,* p.47.

conquered by these hunting and herding tribes: the Semites were herders of goats and sheep and the Indo-Europeans were herders of cattle. These tribes introduced the male warrior gods: Zeus and Yahweh.

Male myths about the sword and death replaced legends about fertility and the goddess. "Particularly the Hebrews really wipe out the goddess," said Joseph Campbell. "The term for the goddess, the Cananite goddess that's used in the Old Testament, is 'the abomination,' and there is a very strong accent *against* the goddess in the Hebrew, which you do not find in the Indo-European where you have Zeus marrying the goddess and the two play together. I think it's an extreme case that we have in the Bible, and our own Western subjugation of the female is really a function of biblical thinking . . . If the male is on top and the female is the subordinate all the way, you have a totally different system from that where the two are facing each other. Particularly if you cut the female out . . . [For] the Hebrew, the male is the total thing, in fact he *takes over* her role."[21]

"From warrior, thinker, child-maker, stockbreeder, he was transformed for the first time into a cultivator, taking over one of the most important of women's tasks and doing it demonstrably better than she had," writes Tannahill. "By the Roman period, certainly, the idea of a Great Goddess had become socially irrelevant. Religion had developed into a branch of government on the one hand, and on the other into an outlet for personal desires and frustrations . . . It was not gods and goddesses who reigned supreme, but legislators and priests. In societies prepared to tolerate many gods – which meant virtually all early societies other than those of the Hebrews and the Zoroastrians of Iran – the varying status of gods and goddesses had more to do with politics and sales promotion than with religious feeling. And when the situation was reversed, so that religion took precedence over politics and both came under the auspices of a single divinity, there was no question of that divinity being anything but male."[22]

The religious myths of God the Father and his Son the Savior were inspired by man's discovery of his role in conception. Once men figured out the biology, they worked out Creation stories and laws that enhance male contribution to the birth process. Thus, the Old Testament is filled with instructions detailing proper observance of "his seed." The world's religions were erected in homage to conception. Knowledge of the biology of fatherhood caused ancient storytellers to cast men as the Sons of God whom the Supreme Father prefers over women. Women were cast as seductive temptresses whose lure of lust subverts *purity* in men.

> *Woman as a symbolic structure was associated in Judaism, as in other Mediterranean cultures, with the unclean, the religiously impure. The male was the symbol for purity.*   – Brandon Scott[23]

---

21. The Power of Myth, *Love and the Goddess,* PBS 3/88.
22. Tannahill, *Sex In History,* pp.48, 55.
23. Brandon Scott, *Hear the Parable: A Commentary on the Parables of Jesus,* (Minneapolis: Fortress Press, 1989), p.326.

Silly women laden with sins, led away with diverse lusts.
                                                                    – Paul: II Timothy 3:6

Do not permit a woman to teach or to have authority over a man. She must be silent, for Adam was born first, then Eve. It was Eve who was completely fooled and sinned. But women will be saved by having children.
                                                                    – Paul: I Timothy 2:12-13

Eve was created out of Adam, from his rib, as if the male "gave birth" to female. Mankind entered the world through man. It's as if, even while demeaning women for being the source of flesh, men can still claim credit for being the source of life, it's like saying that God ordained males to transcend flesh, while the sin of childbirth is left to females.

> *The absurd story of Eve's birth is an excellent example of a process that is prevalent in men's treatment of women and their accomplishments throughout the history of patriarchy. I shall simply call this phenomenon reversal. In some cases it is blatantly silly, as in this case of insistence that a male [Adam] was the original mother . . . Language for millennia has affirmed the fact that Eve was born from Adam, the first among history's unmarried pregnant males who courageously chose childbirth under sedation rather than abortion, consequently obtaining a child-bride . . . priests took Adam as teacher and model. They devised a sacramental system . . . Graciously, they lifted from women the onerous power of childbirth, christening it 'baptism.' Thus they brought the lowly maternal function of birth, incompetently and even grudgingly performed by females, to a higher and more spiritual level . . . Recognizing the ineptitude of females in performing even [such] humble 'feminine' tasks . . . priests raised these functions to the supernatural level in which they alone had competence. Feeding was elevated to become Holy Communion . . . In order to stress the obvious fact that all females are innately disqualified from joining the Sacred Men's Club . . . priests made it a rule that their members should wear skirts . . . They thus became revered models of spiritual transsexualism.*
>   – Mary Daly "[24]

Notions of what a female should be were decreed by men; a "true" woman is a baby-babbling sex receptacle . . . Behavioral codes were designed and defined by men to empower men . . . The word "belief" [means] "to wish".

---

24. Daly, *Beyond God the Father*, pp.95, 195.

. . "religion" amounts to a tradition of wishes forced upon the weaker sex
by the stronger sex for the purpose of sustaining domination.
— A Touch of Hendrix, 1988[25]

"Unlike many of his contemporaries among the deities of the ancient Near East," writes Elaine Pagels, "the God of Israel shared his power with no female divinity, nor was he the divine Husband or Lover of any. He can scarcely be characterized in any but masculine epithets: king, lord, master, judge, and father. Indeed, the absence of feminine symbolism for God marks Judaism, Christianity, and Islam in striking contrast to the world's other religious traditions, whether in Egypt, Babylonia, Greece, and Rome, or in Africa, India, and North America, which abound in feminine symbolism."[26]

The Western ideal is the only formulation of deity that has no relationship with
women at any point in the theological myth . . . Only the god of Western
civilization has no mother, no sister, no female consort, and no daughter.
— Terrence McKenna[27]

Tannahill describes the disaster: "Mans view of himself as superior in all ways to woman was soon enshrined in the law and custom of the world's earliest civilizations, those of the Near East. Woman became a chattel first of her father, then of her husband, then of her son . . . it was the monotheistic strand of Near Eastern culture that won in the end, that of the Hebrews, who had no need to compromise between religious and secular . . . So the attitudes born of the Neolithic era were preserved, and when the Christian Church, solidly based on Hebrew foundations, took over the Western world as successor to Rome, social and sexual relationships became fossilized in the amber of ancient Hebrew custom. To Near Eastern prejudices, the Church Fathers added their own. Sex was transformed into a sin and homosexuality into a danger to the state."[28]

Paul's apparently grudging attitude to marriage provided celibate fanatics
in later Christian generations with plenty of ammunition to support their
body-hating, women-hating philosophies, their monkish despairs, their
flagellations, their hairshirts, their cells and their vows. The monks' attitude
to sex derive as much from Plato as they do from the Jewish tradition, and
from the Greek conception that matter itself, the very world of the physical,
is evil: that God is by definition spiritual.   *— A.N. Wilson*[29]

---

25. Fairchild unpublished manuscript, (1988), pp.163, 16.
26. Pagels, *Gnostic Gospels,* p.48.
27. McKenna, *Food of the Gods,* p.62.
28. Tannahill, *Sex In History,* p.57.
29. A.N. Wilson, *Paul — The Mind of the Apostle,* (New York: W.W. Norton & Co., 1997), p.162.

The exile of Adam and Eve from Eden sets up a split between body and mind that proclaims nature and flesh to be corrupt with sin. With physical life thus decreed inferior to spiritual concerns, men get treMENdous advantages over women. This is the hidden agenda behind biblical tales that portray nature as evil. Eve is vile, she is Ev-ile. Mankind thus enshrined womanhood in a snakepit of sin. Centuries of tradition from male scholars and commentators refer to the Adam and Eve myth as a model for how relationships between men and women should be: male as controller, female as controlled.

> *Your desire shall be for your husband and he will rule over you.*
> — Genesis 3:16

In his book *Counsel for Kings*, eleventh century Islamic philosopher Ghazali reports, "When Eve ate fruit which He had forbidden . . . the Lord . . . punished women with: . . . menstruation; . . . childbirth; . . . pregnancy; not having control over her own person; a lesser share in inheritance; her liability to be divorced and inability to divorce; its being lawful for men to have four wives, but for a woman to have only one husband; the fact that she must stay secluded in the house; the fact that she must keep her head covered inside the house; . . . the fact that she must not go outside of the house unless accompanied by a near relative; . . . disqualification for rulership and judgeship . . ."[30] In short, society became A Man's World.

Of the 1,426 names in the Old Testament Hebrew Bible, only 111 are names of women. The New Testament contains just a few more.[31] The Bible was written specifically to dictate the supremacy of men over women. Even the book's main villain, Satan, was banished to hell because he refused God's order for angels to bow to man. And if angels had to bow to man, woe unto any *woman* who refuses.

Amen.

---

30. *Ghazali's Book of Counsel for Kings* (Nasihat al-Muluk). trs. F.R.C. Bagley (Oxford 1964), II pp.164-5.
31. Mysteries of the Bible, *Scarlet Women of the Bible*, A&E 5/94.

Chapter 7: Messiah/Christ

ح

The Hebrew word "Messiah" means the same as the Greek word "Christ.
— John 1:41

The novel element of the New Testament conception of sin is the presentation of Jesus as the conqueror of sins.
— John McKenzie[1]

Through this man forgiveness of sins is proclaimed to you: by this Jesus everyone who believes is set free from all those sins from which you could not be freed by the law of Moses.
— Paul:Acts 13:38-9

This is the beginning of the Christian religion, the beginning of what makes it distinctive.
— A.N. Wilson[2]

The curious thing about the story of the Fall of Adam and Eve is the way that the Roman Church connects it with the idea of "Messiah," the *anointed one*. For a thousand years before Jesus, the Hebrews waited for someone to replace King David and restore their shattered Jewish nation. David had been anointed of God, just as Aaron was anointed by Moses (Exodus 40:13). Jews waited for a Savior to bring world peace and prosperity. This *Messiah* idea represents a mechanism through which we hope for an improved future. But the concept underwent intense evolution under the new Roman Church.

The woman said to Jesus, I know that the Messiah is coming who is Christ and when he comes he will tell us all things. Jesus said to her, I who speak with you am he.
— John 4:25

Spin doctors in Vatican think tanks stitched together new connections. The result goes like this: Because Eve disobeyed God, and Adam ate forbidden fruit, all people are therefore born with the original sin of Adam and Eve, and condemned to hell unless we

---

1. John C. McKenzie, *Redemption: Dictionary of the Bible*, (Milwaukee: S.T. Bruce Publishing Co. , 1965), p.820.
2. Wilson, *Paul – The Mind of the Apostle,* p.122.

are saved by a Messiah sent from God to "take away" our sins. The Messiah/Christ thus becomes a necessary "antidote" or "Savior" who saves us from sin, frees us from hell and purgatory, and leads us into heaven.

> *God set you free when he sent his own Son to be like us sinners and to be a sacrifice for our sin. God used Christ's body to condemn sin. He did this so that we would do what the Law commands by obeying the Spirit instead of the flesh.*
>   – Paul: Romans 8:3

> *. . . while we were yet sinners, Christ died for us . . . Now that God has accepted us because the Messiah sacrificed his life's blood, we will also be kept safe from God's anger . . . Adam sinned, and that sin brought death into the world. Now everyone has sinned, and so everyone must die . . . In some ways Adam is like Christ who came later . . . That one sin brought death to many others. Yet in an even greater way, Christ alone brought God's gift of kindness to many people . . . Death ruled like a king because Adam had sinned . . . God has accepted us because of Christ. And we will live and rule like kings. Everyone was going to be punished because Adam sinned. But because of the good thing Christ has done, God accepts us and gives us the gift of life. Adam disobeyed God and caused many others to be sinners. But Christ obeyed him and will make many people acceptable to God.*
>   – Paul: Romans 5:8-19

> *Unless Christ was raised to life, your faith is useless, and you are still living in your sins...But Christ has been raised to life and become the firstfruits of them that slept* [in hell]. *For since by man came death, by man came also the resurrection of the dead. Adam brought death to all of us, and Christ will bring life to all of us.*
>   – Paul: I Corinthians 15:17-22

Paul's vision of Adam bringing sin and death into the world via Eve inspired Augustine, four centuries after the lifetime of Paul, to create the myth of "original sin." Augustine's idea of original sin is a key connection to the denigration of sex and women. "Adam's fall perverted all humanity," writes Gregory Shaw, ". . . its effects were passed by hereditary transmission from generation to generation. The belief that Adam, as a corporate personality, was responsible for the sins of humanity was never adopted by Judaism and was resisted by Christian thinkers such as Pelagius and Julian of Eclanum (fifth century C.E.), but Augustine's interpretation of the Fall became the accepted doctrine of Catholic Christianity."[3]

---

3. *The Oxford Companion to the Bible,* (Oxford University Press, 1993), p.223.

The Fall is the result of Adam and Eve disobeying God by succumbing to the desires of their flesh. According to Augustine, the couple are symbols of life and they introduce death into the world, causing all people to be guilty of original sin and thus banished from heaven unless we are "redeemed."

In the opposite corner is Christ, a virgin born of a virgin, a new Adam, conceived of the Spirit to be the gateway to eternal life, through whom God allows us to enter Paradise, but *only* if we *worship* the Savior who saves us from God's punishment of eternal fire in hell as revenge for the disobedience of Adam and Eve in Eden.

Augustine's myth, besides depicting "God" as a psychotic sadist, sets up an Adam-Christ (illness/cure) connection through which is enshrined rejection of the body (Eve/illness). Women, being the vessels of flesh and source of bodies, are thus fingered as handmaidens of evil. The critical link in this scheme to demonize women is the *Messiah/Christ*.

JESUS IN HELL

According to Christian belief, the purpose of the Messiah becoming human, the purpose of God being born as a man of flesh, is so that Christ can die a mortal death and descend into Hades to free all souls imprisoned in the pit. Everyone is born with original sin, which condemns us to hell unless we are saved by the Savior. "It was in Sheol, Hades, or Hell," notes John Crossan, "that the souls of holy and righteous, persecuted and martyred Jews awaited their final and promised deliverance. And it was there that Jesus descended in burial to deliver *those that slept*, as they were called, in triumphant resurrection and communal ascension."[4]

> *The dead shall arise, and those who are in the tombs shall be raised up, and those who are under the earth shall rejoice.*   – Isaiah 26:19

"Jerusalem's place of crucifixion, Calvary, an important symbol of Roman imperialism, derived its biblical name from the word skull, which in Aramaic is Golgotha," writes John Romer. ". . . The rock of Calvary emerging from the floor of the church is a cleft, and this crack, according to Christian legend, appeared when Christ was crucified. And down the same crack, the legend says, Jesus' blood flowed to splash on Adam's skull, who was thus given life. In an upheaval of time itself, Christ crucified appears at mans beginning: our history is here transformed into a cosmic drama."[5]

The Messiah dies and goes to hell for the purpose of freeing Adam and mankind from the penalty of original sin so that we may finally enter heaven. Jesus in hell is described in the *Gospel of Nicodemus*. Nicodemus was a Pharisee and a friend of Joseph of Arimathaea. His gospel, also known as the *Acts of Pilate*, is part of the Christian

---

4. Crossan, *Historical Jesus,* p.388.
5. John Romer, *Testament,* (New York: Henry Holt & Co., 1988), p.179.

Apocrypha. *Nicodemus* describes in detail the link between Jesus and the original sin of Adam and Eve. In the excerpts below, notice how Jesus is the hero who frees human souls by ending our exile outside of Paradise, where God had banished everyone as punishment for the disobedience of Adam and Eve.

> *We . . . were in Hades with all who have died since the beginning of the world, and at the hour of midnight there rose upon the darkness there something like the light of the Sun and shone, and light fell upon us all, and we saw one another. And immediately our father, Abraham, along with the patriarchs and the prophets, was filled with joy . . . The prophet Isaiah, who was present there, said: "This shinning comes from the Father and the Son and the Holy Spirit. This I prophesied when I was still living" . . . Then there came into the midst another . . . "I am John, the last of the prophets . . . Behold the Lamb of God, who takes away the sins of the world . . . the only begotten Son of God comes here, in order that whoever believes in him should be saved, and whoever does not believe in him should be condemned." . . . the first father Adam heard, and said to his son Seth, "My son, I wish you to tell the forefathers of the race of men and the prophets where I sent you when I fell into mortal sickness." And Seth said, "Prophets and patriarchs, listen. My father Adam, the first-created, when he fell into mortal sickness, sent me to the very gate of Paradise to pray to God that he might lead me by an angel to the tree of mercy, that I might take oil and anoint my father, and he arise from his sickness. This also I did. And after my prayer Michael the Archangel came and asked me: What do you desire, Seth? Do you desire, because of the sickness of your father, the oil that raises up the sick, or the tree from which flows such oil? This cannot be found now. Therefore go and tell your father that after the completion of fifty-five hundred years from the creation of the world, the only-begotten Son of God shall become man and shall descend below the earth. And he shall anoint him with that oil. And he shall arise and wash him and his descendants with water and the Holy Spirit. And then he shall be healed of every disease . . . "*
>
> *Satan the heir of darkness came and said to Hades . . . There is one of the race of the Jews, Jesus by name, who boasts himself the Son of God . . . now that he is dead, be prepared that we may secure him here . . . Hades answered, "O heir of darkness, son of perdition, devil, you have just told me that many who made ready to be buried be made alive again with only a word . . . If, therefore, we receive him here, I fear lest we run the risk of losing the others also . . . do not bring him here. For I believe that he comes here to set free all that are shut up in the hard prison and bound in the chains of their sins that cannot be broken. And I tell you this: By the darkness which surrounds us, if you bring him here, none of the dead will be left for me."*

While Satan and Hades were speaking thus to one another, a loud voice like thunder sounded: "Lift up your gates, O rulers, and be lifted up, O everlasting doors, and the King of glory shall come in." [Ps.23:7] . . . Then Hades said to his demons, "Make fast well and strongly the gates of brass and the bars of iron, and hold my locks, and stand upright and watch every point. For if he comes in, woe will seize us". . . the voice sounded: "Lift up the gates." When Hades heard the voice the second time, he answered as if he did not know it and said, "Who are thou that set free the prisoners that are held bound by original sin and restore them to their former liberty? Who is this King of glory?" The angels of the Lord said, "The Lord strong and mighty, the Lord mighty in battle." [Ps. 23:8] And immediately at this answer the gates of brass were broken in pieces and the bars of iron were crushed and all the dead who were bound were loosed from their chains, and we with them. And the King of glory entered in like a man, and all the dark places of Hades were illumined.

Hades at once cried out, "We are defeated, woe to us". . . Then the King of glory seized the chief ruler Satan by the head and handed him over to the angels, saying, "Bind with iron fetters his hands and his feet and his neck and his mouth." Then he gave him to Hades and said, "Take him and hold him fast until my second coming."

And Hades took Satan and said to him, "O Beelzebub, heir of fire and torment . . . Turn and see that not one dead man is left in me, but that all which you gained through the Tree of Knowledge you have lost through the tree of the cross . . . what evil did you find in Jesus that you went about to destroy him? . . . How were you bent on bringing down such a man into this darkness, through whom you have deprived of all who have died since the beginning?"

While Hades was thus speaking with Satan, the King of glory stretched out his right hand, and took hold of our forefather Adam and raised him up. Then he turned also to the rest and said, "Come with me, all of you who have suffered death through the tree which this man touched. For behold, I raise you all up again through the tree of the cross." With that he put them all out. And our forefather Adam was seen to be full of joy, and said, "I give thanks to your majesty, O Lord, because you have brought me up from the lowest depths of hell and delivered me from them that go down to the pit." Likewise also all the prophets and the saints said, "We give you thanks, O Christ, Savior of the world, because you have brought up our life from destruction."

When they had said this, the Savior blessed Adam with the sign of the cross on his forehead. And he did this also to the patriarchs and prophets and martyrs and forefathers, and he took them and leaped up out of Hades . . . Thus he went into Paradise holding our forefather Adam by the

*hand, and he handed him over and all the righteous to Michael the
Archangel . . . There came another, a humble man, carrying a cross on his
shoulder. The holy fathers asked him, "Who are you . . . " He answered, "I
was a robber and a thief in the world, and therefore the Jews took me and
delivered me to the death of the cross together with our Lord Jesus Christ
. . . and he said to me, 'Truly, today, I say to you, you shall be with me in
Paradise.' So I came into Paradise carrying my cross, and found Michael
the Archangel, and said to him, 'Our Lord Jesus Christ, who was crucified,
has sent me here. Lead me, therefore, to the gate of Eden.' And when the
flaming sword saw the sign of the cross, it opened to me and I went in.
Then Michael the Archangel said to me, 'Wait a short while, for Adam also,
the forefather of the race of men, comes with the righteous, that they also
may enter in.'"* — Gospel of Nicodemus[6]

The Messiah/Christ is an antidote for original sin. The Christian Church, centuries after Jesus died, came to define Christ, not as the Messiah who liberates Jews from oppression, but as God's response to Adam and Eve's disobedient act of satisfying themselves with forbidden fruit. In *Church History*, written in the third century, Eusebius described how Jesus "was crucified, and descended into Hades, and burst the bars which from eternity had not been broken, and raised the dead; for he descended alone, but rose with many and thus ascended to his Father."[7]

"This is probably the earliest distinct and formal statement of the descent into Hades," observes Arthur McGiffert, "but no special stress is laid upon it as a new doctrine, and it is stated so much as a matter of course as to show that it was commonly accepted at Edessa at the time of the writing of these records, that is certainly as early as the third century. Justin, Irenaeus, Clement of Alexandria, Origen, Tertullian, etc., all witness to the belief of the Church in this doctrine [of Jesus in hell], though it did not form an article in any of the older creeds, and appeared in the East first in the Aquileian creed, from which it was transferred to the Apostle's Creed in the fifth century or later."[8]

*. . . Jesus Christ, His only Son, Our Lord, who was conceived of the Holy Spirit;
born of the Virgin Mary, suffered under Pontius Pilate, was crucified died and
was buried. <u>He descended into hell</u>; the third day he rose again from the dead:
He ascended into Heaven, siteth at the right hand of God, the Father Almighty,
from thence he shall come to judge the living and the dead . . .*
— Apostle's Creed

6. *The Other Bible*, edited by Willis Barnstone, (San Francisco: Harper, 1984), *The Gospel of Nicodemus-Christ's Descent Into Hell*, pp.374-8.

7. *Nicene and Post-Nicene Fathers of the Christian Church*, under the editorial supervision of Philip Schaff and Henry Wace, notes by Arthur C. McGiffert. *Eusebius: Church History & Life of Constantine the Great*, (Grand Rapids: Wm. B. Eerdmans Publishing Company, 1890), p.102.

8. Ibid. p.102.

"It is the harrowing of hell," notes Crossan, "the despoiling of the demonic regions, that is used to explain why Jesus must die and be buried and still, in the genre of *innocence rescued*, be saved 'from death' before the very eyes of his enemies." Crossan lists three key themes enacted by the Messiah: "a *deception* in which the demons were allowed to crucify Jesus not knowing who he was; a *descent* that was the actual reason for his death and burial; and a *despoiling* whereby Jesus, as Son of God, broke open the prison of Hell and released both himself and all the righteous ones who had preceded him there."[9]

> *The harrowing of Hades was the decisive moment in the redemptive process.*
> — Henry Chadwick[10]

> *Christ then preached to the spirits in hell. They had disobeyed God while Noah was building the boat, but God had been patient with them. Eight people went into that boat and were brought safely through the flood. Those flood waters were like baptism that now saves you. But baptism is more than just washing the filth of the flesh. It means turning to God with a clear conscience, because Christ was raised from death.* — I Peter 3:19-21

The Hebrew term for hell is *She*-ol. According to the Messiah story the main reason for Christ's birth and death was to go to hell and liberate the sinful souls in *She*-ol. The soul of every human who had ever died was imprisoned there. After Christ burst open the gates of Hades, he was then resurrected from death on Easter Sunday. This is the Christian interpretation of the Messiah: By "dying for our sins" Christ inspires God to forgive us for Eve's disobedience in Eden and then lets us enter heaven again. God had closed the gates to man after Adam ate forbidden fruit. This sin is forgiven through baptism and belief in Christ; thus the Savior "saves" us by paving our way back to Paradise. This is what Christians call salvation.

> *Christ came into the world to save sinners.*
> — Paul: I Timothy 1:15

> *Christ never sinned, but God treated him as a sinner so that Christ could make us acceptable to God.* — Paul: II Corinthians 5:21

"The coming of the Messiah brings salvation and forgiveness of sin," explains John McKenzie. "Through the knowledge of salvation Christians escape from the defilements of the world."[11]

---

9. Crossan, *Historical Jesus,* pp.388-9.
10. *Some Reflections on the Character and Theology of the Odes of Solomon,* vol. I, (Munster: Aschendorff, 1970), p.268.
11. McKenzie, *Redemption: Dictionary of the Bible,* p.762.

There is a formula progression to this Messiah story, a specific intent to link "Jesus" with Eden, and original sin, and the resulting denigration of sex:

Eden + original sin + human exile from Paradise = the birth of Christ and his mission in hell.

These themes link Jesus with Eden when the title "Christ" is tacked on by the Church as Jesus' last name. His function thus becomes the forgiver of sins, which connects him with a condemning of flesh. But religions that reject flesh condemn ladies who make babies. Men then get imMENse advantages.

The myth of Eden explains the *need* for a Messiah: if Eve had not caused sin, we would not be banished from Paradise. If she had not disobeyed God, our bodies would not be the source of sin. If she hadn't provoked God, a Savior wouldn't be needed for us to get to heaven.

> *In the Garden, the fall of man into the field of time, out of the timeless rapture, you might say, of Eden, was followed then by the coming of the Savior, who represents a sublimation, a higher manifestation of the consciousness of humanity than that which had been represented in the Garden. So without the Fall there would have been no Savior. All of this is really mystic language from the Greek mysteries . . . the essence of the spiritual experience intended is that of shifting consciousness from the purely phenomenal* [physical, temporary] *aspect of ones life, to the spiritual – the deep, energetic, eternal aspect.*   – Joseph Campbell[12]

For their original sin of eating forbidden fruit from the Tree of Knowledge and becoming aware of opposites – good and evil, life and death – Adam and Eve were exiled out of Paradise and into shame. Against God's command they indulged pleasures of the flesh, and so mankind was cast out of never-ending Eden and into a world where everything dies. We became mortal; we experience time, our bodies pass away and decay. We became aware of opposites: eternal spirit vs. temporary flesh. A split was thus set up: spirit against matter. Our bodies, grown out of our mothers, are vehicles for evil and death, while the spiritual realm of the Heavenly Father is the way to eternal bliss.

> *They that are in the flesh cannot please God. You are no longer ruled by the flesh, but by the Spirit . . . the body is dead because of sin, but the Spirit is life because of righteousness.*   – Paul: Romans 8:8-10
>
> *Let not sin reign in your mortal body, that you should obey it in the lusts thereof . . . as you have yielded your members servants to uncleanness and*

---

12. *Mythos - the Mystical Life*, PBS 12/1/96.

> *to iniquity unto iniquity, now yield your members servants to righteousness*
> *unto holiness ... For the wages of sin is death, but the gift of God is eternal*
> *life through Christ.*　　　　　　　　　　　　　– Paul: Romans 6:12,19,23

> *... who shall deliver me from the body of this death? I thank God through*
> *Christ our Lord. So then with the mind I myself serve the law of God, but*
> *with the flesh the law of sin.*　　　　　　　　　– Paul: Romans 7:24-25

The Fall of Eve from Eden is the first domino that topples this progression. The Hebrew word for sin, *hamartia*, comes from the sport of archery, it literally means "missing the mark,"[13] as if we miss the entrance to heaven if we have sin – we veer off course and end up in hell or purgatory. But the Messiah arrives to steer us back through the gates of Eden. Christ is the antidote for original sin, a human sacrifice, an exchange – the Savior dies so that we can live forever. We can re-aim for the mark through *atonement*, at-one-ment, agreement with the beliefs of this religion and alignment with its ideas and deeds. The result is that we "hit the mark" *if* we reject flesh, and rejecting flesh paves the way for condemning women.

The concept of Christian salvation is meant to condemn women. That's the main concern of the Messiah/Christ complex: God's Son is sacrificed, killed by humans, but instead of being angry, God opens the gates of heaven for us because Christ, by dying, somehow removes sins from the world. We're told that the Messiah is the antidote for our sin and we have all sinned simply by being born. The implication is that God *prefers* males because men don't give birth. God created man in His own image: *spiritual*.

> *Divinity is of one sex, the male sex ... males are the same sex as God. This*
> *is a very, very deep lesson that children pick up on as soon as they're*
> *inculcated into society and it stays with them from cradle to grave. People*
> *today will say, well, how quaint, what does that have to do with our*
> *situation? Well, an awful lot.*　　　　　　　　　　– Sharleen Spretnek[14]

It's called the *Messiah/Christ complex*:

Christ = Messiah = Original Sin = Sex Denigrate = Control of Women

The story of Jesus was not about original sin or the fate of Adam and Eve. Jesus didn't speak ideas that denigrate sex. But then long after he died, writers for the Church created the story of the Messiah/Christ who erases original sin. Elaine Pagels cites biblical scholars "who are convinced that the titles Messiah and Son of God emerged later, from

13. Pagels, *Gnostic Gospels*, p.123.
14. *Full Circle*, National Film Board of Canada, PBS 8/96.

Christian communities."[15] Long after his crucifixion, Jesus was recast as the Messiah/Christ of Eden. But to him, the word Messiah held a different significance.

"In Jesus' time there was much talk of a Messiah who would liberate the Jews by force," writes John Romer, ". . . This label of Messiah automatically challenged both Roman and Jewish authority in Judaea and Galilee; for the belief that a Messiah would arise and, with the help of God, expel the godless, was often expressed in Hebrew Scripture . . . Many of the Gospel stories are designed to show how Jesus' life fulfilled the Messianic predictions of the Hebrew Prophets."[16]

The original meaning of Messiah has nothing to do with sex and redemption from original sin. It's much more a metaphor for politics and justice. Elaine Pagels points out that, prior to the crucifixion, "Some among the uneducated masses already acclaimed Jesus as Messiah – the 'anointed king' who they expected would liberate Israel from foreign imperialism and restore the Jewish state." Pagels explains how the Hebrews "maintained that human destiny depends upon the events of 'salvation history' – the history of Israel, especially the prophets' predictions of Christ and then his actual coming . . . All of the New Testament Gospels . . . rely on the prophet's predictions to prove the validity of the Christian message . . . But according to the *Gospel of Thomas,* Jesus dismisses as irrelevant the prophet's predictions."[17]

> His disciples said to him, "Twenty-four prophets spoke in Israel, and they all spoke of you." He said to them, "You have ignored the one living in your presence, and have spoken only of the dead."   – Thomas:52

Early Christians regarded Jesus as the Messiah who came to free the Jews from Rome. But later Christians fell under the influence of Roman Catholic theologians who invented the concept of original sin. Jesus, they said, had died and gone to hell to free all souls and re-open the gates of Paradise for man. With this new original sin story, Jesus was transformed from a Messiah who saves Jews from Rome into a Christ who saves man from hell. And both interpretations are rooted in predictions from the Old Testament.

Connecting Jesus with the Old Testament was useful to the early Church because the story of Jesus was just a few decades old when the gospels were written, and this was "one of the principal objections raised against Christianity," notes Arthur McGiffert. "Antiquity was considered a prime requisite in a religion which claimed to be true, and no reproach was greater than the reproach of novelty. Hence the apologists laid great stress upon the antiquity of Christianity, and this was one of the reasons why they appropriated the Old Testament as a Christian book."[18]

---

15. Pagels, *The Origin of Satan,* p.95.
16. Romer, *Testament,* p.173.
17. Pagels, *Gnostic Gospels,* pp.132, 71.
18. *Nicene and Post-Nicene Fathers of the Christian Church,* ed: Schaff and Wace, *Eusebius: Church History & Life of Constantine the Great,* p.82.

John Crossan describes the strategy used by gospel writers to connect Jesus with the Old Testament: "Jesus' first followers knew almost nothing whatsoever about the details of his crucifixion, death, or burial. [Because they all fled in fear after the Romans arrested him.] What we have now in those detailed passion accounts . . . [are] units sought out *backwards*, as it were, sought out *after* the events of Jesus' life were already known and his followers declared that texts from the Hebrew Scriptures had been written with him in mind. Prophecy, in this sense, is known after rather than before the fact . . . [from] the search by scribally learned followers . . . to find basis or justification in the Hebrew Scriptures for such a shocking eventuality. How could God's Chosen One have been so treated, and if he had been so treated, could he still be God's Chosen One? Finally came the . . . placing of such prophetic fulfillments into a sequential narrative with its origins well hidden within a plausible historical framework . . . Imagine . . . learned followers of Jesus beginning to search their scriptures *immediately* after the crucifixion . . . the followers of Jesus . . . are very, very interested in studying the scriptures . . . You know, first of all, exactly what you are looking for. You search for texts that show death not as end but as beginning, not as divine judgement but as divine plan, not as ultimate defeat but as postponed victory for Jesus. You are, therefore, especially looking for [Old Testament] texts with a certain duality, a certain hint of two stages, two moments, two phases, or two levels."[19]

OLD TESTAMENT

Some of the old Hebrew passages that these gospel writers snatched to attach to Jesus are shown below.

> *A child has been born for us. We have been given a son who will be our ruler. His names will be Wonderful Advisor and Mighty God, Eternal Father and Prince of Peace . . .*   — Isaiah 9:6

> *He was hated and rejected; his life was filled with sorrow and terrible suffering . . . He suffered and endured great pain for us . . . He was wounded and crushed because of our sins; by taking our punishment, he made us completely well . . . He was painfully abused, but he did not complain. He was silent like a lamb being led to the butcher . . . He was condemned to death without a fair trial . . . he suffered for our sins and asked God to forgive us.*   — Isaiah 53:3-12

> *Thy dead men shall live, together with my dead body shall they arise.*
>   — Isaiah 26:19

19. Crossan, *Historical Jesus*, pp.145-6.

Forty years after the death of Jesus, the gospels were being written in reaction to the Roman Jewish War of 66-70 C.E. Gospel stories had a therapeutic effect on a Jewish society then devastated by Rome. But hundreds of years later, after Roman emperors co-opted and redefined the Christian religion, Augustine compared the gospels with the Old Testament, and for the Roman Catholic Church he invented the story of original sin. By the time Augustine went looking for links in Bible stories that could connect Jesus with the denigration of sex and condemnation of women, the Church had long since degenerated into a fraternity for men only.

Rome itself degenerated as Christianity rose and spread around the Mediterranean. One could say that the fall of Rome was caused by the new Christian religion. In a desperate attempt to save the crumbling empire, the emperor seized upon the idea of "Church." The State took over the religion and redefined it to suit the leaders of the empire. The religion had to attract soldiers to Rome, the emperor needed bait, he needed beliefs that persuaded women to obey men. So Augustine, a Vatican writer, dreamed up the idea of original sin to link Jesus with Eden and the denigration of sex. With this creed the Church of the Empire offered men authority to order women into submission. Rome offered a religion that defined females as a race of slaves. Thus Bible stories became a way to lure men to fight for a corrupt and decayed Empire. Vatican writers began to portray Jesus as an antidote for the sexual "evils" of women and gays. The meaning of Messiah was changed, no longer did it mean a Savior for Jews under Rome, but rather a Savior for men over women. This is how the Vatican interpreted the four gospels that its members selected out of many to become the New Testament.

But there were dozens of other gospels that were banned by the Church. Elaine Pagels points out that in these "rejected" gospels Jesus "speaks of illusions and enlightenment, and not of sin and repentance, like the Jesus of the New Testament. Instead of coming to save us from sin, he comes as a guide who opens access to spiritual understanding. But when a disciple attains enlightenment, Jesus no longer serves as the spiritual master; the two have become equal – even identical."[20]

According to the Roman Church, Jesus was born *because* of the original sin of Adam and Eve. Although Judaism doesn't hold Adam and Eve responsible for the sins of humanity,[21] Hebrew beliefs do describe a hell in which "the souls of holy and righteous, persecuted and martyred Jews await their final and promised deliverance."[22] So even if Judaism doesn't blame Eve for our enslavement to sin, the religion does set up this theme of humanity awaiting a savior, a Messiah/Christ, who delivers us from evil and into Paradise.

Two thousand years ago, Jews awaited a Messiah who would free them from the hell

20. Pagels, *Gnostic Gospels,* p.xx.
21. Gregory Shaw writes, "Paul's view that Adam's fall introduced sin and death led Augustine (fifth century C.E..) to develop the doctrine of original sin: that Adam's fall perverted all humanity and that its effects were passed by hereditary transmission from generation to generation. The belief that Adam…was responsible for the sins of humanity was never adopted by Judaism…but Augustine's interpretation of the Fall became the accepted doctrine of Catholic Christianity." *The Oxford Companion to the Bible,* p.223.
22. Crossan, *Historical Jesus,* p.388.

of bondage to Rome. Three centuries later, the Church of Rome took over Christianity and redefined the Messiah as Christ freeing us from original sin. Without Christ, said the Church, original sin takes us to Hades. It's this connection between original sin, hell, and Christ that Rome found so useful.

When Augustine invented the story of original sin it's as if he *intended* that, as long as we believe we are condemned sinners in need of a Messiah, women will remain *blamed* for bringing bodies into the world and *blamed* for tempting men with sexual pleasures. As long as we need a Christ who leads us to heaven by erasing sins, then women, the source of life and sin, remain villains at a disadvantage to men. So whether or not you "believe in Jesus," what really counts is whether or not you accept the *idea* of a Messiah as defined by the Roman Church.

The first followers of Jesus may have been looking for someone to lead a revolt against Rome, but when Rome took over the Christian religion three hundred years later, it was the sexual aspect of original sin and the Messiah that served the needs of Imperial power. Men are *motivated* to believe in the story of original sin because it casts women in opposition with God. The story often inspires women to seek God's forgiveness by serving men. Such beliefs are used as tools to MANipulate women.

After the spread of male religions, females ceased to be the regulators of mating that they had always been because the new religions now *justified* the supremacy of men, which meant that males had more leverage with which to access sex from women. This is what the inventors of the religions intended all along.

> *It has been the physically strongest and most violent groups among us who have forced their own preferences on civilization by interpreting religious revelations to suit their own urges. Theological decrees – "the word of God" – have been a means by which the dominant group maintains exclusive access to pleasures. Weaker groups and minorities have been coerced into worshipping creeds that uphold the lifestyle of the dominant group . . . Only the most brutal, only the brutal pre-history elite, could define the faiths that conspire against minority interests. The elite sustain tyranny by the design of their religions, and traumatize our race with fears of damnation.*
> – A Touch of Hendrix, 1988[23]

NATURE'S BOUQUET OF LEAVES AND MUSHROOMS

Christians consider our world to be a punishment for becoming aware of pairs of opposites. Against God's will man ate from this Tree of Knowledge and was therefore banished into a world of duality; life is the opposite of death, and physical matter is separate from and opposed to the eternal spirit. Discussing the legend of the Holy Grail and the Grail King, Joseph Campbell explains how "the Christian separation of matter and

23. Fairchild, unpublished manuscript, (1988), pp.294, 16.

spirit – of the dynamism of life [against] the spiritual, natural grace and supernatural grace – has really castrated nature and the European mind. The European life has been emasculated by this. *True* spirituality, which would've come from [natural life], has been killed. What does the pagan represent? He was a person from the suburbs of Eden, he was regarded as a nature man and on the head of his lance was written the word 'Grail' – that is to say, nature *intends* the Grail – spiritual life is the *bouquet* of natural life, *not* a supernatural thing *imposed* upon it. And so, the impulses of nature are what give authenticity to life, not obeying rules coming from a supernatural authority. That is the sense of the Grail."[24]

"Pagan" comes from the Latin word *pagani*, which means a person who lives in the country. Pagan shamans throughout history have been aware that the world of spirituality is the "bouquet" of the natural world. Shamans access the spirit world *through* the natural world via a *bouquet* of leaves, seeds, bark, cactus, and mushrooms – the psychoactive plants of nature. "The Amanita muscaria [mushroom]," writes Tom Robbins, "[is] the direct inspiration for every major religion on Earth except Buddhism . . . the musicaria has been eaten since at least 4000 B.C. . . . At least eight Siberian tribes gobbled the musicaria regularly at ceremonies . . . tribal elders always ate the musicaria first. Their urine would then be saved and drunk by other males, and it is said that the urine high was better than the original. Women were prohibited to touch the stuff, and occasionally a male might be denied right to the urine cup . . . The mushroom was fraught with sexual allusions. It thrust from the ground like an aroused phallus. Later, its cap, as it flattened, would resemble a vagina receiving an erect penis. The mushroom was both cock and cunt. Often it was coated with a slimy mucus . . . Fertility was of prime concern to those folks, and most of their magic and ritual consisted of trying to induce lust and promote fecundity in human, beast and vegetable . . . plants were the babes of the Earth, as early people saw them. The Earth was a kind of womb, sometimes fruitful, sometimes barren. And the spilling rain made the Earth bear, just as the spurting semen made humans and animals bear. God hung out in the sky, where the head of his penis was clearly visible – we moderns call it the Sun. When God had coitus with the Earth, he showered the hills and fields with his vital semen – rain. So, through art, dance, song and elaborate outdoor fucking, humans tried to entice God and Mother Earth to get it on. In an effort to gain more influence over God's passions, the ancients attempted to find links with him on Earth. They regarded bodies of water as holy not only because of their life-enhancing moistures, but because they were considered to be pools of God's cum."[25]

The point is that pagans of pre-history knew that *true* spirituality *includes* sex, sensuality and nature. With magic plants and impassioned dances of possession frenzy, they elevated their awareness of immortality and ascribed meaning to the mysteries of divinity. "Only shamanic approaches will be able to give us answers to the questions we find most interesting," claims Terrence McKenna, "who are we, where did we come from,

---

24. The Power of Myth, *Love and the Goddess*, PBS 3/88, emphasis added.
25. High Times 12/76, pp.93-4.

and toward what fate do we move? . . . shamanism as an interdisciplinary and professional approach to these realities . . . Without such a visionary relationship to psychedelic exopheromones that regulate our symbiotic relationship with the plant kingdom, we stand outside of an understanding of planetary purpose . . . Our sense of political obligation, of the need to reform or save the collective soul of humanity, our wish to connect the end of history with the beginning of history – all of this should impel us to look at shamanism as an exemplary model."[26]

In opposition with shamanism is Western rationalism in which mind and body are separated while nature is opposed. In the West, shamans are persecuted and hallucinogens are banned. How did the ancient cultures that routinely used psychoactive plants become replaced by today's anti-hallucinogen governments? McKenna theorizes that "mushroom ecologies grew more rare . . . there may have been efforts to preserve mushrooms by drying and preserving them in honey . . . Honey . . . easily ferments into [alcohol] . . . Over time . . . the mushroom cult [was replaced] with a cult of mead [alcohol]. No greater shift of social values is possible to imagine than that which would accompany the gradual changeover of a psilocybin cult to an alcohol cult . . . the second step is the substitution of completely inactive materials for active ones . . . the substitutes, though usually still plants, are really no more than symbols of the former [mushroom] power of the mystery to authentically move initiates. And in the third stage of the process, symbols are all that is left . . . plants of any sort have disappeared, and in their place are esoteric teachings and dogma, rituals, stress on lineages, gestures, and cosmogonic diagrams. Today's major world religions are typical of this stage . . . another stage [is] . . . the complete abandonment of even the pretense of remembering the felt experience of the mystery. This last stage is typified by secular scientism as perfected in the twentieth century . . . in the process of abandonment: the rediscovery of the mystery and its interpretation as evil and threatening to social values."[27]

Dominator governments today sponsor anti-hallucinogen propaganda and persecute/prosecute people who eat the Earth's natural plants. But use of hallucinogens in ancient societies inspired insights about human origins and purpose. As mushrooms became scarce, these visions vanished. Without the plants with which to expand perceptions and promote partnership traditions, a new breed of theologian invented creeds in praise to the supremacy of men.

World religions today explain and justify reasons why societies are ruled by men. We've been trained to relate to nature with logic that denigrates sex and condemns women. People raised under Judaism, Christianity or Islam sometimes glimpse the sexist connections of their religion and experience the anxiety of *anomy*. Anomy is the sense of uprootedness that occurs when what was previously accepted as normal is shown to be destructive to everyone. Southern slaveholders experienced anomy when slavery was abolished and condemned by the majority of Americans. What was once accepted is now

---

26. McKenna, *Food of the Gods*, pp.8, 245, 92, 253.
27. Ibid. p.122.

rejected. But when we've been trained since birth to expect damnation if we reject a religion, and if we're conditioned with religion as a way to stay "stable," then it might be dangerous to abandon that religion. If the "Messiah" is explained as a belief system designed to dominate women, anomy is unleashed among people trained to worship Christ, and the explanation is labeled "evil and threatening to social values."

No matter how well explained, no matter how true, any suggestion that "Christ" is a destructive symbol for society will be interpreted by Christians as *evil* reasoning. "A rejection of Christolatrous symbols in the rising woman-consciousness has an organic consequence in the rejection of sexist rituals," notes Mary Daly. "[Peter] Berger has pointed out that the sacred cosmos provides the 'ultimate shield against the terror of anomy.' To be in a position of confronting the Christocentric cosmos that shields many from facing 'the terror of anomy' is to be exposed to the wrath of those who fear their own latent madness and therefore will inflict madness upon those who threaten their fragile sanity.'"[28]

In other words, the binding of our minds by dominator society cannot be unknotted without treMENdous upheaval. A certain type of "madness" is required for so many people to expend so much energy denying that world religions incite harm against women and gays. Masses of people have been braintrained all of their lives to resist any explanation that lessens the supremacy of heterosexual men. To effectively discredit a male religion will threaten the mental stability of its followers.

Likewise, to claim that religions are derived from visions induced with psychoactive plants is a claim that will be "interpreted as evil and threatening to social values." But without the effects of such plants, today's sober consumers are a nightmare of anxiety. It's as if the Earth's scream of warning is gagged by taboos against hallucinogens; without the plants we can't hear the message, and the plants are banned because they induce in humans an unaggressive state of compliant partnership, the opposite of competition. The plants produce a sort of "feminine intuition" that enables us to sense the Earth's concern. But in a culture that condemns the feminine, and instead empowers men, the effects of hallucinogens have been outlawed – users are persecuted, seers are silenced. Written into world religions is this prescription for destruction. We are today unable to handle asteroids because our ancestors were so preoccupied with brutalizing women and gays.

Shamans are the agents through whom we come to sense hidden intentions behind these creeds we've been led to believe. The Hebrew scheme against women may be, as Campbell points out, "an extreme case," but it is not an isolated one. Most world religions are schemes of male supremacy. By enshrining the spirit as a separate realm held to be "higher" than physical desires, we cast sex as unacceptably "lower." World religions thus condemn the two groups most *associated* with sex/sensuality: 1) women, the physical bearers of life, and 2) gay people, a group defined in terms of sexual behavior.

---

28. Daly, *Beyond God the Father*, p.141.

A RACIST-SEXIST CONNECTION

Many past African societies maintained goddess traditions and practiced dance rituals around bodily possession and ecstatic abandon. Nature religions and possession dances of Africans are physical, bodily celebrations denounced by Judeo-Christian traditions. When male religions sought to control women by condemning sex, they likewise vilified black Africans and native nature religions. For example, the Hebrew story of Noah and the Flood associates Africa with sexual corruption.

Genesis 9:20 describes how Noah "planted a vineyard and he drank of the wine and was drunken; and he was uncovered within his tent." He falls asleep and his son Ham enters the tent. Ham sees his father naked. Something happens, but the Bible is vague. Ham tells his older brother Shem what happened and Shem goes into the tent and covers his father's naked body with a robe without looking at him. "Noah awoke from his wine and knew what his younger son had done to him." (Genesis 9:24) Noah threatens, "I now put a curse on Ham's son. He will be the lowest slave of his brothers."

Dr. Nahum Sarna notes, "There are some external sources that suggest that what happened was that his son and/or his grandson sodomized the father when he was lying naked."[29]

"The peculiar disrespect and sexual implications of what Noah's children do," explains David Wolper, "is intended to tell us that they too were influenced by the world from which they had come, that it was impossible to grow up in such a corrupt world and not have tainted behavior."[30] But the clincher in this story of Noah is that Shem, who covered his naked father, goes on in the Bible to become the father of all Semitic people, but lusty Ham, the son who buggered ol' Noah, becomes the father of black Africans!

When a religion denigrates sensuality, it condemns three groups: women, gays, and blacks. This is the racist-sexist connection. And Hendrix, the sensual black shaman of possession frenzy, denounced with his group for appearing "like big women,"[31] looms as the boogey-man devil to dominators in our time.

---

29. Mysteries of the Bible, *Noah and the Flood*, A&E 5/94.
30. Ibid.
31. *See My Music Talking*, Produced by John Marshall 12/67.

Chapter 8: World Creeds/Male Needs

෴

What a lot of people forget is, they think that humanism means Protestants having tea together, or if you're really far out, Catholics and Buddhists praying together. They've forgotten the women's religion. When we use the word "World Religions" today, every one of them that we have in mind is a religion that grew up during the patriarchal times.

— Matthew Fox[1]

It has been possible for scholars to be aware of the most crudely dehumanizing texts concerning women in the writings of religious "authorities" and theologians – from Augustine to Aquinas, to Luther, to Knox, to Barth – and ... treat their unverified opinions ... with utmost reverence and respect ... the blatant misogyny of these men has not been the occasion of a serious credibility gap. It has simply been ignored or dismissed as trivial.

— Mary Daly[2]

I think religion is just a bunch of crap. It's only man-made stuff, man trying to be what he can't, and there's so many broken-down variations, all trying to say the same thing, but they're so cheeky, all the time adding in their own bits and pieces ... I'm working on my own religion, which is life. I'm just trying to push the natural arts: rhythm, dancing, music – getting it all together is my thing.

— Jimi[3]

Most world creeds are obsessed with rules about sex. Everyone is exposed to these beliefs repeatedly from birth. Humans are the only species for whom youthful years are comprised of thousands of hours spent being told what to believe, what to think and what attitudes to accept. "The number of impressions that get laid down inside us is staggering," notes Deepak Chopra. "Behavioral psychologists have estimated that just the verbal cues said to us by our parents in early childhood, which still runs inside our heads like muffled tape loops, amount to over twenty-five thousand hours of pure conditioning."[4]

1. *Full Circle*, National Film Board of Canada, PBS 8/96.
2. Daly, *Beyond God the Father*, p.22.
3. Hit Parader 1/70.
4. *Ageless Body, Timeless Mind*, audio lecture, tape 2, 1994.

Children undergo constant direct and indirect exposure to religion. Everyone's thoughts have been trained by symbols designed to empower men over women. "We *don't have to be* conversant with the Creation myth," notes Susan Griffin, "and the idea that Eve ate the apple through her sensuality and brought death into the world. We don't even have to know these ideas, because *they are picked up* now through advertisements, films, and just the attitude of other people in your life, and through the family system that's also taken in these ideas and been shaped to these ideas. And all of this becomes almost second nature, we don't even think about it . . . When you think about the degree of self-hatred and fear that most woman carry, you have to understand that there's something very large behind it, and what's behind it is the terrible splitting, in this culture, between spirit and matter, between the two halves of ourselves, which expresses itself in many different ways."[5]

Matter = m*other* = *other*.

Physical life begins with women. A mother who gives birth is *other* than spirit, and this is a prescription for self-hatred. In 1997, *The New York Times* and ABC News reported that, "As many as three million Americans, mostly women, are believed to be suffering from [a] psychiatric disorder . . . called self-mutilation, or self-abuse . . . Women who express their hurt and alienation by injuring themselves . . . these women seem not to be able to express their anger outward, so when they feel terrible anger they turn it against themselves and take it out on themselves."[6]

MARY: IDOL IDEAL

> *A particular woman might have been regarded as sacred, yet the entire female sex would still be considered vessels of sin.*   – Max Weber[7]

> *While Catholics revere Mary as the mother of Jesus, they never identify her as divine in her own right: if she is "mother of God," she is not "God the Mother" on an equal footing with God the Father.*   – Elaine Pagels[8]

"In the case of the ideal of goodness foisted upon women," notes Mary Daly, "there is a special aura of glorification of the ideal, as symbolized in [the Virgin] Mary, for example. This impossible ideal ultimately has a punitive function, since, of course, no woman can really live 'up' to it. (Consider the impossibility of being both virgin and mother.) It throws all women back into the status of Eve and essentially

---

5. *The Famine Within – A Film by Katherine Gilday*, Direct Cinema Limited, 1990.

6. ABC World News 7/26/97.

7. Daly, *Beyond God the Father*, p.163.

8. Pagels, *Gnostic Gospels*, p.48.

reinforces the universality of women's low status . . . [Mary] reinforces sexual caste. The inimitability of 'Mary conceived without sin' ensures that all women as women are in the caste with Eve."[9]

TORTURE IN THE NAME OF GOD

The belief that women are "explosive sexual beings" is not unique to Hebrew and Muslim myths. Throughout the world, this stigma has produced hundreds of societies in which millions of women have faced, and continue to face, tortures that are sanctioned by religious customs. In many countries, girls – from infancy to adolescence – undergo the ritual cutting away of their clitoris with knives and blades. The external labia are stitched together, leaving only a tiny opening for urine and blood to pass through. The mutilation is usually done without anesthetics. Its purpose is to provide evidence to the girl's future husband that she is still a virgin, as if her vagina were a box that had been gift wrapped with stitches and stamped "unused." Anti-sensual religions of men have coerced these women into accepting the mutilation of their own genitals. The women are told that this custom exists for their own good, to curtail their *explosive* sexuality.

> *What is often (inaccurately) called female circumcision . . . is painful and dangerous, both physically and psychologically. The purpose appears to have been to discourage promiscuity by depriving the woman of the areas most susceptible to pleasurable stimulus. In a recent survey conducted by the Cairo Family Planning Association, 90 percent of the young (Egyptian) women interviewed had had some part of the clitoris and labia removed.*
> — Reay Tannahill[10]

More than 100 million women alive today have undergone this ritual. But the torture of females by mutilating their genitals dates back to the time of the Pharaohs, at least three, possibly four thousand years ago. Such torture is ingrained in the cultures of more than thirty countries throughout Africa, the Middle East and Southeast Asia. It is practiced throughout a wide area of Africa among Christians, Muslims and Jews. It is also practiced in parts of Australia and the Highlands of Peru.[11]

The male religions persuade women to regard genital mutilation as a routine rite of passage. Brides must be virgins and only the concerns of the male matter. A man can be promiscuous as often as he pleases; there is no ritual genital mutilation to prevent him from having sex, as there is for women. For men the equivalent would be partial or total removal of the penis. However, whereas male circumcision is similar, its function is basically cosmetic rather than intentionally disruptive of a man's sex life in the way that female mutilations are.

---

9. Daly, *Beyond God the Father*, pp.62, 82.
10. Tannahill, *Sex In History*, p.68.
11. ABC News Nightline 2/9/94.

Male circumcisions are also reversible. Describing the use of circumcision in ancient Greece, and the history of the Bible, John Romer explains, "Everybody wanted to be Greek . . . The Jews wanted to join in that too . . . Greekness . . . [was] an attitude of mind, of thought, a way of talking, also a way of being, in body as well as mind . . . a particular sort of body image that has come down to us today . . . If you didn't join them down in the gymnasium you'd never become a man of substance and position in Hellenistic society. For a young Jewish chap . . . a major individual and personal problem would arise because all these events, all the training, was done in the nude, and our poor Jewish chap had been circumcised when he was a lad. He would have stood out like a sore thumb! . . . So they had an extraordinary operation devised call an *epsipadian*. This consisted of actually disguising the effects of circumcision. That's an extraordinary thing, it's one of those terrible cultural distortions so depressing to read about in any period of history."[12]

"Epispadians," meaning *those who have made themselves foreskins*, were the recipients of a surgical procedure devised by Arelius Cornelius Celsus around the time of the birth of Jesus. The procedure involves peeling back the skin on the shaft of the penis and then bandaging the head, or *glans*, so that the peeled tissue heals into a new foreskin over the top of the bandage, which is then removed.

CIRCUMCISION – SNAKEPIT OF SYMBOLISMS

Such a strange mutilation, found among the most primitive and the most highly civilized people, and on all continents, must reflect profound needs.
— Bruno Bettelheim[13]

The circumcision ritual goes back possibly before the dawn of recorded history. The circumcised phallus has been observed on mummies in ancient Egypt dating as far back as 1614 B.C.E. Nicholas Carter, in his climactic expose, *Circumcision: The Tragic Myth*, reports, "It is difficult to indicate exactly where any one motivation for the procedure has ruled to the exclusion of all others . . . many of the cultures that have practiced the ritual have probably embraced differing tribal and religious justifications for the procedure at different times in their history . . . Male circumcision is now known to have existed in Asia, Africa, and among the Moslem peoples of India. It has been practiced among the Arabs, Christians, Abyssinians, dwarf tribes of Gabon, Malays, Men of Borneo, Mayas, Aztecs, Caribs, Mohammedans and Jews. In Pagan Africa, the custom was known to the Zulu, Zhosa, Bechuana and Falasha. It was the custom of the aborigines of Fiji, New Caledonia, Samoa, New Hebrides and Madagascar . . . Babylonians were also infatuated with the rite."[14]

The role of circumcision in the battle of the sexes might be that of a ritual carried over from Paleolithic times that was invented by men to mimic female menstruation.

12. Romer, *Testament*, PBS 10/91.
13. *Symbolic Wounds*, (New York: Collier Books, 1962), p.16.
14. Carter, *Routine Circumcision- the Tragic Myth*, pp.25, 10.

Menstruation brought forth blood, which prehistoric people regarded as a mystical substance. Menstruation also marked the divide between barren girls and child-bearing women; it represents physical maturity. Prehistoric men may have reacted to female bleeding by devising a corresponding male-only genital blood ritual. Prehistoric people may have reasoned that bleeding the penis might enable men to bear children, just as menstrual blood seemed to enable females to be fertile. Circumcision in early societies was instituted as a puberty rite for boys who reached the same age as girls who begin to menstruate, marking the transition from pre-pubescence to sexual maturity. But circumcision, as Reay Tannahill notes in *Sex In History*, "was not practiced in Mesopotamia until the Hebrews made it an article of faith. Possibly, they brought the idea back from Egypt at the time of the exodus. Israel's law givers, however, transferred it from adolescence to infancy, made it mandatory, and represented it as an eternal symbol of God's covenant with the Jewish people, thus turning a pagan rite into an index of grace."[15]

> *You shall circumcise the flesh of your foreskin and it shall be a token of the covenant between me and you. Your family must circumcise every baby boy when he is eight days old.*   — Genesis 17:11-12

According to Carter, "When Jews accepted the rite as a special mark they gave to it . . . a new and unheard-of-meaning – that is, as a covenant or free promise of God's blessing between them and Yahweh, with the procedure becoming a distinctive mark of Yahweh-worship . . . If circumcision had a hygienic origin with the Jews, the oldest legal codes of the Hebrews would have noted that significant fact. But they do not . . . There is absolutely no mention of hygienic purposes in the biblical text . . . Spinoza mirrored the view of Tacitus, the Roman historian, who referred to circumcision as the distinctive racial stamp of the Jewish people. The Bible too bears out the belief that the rite was a means of identification."[16]

The circumcision ritual itself indicates that we are a species deeply confused about sexuality. Anthropologist Margaret Mead noted in *Male and Female* that "women's lives are arranged in sharp, discontinuous steps with the emphasis almost inevitably on being: a virgin, a girl who has ceased to be a virgin, a childless woman, a woman who has borne a child, and a woman (past menopause) who can no longer bear a child."[17] Men likely sought to mark and distinguish corresponding sequential periods of male growth with permanent bodily alterations and scars, therefore boys were circumcised when they reached adolescence.

But this doesn't explain why modern mothers, mainly in America, are so accepting of circumcision for infants. Studies of American hospitals reveal that by the mid-1950s, around 90 percent of all non-Jewish males were being circumcised at birth. Women are

---

15. Tannahill, *Sex In History*, p.68.
16. Carter, *Routine Circumcision – the Tragic Myth*, p.12.
17. Ibid. p.22.

often the ones who make the decision to circumcise. It's as if a kind of collective revenge is being imposed on boys, by mothers in protest of male domination of society.

> *It is the one way an intensely matriarchal society can permanently influence the physical characteristics of its males.*
> — Dr. William Morgan[18]

From 1900 to 1950, the incidence of routine circumcision jumped from a mere 6 percent to nearly 100 percent, becoming the most common medical procedure in the United States. "The overwhelming majority of non-Semitic Americans have become infatuated with circumcision for non-ritual reasons," writes Carter. "The typical mother will dedicate a lot of time and effort to teaching her boy to brush his teeth and wash behind his ears. But when it comes to the care of his genitals Victorian taboos and fears stand in the way. Consequently, circumcision is chosen to relieve the parent of her anxieties and discomfort . . . many a mother turns to the operation as a practical means of avoiding situations with which she fears she will be unable to cope . . . the majority of them believed that it would *relieve* them and the child of the *bother* of cleanliness."[19]

NO HYGIENE PROBLEM

> *Some people worry because they think it may be unwholesome to stimulate the penis so regularly.*
> — Dr. Benjamin Spock[20]

"One reason for the obsessive worry," explains Carter, "is that old devil 'masturbation' . . . the widely held fear that the handling of the uncircumcised genitals will lead to masturbation . . . it is highly probable that this is the primary reason for the entire penile cleanliness dilemma . . . [since] there is no hygienic problem in the young male . . . Our society is still strongly under the influence of the tradition established by the religious rites and doctrines of Judaism and Christianity – traditions that have led to many beliefs in opposition to biological facts. The conception of sex as sinful, along with many specific prohibitions and enactments, have survived until modern times resulting in guilt and shame because of the feeling that sexual activity is sinful and dirty. Out of these attitudes have sprung taboos . . . sex is associated by nature with the excremental process, and because these processes are treated by many with disgust, it follows that some residue of that disgust will in turn detrimentally effect the climate in which a society must function. Growing to maturity immersed in a climate of sexual repression, many people – in their subconscious minds – hate or fear the organs of sex because of the things they have been brought up to look upon as 'dirty' or 'questionable' and yet cannot

---

18. Ibid. p.93.
19. Ibid. pp.26, 50.
20. Ibid. p.97.

do without. Because of 'penis hate' or 'penis fear' for example, there are those people who automatically 'believe in' circumcision; if you cannot cut off that nasty offending member, at least you can mutilate it."[21]

> *The sadism (or the catatonia) of nurses . . . has allowed them to witness and aggravate the suffering of circumcised babies . . . I worked as a volunteer nurses' aid...[and saw] the ghastly appearance of circumcised babies . . . the reaction of extreme pain and shock. The babies would scream and quiver with shock. What psychotic monsters we are!*
>
> — letter to *Fact* magazine[22]

Deep within the snakepit of hysterical revulsion against sex, many parents subconsciously regard circumcision as a symbolic form of castration. It's as if the purifying waters of baptism were just not enough to cleanse the soul of original sin, so just to make sure that the body pays for whatever pleasure it has in store, let us begin each newborn life with a corrective measure of pious punishment. "There is something terrifyingly evangelical about the American infatuation with circumcision," concludes Carter, "and this explains perhaps, in part, why physicians as well as parents endorse the . . . delusion that circumcision is painless . . . Child mutilation and child torture are being practiced in 20th century America to a degree unprecedented in the civilized world . . . the uselessness, the brutality and the harm of this surgical assault upon normal physiology . . . a surgical operation that has absolutely no medical basis for performance ...Complications and deaths . . . due to circumcision are successfully concealed."[23]

> *Circumcision's origins, even religiously speaking, are primitive and barbaric . . . It is too deeply entwined with conscious and unconscious feelings of Jewish identification, Jewish loyalties, and a stubborn resistance to doing voluntarily that which millennia of persecution have not succeeded in getting us to do (or not to do).*
>
> — Board of Jewish Education, Baltimore[24]

Moses Maimonides, the 12th century rabbinical scholar, considered circumcision to be a means of restricting men from the sin of pleasure. The purpose of cutting flesh from the penis, said Moses, was to "lessen the power of passion and of too great desire. An organ that is bled after birth and its covering removed is undoubtedly weakened."[25] Augustine, too, advocated penis dismemberment as a means of cleansing the body of original sin.

---

21. Ibid. pp.51, 16.
22. Ibid. p 58.
23. Ibid. pp.59, 120, 118.
24. Ibid. p.112.
25. Ibid. p.122.

Nature intends that the adolescent male shall copulate as often and as promiscuously as possible, and to that end covers the sensitive glans so that it shall be ever ready to receive stimuli. Civilization, on the contrary, requires chastity, and the glans of the circumcised rapidly assumes a leathery texture less sensitive than skin. Thus the adolescent has his attention drawn to his penis much less often.

– R.W. Cockshut, *British Medical Journal*, 1935[26]

I should have thought that the exposed glans would have attracted the adolescent's attention more than the covered one.

– Dr. M.P. Menon, *British Medical Journal*, 1935[27]

The comments of Cockshut and Menon reveal a double-edged irony which has resulted in near universal acceptance of circumcision in 20th century America: a circumcised penis satisfies the urges of Puritans who seek some punishment for sex, while at the same time satisfying the tastes of men and women who prefer the *appearance* of an uncovered phallus.

NAKED GLANS

In the ancient *Babylonian Magical Text*, circumcisions are described as being for "the shaping of the phallus."[28] And although the Koran contains no instructions or requirement for circumcision, the practice is universal among Muslims. The Prophet Mohammed considered the procedure to be "an observance of natural impulsion with no special religious character."[29]

The point is that in prehistory the *urge* for circumcision came first. Men later offered explanations to justify the ritual with reasons other than "it looks better." My proposal is that a larger percentage of the human population is more erotically aroused by the appearance of a naked glans as opposed to a covered one; therefore, foreskins are removed for cosmetic/erotic reasons. "Modern scholars sometimes argue that circumcision . . . was originally carried out for reasons of hygiene," notes Tannahill, "[but] the operation was most common in Egypt and Africa, and was not performed until just before adolescence – rather late in the day if hygiene was the object. Everything, in fact, points to a puberty rite: the age of the patient, the triumphant exposure of the masculine glans, and the removal of the flaccid folds of skin that to the envious primitive male may have had something of a feminine look about them ...Of multi-partnered women surveyed in the 1980s, 90% declared a preference for intercourse with circumcised lovers."[30]

---

26. Ibid. p.127.
27. Ibid.
28. Ibid. p.11.
29. Ibid. p.19.
30. Tannahill, *Sex In History*, p.67.

Carter cites a study conducted at the Ohio State University College of Medicine in which 80 mothers were asked about their reasons for requesting circumcision for their boys. Many of the women answered, "because it looks better."[31]

> *I was circumcised at birth and much prefer the clean, graceful appearance of my "bareheaded" penis compared with penises retaining the usual dirty-looking foreskin.*   – letter to *Fact* magazine[32]

In his book *Commonsense Childbirth*, Lester Hazell observes, "In a way circumcision has become cosmetic surgery."[33] Foreskin removal has from the start always been "cosmetic surgery," with a lot of other explanations offered throughout history to disguise this fact for people who won't admit that they are more turned on by a naked glans. Controversy surrounds this assertion because many other people are indifferent with regards to whether a glans is covered or uncovered, while still others consider the foreskin to be most appealing.

> *Dr. Frank Zimmerman, Ph.D, . . . infers that both phallic worship and a sacrifice to fertility were involved in the establishment of the custom. He emphasizes that the Jews would have been very conscious that the erect penis was a strong symbol of sexual power and fertility. Therefore, he maintains, the intent of circumcision becomes very clear for the following reason: A circumcised penis is a copy of a penis in erection. In other words, the ancient Hebrew unconsciously thought as follows: May the penis of this infant now circumcised be always sexually potent and fertile, and ready to fertilize as if in perpetual erection . . . the "worship of Priapus" dates back thousands of years before the present-day conception of deity was even developed . . . Primitive man was proud of the strength of his penis. To him it represented the essence of some Divine principle of which he was a part; and in many countries – Egypt, Arabia, India, England, Ireland and America, among them – he erected monuments in the shape of the phallus.*
> – Nicholas Carter[34]

Removal of the foreskin should be a choice made by adult males, but typically the decision is made for us when as infants we're forced to undergo the "barbarous mutilation." Most scholars agree that hygiene is not the reason nor even the issue. However, the anti-sex beliefs of Judaism, Christianity, and Islam inspire denial of the idea that this custom is rooted it eroticism.

---

31. Carter, *Routine Circumcision – the Tragic Myth*,   p.39.
32. Ibid. p.123.
33. Ibid. p.34.
34. Ibid. pp.14-14, 22.

The difference between circumcision and female genital mutilation is one of *intention*: whereas women are sexually scarred to ensure their virginity, men are sexually sculpted to enhance their appeal. The dimensions of this difference became clear in 1993 when John Bobbitt's wife cut off his cock. American media fixated for weeks on the single penis of one male, while each and every year more than 100 million women are victims of similar mutilations while few bystanders notice nor protest.

> *There's a lot of discrimination on women today . . . You feel to yourself, damn, there's really a responsibility to some of these girls because they're the ones that are gonna get screwed.* — Jimi[35]

While men legally mutilate millions of women each year throughout Asia and South America, in other cultures females are being exterminated under policies that approach genocide. For example, in India, a nation one-third the size of the United States and with three times the population, almost all infanticide victims are girls. The killing of female infants is an ancient practice promoted by Hindu customs. The birth of a daughter in India is considered a curse because of the dowry custom. When a girl is married her family must pay to the groom a fee, or dowry, of whatever he asks, sometimes as much as fifteen years' worth of income. The dowry system was officially outlawed in India decades ago, but today the tradition is more widespread than ever.[36]

In Hindu society, the first rule of correct behavior for a wife is to please her husband. But according to India's tradition, if there isn't a continuous flow of gifts from the woman to the man in exchange for her having been accepted within the man's home, it is customary for him to get rid of her. Bride burning is a traditional means for a man to "leave" his wife – he sets her on fire. In New Delhi, the capital city of India, a woman is burned to death every 12 hours. Official statistics show that 5000 dowry murders took place in 1991, and unofficial figures are higher. Often the burnings are planned to look like cooking accidents.[37]

> *A woman must never be free of subjugation.*
> — The Hindu Code Of Manu, V

> *With rare exceptions, to be a woman in India is to be something less than a slave, property of no worth beyond what she can cook, or fetch, or carry, or can bring as dowry to a marriage. Her purpose is to bear a treasured son.*
> — 60 Minutes[38]

---

35. Hall and Clark, *The Superstars – In Their Own Words*, pp.134-5.
36. Investigative Reports, *Let Her Die*, A&E 2/94.
37. CBS News 60 Minutes 1/24/93.
38. Ibid.

Hindu and Muslim customs prevent most women from achieving financial independence. Brides are kept dependent on husbands and laden with dowry debt. In a society where so many women are forced to endure lifetimes of abuse, it isn't surprising that killing girls at birth is considered the kinder option. Each year in India thousands of female infants are murdered by their own families. It is customary to either suffocate the baby by putting a sandbag over her nose, giving her a double dose of opium in liquid form, poisoning her with the juice of toxic plants, or feeding her unhusked rice grains to induce choking. Government health clinics estimate that four in every ten girls in India are killed at birth. In the village of Kumla, out of one hundred children only fourteen are girls.[39] Today in India, millions of pregnant mothers use ultrasound to discover the gender of their fetus. Unborn girls are routinely aborted.

India is a country starved for medical technology, yet there is no shortage of ultrasound machines. Ultrasound is meant to be used for detecting fetal abnormalities, but in India it is used almost exclusively to study the genitals of fetuses in the womb. A 1990 U.N. survey of 8000 legal abortions in Bombay records just one baby boy aborted. In some villages, ultrasound tests are more available than running water. But the cost of the test is relatively expensive, driving most families deep into debt. And ultrasound is reliable only when the fetus is four months or older, meaning that abortions usually take place after the sixteenth week of pregnancy, which is extremely dangerous for the mother. Nonetheless, in India 3000 female fetuses are aborted every day after sex determination tests. There are over one million abortions per year throughout the country. A huge gender gap has developed. Population statistics for 1993 reveal an estimated loss of 25 million girls.[40]

"It is because of the low political significance of women in our society." states Dehli lawyer Rani Jeth Malani. "It is a very strongly entrenched patriarchal society and women are a secondary sub-caste, almost, within our society, there is no doubt about that. It is difficult to imagine, but that is the brutality of this culture and I think it is really getting to be quite a sick society."[41]

CONFUCIAN CONFUSION

Ultrasound technology also enables Asians to pursue sexual genocide. Ancient religions train parents to feel blessed by sons and cursed by daughters. Girls are either aborted or murdered at birth.

Those who survive face lifetimes of institutionalized violence against women. Nowhere is such torture more refined than in China. For centuries the entire culture was obsessed with an urge to force women to walk with crushed feet! Billions of Chinese girls endured an excruciating practice called "footbinding." In ancient times, an emperor with a fetish for tiny feet began a practice of requiring girls to have four of their toes pressed

---

39. Investigative Reports, *Let Her Die*, A&E 2/94.
40. Ibid.
41. CBS News 60 Minutes 1/24/93.

together under the soles of their foot, with heel and instep drawn tightly together and bound up in long strips of fabric. It was common for woman to reach adulthood with feet compressed into five-inch, four-inch, and even three-inch stubs of crushed flesh and permanently deformed lumps of bone. Men insisted that women regard the footbinding mutilations as marks of beauty. It was common for a groom to choose his wife based on the smallness of her feet! Marriage contracts were broken if the foot turned out to be larger than advertised.

"It is estimated that there are about two million mature Chinese women today who started life with bound feet," reports foot-binding historian Glenn Roberts. "The foot never grows out and it can be very, very painful when it is let out. This had a great deal to do with the society and the culture . . . it's a whole social, almost religious, ritual . . . Women with bound feet did work in the fields, but probably on their knees. It was a whole country that had a male population with a foot fetish. It was such a forbidden subject, little boys grew up thinking that it's erotic."[42]

Boys also learned that the feelings of females are expendable when in service to male needs. The extent of such expendability surfaced in recent decades when the Chinese government sought to reduce China's population of 1.2 billion people by limiting each family to one child. Millions of parents reacted by abandoning their baby girls. Orphanages overflow today. The death rate among young girls approaches fifty percent.[43]

> *The female half of China harbors serious concerns about legacies of the past. Many women worry that age-old Confucian prejudices will take new forms, such as male-oriented population control practices, and male-dominated employment policies . . . There is a cultural imperative for boy [babies] . . . With a one-child policy in effect . . . this has contributed to China's so-called "missing girls" problem. Over the past decade ultrasound technology has become a vehicle for the sex selection of infants . . . According to China's own census data in 1990, 114 boys were born for every 100 girls . . . "For a child that is delivered at home . . . they bribe the midwife. They say, 'oh, this is a baby girl, pity, a still-birth,' and she's dead when she's out of the delivery room."*   – MacNeil-Lehrer News Hour[44]

> *It is a violation of human rights when babies are denied food or drowned or suffocated or their spines broken simply because they are born girls.*   – Hillary Clinton in China[45]

---

42. The Phil Donahue Show, ABC 7/23/96.
43. ABC World News 9/95.
44. McNeil/Lehrer News Hour, PBS 9/95.
45. ABC World News 9/95.

GLOBAL HORROR

In our global culture of male supremacy, most women live with a constant threat of violence from men. A 1995 NBC News report revealed that "at least one in two Arab women are beaten by their husbands and it is justified by religion and society."[46] Arab women are subservient in their homes. Divorce is rare and the few women who do find employment outside the home are paid little. The NBC report profiled an Arab man whose "daughter was raped, or committed adultery, the facts aren't clear, so he restored the family honor . . . he allegedly strangled his daughter, then killed his wife for bringing her up wrong . . . Even his sons expect him to get a light sentence from the Palestinian court."[47]

"It's the right thing to do to a woman who betrays her husband or who commits adultery," said the man's neighbor, "because it's what Islam tells us."

"Mohammed himself said that men should be more controlling, more dominant, and women should be more submissive," notes Dr. Mohammed Haj Yiyha of Hebrew University. "Family peace is more important than women's peace."[48]

The major religions of the world restrict options for women and set the stage for laws like those in African societies that deny a wife the right to refuse intercourse with her AIDS-infected husband.[49] South American machismo customs are likewise legendary for mythologizing the abuse of females. CBS News *60 Minutes* reports, "No place on earth degrades women quite the way Brazil does . . . in defending his honor a man can get away with murder, particularly if the victim is his woman . . . Throughout Latin America it is called 'machismo' . . . and it pervades all of society, including the courtroom . . . In a domestic dispute the man's position will prevail. His wife may not sell her property without his permission. He may annul a marriage if he discovers his wife is not a virgin . . . A man can have as many mistresses as he wants, it's a proud point if he has a mistress. But for a woman, if she has a lover, she is in disgrace . . . The defense of honor is generally accepted by the jury . . . the remarkable thing is that so many of the murderers are not backwoods primitives but professional, educated men . . . A prominent engineer here . . . murdered his wife . . . then confessed. He killed her, he said, because she offended him, she was too independent. He was tried, given a suspended sentence, and set free. The packed courtroom applauded the verdict. The judge said [the killer] had defended his honor. His case was just one more in a long list of men, rich and educated, poor and peasant, who literally have gotten away with murder or mayhem. The courts merely frown on such 'domestic incidents.' Under Brazilian law, a man may commit a murder and if he is not caught within 24 hours . . . he may . . . walk into a police station and confess his crime and he will be free until he goes to trial. In

---

46. NBC Nightly News 9/9/95.
47. Ibid.
48. Ibid.
49. McLaughlin Group, Eleanor Clift comment, PBS, 9/15/95.

cases of wife murder that could take years and possibly never . . . It is more than sexual aggression. It is sexual tyranny in which the prevailing attitude dismisses murder as a simple act of purification."[50]

"We are the world champions in impunity to violence against women," says a member of the Brazilian legislature.[51] Under Portuguese colonial law, men were permitted to kill their unfaithful wives. The "honor defense" remained legal as recently as 1991. Then, after decades of protest, Brazil's Appeals Court struck down the right of wife-killers to argue that they murdered in defense of their honor. But the custom continues under a legal loophole: after the men kill their wives they check into a psychiatric clinic and announce that they acted under a disturbed mental state. Statistics from 1992 reveal that men convicted of murdering women in Brazil serve an average of only four years in prison. In 1993, the U.S. State Department singled out Brazil's "high incidence of violence against women."[52]

> *The impunity for crimes of violence against women has remained. Batterers, assassins, and rapists of women rarely are taken to the tribunals and condemned. And, when they are, they remain free and pose a constant threat to society . . . The public authorities and, in particular, the Judiciary, have not changed. They continue to absolve the criminals . . . [Brazil's] penal code, for example, still defines rape as "a crime against custom" rather than a crime against an individual person.*
>
> – Jane Jaquette[53]

> *I have been tried by law made by men, interpreted by men, administered by men, in favor of men, and against women.* – Susan B. Anthony[54]

In the United States, where as recently as 1920 women were still forbidden to vote, the legal status of females was once close to a condition of slavery. Historian Sally Roesch Wagner explains, "When a woman married, everything that she owned became her husband's. She ceased to exist legally. Women had no rights to their own property. They had no rights to their children. They had no rights to the safety of their own bodies. One of the states upheld the right of the husband to beat his wife, saying that to do otherwise would be to upset the domestic harmony of the home."[55]

"Family peace," as the Arabs like to say, "is more important than women's peace."

---

50. *Machismo*, CBS News 60 Minutes 2/21/88.
51. *Battered By the Myth of Machismo - Violence Against Women Is Endemic In Brazil - The War Against Women*, U.S. News & World Report 4/4/94.
52. Ibid.
53. Jane S. Jaquette, *The Women's Movement in Latin America – Participation and Democracy*, (Westview Press, 1994), p.47.
54. *One Woman, One Vote*, PBS, 12/18/95.
55. Ibid.

I thank thee, O Lord, that thou has not created me a woman.
— Daily Orthodox Jewish Prayer[56]

Customs that were widely practiced a few decades ago still pervade daily life in America. For example, in American universities in 1995 there were only three women deans in the entire country. Less than three percent of over two thousand departmental chairs are occupied by women, and only about nine percent of all full professors who are tenured are women.[57]

The educational system has been effectively appropriated by the upper strata and transformed into an instrument which tends to reproduce the class structure and transmit inequality. — Paul Blumberg[58]

One measure of this inequality is women's private pensions, which average about half those of men: four thousand dollars for women versus eight thousand dollars for men.[59] And of the CEOs of Fortune 500 companies in America in 1997, 498 were men and just 2 were women.[60] Until recently, if you walked into the rotunda of the U.S. Capitol building, you were surrounded by statues of all male figures. It took until the summer of 1997 before a memorial was accepted to represent the contributions of women in America. And it took female Senators *seventy-two years* just to get a women's bathroom near the Senate floor.[61]

Beyond the United States government is the United Nations, a world organization in which, in the 1990s, only five of more than 180 ambassadors are women. In 1995, the U.N. reported that females make up 70 percent of the world's poor.[62] At the same time, on a global scale, of nearly one million pornographic images on the Internet, one quarter of all the images involve the torture of women. A 1995 study by Carnegie Mellon University revealed that the best way for the Internet's merchants of porn to guarantee big sales was to offer sex that tortured or humiliated women. A writer for *Time* magazine reported that "if you just described an act of oral sex, or a photograph of straight oral sex, it wasn't a particularly popular picture. Not a lot of people chose to download it. But if in his description he included the word 'choke,' or 'choking,' he would double the number of hits."[63]

The history of mankind is a history of repeated indigence on the part of men toward women, having in direct object the establishment of an absolute tyranny over her. — Elizabeth Cady Stanton[64]

56. Daly, *Beyond God the Father*, p.132.
57. Susan Blumenthal, U.S. Assistant to Attorney General, Deputy Assistant Secretary for Women's Health, Commonwealth Club of CA, NPR 8/15/95.
58. Paul Fussel, *Class*, (New York: Ballantine Books, 1983), p.154.
59. NBC Nightly News 6/25/97.
60. *The Sex Wars*, NBC Nightly News 10/23/97.
61. NBC Nightly News 8/95.
62. Ibid.
63. ABC News Nightline 6/29/95.
64. *One Woman, One Vote*, PBS 12/18/95.

Chapter 9: Herd Thinners

જી

The establishMENt establishes tyranny which is sustained by superstitious religions, and nowhere do established beliefs reach such pinnacles of ignorance than in religious literature used to oppose homosexuals. "If any one man was responsible for the hardening of the Church's attitude toward homosexuals," reports Tannahill, "it was the . . . theologian of the thirteenth century, St. Thomas Aquinas . . . Aquinas consolidated traditional fears of homosexuality as the crime that had brought down fire and brimstone on Sodom and Gomorrah, by 'proving' what every heterosexual male had always believed – that it was unnatural in the sight of God as of man . . . From the fourteenth century on, homosexuals as a group were to find neither refuge nor tolerance anywhere in the Western Church or state."[1]

In 1993 Dr. Dean Hamer of the National Cancer Institute studied DNA from the genes of forty gay brothers and discovered that a portion of DNA in their genes, a same stretch of DNA that the researchers found over and over again, appears to determine sexual orientation. "An unexpectedly high proportion of those gay brothers shared DNA markers on one small region of the X chromosome," announced Dr. Hamer, "which suggests that there is a gene or genes located there that affect the sexual development in these men."[2]

Hamer believes that a breakthrough in finding the "gay gene" is forthcoming. "We submitted our papers to science when we had reached an appropriate statistical confidence level of more than ninety-nine percent...Previous studies have suggested that genes play about fifty percent of a role in whether a person is gay or heterosexual. The particular gene region that we've isolated plays about half again of that. So there is clearly a substantial component which is inherited. We can measure it, we can accurately assess it in the laboratory...[we have] proof that there is such a component."[3]

In 1995, Hamer's team announced the results of a separate second study of 33 sets of brothers who were all homosexual. As in 1993, scientists again found the marker on the X chromosome that these gay men carried in common. Scientific evidence is becoming conclusive: hereditary factors do predispose men to homosexuality.

---

1. Tannahill, *Sex In History*, pp.159-60.
2. CNN 7/93.
3. ABC News Nightline 7/15/93.

> *Throughout the world, limitations in the carrying capacity of a given environment have demanded from people cultural as well as biological responses.*
> — Marlene Dobkin de Rios[4]

Could it be that Nature, and natural selection, *intends* homosexuality as a means of reducing the number of people when a population grows too large for an environment to feed or sustain it? Is the "purpose" of a gay person to avert another birth by diverting human conception? Sex between gay couples does not conceive offspring, which suggests that homosexuality is nature's way of thinning the herd and slowing down the rate of reproduction when there are *"limitations in the carrying capacity of a given environment."* In this sense gay people help stabilize human interaction with the eco-system by decreasing the population when needed, and in a natural way.

Homosexuality is manifest in human societies in a *multi-generational* way. It is triggered in one generation to become expressed in their offspring. For example, when food shortages, droughts, floods, or changes in climate create conditions hostile for human life, reproductive biology in some people starts to change. We struggle when our environment puts us under *stress*. When we become strained to a certain point, a threshold that is different for each person, the stress triggers a signal in the body. Some people are rendered infertile from stress, others remain fertile but conceive offspring which nature *intends* to be infertile. Such progeny are homosexuals, people predisposed to a form of sex that produces no children.

AVERT-A-BIRTH

When the human herd overpopulates an environment there is not enough food, shelter, relaxation, or time. People get anxious, exhausted, and stressed. But we've evolved a biological corrective mechanism, and it's activated by stress. Couples start to conceive offspring who grow up and don't reproduce because they're gay. Over several decades the population of the next generation is reduced. This is nature's way of adapting humans to conditions of scarcity, giving the environment time to recover.

"How can stress inhibit conception?" asks Dr. Alice Domar, a psychologist who specializes in human infertility. "We're not sure. But we know that stress can definitely impact ovulation, stress can cause tubal spasms, and we know that stress can impair sperm production. That's about as much as we know right now."[5]

Professor Robert Chatterton adds, "New mothers who have premature infants often have difficulty with lactation and we know that stress is one of the factors that inhibits milk let down."[6]

---

4. Marlene Dobkin de Rios, *Hallucinogens – Cross Cultural Perspectives,* (University of New Mexico Press, 1984), p.107.
5. Dateline NBC 6/4/96.
6. WROC News, Rochester, NY 6/11/97.

Dr. Domar discovered evidence of a link between stress and infertility. To further define this connection the National Institute of Mental Health is funding a five year study headed by Domar. So far the studies suggest that the hypothalamus, the master gland of the brain that controls reproduction, is the organ affected by stress. And earlier studies have identified structural differences in the hypothalamus between gay men and heterosexual men.

In 1991, prior to Dean Hamer's breakthrough, neurobiologist Simon Lavey completed a study of brain structure in nineteen gay males. Lavey discovered that a portion of the hypothalamus, the part of the brain responsible for sex drive, is smaller in gay men than in heterosexual men. This was the first time that science had identified biological differences that distinguish homosexual men from heterosexual men. But at Harvard University, neurobiologist Evan Balaban cast doubts, saying that Levay's study was "really not up to the standard that you would want to be able to accept the conclusions." Balaban argued that structural differences in the hypothalamus might result from something as simple as "stress levels" among the men.[7]

But could it be that nature accomplishes "birth control" when a society gets so stressed it produces a new generation that numbers many non-reproducers – gay people – instilled by nature with an innate tendency not to multiply? This is the *purpose* of homosexuality: intended to avert births, nature's *herd thinners*. Humans have a built in biological monitor which senses when the herd needs thinning and automatically adjusts the rate of reproduction through the number of gays being born.

Dr. Domar's research has revealed that of 284 women who tried unsuccessfully for an average of 3 years to get pregnant, 42% conceived shortly after completing a program of anti-stress relaxation techniques.[8] Stress is always present at various levels among all people at any given time. During bad times we struggle and our stress increases. Our bodies respond to stress and something in us, possibly genetic, changes so that we conceive kids who are gay and tend not to have children of their own. Population is thus lowered according to nature's plan. It's as if our bodies are programmed to interpret stress as a signal to thin the herd. This is not to imply that, as homosexuals, we are the result of a "malady" or something gone "wrong" with people who are stressed. On the contrary, herd thinners are very *helpful* to humans and the environment.

In 1995 human population grew by 100 million people to a record 5.75 billion, the largest increase ever. (In October 1999 it hit six billion.) Ninety percent of this growth was in poor countries. In December of 1995 the Population Institute announced: "Some three billion young people will be entering their reproductive years in this coming generation. How well these young people are able to implement the awesome responsibility of parenting will make the difference between our setting course for an environmental Armageddon in the 21st century or a better quality of life."[9]

---

7. McNeil/Lehrer News Hour, PBS 7/93.

8. Dateline NBC 6/4/96.

9. *Population Grows at Record Pace,* Associated Press 12/28/95.

SUSCEPTIBLE—BORN WITH PREDISPOSED *TENDENCY*

> *What we found is that one specific region of one chromosome is linked to*
> *homosexuality at least in some men, and what that demonstrates is that part*
> *of being gay, or part of being straight, is determined in the genes ... We found*
> *a linkage between sexual orientation in men and a small genetic segment of*
> *the X chromosome. What our data suggests is that whether a person is gay or*
> *heterosexual depends at least in part on the genes that they inherit.*
>
> – Dr. Dean Hamer[10]

Hamer studied forty pairs of gay brothers. Two thirds of them had the same type of genetic material along the same section of the X chromosome. A male born with such genes is twice as likely to be homosexual. He is not one hundred percent certain to turn out gay because a third of the brothers in Hamer's study did not share the genetic markers and yet were gay anyway. "[The scientists] don't see [the material] in every gay man," reports Richard Harris. "They find it in some of the brothers who are not gay, so it's not exclusively a homosexual thing . . . There's not going to be a 'gay gene' . . . because even with identical twins, one is gay and one is not, so you know that homosexuality is not 100% genetic at all. It is genes interacting with other things . . . but this is perhaps susceptibility . . . if they can find a gene . . . maybe it's a gene that tells the body about hormone balance or maybe it's a gene that has some other function that we can't even guess right now."[11]

Maybe it's function is to respond to stress. If homosexuality is influenced by genetics, then some aspect of the genetic process may be affected by stress. But a hundred different people experience stress in a hundred different ways. Some couples, following just one prolonged period of stress, may affect their biology enough to produce a gay child. Other people might endure many times more stress before they will conceive gay offspring. And a parent may respond to stress differently during different phases of life; whereas mild stress may trigger the gay trait from a 20-year-old parent, more intense stress might be needed to activate it in that same parent at age 30. In other words, the biological *threshold* for stress, beyond which is triggered gay offspring, fluctuates up and down not only from person to person, but also from time to time in us all.

> *There are definitely inherited characteristics which are very important . . .*
> *homosexuality is not simply determined by some single gene in the same*
> *simple sort of way that, for example, your eye color is determined by one*
> *gene . . . There may be other genes or other factors or perhaps even voluntary*
> *sorts of factors that are involved. What's important today is that we clearly*

---

10. ABC News Nightline 7/15/93.
11. News Hour with Jim Lehrer, PBS 10/31/95.

> *demonstrated that genes are involved . . . The important question is whether*
> *or not there's a defined genetic component and if we can ultimately*
> *understand how that works.*   – Dr. Dean Hamer[12]

The gay trait may be triggered by some alteration to DNA in a father, or by something that happens biologically to a mother. Dr. Michael Bailey studies the genetics of twins and reports, "I found in several studies that identical twins are more similar in their sexual orientations than fraternal twins and this suggests that genes are at least partially the story, but they can't be the whole story because we often have identical twins who have different sexual orientations, and that can only happen for environmental reasons. In many cases the environment does seem to matter. But I want to emphasize that the environment begins at conception: there is a biological environment and a pre-natal environment, and science has shown that, for example, we can alter the sexuality of animals and even humans by, for example, pre-natal hormones. So identical twins may be different in their sexuality due to things that happen early in development."[13]

"If environments could create heterosexuals, we'd all be heterosexual," says science journalist Chandler Burr. "When scientists say 'environment' they are talking about, in this case, non-genetic, but biological factors. Something can be 'non-genetic,' but can be purely *biological*. [Dr. Bailey's] study has given about a 50% concordance for twins, showing that 50% of the twins are going to share the same sexual orientation, and 50% are not. You know what the concordance is for left handedness? Twelve percent. You know what the concordance is for auto-immune diabetes? Thirty percent. Both of them well under the concordance for homosexuality, which suggests, if anything, that there's actually a larger genetic component to homosexuality than there is to either left handedness or auto-immune diabetes."[14]

Stress caused by events in our environment alters the reproductive process in humans. If both parents are altered by stress, gay offspring may result. If one parent, and not the other, has been changed by stress, a bisexual child may be conceived. The degree to which an offspring becomes homosexual, heterosexual or bisexual is determined by the combined stress level of both parents. But all such ratios exist in flux because people are born who break the mold. Some contented, unstressed people might trigger the gay trait for other reasons, but such instances are likely exceptions to the rule.

Evidence that stress levels determine sexuality is seen in increased numbers of circumcisions in recent decades. In the 1940s, Menlitta Schmideberg theorized that "circumcision is an important factor in the development of . . . homosexuality."[15] Is it more likely that homosexuals are key to the rise in circumcisions? Gay men and straight women are the two groups most concerned with whether or not a penis has a foreskin.

---

12. ABC News Nightline 7/15/93.
13. Oprah Winfrey Show, CBS 5/5/97.
14. Ibid.
15. Nicholas Carter, *Routine Circumcision – the Tragic Myth*, p.91.

And there has been an increased population percentage of gay men (including homosexuals who pretend to be straight) in recent centuries. As the industrial age brought ever higher levels of stress to working people, a resulting rise in the number of gay men has increased the demand for circumcisions.

Today's society is extremely stressed. A much larger population of herd thinners is being born. Because there are more gay men today – most of whom prefer a bare glans – circumcision is now nearly universal. "Prior to the turn of the century," notes Carter, "circumcision was a rare operation in America, occurring in only 6.8 percent of the better class families in the urban areas, and even less among those born on farms. From 1900 to 1910 the number of operations increased until an estimated 18.6 percent of white gentiles were circumcised. It was still confined primarily to urban males from the upper classes. The trend continued until 1930 . . . with the rate of the operations reaching twenty percent or more during this period. During the early 1930s, the increase in surgical circumcision began the sharp upward spiral that was to carry it to nearly universal acceptance in the United States."[16]

The rise of industrialized urban life in the 20th century brought with it a great increase in stress among city dwellers. Our high anxiety lifestyles have resulted in an explosion of homosexual progeny. Events like the Great Depression of the 1930s and World War II in the '40s produced millions of conceptions under conditions of prolonged stress. Many of the boys conceived during this period grew up to become gay men. Today, circumcised cocks are in demand more than ever before. The increase of stress in America is paralleled by an increase in circumcisions. "Routine circumcision skyrocketed from a mere 6 percent to nearly 100 percent in little more than 50 years," reports Carter.[17] Did an increase in homosexual/bisexual men create a social climate in which routine circumcision is preferred? Today's population of men are mostly free of foreskins (and more appealing to the majority of gay men who prefer the "cut" look).

Widespread circumcision is evidence of an increase in numbers of gay men. Overpopulation produces increased stress in our lives. Homosexuals are nature's corrective defense against extinction, because without herd thinners, population will increase unchecked until our numbers consume all resources. Benefits from herd thinners have been recognized by many societies throughout history.

> *The two centuries during which [Greek] pederasty was in fashion were also the finest period of Classical achievement. If homosexuality had been kept underground, it might be argued that the magnificence of Athenian art and architecture was a sublimation . . . In Sparta, on the Greek island of Euboea, and in the Boeotian city of Thebes, [homosexuality] was directly associated*

16. Ibid. p.27.
17. Ibid. p.132.

> *with success in war. As Plato said . . . 'A handful of lovers and loved ones,*
> *fighting shoulder to shoulder, could rout a whole army . . . ' The famous*
> *Sacred Battalion of Thebes was entirely composed of pairs of lovers. One*
> *study of modern tribes (made in 1952) showed that two-thirds of them*
> *considered adolescent homosexuality as normal and acceptable, and other*
> *researchers have found it institutionalized among the Cubeo on the*
> *Amazon, and the Mohaves and Zuni, among others, in North America.*
> — Reay Tannahill[18]

Same-sex attraction occurs so naturally that in some cultures homosexual behavior is celebrated as the *primary* way of life. For example, the Sambia tribe in New Guinea's highlands is known for its warriors. Young boys are removed from the softening influence of their mothers to be toughened and trained by older males. Initiation rites include teaching the boys that true masculinity is acquired by drinking semen. The Sambia tribesmen believe that all things feminine weaken a man, and mother's milk is replaced by semen to nourish the future warriors. The men and the boys of the tribe maintain gay relations with one another throughout their lives. They engage in heterosexual intercourse only to reproduce.[19]

Similarly, in northern Peru there existed the Mochica Indians, a civilization renowned for its art. Marlene Dobkin de Rios reports, "None of the Mochica art shows any practice that would lead to insemination and subsequent childbirth . . . only anal intercourse is shown . . . 17th century Catholic priests found sodomic practices prevalent and had instructions from Rome to extirpate such 'ungodly' acts. Yet it may be that the representation of sodomy in the religious art of a people (and most art in non-Western societies is linked to religious beliefs and rituals) may be seen as an important mechanism for spacing births in areas where seasonal fluctuations in rainfall, food harvests, available fish resources, and so on, can be crucial. Throughout the world, limitations in the carrying capacity of a given environment have demanded from people cultural as well as biological responses. Postpartum sexual abstention of up to three years is a generally cited worldwide average, to ensure that a nursing infant will not die because of malnutrition when his mother becomes pregnant again and another baby displaces him at the breast. Sodomy can be viewed as still another cultural mechanism to achieve spacing of births."[20]

Gays are nature's gentle way of decreasing populations during periods when an environment is losing its capacity to nourish the numbers of people that inhabit it. If too many people struggle under stress in that environment, many will conceive gay offspring and reduce their numbers as these homosexuals have no children. The reduced human population thus decreases its strain on the environment. Nature intends this to allow environments time to replenish themselves, which in turn supports more life.

---

18. Tannahill, *Sex In History,* pp.90, 92, 292.
19. *The Opposite Sex,* A&E 3/95.
20. Dobkin de Rios, *Hallucinogens – Cross Cultural Perspectives,* p.107.

Although modern science allows lesbians to reproduce via artificial insemination, and technology supports today's overpopulated planet, the *purpose* and *intent* behind nature's creation of gays was and is as a way of thinning the herd when food and relaxation are scarce. In this sense, it can be said that nature *intends* gays as a remedy for overpopulation.

> *Biologists are interested in this biological trait. This is a fascinating trait from a biological perspective and it's going to teach us a hell of a lot about the way that genes and molecules and the endocrine system comes out and creates us as human beings. That is why biologists are researching it.*
>
> — Chandler Burr[21]

---

21. Oprah Winfrey Show, CBS 5/5/97.

Chapter 10: Genesis Edits

꒳

As human populations stretch the limits of our planet's capacity to support us, homosexuality is a natural answer meant to benefit our species. God *did* create "Adam and Steve." The Creation story of *Adamas* was preserved by churches in ancient Greece, it is one of the many gospels deleted and excluded from the official Bible. This gay Creation myth is described by Hippolytus (170-236 C.E.), he writes of "the Naassenes, who are so called after the Hebrew language, in which 'naas' is the word for the serpent. But after this they call themselves Gnostics, alleging that they alone 'knew the deep things' (Rev. 2:24)."[1]

> *These men, according to their own doctrine, reverence beyond all others Man and the Son of Man. Now this man is bisexual and is called by them Adamas . . . the intercourse of women with man is in their teaching shown to be most wicked and prohibited . . . 'men, giving up natural intercourse with women, have been inflamed with passion for one another; men behaving shamelessly with men' – and shamelessness for them is primal, blessed, formless [semen], which is the cause of all forms in the things that are formed – 'and receiving in themselves the due reward of their error' (Rom 1:20-7). For these words spoken by Paul, they say, contain the whole secret and unspeakable mystery of blessed enjoyment. For the promise of the washing (in baptism) is, they say, nothing less than the introduction into unfading enjoyment of him who in their fashion is washed in living water and anointed with unutterable [semen] anointing . . . the Samothracians clearly commemorate the same Adam, the primal man, in the mysteries performed among them. And there are two statues standing in the Samothracians' temple, statues of naked men, having both hands stretched upwards towards heaven and their male members turned upwards, like the statue of Hermes in Cyllene. And these statues which I have described are images of the primal man and of the spiritual man who is reborn, essentially the same in all respects with that of (primal) man.*
>
> – Hippolytus[2]

---

1. *Gnosis – A Selection of Gnostic Texts* (Oxford University Press, 1969), p.263.
2. Ibid. pp.263-7, 272.

What happened to these lost chapters from the Bible? Who destroyed the testaments of the Naassenes and the Samothracians? John Romer explains that in the decade after the death of Jesus, "there was a multiplicity of churches, of teachings, of holy books; it was a world with no clear Christian creed, no single body of accepted truth and no New Testament. This book, like the faith itself, was still a soup with many exotic ingredients – a mixture that went right back to the church's early years . . . these churches still lacked 'orthodox' identity."[3]

Jerusalem was destroyed by Roman troops forty years after Jesus died. No New Testament gospels are known to have existed prior to the destruction. The Roman Jewish War from 66-70 C.E. is the violent trauma that inflamed the person(s) who wrote the first story of Jesus, later titled the Gospel of Mark. That story was the blockbuster hit of its time around the Mediterranean, inspiring hundreds of spin-offs for many decades. "Matthew," "Luke," and "John" are titles given to just three of the sequels. The gospels written by churches of the Naassenes and Samothracians were among the many spin-offs inspired by the Gospel of Mark.

The Roman Jewish War also compelled the leaders of Judaism to compile a list of Hebrew books to include in the Old Testament. The "Bible" did not exist prior to this time.[4] The priests of Judaea decided what texts would make up their book. "They obviously had no trouble with the Book of Kings and the Book of Judges," notes Romer. "These great books automatically could not but be included in the cannon of religious texts. But there were later books that caused much more problems. The book of Esther, for example, had been written by a woman, that was a bit doggy in itself, so they cut it in half and kicked half out . . . In fact there's quite a collection of [books] that went out . . . You don't have any proper record of what went on. What you have is dozens and dozens of marvelous stories, especially of the rabbis that seemed to dominate the proceedings . . . So it's through these legendary debates that the Bible has come down to us today, through men."[5]

Much of what we know about Palestine during this period comes from the writings of Flavius Josephus, the Jewish historian, especially his *Antiquities*. But in the decades and centuries after Josephus published his studies, later copies of it were altered. "There are sentences in it that could hardly have been written by a Jewish writer," notes John Crossan, "sentences that assert Christian beliefs, sentences that could only have been written by a Christian believer. Remember that Josephus' works were preserved and copied by Christian rather than Jewish editors; such additions would have been easy to insert . . . [Josephus] was cautiously impartial and some later Christian editor delicately Christianized his account."[6]

The history of biblical texts is fraught with editorial tamperings. "We know only what later churches wanted to tell us," writes Romer, "and this is also true of the beginnings of the Gospels."[7]

---

3. Romer, *Testament*, p.196.
4. *Who Wrote the Bible?*, A&E 3/95.
5. Romer, *Testament*, PBS 10/91.
6. Crossan, *Historical Jesus*, pp.161-2.
7. Romer, *Testament*, p.188.

Canon is a term derived from the Greek word *kanon*, meaning rules or guidelines. A century and a half after Jesus died, his followers began to debate and argue about which gospels to include in, and which to exclude from, the "official" canon of the faith. "The four gospels collected into the New Testament were canonized around 200 C.E.," writes Elaine Pagels, ". . . they were chosen not necessarily because they were the earliest or the most accurate accounts of Jesus' life and teaching but precisely because they could form the basis for church communities."[8] The men who chose the stories were looking for writings that justified a certain *type* of community.

In the year 177 C.E., a man in Lyons, France named Irenaeus (130-202 C.E.) reasoned that, because he had been a friend of Polycarp, who had known the Apostle John, he was therefore possessed by the authority of "apostolic succession." Irenaeus declared himself a "bishop" whose right it was to dictate beliefs to people who worshiped Jesus. But dissenters protested. They called themselves *Gnostics*, derived from the Greek word *gnosis*, which means knowledge. *A*gnostic refers to those who regard ultimate reality as unknowable. Gnostic refers to those who *know*.

But Irenaeus had an imaginative plan with which to influence the congregation at Lyons. He invented the term "New Testament" to designate writings that, like the Book of Moses, were the word of God and therefore belonged in a book along with the Old Testament. He drew up a list of the gospels that reflected his prejudices and declared that all other gospels were the work of "heretics" – a Greek word for "one who makes a choice." No "choices" were to be made under Irenaeus. His plan of propaganda aimed to sanction only heterosexual men, and condemn the rest, especially women and gays. Like Paul of Tarsus, Irenaeus understood the value of denigrating sex; he understood that condemning flesh automatically disfavors women and gays. He therefore warned that those who oppose him "yield themselves up to lusts of the flesh with utmost greed."[9] Iranaeus began a crusade to see that all sacred writings favoring women and gays be banned as *heresy*.

"The gospels he endorsed helped institutionalize the Christian movement," writes Pagels. "Those he denounced as heresy did not serve the purposes of institutionalization. Some, on the contrary, urged people to seek direct access to God, unmediated by church or clergy."[10] Irenaeus advanced an interpretation of Jesus which "legitimized a hierarchy of persons through whose authority all others must approach God. Gnostic teaching, as Irenaeus and Tertullian realized, was potentially subversive of this order: it claimed to offer to every initiate direct access to God of which the priests and bishops themselves might be ignorant."[11]

Irenaeus told sinners to pay tribute to his church in order to get to heaven. But for doing this same thing, moneychangers in the Jerusalem Temple were cursed by Jesus. "Jesus promised redemption from earthly sin," writes Romer, "not by the orthodox Jewish method of making offerings at the Jerusalem Temple, but by the simple gesture of

---

8. Pagels, *The Origin of Satan*, p.65

9. Ibid. p.155.

10. Ibid. p.70.

11. Pagels, *Gnostic Gospels*, p.27.

genuine personal repentance. The acceptance of God was signified not by an expensive journey to Jerusalem and an offering to the Temple but . . . by baptism in the free-flowing waters . . . an internal act of will and faith . . . Most ancient kings raised revenues through taxation which was often called an offering to the state gods. In Jerusalem also the elaborate system of Temple offerings was central to the fiscal power of the state. By proposing the redemption of sin outside the Temple and its system of offerings, both Jesus and John [the Baptist] not only denied the spiritual efficiency of the priests but also hit at the source of their wealth."[12]

A century and a half after the Temple priests plotted to kill Jesus for promoting free redemption, another group of priests under Irenaeus ordered everyone in Lyons to pay tribute to *them* to get to Jesus! "Whoever refuses to 'bow the neck' and obey the church leaders is guilty of insubordination against the divine master himself," writes Pagels, noting that Irenaeus divided the clergy into ranks of bishops, priests and deacons "as a hierarchical order that mirrors the divine hierarchy in heaven. As there is only one God in heaven . . . so there can be only one bishop in the church. 'One God, one bishop' – this became the orthodox slogan . . . 'the laity' [is warned] to revere, honor, and obey the bishop 'as if he were God.'"[13]

"Gnostic Christians, on the contrary, assert that what distinguishes the false from the true church is not its relationship to the clergy," explains Pagels, "but the level of understanding of its members, and the quality of their relationship with one another . . . they neither attempt to dominate others nor do they subject themselves to the bishops and deacons."[14] Followers of Irenaeus proposed the death penalty for anyone who disobeys the leaders of the church. But the Gnostics resisted hierarchy. "*Gnosis* offers nothing less than a theological justification for refusing to obey the bishops and priests!" observes Pagels. "All who had received *gnosis*, they say, had gone beyond the church's teachings and had transcended the authority of its hierarchy . . . They celebrated every form of creative invention as evidence that a person has become spiritually alive. On this theory, the structure of authority can never be fixed into an institutional framework: it must remain spontaneous, charismatic, and open."[15]

Romer points out, "The Gnostics believed that the church itself was a device of the devil, made to keep man from God and from realizing his true nature . . . They preached as confidently as did Paul, who also had never seen Jesus, and they felt secure enough in their understanding of the true religion to claim their faith as divine."[16]

The Gnostics, persecuted and martyred under Irenaeus, preserved and protected the *best* Christian literature – the gospels that the bishop sought to destroy. "Instead of describing a monistic and masculine God, many of these texts speak of God as a dyad who embraces both masculine and feminine elements," explains Pagels. "Among such

12. Romer, *Testament*, p.172.
13. Pagels, *Gnostic Gospels*, pp.34-5.
14. Ibid. p.106.
15. Ibid. pp.38, 25.
16. Romer, *Testament*, PBS 10/91.

Gnostic groups as the Valentinians, women were considered equal to men; some were revered as prophets; others acted as teachers, traveling evangelists, healers, priests, perhaps even bishops."[17]

"This is Christian literature seen through thousands of years of religious experience," adds Romer, "interpretations of Jesus, not straight forward Christianity . . . We get a wondrous poem that tells us that God is actually a woman, the poem is called *The Thunder: Perfect Mind*."[18]

> *I am the whore and the holy one. I am the wife and the virgin. I am the*
> *mother and the daughter. I am the members of my mother. I am the barren*
> *one and many are her sons. I am she whose wedding is great, and I have not*
> *taken a husband . . .*   *– The Thunder: Perfect Mind*

"Bishop Irenaeus notes with dismay that women especially are attracted to heretical groups," writes Pagels. "What concerns the bishop . . . is the enormous appeal that Valentinian teaching had for women believers, who were increasingly excluded during the second century from active participation in Irenaeus's church . . . by the late second century, the orthodox community came to accept the domination of men over women as the divinely ordained order – not only for social and family life, but also for the Christian churches . . . Every one of the secret texts which Gnostic groups revered was omitted from the canonical collection, and branded as heretical by those who called themselves orthodox Christians. By the time the process of sorting the various writings ended – probably as late as the year 200 – virtually all feminine imagery for God had disappeared from orthodox Christian tradition."[19]

> *[The] four gospels do not represent all the early gospels available or even a*
> *random sample within them but are instead a calculated collection known as*
> *the canonical gospels...The existence of such **other** gospels means that the*
> *canonical foursome is a spectrum of approved interpretation forming a strong*
> *central vision that was later able to render apocryphal, hidden, or censored,*
> *any other gospels too far off its right or left wing.*   *– John Crossan*[20]

"From the year 200, we have no evidence for women taking prophetic, priestly, and episcopal roles among orthodox churches," continues Pagels. "This is an extraordinary development, considering that in its earliest years the Christian movement showed a remarkable openness toward women. Jesus himself violated Jewish convention by talking openly with women, and he included them among his companions . . . Some ten to twenty

17. Pagels, *Gnostic Gospels*, pp.49, 60.
18. Romer, *Testament*, PBS 10/91.
19. Pagels, *Gnostic Gospels*, pp.59, 66, 57, *The Origin of Satan*, 170.
20. John Dominic Crossan, *Jesus – A Revolutionary Biography*, (San Francisco: Harper, 1994), pp.x-xi.

years after Jesus' death, certain women acted as prophets, teachers, and evangelists . . . [But] by the end of the second century, women's participation in worship was explicitly condemned: groups in which women continued on to leadership were branded as heretical."[21]

SECRET MARK – HETEROSEXUAL REVISION

Women and gays were excluded. Groups of them struggled to protect their condemned gospels.

> *These secret sects wrote and wrote and wrote . . . They were starting to write Christian literature in with all this other strange stuff that's going on . . . and so you get a most extraordinary body of literature going on – you get twelve gospels, one of them tells us that Jesus was gay.*   – John Romer[22]

Of the four gospels in the New Testament, the Gospel of Mark was the first to be written. But the version that appears in our modern Bible has been edited. Originally, between verses 10:34 and 35 and after 10:46a, scenes were included which depict "the sacred homosexuality of baptismal eroticism."[23] This deleted text was rediscovered in 1958 at the Monastery of Mar Saba in a letter that Clement of Alexandria had written to "Theodore" 150 years after Jesus died. Theodore had inquired of Clement about the Gospel of the Carpocratians in which Jesus conducts baptismals "naked man with naked man." Clement's letter of reply to Theodore reproduces passages from the original Gospel of Mark that the Carpocratians questioned, passages that the early Church deleted from the Bible and kept "secret" until 1958:

> *Jesus, being angered, went off with her into the garden where the tomb was, and straightway a great cry was heard from the tomb. And going near, Jesus rolled away the stone from the door of the tomb. And straightway, going in where the youth was, he stretched forth his hand and raised him, seizing his hand. But the youth, looking upon him, loved him and began to beseech him that he might be with him. And going out of the tomb they came into the house of the youth, for he was rich. And after six days Jesus told him what to do and in the evening the youth comes to him, wearing a linen cloth over his naked body. And he remained with him that night, for Jesus taught him the mystery of the Kingdom of God. And thence, arising, he returned to the other side of the Jordan . . . And he comes into Jericho. And the sister of the youth whom Jesus loved and his mother and Salome were there, and Jesus did not receive them.*
> – The Complete Gospels (HarperSanFrancisco, 1994), p.411.

---

21. Pagels, *Gnostic Gospels,* pp.60-61, 63.
22. Romer, *Testament,* PBS 10/91.
23. Crossan, *Historical Jesus*, p.330.

The Secret Gospel of Mark was written forty years after Jesus died, but then, Crossan points out, "the second version of Mark . . . the Gospel of Mark . . . expurgated those passages . . . canonical Mark is a censored version of Secret Mark . . . that censorship not only excised the story, it dismembered it."[24] Crossan notes that the original version was likely read during nude baptismal rituals of early Christians "and thereby received an erotic interpretation among some believers. The second-century Carpocratians . . . were not . . . the only or even the first early Christians with homosexual understandings of such baptisms . . . it could easily – very, very easily – be interpreted along the lines of sacred sexuality and even homosexual intimacy as initiation ritual. It was such an interpretation that necessitated the drastic textual dismemberment . . . as Helmut Koester put it, 'Canonical Mark is derived from Secret Mark . . . 'canonical' Mark was a purified version of that 'secret' Gospel . . .' Koester is surely correct that 'textual critics of the New Testament writings have been surprisingly naive' in presuming that our earliest Markan manuscripts accurately reflect their autographical archetype."[25]

The Secret Gospel of Mark, with its homoerotic scenes, was the original story that early Christians learned during baptismal rituals. "Second century bishops writing of these secret Gospels say that they were only to be shown to initiates," notes Romer. "One passages describes Jesus taking naked young men off to secret initiation rites in the Garden of Gethsemene, rites that could be duplicated in the underground lodges of the Gnostics[26] . . . Early Christians would take up even very special diets. They thought that food itself was divided into good and evil, into light and dark, so you'd only eat good food, light food, drink white wine. Cucumbers were very fashionable food . . . it would go through your body and the wicked sin will come out as excrement, and the light will come out in orgasm, as semen. So your lusty Christians, and lots of them were doing this, were having orgiastic rituals in their churches: drinking of semen, anointing statues and each other with it as part of a love of God itself. That's a very shocking idea to modern Christians."[27]

Bishop Epiphanius of Salamis (315-403 C.E.) wrote a book called *Panarion* which describes the beliefs and rituals of these early, persecuted Christians:

> *[Barbelo] always appears to the Archons in beauty and takes from them their seed through pleasure (causing) its emission, in order that by so doing she may recover again her own power that was inseminated into those various beings . . . Others honor a certain Prunicus . . . they say, 'We are collecting the power of Prunicus from bodies by their fluids' – which means the semen and the periods. . . What was taken from the Mother on high . . . must be collected from the power that is in bodies, through the emissions of men and women . . . they give themselves over to passion. For the husband withdraws from his wife,*

24. Ibid. pp.430, 329.
25.   "   pp.412-413.
26. Romer, *Testament*, p.196.
27. Romer, *Testament*, PBS 10/91.

and says these words to his own wife: 'Rise up, make the love (feast) with the brother.' And when the wretches have had intercourse out of passion of fornication, then, holding up their own blasphemy before heaven, the woman and the man take the mans emission in their own hands, and stand there looking up towards heaven. And while they have uncleanness [semen] in their hands they (profess to) pray, the so-called Stratiotici and Gnostics, offering to the natural Father of the Universe that which is in their hands, and saying 'We offer thee this gift, the body of Christ.' And so they eat it, partaking of their own shame and saying, 'This is the body of Christ, and this is the Passover; hence our bodies are given over to passion and compelled to confess the passion of Christ.' Similarly with the woman's emission at her period, they collect the menstrual blood which is unclean, take it and eat it together, and say 'This is the blood of Christ.' For this reason when they read in the apocryphal writings: 'I saw a tree which bears twelve fruits each year, and he said to me, 'This is the tree of life,' they allegorize this to refer to the woman's monthly emission . . . They have their pleasure, and take for themselves their seed which is unclean, not implanting it for the bearing of children, but themselves eating the shameful thing . . . they pray to God and say, 'We have not been deceived by the Archon of lust, but we have retrieved our brother's transgressions.' And this they consider the perfect passover. And they have other outrageous practices. When they are excited to madness they moisten their own hands with the shamefulness of their own emissions and get up and with their own hands thus polluted they pray with their whole bodies naked, as if by such a practice they could gain free access to God. And they tend their bodies night and day, the contemptible objects, both women and men, they anoint themselves, wash themselves, feast themselves, devoting themselves to bedding and drinking . . . and they say that this is what is spoken in the Gospel . . . 'When you see the Son of Man coming up where he was before' (John 6:62) means the emission which is taken up to the place from which it came, saying, 'Unless you eat my flesh and drink my blood' (John 6:53)…And when David says, 'He shall be as a tree that is planted by the springs of the waters, which shall give forth its fruit in due season' (Ps. 1:3), he refers, he says, to the male member. 'By the water-springs' and 'which shall give forth its fruit' refers, he says, to the emission with its pleasure, and 'his leaf shall not fall,' because, he says, we do not allow it to drop upon the ground, but eat it ourselves . . . Some of them do not consort with women, but corrupt themselves with their own hands, and they take their own corruption in their hands, and so eat it, using a falsified proof-text, namely, 'These hands were sufficient, not only for me but for those with me' (Acts 20:34), and again: 'Working with your own hands, so that you may have something to share with those who have nothing' (Eph. 4:28) . . . For those who corrupt themselves with their own hands, and not only they, but also those who consort with women, since they are not satiated with their promiscuous

> *intercourse with women, are inflamed towards one another, men with men, as it is written (Rom. 1:27) . . . For these, who are utterly abandoned, congratulate each other, as if they had received the choicest distinction . . . The more infamous a man is in his conduct among them, the more he is honored among them, too. And they give the name of 'virgin' to women who . . . are constantly copulating and fornicating, but before their pleasure finds its natural outcome let go the wicked corrupter of their intercourse and take the aforesaid indecency to be eaten . . . they say there is a book called 'The Birth of Mary' into which they made outrageous and depraved interpolations . . . Those who among them who are called Levites do not have intercourse with women, but with each other. And it is these who are actually distinguished and honored among them.*
> — Epiphanius[28]

It is ironic that such early Christian traditions – as described above from Epiphanius sixteen hundred years ago, and consistent with the long lost Secret Gospel of Mark – are today considered the *opposite* of what Jesus represents. Ironic because it is likely that the original Jesus movement was heavily homosexual, and Jesus stories were then "revised" by heterosexual men decades later. But still, the outline of Jesus' story suggests a personality prone to *homosexual panic*: "He demanded that those who follow him must give up everything – family, home, children, ordinary work, wealth – to join him," writes Pagels. "And he himself, as prototype, was a homeless man who rejected his own family, avoided marriage and family life, a mysterious wanderer who insisted on truth at all costs, even the cost of his own life. Mark relates that Jesus concealed his teachings from the masses and entrusted it only to the few he considered worthy to receive it."[29]

Outside the walls of Jerusalem, Jesus revealed his secrets in the Garden of *Get semen e*. Following the Roman Jewish War, the followers of Jesus wrote down his story, including the gay scenes. Biblical scholars agree that the Gospel of Mark contains the source material from which the gospels of "Matthew" and "Luke" were derived. But Crossan points out, "Agreements of Matthew and Luke against Mark cannot automatically be taken as evidence for their Markan source . . . coincidental redaction by both of them must be weighed against later corruption in the Markan tradition . . . I take it for granted that [Helmut] Koester is quite correct on the inevitability of such scribal corruption [changes in text] . . . both Matthew and Luke . . . did not . . . like Mark as a narrative Gospel. They rewrote it and would probably be very surprised to find it today wedged in between them. The more Markan something is . . . the more likely Matthew and Luke are to change it . . . The young mans raising and naked initiation . . . led, I presume immediately, to erotic interpretations . . . It was not enough simply to excise the offending passage from a new 'edition' of Mark. Opponents already had the fuller text and could easily prove, however we are to imagine

28. *Gnosis – A Selection of Gnostic Texts* (Oxford University Press, 1969), pp.316-24.
29. Pagels, *Gnostic Gospels*, p 148.

such a textual war, that they were right in their interpretation since they were right in their text. The solution . . . was not only to remove the offending text but to scatter its dismembered parts throughout the Markan Gospel. Thereafter, its presence in any version of Mark could be counterclaimed as pastiche from such residue . . . redoing the ending of Mark became a small industry in the early church."[30]

> *We must learn to consider the gospels of the New Testament canon, in the form in which they existed before 180 C.E., in the same light in which we consider the apocrypha. At this earlier time the gospels were what the apocrypha never ceased to be. Like the apocrypha, the gospels of the New Testament were not yet canonical; they did not circulate together . . . and when they did, they did not always appear in the same sequence.* — Francois Brown[31]

Early Christian writers, who edited the letters ascribed to "Paul," not only removed homoerotic stories, they turned Paul of Tarsus into the *antigay*, obsessed by homophobia. Jimi Hendrix tells us that the gospels writers "*twisted so many of the best things*" that Jesus said,[32] and evidence of scribal tampering with New Testament texts is plentiful. For example, Jesus never condemned homosexuality. Antigay thoughts appear only in letters from Paul, who never met Jesus and never heard his sermons. Paul is described as a persecutor of Christians until he joined the Jesus movement and began putting words in Jesus' mouth. "Paul" is a rewriting of the legend of Christ into a version that became our modern Bible, and this rewrite carries prejudiced edits against women and gays.

"Paul used a secretary," explains professor of religion David Barr. "Dictation had already been invented . . . a system of shorthand [to] take down notes and then transcribe them, and it's clear that Paul used that because in a couple of letters [the secretary] adds things at the end . . . in one of his letters one of his scribes . . . adds his greeting to Paul's greeting [Rom. 16:22]. Ancient authorship is more of a community concept than an individual concept, and so a disciple could write in the master's name and still believe he's doing the master's work. Plato, for example, wrote all his dialogue as if Socrates were speaking, but in fact it's Plato's work, not Socrates that we're hearing."[33]

The authors of "Paul" transform Paul of Tarsus from a brutalizer of Christians into a persecutor of women and gays. "Writing to the various congregations as he traveled," writes Pagels, "Paul sometimes invoked a 'saying of the Lord.' Once he invoked Jesus' authority to prohibit divorce (I Cor. 7:10)."[34] The authors of the story use Paul as a mouthpiece for Jesus. Words of the antigay, ascribed to Paul, are the only editorials against homosexuals inserted

30. Crossan, *Historical Jesus*, pp.412-416.
31. Ibid. p.425.
32. Melody Maker 3/1/69.
33. *Who Wrote the Bible?*, A&E 3/95.
34. Pagels, *The Origin of Satan*, p.66.

into the New Testament. But Paul had nothing to do with Jesus. Antigay rantings in letters ascribed to Paul proclaim the opposite of what Jesus preached. Early Christians who quoted gospels about Jesus' ministry to gays are attacked by "Paul" as being "false apostles, deceptive workers, disguising themselves as apostles of Christ" (2 Cor. 11:13), which, of course, is just what the writers of "Paul" are.

The reputation of Jesus was changed in the years following his death. Opportunists, like those who wrote "Paul," crawled out of the woodwork claiming to have been in direct communication with the famous man from Nazareth. The writings of "Paul" inspired a second generation of self-appointed "apostles" who inserted their own words and prejudices into early church literature. A century and a half later, Irenaeus, Bishop of Lyons, had more than enough manuscripts from which to edit various versions of Jesus' story. Among the manuscripts, the gospels that favored women and gays were suppressed. As Pagels points out, "What Jesus actually taught often became a matter of bitter dispute, as we can see from the Gospel of Mary Magdalene . . . [which] depicts Mary Magdalene among the disciples – indeed, as one of Jesus' most beloved disciples, to whom he entrusted secret teachings . . . Mary admits to Jesus that she hardly dares to speak to [Peter] freely because, in her words, 'Peter makes me hesitate; I am afraid of him, because he hates the female race.' [*Pistis Sophia* 36:71] Jesus replies that whoever the Spirit inspires is divinely ordained to speak, whether man or woman. Orthodox Christians retaliated with alleged 'apostolic' letters and dialogues that make the opposite point."[35]

> *In the first century and early second century the number of gospels in circulation must have been much larger, at least a good dozen of which we at least have some pieces, and everybody could and did rewrite, edit, revise, and combine, however he saw fit.*   – Helmut Koester[36]

> *It is extremely unlikely that Paul wrote some of the letters which are attributed to him in the New Testament. That there was some kind of 'school of Paul', even in his lifetime, seems overwhelmingly likely, and . . . the school which he has founded . . . could propagate and develop his ideas. It was not considered dishonest in the ancient world to write something and then attribute it to the pen of someone you greatly admire. A modern might think it was 'forgery' to write, say, the letter we know as Ephesians and then claim that its author was Paul. The modern concept of authorship, and the jealousy a modern author would feel of her or his own words being written down unaltered, is really entirely post-medieval, in many cases a post Enlightenment phenomenon.*   – A.N. Wilson[37]

---

35. Pagels, *Gnostic Gospels,* pp.67, 65.
36. Crossan, *Historical Jesus,* p.xxxi.
37. Wilson, *Paul – The Mind of the Apostle,* p.231.

In place of the gospels that celebrate gays and women, *hate*rosexual men substituted stories of glory in praise of straight men. "Some Christians," continues Pagels, "two or three generations after Paul, wrote letters attributed to Peter and Paul, including First Peter and the letters of Paul to Timothy. These letters, later included in the New Testament and widely believed to have been written by the apostles themselves, attempted to construct a bridge between the apostles and Christians of later generations..."[38]

> *Women should keep silence in the churches. For they are not permitted to speak, but they should be subordinate . . . it is shameful for a woman to speak in church.*   – Paul – I Cor.14:34-35

"By the year 200," concludes Pagels, "the majority of Christian communities endorsed as canonical the pseudo-Pauline letters of Timothy, which stresses (and exaggerates) the anti-feminist element in Paul's views . . . [and] also accepted as Pauline the letters to the Colossians and to the Ephesians."[39]

> *Let a woman learn in silence with all submissiveness. I permit no woman to teach or to have authority over men; she is to keep silent.*
> – Paul – I Tim. 2:11-12

> *A husband is the head of his wife, as Christ is the head and the Savior of the church . . . Wives should always put their husbands first, as the church puts Christ first.*   – Paul – Eph. 5:22-24

By claiming to have seen Jesus, Paul claimed authority to demand the submission of women and dismissal of gays. Decades after Jesus died, "Paul" became a code name to promote homophobia:

> *God gave them up to uncleanness through the lusts of their own hearts, to dishonor their own bodies between themselves . . . God let them follow their own evil desires. Women no longer wanted to have sex in a natural way, and they did things with each other that were not natural. Men behaved in the same way. They stopped wanting to have sex with women and had strong desires for sex with other men. They did shameful things with each other . . . men with men working that which is unseemly . . . God gave them over to a reprobate mind, to do those things which are not convenient, without understanding, covenant breakers, without natural affection . . . God has said that anyone who acts this way deserves to die.*
> – Paul – Rom. 1:24, 26-28, 31-32

---

38. Pagels, *The Origin of Satan*, p.151.
39. Pagels, *Gnostic Gospels*, p.63.

This language, ritualized by *hate*rosexual men and sadistically used today to persecute gays, tells us all about the writers of "Paul" and nothing at all about Jesus.

> *There are many reasons to suppose that the letters in which these sentences occur belong to a period later than Paul's, and that they were written in a so-called school of Paul, perhaps by one of his converts.* — A.N. Wilson[40]

Pagels points out how "dissenting Christians ever since the second century have claimed that the gospel itself has been co-opted by the forces of evil."[41]

THE ANTIGAY

If gays are nature's way of thinning the herd by reducing the number of births, then homosexuality is natural and intended by God. Herd thinners are proof that the Bible edited together by Rome cannot be the "word of God," and stories in it were written, edited, and tailored in favor of straight men, with explicit intent to direct harm towards homosexuals:

> *Thou shalt not lie with mankind, as with womankind, it is abomination. Those who do will be put to death, just as they deserve.*
> — Leviticus 20:13

Revered Mel White, who ghostwrote the autobiographies of Jerry Fallwell and Pat Robertson, points out, "Leviticus is clear that a man who lies with another man is an abomination and should be killed. Of course it also says a man who handles a pigskin is an abomination [Leviticus 5:2, 11:7-8, 11:26]. What will that do to American football?"[42]

Dominators dwell on anti-gay passages in Leviticus because those words were inserted by men with intent to degrade sex and flesh. In today's overpopulated world, those who oppose homosexuality are in opposition with nature. They represent the antigay.

> *God hates homosexuality.*
> — Jerry Fallwell[43]

> *Homosexuality is an abomination . . . It is a pathology. It is a sickness . . . The same thing will happen here that happened in Nazi Germany, because many of those people involved with Adolph Hitler were Satanists, many of them were homosexuals, the two things seem to go together.* — Pat Robertson[44]

---

40. Wilson, *Paul – The Mind of the Apostle*, p.142.
41. Pagels, *The Origin of Satan*, p.158.
42. CBS News 60 Minutes 9/94.
43. CBS Evening News 11/27/95.
44. Ibid. and CBS News 60 Minutes 9/94.

"When you hear that rhetoric trickling down," warns Rev. White, "by the time it gets down to people with clubs it says 'Better we abolish these people, better we kill them than it is that they live with us.'"[45]

The Bible is a guidebook for enshrining male heterosexuals and targeting gays for hate. Antigay language in the Bible has turned organized religions into camouflaged fronts sheltering hate groups in disguise. Gay bashing and words in the Bible that condemn homosexuality are "the two things" that "seem to go together."

> *You're more likely to bash a gay in direct proportion to the amount of church you attend.*   — Mel White[46]

LET MY PEOPLE GO

A holocaust against gays was instigated by the Bible. In 1995, an organization called Parents, Families & Friends of Lesbians & Gays produced a TV commercial that shows how attacks on homosexuals can be linked to the rhetoric of the religious right. Pat Robertson's Christian Broadcasting Network (CBN) sent letters to TV stations that planned to broadcast the ads. Robertson's network threatened "we will immediately seek judicial redress against your station."[47] As a result of this CBN threat, TV stations turned down the gay-friendly ads. Some of the stations cited "creative differences" as the reason for refusing the ad. But advocates of free speech suspect that the real reason is intimidation. Although the First Amendment theoretically protects our right to report truth, threats of lawsuits from monied organizations like CBN prevent all but the wealthiest of TV stations from airing ads critical of CBN's language against homosexuality.

But language in the Bible is also a source of dispute. In recent years, new translations of source manuscripts have reworded much of the book. For example, the King James translation of Paul reads:

> *Neither . . . effeminate, nor abusers of themselves with mankind, nor thieves, nor covetous, nor drunkards, nor revilers, nor extortioners, shall inherit the Kingdom of God.*   — Paul — I Corinthians 6:9-10

In 1996, ABC World News aired a report[48] on gays in the church that included a new translation of the above Bible passage:

> *Neither . . . homosexuals, nor thieves, nor the covetous, nor drunkards, nor revilers, nor swindlers, shall inherit the Kingdom of God.*
>   — Corinthians 6:9-10

45. CBS News 60 Minutes, 9/94.
46. Ibid.
47. CBS Evening News 11/27/95.
48. ABC World News 2/28/96.

"Effeminate" and "abusers," which appear in the King James version, are replaced with "homosexuals" in the new translation. The translation used by ABC TV singles out "homosexuals" – a term not found in the traditional King James Bible. A case can be made that the original Greek translation of Paul's letter to the Corinthians doesn't really condemn gay people at all because "effeminate" and "abusers of themselves with mankind" are not the same as *homosexual*. The change of words is reminiscent of George Orwell's *Animal Farm*, where rules of the farm are gradually reworded so that no one perceives how the laws of the land keep changing.

> *The New English Bible, for example, loves to intrude the word 'Christian' into Paul's writings, even through it never once appears in anything he wrote!*
> *   – A.N. Wilson* [49]

> *Jesus shouldn't have died so early, then he could've got twice as much across. They killed him and then twisted so many of the best things he said. Human hands started messing it all up and now so much of religion is bogwash. So much of it is negative – Thou Shalt Not. Look at sex, it's been screwed around so much I'm surprised babies are still being born.*   *– Jimi* [50]

In the centuries following the Crucifixion, writings about Jesus were altered by many people. Pagels reminds us, "Antagonists on both sides resorted to the polemical technique of writing literature that allegedly derived from apostolic times, professing to give the original apostle's views."[51] History leaves us with a *deconstruction* of Jesus, with words and ideas that have been assembled to reflect the interests of the men who edited them.

The earliest known list of texts that were proposed for inclusion in the New Testament was compiled in the second century by Marcion. Marcion excluded Jewish stories. The point here is that, from the start, the New Testament has been a vehicle for promoting prejudices. When considering the way its stories are arranged to condemn gays, it's revealing to see in the book other selective edits used to condemn Jews.

The Hebrews who wrote the gospels blamed Jews, and not Romans, for the death of Jesus. They whitewashed the role of the Roman governor, Pontius Pilate, because they wanted readers to condemn Jews instead. "The more intimate the conflict," notes Pagels, "the more intense and bitter it becomes."[52] The authors of the gospels were angry with their fellow Jews for rejecting Jesus as the Messiah. The Bible writers were also angry at Jews for provoking violence that led to the Roman Jewish War of 66-70 C.E. In the aftermath of that war, the gospels were written with intent to vilify Jews. The story of Barabbas is an example of how they achieved this.

---

49. Wilson, *Paul – The Mind of the Apostle*, p.176.
50. Melody Maker 3/1/69.
51. Pagels, *Gnostic Gospels*, p.64.
52. Pagels, *The Origin of Satan*, p.15.

The Gospel of Mark (15:6) describes how Pilate invoked an ancient custom honoring Passover by which the procurator "frees one prisoner chosen by the people." Pilate lets the Jews of Jerusalem choose freedom for either the prisoner Barabbas, a hometown hero, or the stranger Jesus, who is ridiculed as "King of the Jews." The gospel describes how the Jews cheered Barabbas and jeered Jesus. Pilate escapes blame. "I judge that narrative to be absolutely unhistorical," claims Crossan, ". . . its picture of Pilate, meekly acquiescent to a shouting crowd is exactly the opposite of what we know about him from Josephus. Brutal crowd control was his specialty . . . A custom such as *open* amnesty, the release of *any* requested prisoner at the time of the Passover festival, is against any administrative wisdom . . . Mark wants to have it both ways. Pilate must be in charge, since nothing else is historically plausible, but he must also be innocent of any wrongdoing in the unjust sentencing of Jesus. Mark's solution is to create the Barabbas incident in 15:6-15. I do not believe for a second that it actually happened, that there ever was or ever could be any such open and preset Passover amnesty, or that Pilate deviated on this occasion from his normal crowd-control tactics . . . I do not presume any trial before Ciaphas or any dialogue in which Pilate is discussing with Jesus, nor that there was a crowd outside shouting 'Crucify him' and Pilate was saying 'He's innocent, I want to let him go.' That is Christian fiction, writing the story years later . . . I doubt that 'trial' is even a good description of that process even when taken at its most minimal connotation . . . I would presume that there were standing orders for the soldiers, an agreement between Chiaphas and Pilate of what to do with anyone who causes trouble at Passover in the Temple. Chiaphas and Pilate would say, 'Don't ask silly questions, you know what to do with a peasant who causes trouble in the Temple: you kill him, you execute him. Do you have to come back and ask us? No!' It probably goes no higher up the chain of command than a centurion . . . It is difficult for the Christian imagination, then or now, to accept the brutal informality with which Jesus was probably condemned and crucified . . . There is no way, I believe, that Pilate, or any other Roman governor, could allow out of prison on a festival occasion *anyone the crowd demanded* . . . The idea of the crowd shouting down Pilate is quite inconceivable to me. This reads to me like Christian propaganda, it is the early sect, the Jewish sect of Christians saying to themselves, 'We think the enemy is the Jewish authorities and we think the Roman authorities are better to go with. We will play to the Roman authorities' . . . It is magnificent theological fiction, to be sure, but entailing a dreadful price for Judaism."[53]

That "price for Judaism" is what the writers were seeking, they invented a story that condemns Jews, just as the story of Paul, and the story of Sodom and Gomorrah, were written to condemn gays.

53. Crossan, *Historical Jesus*, p.390, and *Jesus – A Revolutionary Biography*, p.141, and A&E, *Biography of Jesus* 4/95.

"The Pilate who appears in the gospels . . . has little to do with the historical Pilate," agrees Pagels. ". . . Mark's benign portrait of Pilate increases the culpability of the Jewish leaders and supports Mark's contention that Jews, not Romans, were the primary force behind Jesus' crucifixion. Throughout the following decades, as bitterness between the Jewish majority and Jesus' followers increased, the gospels came to depict Pilate in an increasingly favorable light . . . [while] the Jews [depicted] become increasingly antagonistic [towards Christians] . . . John, like Luke, suppresses all traces of Roman initiative in Jesus' execution. In nearly every episode, John displays what one scholar calls 'bizarre exaggeration' to insist that the blame for initiating, ordering, and carrying out the crucifixion falls upon Jesus' *intimate* enemies, his fellow Jews."[54]

Jimi Hendrix, speaking of being persecuted by blacks in Harlem, said "your own people hurt you more."[55] The gospel writers intended to make their "own people," Jerusalem Jews, look bad. The story of Jesus was revised to fulfill this goal.

Descriptions of Barabbas and Pilate frame the Jews as executioners of the Son of God. Because of this Bible story, centuries of persecutions against Jews climaxed in the Nazi holocaust. Likewise, the story of Adam and Eve frame women and gays as agents of Satan. But whereas the story of Barabbas and Pilate empower Christians over Jews, the story of original sin and Eden empowers heterosexual men with honor and approval. Again, gospels written in praise of gays and females were weeded out and deleted by the men who edited the Bible.

There was so much time and opportunity within which to alter the original written stories about Jesus: Jesus died around 30 C.E. Forty years later his story, in the form of the first gospel (Mark), was written. During the next thirty years three more of the gospels that came to be included in our modern Bible were written. Within a thirty-year period between the end of the Roman Jewish War in 70 C.E. and the end of the first century in 100 C.E., decades after Jesus died, the four gospels called Mark, Matthew, Luke and John were written. The Gospels are far removed in decades from the lifetime of Jesus. For dozens of years after Jesus died, the stories had been passed along by word of mouth before they were written down. Worse yet is the fact that over the next 100 years after they were written, up until around 200 C.E., all of the original manuscripts were lost or destroyed. Biblical scholar Helmut Koester points out, "The problems for the reconstruction of the textual history of the canonical Gospels in the first century of transmission are immense. The assumption that the reconstruction of the best archetype for the manuscript tradition is more or less identical with the assumed autograph is precarious. The oldest known archetypes are separated from the autographs by more than a century. Textual critics of classical texts know that the first century of their transmission is the period in which the most serious corruptions occur."[56]

---

54. Pagels, *The Origin of Satan*, pp.29, 33, 110, 106-7.

55. The New York Times 2/25/68.

56. "The Text of the Synoptic Gospels in the Second Century," in *Gospel Traditions in the Second Century: Origins, Recensions, Text, and Transmission, Christianity and Judaism in Antiquity 3*, edited by William L. Petersen, (Notre Dame: Univ. of Notre Dame Press. 1989), p.19.

Crossan elaborates, "What those first Christians experienced as . . . the abiding empowerment of the Spirit gave the transmitters of the Jesus tradition a creative freedom we would never have dared postulate had such a conclusion not been forced upon us by the evidence . . . They are unnervingly free about omission and addition, about change, correction, or creation in their own individual accounts . . . subject to their own particular interpretations of Jesus. The gospels are neither histories nor biographies, even within the ancient tolerances for those genres."[57]

The earliest copies of the gospels that survive today come from the third century. Prior to that no original text is known to exist. From the time that the first gospel (Mark) was written around 70 C.E., and for the next 130 years, until around 200 C.E., no manuscripts survive.

202 C.E COINCIDENCE:

In 202 C.E. Irenaeus died. Is it coincidence that only *after* his death we find preserved written versions of the gospels? It is likely that for more than a century prior to 202 C.E., gospel manuscripts underwent alterations, additions and deletions. And then during the years of Irenaeus's reign of terror against women and gays, every gospel passage labeled "heresy" by Irenaeus was rewritten or removed. There are no copies of any manuscripts that predate the reign of Irenaeus as Bishop of Lyons. Irenaeus grew up in Asia Minor, the area where the original gospels were written. I propose that Irenaeus and his churches destroyed all original manuscripts in order to cover up the changes they made to these stories. Romer reminds us that "we know only what later churches wanted to tell us."[58]

> *The four gospels collected into the New Testament were canonized around 200 C.E. . . . By the time the process of sorting the various writings ended – probably as late as the year 200 – virtually all feminine imagery for God had disappeared from orthodox Christian tradition . . . From the year 200, we have no evidence for women taking prophetic, priestly, and episcopal roles among orthodox churches . . . By the year 200, the majority of Christian communities endorsed as canonical the pseudo-Pauline letters . . . which stresses (and exaggerates) the antifeminist element in Paul's views.*   – Elaine Pagels[59]

> *By the year 200, someone had gathered all these letters up and attributed them to Paul.*   – A.N. Wilson[60]

57. Crossan, *Jesus – A Revolutionary Biography,* p xiii.
58. Romer, *Testament,* p.188.
59. Pagels, *The Origin of Satan,* p, 65, *Gnostic Gospels,* pp.57, 60-1, 63.
60. Wilson, *Paul – The Mind of the Apostle,* pp.231-2.

That "someone" was Irenaeus, a male supremacist who rewrote the gospels in his own hateful image and destroyed the original manuscripts before his death in 202 C.E.

When the long hidden Gnostic gospels were dug up and discovered at Nag Hammadi in Egypt in 1945, the world observed ancient accounts of the Jesus movement – two-thousand-year-old writings that praise women and gays. All of these sacred texts had been suppressed for millennia. When comparing these gospels of the Gnostics with the gospels that are promoted by the Vatican Bible, it becomes clear that what Irenaeus and the "later churches wanted to tell us" is that the Christian faith glorifies straight males and condemns women and homosexuals. The gospels of gays, and stories of the Gaian goddess, were deleted and destroyed by Irenaeus.

The discoveries at Nag Hammadi provide evidence that Bible passages which condemn women and gays are editorial reversals of what Jesus preached. The original followers of Jesus in 30 C.E. were people seeking freedom from dominators.

Chapter 11: Churchianity

ى

The orderliness of the Pastoral Epistles and the writings of the School of Paul would have enraged [Jesus] – it is the replacement of one religious enslavement for another, the idolatry toward Torah replaced by idolatry towards Church.
— A.N. Wilson[1]

By the end of the second century, Christianity had been institutionalized into "Churchianity" – a hierarchy of deacons, priests and bishops. For the next two hundred years they established a cult around arcane rules and regulations. But by the start of the fourth century, Christians were still an obscure and persecuted minority struggling to survive within a vast and hostile Empire. The rise of Christianity in the fourth century and beyond parallels the fall of Rome. Romer points out that the Empire "was more prosperous in the two centuries after Christ than it would be under the later Christian emperors, when slavery along with poverty would become more common."[2]

At it's height the Empire extended from Hadrian's Wall in Scotland to the Persian Gulf and you could call yourself a citizen of Rome whether you lived in Manchester, Athens, Luxor, or even briefly Uruk in the baking South of Iraq. But unlike India or China, there was no binding religious or social ethic to hold its disparate parts together, and in the fourth century it entered a great crisis: economic, social, and especially spiritual. And the vacuum was filled by an obscure cult – one of many new religions arising out of the spiritual ferment of the late antique world: Christianity.
— Michael Woods[3]

During the reign of the last successful pagan emperor of Rome, Diocletian (284-305 C.E.), Christianity grew and spread around the Mediterranean. Its bishops now patterned their Church after the cult of the emperor. Diocletian became the first Roman Emperor to resign rather than be overthrown by a rival military ruler. "He almost seemed to acknowledge the impossibility of holding the empire together," writes Romer. "In his last years he had seen the disintegration of his great creation . . . The Empire had slipped away into its separate provinces. The center had been hollow; no common bond had held the

1. Wilson, *Paul – The Mind of the Apostle*, p.239.
2. Romer, *Testament*, PBS 10/91.
3. Legacy: The Origins of Civilization, *The Barbarian West*, 1992 PBS, Ambrose Video Publishing 1995.

people of this commonwealth, only abstract civic duty inside a faceless state . . . In the new Empire of Diocletian and Constantine, slavery and poverty had greatly increased; life inside this Empire was harder than it had ever been before."[4] In 312 C.E., Constantine succeeded Diocletian as Emperor of a crumbling Empire.

CONSTANTINE'S FRANKENSTEIN

> *With Constantine around 327 A.D., Christianity was recognized as one of the permitted religions in the Roman Empire, and very shortly later, with Theodosius, at the end of the fourth century and beginning of the fifth, Christianity was declared to be the **only** permitted religion in the Roman Empire, and not only Christianity, but a specific form of Christianity, which was that of the Byzantine throne. And so a system of violent persecutions and vandalism begins with the destruction of shrines, and the more sacred the shrine the more violent the destruction.*
>
> — Joseph Campbell[5]

Constantine had a plan: he plotted to co-opt the growing Christian religion and use it to rejuvenate his rule over what would become the Christian Roman Empire. Constantine's designs for power led him to order the death of his own son. The Emperor, wrote his biographer Eusebius, was "exceedingly ambitious of military glory . . . aspiring to the sovereignty of the whole world . . . he alone of all rulers pursued a continual course of conquest."[6]

Constantine's campaign went beyond earthly realms to include heaven as well. He sought to position himself as an actual apostle of Jesus and patterned his effort after the famous story of Paul. Paul was not among the twelve apostles of Jesus' entourage. He had never seen Jesus. In the years after Jesus died, Paul persecuted Christians. But as the new religion spread to large numbers of people, he saw an opportunity to gain influence over believers. Decades after the crucifixion, Paul claimed that while walking down the street he saw Jesus floating by on a cloud. Paul therefore proclaimed himself the 13th apostle, and his tale about *Jesus In the Sky With Diamonds* set the stage for Constantine's sequel. The Emperor went Paul one better: a hallucination that preserves history's first officially recorded siting of an Unidentified Flying Object, identified by Constantine as a levitating crucifix. "He said that about noon he saw with his own eyes the trophy of a cross of light in the heavens above the Sun," recalls Eusebius, "and bearing the inscription, *Conquer By This*."[7]

---

4. Romer, *Testament*, pp.208-9.
5. *Mythos - the Mystical Life*, PBS 12/1/96.
6. *Nicene and Post-Nicene Fathers of the Christian Church*, ed: Schaff and Wace, *Eusebius: Church History & Life of Constantine the Great*, p.423.
7. Ibid. p.490.

Constantine thereby announced his conversion to the obscure cult of Christianity, which he proceeded to conquer and dominate. And like Paul, instead of persecuting Christians, the Emperor now used the new religion to his advantage. But Constantine aimed to upstage Paul altogether and give himself top billing as the *13th Apostle*. It was a publicity stunt made in heaven. "He erected his own Sepulchral Monument," wrote Eusebius, "anticipating with extraordinary fervor of faith that his body would share their title with the apostles themselves, and that he should thus even after death become the subject, with them, of the devotions which should be performed to their honor in this place. He accordingly caused twelve coffins to be set up in this church, like sacred pillars in honor and memory of the apostolic number, in the center of which his own was placed, having six of theirs on either side of it. Thus he had provided with prudent foresight an honorable resting-place for his body after death."[8]

Apostledom was just the beginning. Constantine's ambitions were more grandiose than a Microsoft-Donald Trump development scheme. After his conversion was announced with a flying crucifix media blitz, the Emperor "marched with his whole forces, trying to obtain again for the Romans the freedom they had inherited from their ancestors."[9] The Emperor had a *plan* to revive the crumbling Empire; he envisioned a Palestinian showplace, boasting monumental tourist attractions over the sites of Jesus' birth and death. Constantine oversaw the production of a Middle East theme park, a sort of Christian Disneyland. With his new religion and its attendant attractions, the Emperor shrewdly maneuvered to put his Empire back on the map. Through Jesus memorabilia, Jerusalem became the center of a happening Holyland, all according to the plan of an Emperor's Roman renewal project. A Bethlehem temple was erected to enshrine the Nativity site. A hundred Inns were built to house streams of vacationing pilgrims.

Eusebius composed a theme song jingle, *The Nicean Creed*, which advertised the four key attractions built by Constantine in the Holyland Theme Park. First, the Creed's verse "*born of the Virgin Mary*" refers to a Bethlehem site enshrined by the Nativity Church. "*Crucified, died, and was buried and on the third day rose again*" refer to the second and third attractions, the church on Calvary and the tomb under Jerusalem's Church of the Holy Sepulchre. "*He ascended into heaven*" from atop the Mount of Olives, a site preserved like a launch pad over the Church of the Ascension, which is the fourth attraction in Palestine advertised by *The Nicean Creed.* Under Constantine's plan, the four cornerstone pillars of the faith were now enshrined by monumental castles erected in the center of a thriving tourist industry. The Empire was back in business.

Today, after more than a millennium, the theme park still rakes in revenues. So successful is this formula that even Buddhists now take notice. On the eve of Christianity's third millennium, the erection of a similar theme park scheme is already giving the sacred sites of Buddha a makeover. It wasn't until 1834 that British archaeologists discovered inscriptions that showed Buddha to be a man and not a god. Ever since then,

8. Ibid. p.555.
9. Ibid. p.492.

a tourist industry around Buddha's hometown has grown steadily. Today the place attracts Constantine-like benefactors. In the 1990s, real estate developers were well on the way to emulating Israel's Holyland example.

The birthplace of Buddha (born to Queen Mayadevi) at Lumbini is quickly becoming "Bethlehem East." In cooperation with Japan's Buddhist Federation, the Lumbini Development Trust today sponsors the Mayadevi Temple Restoration Project: a $100 million theme park covering three square miles of Buddhaland. Currently under construction are 41 monasteries surrounding an international visitor's center with 8 blocks of shops and restaurants, world class hotels, banks, post office, parking lots and jet airport, all topped off with the world's largest golf course. Holyland East takes in the sites of Buddha's first sermon at Sarnath, as well as his enlightenment at Bodh Gaya, where real estate today costs $100,000 an acre.[10] Galilee has the Church on the Mt. of the Beatitudes (where Jesus' Sermon on the Mount vies with Moses on Sinai), but Bodh Gaya boasts the Mahabodhi Temple, enshrining a Bodhi tree like the one under which Buddha sat when he gained enlightenment.

> *Being free, I make others free, being perfectly at rest, I lead others to rest.*
> – Buddha

New discos at Bodh Gaya (Body Gay?) may outclass Monte Carlo. Constantine would be proud. He too had plotted, like a Walt Disney of religion, to consolidate his assets by developing a theme park. Constantine seemed to sense that the fall of the Roman Empire was *related* to the spread of Christianity, so at the top of his agenda was conquest of this religion and a reworking of its rules. His whole Holyland plan revolved around a book that redefined Jesus in Emperor-friendly terms. Constantine's spin doctors were ordered to construct an official New Testament, spelled out along the lines that Irenaeus dictated long ago: all power to men, condemn all women and gays. A list of books that Eusebius approved were included in Constantine's new Bible of the Roman Empire. The story of Jesus was now finally revised. Anyone who disagreed was persecuted or killed.

In the summer of 325 C.E., Constantine ordered three hundred Christian bishops to the town of Nicea to settle disputes about the religion's meaning and procedures. "In return for the imperial acceptance of the bishops and their faith, the Council tacitly validated the Emperor's earthly rule," notes Romer. ". . . Christ's birthday, fixed on 25 December, took over the feast day of an earlier favored deity of Constantine, *Sol Invictus* . . . [Dec. 25] was also . . . Constantine's birthday."[11]

The Emperor decreed Sol's weekly festival, *Sol-day*, to be Sunday, a Sabbath for Christians. The Council of Nicea proceeded to agree to twenty Canons (or "guidelines") for their Roman Catholic Church. The very first Canon addressed the urgent issue of "Self-mutilation incompatible with clerical office":

---

10. *On the Buddha Trail*, PBS 4/96.
11. Romer, *Testament*, pp.215, 231.

If a man in good health has castrated himself, he must withdraw, even though he is registered among the clergy; and from this time on, no one who has thus acted should be promoted. And clear as it is, that what has been said refers to those who have intentionally acted thus and have dared to castrate themselves, it is equally clear that the rule of discipline admits to the ranks of the clergy those who have been made eunuchs by barbarians or by their masters, provided they are in other respects found worthy.

– Council of Nicea[12]

The third hot topic on the agenda at Nicea, titled "Sub-introduced women not to dwell with clerics," was written to limit contact between priests and women:

The great Synod has wholly denied permission to either bishops, or presbyter or deacon, or any one at all of the clergy, to have an intimate female house companion, except she be a mother, or a sister, or an aunt, or such other woman as has escaped all suspicions.

– Council of Nicea[13]

This new Church was defined by a cult of very strange men. Aware that the control of females depended upon the denigration of sex, they suppressed all gospels that told stories of women and gays. "When orthodoxy finally came," writes Romer, "it was defined, almost inadvertently, in argument against many of these Gnostic sects."[14] Constantine's Holyland theme park was meant to recapture the riches that had once supported imperial Rome. Therefore, in deference to the men who would fight the wars of Rome and its new religion, all writings that favored women and gays were banned.

About Constantine's decrees Eusebius writes, "All who had been compelled by way of disgrace and insult to serve in the employment of women, he likewise freed . . . So did he . . . discover . . . a grove and temple . . . a hidden and fateful snare of souls . . . such as destroyed their bodies with effeminacy. Here men undeserving of the name forgot the dignity of their sex, and propitiated the demon by their effeminate conduct . . . Our august emperor . . . gave orders that the building with its offerings should be utterly destroyed . . . Now a new statue, breathing the very spirit of modesty, proceeded from the emperor, who forbade the continuance of former practices. And besides this, he sent them also written exhortations, as though he had been especially ordained by God for this end, that he might instruct all men in the principles of chastity . . . And inasmuch as the Egyptians, especially those of Alexandria, had been accustomed to honor their river through a priesthood composed of effeminate men, a further law was passed commanding the extermination of the whole class as vicious, that no one might

12. *The Canons of the First Four General Councils: Nicaea, Constantinople, Ephesus and Chalcedon* - edited by Edwin Knox Mitchell, D.D., (University of Pennsylvania, 1897), p.4.
13. Ibid. p.5.
14. Romer, *Testament*, p.196.

thenceforward be found tainted with the like impurity . . . those who had defiled the cities by their vicious conduct were indeed seen no more . . . Women, too, consecrated to the service of God, have maintained a pure and spotless virginity, and have devoted themselves, soul and body, to a life of entire chastity and holiness."[15]

These observations from Eusebius set the stage for an age of Inquisitions, witch hunts, and burnings. "When the orthodox gained military support," notes Pagels, "sometime after the Emperor Constantine became Christian in the fourth century, the penalty for heresy escalated."[16] This trend climaxed hundreds of years later when the Gnostics, and anyone who followed goddess beliefs, became the targets of holocaust. Throughout Europe from the 15th to the 17th centuries, nine million people were accused of being witches. Eighty-five percent of those killed for the crime of witchcraft were women.[17]

This women's holocaust has roots at the Council of Nicea, the world's first EcuMENical gathering. At Nicea, and several later gatherings of church "fathers," editorial members defined the faith in ways that enshrined heterosexual men as God's preferred people. Constantine, like Irenaeus, ordered that the writings about Jesus that favored straight men be tacked onto sections of old Hebrew scriptures. The Bible, now with two TestaMENts, was thus sealed. The official Canon of "books" to be included was closed.

> *The four New Testament gospels are neither a total collection of all those available nor a random sampling from among them. They are, rather, a deliberate arrangement in which some gospels were accepted and included while others were rejected and excluded . . . differences and discrepancies between accounts and versions are not due primarily to vagaries of memory or divergences in emphasis but to quite deliberate theological interpretations of Jesus.* — John Crossan[18]

THE GHOSTLY TRIO – SEEDS OF ELITISM

> *The voices that speak to us from antiquity are overwhelmingly those of the cultured few, the elites. The modern voices that carry on their tale are overwhelmingly those of white, middle-class, European and North American males. These men can, and do, laud imperialistic, authoritarian slave societies . . . The peasants form no part of the literate world on which most reconstructions of ancient history focus.* — Thomas Carney[19]

---

15. *Nicene and Post-Nicene Fathers of the Christian Church*, ed: Schaff and Wace, *Eusebius: Church History & Life of Constantine the Great*, pp.505, 434-6, 546.

16. Pagels, *Gnostic Gospels*, p.xxiii.

17. *Burning Times*, National Film Board of Canada, PBS 8/19/96.

18. Crossan, *Jesus – A Revolutionary Biography*, pp xii-xiii.

19. *The Shape of the Past: Models and Antiquity*, (Lawrence: Koronado Press, 1975), pp.xiv, 231, note 123.

> *Ideology became one of the driving forces in the development of civilization*
> *– religious, social, political . . . and ideology is also the key to*
> *understanding that fateful change which came over humanity with the*
> *beginning of civilization, by which the few came to dominate the many –*
> *as is still the case across much of the world today.*
>
> – Michael Woods[20]

Elitism – the practice of privileges for a select few who are favored by authority under law – is the system that underlies our beliefs about *deservedness*. Who deserves what, and why?

> *Ultimately, the system which all liberation movements seek to dismantle is*
> *contained within the concept of elitism. Elitism, the phenomenon of placing*
> *oneself at privilege – above another person on the pretext that one is*
> *"better" – is the umbrella concept under which capitalism, racism and*
> *sexism are subcategory derivatives . . . Racism, sexism and financial*
> *inequality are all sub-categories of elitism. Delusions about deservedness*
> *and privilege that afflict elitists are symptoms of a mental illness that has*
> *inspired every inequity scheme throughout history. Societies that maintain*
> *laws designed to financially reward elitists are societies deservedly doomed*
> *to violence from the victims of elitist thievery.*
>
> – A Touch of Hendrix, 1988[21]

The enslavement of civilization under a hierarchy that favors a few at the expense of the rest was sanctified and enshrined by Constantine at Nicea. It was done with a philosophical twist which to understand requires some background.

Gnostics believed that Jesus was impervious to pain on the cross. His powers of miracle healing, his nonhuman aspect, they reasoned, allowed him to transcend suffering. The Gnostics regarded Jesus as a spiritual being. Pagels notes that this idea "became central to Christian theology some two hundred years later – the question of how Christ could be simultaneously human and divine." In the fourth century at the Council of Nicea, Constantine and his bishops realized that the resolution of this dispute held the key to endless power for the ruling class and its Vatican.

"Rejecting the Gnostic view that Jesus was a spiritual being," writes Pagels, "the orthodox insisted that he, like the rest of humanity, was born, lived in a family, became hungry and tired, ate and drank wine, suffered and died. They even went so far as to insist that he rose *bodily* from the dead."[22]

---

20. Legacy: The Origins of Civilization - *Central America: The Burden of Time*, 1992 PBS, Ambrose Video Publishing 1995.
21. Fairchild, unpublished manuscript (1988), pp.46, 36.
22. Pagels, *Gnostic Gospels*, p.101.

"There was a great deal of discretion in the first four centuries," observed Joseph Campbell, "as to whether Christianity had anything to do with Judaism, that is to say: was the Son Jesus the Son of Yahweh? Or Son of a higher power of which Yahweh was ignorant? Yahweh was called the Fool because he didn't realize there was a higher power than himself. He thought he was God. The Son, then, who was to carry us past that, was the revelation of a higher light. And so, Yahweh was associated with the demiurge who brought about all the agony and evil and sorrow in the world. This is a very definite thrust in the early Christian tradition . . . With Christianity in those early centuries, what happened was a conflict between interpretations of Christ: either as an example of the mystery hero who dies to be resurrected, or, as the unique incarnation. That was the big argument between the Gnostics and the orthodox community. And the orthodox community opted for the importance of the historicity of the [unique] incarnation."[23]

"The argument concerned the precise nature of divinity," explains Romer. "Theologians were interested in the nature of God, but Constantine was concerned with the extent of divinity . . . Constantine talked about the nature of power and where the demarcation was: power in heaven and power on Earth . . . Constantine was after something more than just abstract theology. It has to do with the *shape* of God: if you have God as a Father, a great power in the sky, and then you have this divinity that sort of trickles down so that you have Jesus his Son, and you have saints and holy men and popes and bishops and emperors – and everybody has this little bit of divine power – it makes a very muddy picture for Constantine. *He* wants to be the main act on Earth, and that means cutting out all these little trickle downs of power and stuffing God clear up into heaven. This issue comes over very clearly with Jesus Christ. There were many bishops [at Nicea] who would have died for the belief that Jesus had been a man and a god in one person on Earth, and that means that there could be other men who had become gods as well, and these could then be set up as opposition or as confusers to Constantine's supreme position of power."[24]

But instead they chose to isolate Jesus alone as the only Son of God. The problem for the Council of Nicea was to explain how Christians can worship the God of the Israelites, *and* the Son of God Jesus, too, and still claim to believe in just *one* divinity. The problem was solved when the Council adopted the doctrine of the *Holy Trinity* – God the Father, Son the Savior, and Holy Ghost – three divinities "of one substance," a Ghostly Trio.

> *We believe in one God, the FATHER Almighty, Maker of all things visible and invisible. And in one Lord, Jesus Christ, the SON of God, begotten of the Father, the only-begotten . . . being of one substance with the Father . . . who for us men, and for our salvation, came down and was incarnate and was made man . . . And in the HOLY GHOST, the Lord and*

23. *Mythos - the Mystical Life*, PBS 12/1/96.
24. Romer, *Testament*, PBS 10/91.

> *Giver of life, who proceeds from the Father, who with the Father and the*
> *Son TOGETHER is worshipped and glorified . . . But those who say . . .*
> *'He is of another substance or essence'. . . they are condemned by the*
> *holy catholic and apostolic church.*   — Nicean Creed

ZEN SPIN DOCTORS

There is an aspect of Zen in the Council's logic. Zen teachers give their students "koans," problems upon which a student's meditation can focus. A typical koan is a question, like "what is the sound of one hand clapping?" or "what did your face look like before your parents were born?" Houston Smith said that "Koans are like Shaggy Dog stories – they make no sense." Smith, a scholar of world religions, described his own Zen education. His instructor told him to figure out why a certain monk had said that a dog doesn't have a "Buddha nature." "Now every Buddhist would know," recalls Smith, "that the Buddha had said even grass has a Buddha nature; presumably a dog is on a higher scale of being than grass. How can it be that grass has Buddha nature and a dog doesn't? . . . So I had a problem. Somehow, by redefining the words – maybe by 'Buddha nature' he didn't quite mean that, or 'the dog' didn't mean that – you know, when you get a contradiction you fiddle with the terms so that they'll fit."

The Council of Nicea was presented with a contradiction, a sort of Zen koan: If God the Father is a divinity, and God the Son is a divinity, and God the Holy Ghost is a divinity, what is the single God that we worship? In Zen, the answer to such questions, says Smith, "needn't be determined definitively . . . The answer to . . . koans is not a verbal answer, it is an experience. These are conundrums set up in such a way . . . that it presents you with a contradiction before which reason feels helpless . . . it is to bring the other world into this world in the nitty gritty of daily life."[25]

The Trinity was Constantine's answer to the conundrum of how to relate Jesus with God in heaven and leave the Emperor to rule the Church and the Empire. At Nicea, Constantine's bishops turned a three-headed God into one. They set out to "fiddle with the terms so that they'll fit." With the verbal acrobatics of intellectual contortionists, they forced a square peg into the round hole. The Church decreed it illegal to preach that Jesus and God are not the same: *"Those who say . . . 'He is of another substance or essence' . . . are condemned."*

"So the Holy Trinity," notes Romer, ". . . actually served Constantine to push all this up into heaven. God, you could say, was composed of the Father and the Son and the Holy Ghost. It's very mysterious, but its sure enough way up in the sky, far away from power, while Constantine is down here on his throne."[26]

---

25. Houston Smith: *Hinduism & Buddhism*, interview with Bill Moyers, PBS 3/96.
26. Romer, *Testament*, PBS 10/91.

Because the Trinity is such an important part of later Christian doctrine, it is striking that the term does not appear in the New Testament. Likewise, the developed concept of three coequal partners in the Godhead found in later creedal formulations cannot be clearly detected within the confines of the canon. Later believers systematized the diverse references to God, Jesus, and the Spirit found in the New Testament in order to fight against heretical tendencies of how the three are related. Elaboration on the concept of a Trinity also serves to defend the church against charges of di– or tritheism. Since the Christians have come to worship Jesus as a god, how can they claim to be continuing the monotheistic tradition of the God of Israel? Various answers are suggested, debated, and rejected, as heretical, but the idea of a Trinity – one God subsisting in three persons and one substance – ultimately prevails . . . no New Testament writer expounds on the relationship among the three in the detail that later Christian writers do . . . It is possible that this three-part formula derives from later liturgical usage and was added to the text of 2 Corinthians as it was copied . . . The word 'holy' does not appear before 'spirit' in the earliest manuscript evidence for this passage . . . it is important to avoid reading the Trinity into places where it does not appear. — Daniel Schowalter[27]

The Trinity didn't exist prior to the Council of Nicea in 325 C.E. This notion of a Ghostly Trio was foreign to the Jesus tradition until then. Jimi noted that men had "*twisted so many of the best things*" that Jesus had said, and Constantine's Trinity was a major twist on these teachings. The idea behind the Trinity is to isolate Christ with God in heaven as a special and unapproachable being whom no human can hope to aspire to. The Trinity puts Jesus on an elite pedestal as the *only* Son of God. "I think he would have been completely horrified," states theology professor Robert Eisenman. "That's the very opposite of everything that he would, or could, have represented in Palestine . . . The Dead Sea Scrolls speak of the Sons of God in a *plural* way."[28]

The Church of Rome decreed that God existed as a Trinity of Father, Son, and Holy Ghost. But Gnostics knew that such logic defines Jesus in ways that favor what they call the *demiurge* – the demon's urge to dominate. "It is...the demiurge who reigns as King and Lord, who acts as military commander," wrote Valentinius.[29] The way that Jesus is interpreted holds implications for the type of society that Christians have. Gnostics were in opposition with the Church's version of Jesus. The Church represents elitist dominators, Gnostics represent nurturing equals – *equalitarians*.

"Orthodox Jews and Christians insist that a chasm separates humanity from its creator: God is wholly other," explains Pagels. "But some of the Gnostics who wrote these gospels contradict this: self knowledge is knowledge of God; the self and the divine are

27. *The Oxford Companion to the Bible*, pp.782-3.
28. History's Mysteries, *Origins of the Bible*, The Learning Channel 1/95.
29. Pagels, *Gnostic Gospels*, p.37

identical."[30] Calls for equality in the teachings of Jesus appealed to Gnostic sensibilities. But Constantine revised the story of Christ and added a Trinity scheme to justify privilege for an elite few rulers.

"The Holy Trinity, that supreme mystery of Christian theology which holds that God exists in Three Persons and One Substance, came to serve the cause of the Christian empire," writes Romer. "God had become a remote and ineffable unity of Father, Son and Holy Ghost. His time on Earth as Jesus Christ was fixed precisely to one event in the historical past from which the new imperial calendars would be dated, Christ's birthday . . . In all this, the church and its officers became a vital part of the earthly hierarchy, the organization through which people might reach to God. And at the very top of this worldly pyramid of power stood Constantine, the holy emperor, whose earthly order reflected that of Heaven itself. This is why the Council of Nicea and its Creed, which so carefully defined and separated the heavens from the Earth, was of fundamental importance to Constantine the Christian and to Constantine the empire builder. And for that reason the Council of Nicea may be said to have been about the redefinition of imperial power."[31]

Jesus died trying to oppose such power. He fought for economic and social equality, ideals that he demonstrated through communal sharing of food: *commensality*—from the Latin word *mensa*, meaning table. "It means the rules of association and socialization," explains Crossan. "It means table fellowship as a map of economic discrimination, social hierarchy, and political differentiation . . . The Kingdom of God as a process of open commensality, of a nondiscriminating table depicting in miniature a nondiscriminating society, clashes fundamentally with honor and shame, those basic values of ancient Mediterranean culture and society. Most of American society in the twentieth century is used to *individualism*, with guilt and innocence as sanctions, rather than *groupism*, with honor and shame as sanctions . . . Open commensality is the symbol and embodiment of radical egalitarianism, of an absolute equality of people that denies the validity of any discrimination between them and negates the necessity of any hierarchy among them . . . [a] challenge launched . . . at civilization's eternal inclination to draw lines, invoke boundaries, establish hierarchies, and maintain discriminations . . . No importance was given [by Jesus] to distinctions of Gentile and Jew, female and male, slave and free, poor and rich. Those distinctions were hardly even attacked in theory; they were simply ignored in practice . . . What he was saying and doing was as unacceptable in the first century as in the twentieth century."[32]

I'm for the masses and the underdog. – Jimi[33]

You should stick with the underdog. – Noam Chomsky[34]

30. Ibid. p.xx.
31. Romer, *Testament*, pp.215-216.
32. Crossan, *Jesus – A Revolutionary Biography,* pp.68-71, xii.
33. Circus 3/69 p.40.
34. *Manufacturing Consent,* 1992, PBS 9/95.

Those who proclaim, "blessed are the poor" will find themselves hated
and reviled.   – John Kloppenborg[35]

Jesus, like all reformers, met with hostility . . . [he led] a movement which
reformed an existing religion, which took from Judaism its best elements:
its high monotheism, its high ethical standard, while at the same time
rejecting what Judaism had degenerated into at this time: an obsessive
concern with an imaginary holiness, a rejection of outsiders, a rejection of
gentiles, a rejection of anybody that they didn't think was perfectly pure and
holy. Financial exploitation also. The early Christian church arose from
within this movement – the new Israel, the Kingdom of the Jews – and
reformed it.   – Barbara Thering[36]

Most people seem to agree that distinctions between us in skill, luck, talent or ability should determine who deserves what. But Jesus preached that everyone deserves the same. Constantine's crime at Nicea was to revise these teachings and redefine Jesus as a figurehead of hierarchy. The Roman Empire merged with the church. "The sons of that church were . . . taking on the appearance of a spiritual government," notes Romer, "and they required an earthly hierarchy for themselves, and one that Christian doctrine could affirm. What Constantine sought in all this was a pre-eminent position for his imperial self. The heretical splitting of God into a hierarchy of sacredness served to muddy the issue. For if God was divided into Father, Son and Spirit, then small fractions of this sacredness might still run throughout mans world just as Jesus, the Son had once done. And if sacredness could run unchecked through the order of the world, the role of emperors in such a universe of democratic holiness would come but a poor second! Constantine wanted *his* Emporium to resemble the order of heaven, with the role of emperor echoing the role of God in heaven. Arguments about the nature of God were far from being theological abstractions: they were about power in this world and the next."[37]

So, like Jesus turning water into wine, Constantine turned three deities into one and called it the Holy Trinity. In the process, he enshrined elitism for the Christian church by encasing Jesus on a three-headed pedestal that no person can hope to emulate. Unlike Buddha, or even Mohammed, Jesus was now a figure with whom it is impossible to really relate; in fact, it's *forbidden* to relate yourself with Jesus. Access to God is achieved abstractly, through a maze of church hierarchies that end in the Trinity. Masses of peasants were trained to think that the emperor and his churchmen were like mediums in touch with the deity. To get to heaven it was necessary to obtain (or purchase) approval from the church.

The Christian faith went through a makeover. Its obscure peasant stories were reconstructed and transformed into official religion for an empire. Constantine saw the

35. Crossan, *Historical Jesus*, p.274.
36. *Riddle of the Dead Sea Scrolls*, (Surry Hills: Ariba Pty. Ltd., 1990), The Discovery Channel 8/24/92.
37. Romer, *Testament*, p 215.

Trinity as a way to whitewash the message of equality *out* of the story of Jesus and replace it with complex dogma that only Rome and its Church could interpret. Thus, the Vatican became middlemen who brokered communication between God and the people. "We can see throughout the history of Christianity how varying beliefs about the nature of God inevitably bear different political implications," states Pagels.[38] Constantine's doctrine picked up where Irenaeus left off. Irenaeus claimed authority on grounds that his church represented a single God, the Creator of creation, therefore the Bishop's insight gave his church *exclusive* access to God.[39] But whereas Irenaeus was a Christian bishop in an empire still hostile to Christians, Constantine, two centuries later, was a Christian *Emperor*. In the time of Irenaeus, the argument was over "one God, one bishop." Constantine refined the argument into *one Son of God, one Emperor of men.* "With God in his Heaven now," writes Romer, "and Constantine ruling by God's Grace: Deo Gratia upon the Earth, the imperial power had to be seen as the essential link in the scheme . . . the enthroned Emperor and his bishops appear as the prototype of Western government, for it was at Nicea that this dual order of temporal and spiritual power first received sanction . . . the effects of the Council are still felt in the Christian church and in Western government."[40]

> *The Church, organized on the lines of the imperial administration, with its dioceses and provinces corresponding to Roman divisions, had the makings of a functional authority . . . the Christian church proved itself to be the true successor of imperial Rome.*   – Reay Tannahill[41]

The Roman army ruled the Empire by dividing it into districts called *diocese*, and each diocese was governed by a bureaucracy of overseers and judges called *vicarii*. To this day the Roman Catholic Church maintains this system of dioceses ruled by vicars. "The empire needed a stronger cement than the notion of imperial divinity," explains Romer, "and within two generations it found it in the Christian church. The story of how Diocletian's successors achieved this brand-new balancing between heavenly power and earthly rule is a story of how the Bible was interpreted to justify the Christian empire and its rulers, men who found a new balance of earthly and divine power that would last a thousand years and more."[42]

Living under Roman dominators, Jesus protested inequity. "Jesus incarnates a profound and ancient dream deeply imbedded in the human spirit for a world of radical equality," states Crossan, "for a world not of domination, but of empowerment, and above all for the announcement that that is what God, that is what the holy and sacred, is concerned

---

38. Pagels, *Gnostic Gospels,* p.46.
39. Ibid. pp.106-7.
40. Romer, *Testament,* pp.219, 213, 212.
41. Tannahill, *Sex In History,* p 136.
42. Romer, *Testament,* p.203.

about – not about domination, but about empowerment, about a world of justice. That is the permanent, abiding legacy of Jesus . . . The vision of God which Jesus had is one that can best be described as radical egalitarianism – a refusal to draw discriminations and hierarchies and lines of demarcations separating this one from that one, lower from higher, pure from impure, male from female, slave from free, Pagan from Jew – it's a refusal to accept the basic distinctions which most people in this society accept."[43]

Equality is the centerpiece of Jesus' teachings. But in place of a table of open sharing, Constantine instead instates the Bible as a MANual for men to justify elitist ascent, higher up the hierarchy, on ladders of evermore exclusive privileges, with a pinnacle epitomized by Papal authority. Whereas Jesus demonstrated equality by distributing free food for all, Constantine celebrated elite privilege by inviting his bishops to feast at an imperial banquet in Nicea's exclusive lakeside resort. There was nothing equal about these elitist proceedings. "Detachments of the body-guard and troops surrounded the entrance of the palace with drawn swords," recalled Eusebius, "and through the midst of them the men of God proceeded without fear into the innermost of the Imperial apartments, in which some were the Emperor's companions at table, while others reclined on couches arranged on either side . . . The emperor's entrance: at last he himself proceeded through the midst of the assembly, like some heavenly messenger of God, clothed in raiment which glittered as it were with rays of light, reflecting the glowing radiance of a purple robe, and adorned with the brilliant splendor of gold and precious stones . . . One might have thought that a picture of Christ's kingdom was thus shadowed forth, and a dream rather than reality."[44]

This nightmarish conspiracy thus co-opted the Jesus story and reconstructed its principles to justify wealth, privilege and authority for heterosexual men. The table at Constantine's feast was *closed* to women and gays. The Emperor's ecuMENical ball had inverted the teachings of Jesus on its head. Army battalions of Rome rode forth to proclaim the doctrine of a most unholy Ghostly Trio called the Trinity.

> *What exactly was the content of this preliminary notion of God, that was somehow to be presupposed in every discussion, and in every later development? . . . the doctrine of the Patripassians, that the Father and the Son are the same person, is said to have been based not on the affirmation of the unity of the divine essence, but rather on their determination to safeguard the monarchy. Tertullian, however, saw a grave danger that the mass of simple Christians would be deceived by such an argument . . . Dionysius of Rome, finally, called the doctrine of the monarchy the most august doctrine of the Church.*   – Bernard Lonergan[45]

43. *Biography of Jesus*, A&E 4/95.
44. *Nicene and Post-Nicene Fathers of the Christian Church*, ed: Schaff and Wace, *Eusebius: Church History & Life of Constantine the Great*, p.522.
45. Bernard Lonergan, *The Way to Nicea*, (The Westminister Press, 1976), a translation of pages 17-112 of *De Deo Trino* (Rome: Gregorian University Press, 1964), p.121.

In many churches the bishop was emerging, for the first time, as a "monarch" (literally, "sole ruler"). Increasingly, he claimed the power to act as disciplinarian and judge over those he called "the laity."

— Elaine Pagels[46]

The Church's convoluted logic used *Christ* to justify inequality and institute monarchy over the peasants. For centuries to come, right up to the time of Jimi Hendrix, the masses of humanity were MANipulated with stories revised and labeled "sacred" by the Church. "Literacy and learning were two of the most important victims in the collapse of the Classical world," writes Tannahill. "What was read and what was written were virtually at the sole discretion of the Church . . . the words and conclusions of the Church Fathers remained unassailed, and so, in time, became unassailable. Their deliberations – products often of a highly personal and highly prejudiced view of life and society – took on an aura of revealed truth, and their morality, almost entirely relative in its origins, achieved the status of the absolute . . . much of what the modern world still understands by 'sin' stems not from the teachings of Jesus of Nazareth, or from the tablets handed down from Sinai, but from the early sexual vicissitudes of a handful of men who lived in the twilight days of imperial Rome."[47]

Romer describes what happened: "[At Nicea] they also used [the Bible] to buttress the idea of earthly power . . . That's what the next 1500 years of history is all about . . . The idea is that [the Emperor] rules by divine right and if you go against him you go against God . . . The ancient Bible stories were used to organize the lives of men . . . they became the justification of nations, of capitalism too, the root of law and the seed perhaps of all the writhing power of the West"[48]

Jesus' message of equality was modified, rewritten and de-emphasized by the Council's decrees. The Church adapted Irenaeus's example of banning all gospels that praise gays and women. Constantine promoted the Trinity to justify a society structured in favor of *dominator* men. "These religious debates," observed Pagels, "questions of the nature of God, or of Christ – simultaneously bear social and political implications that are crucial to the development of Christianity as an institutional religion . . . ideas which bear implications contrary to that development come to be labeled as 'heresy'; ideas which implicitly support it become 'orthodox' . . . Orthodox Jews and Christians insist…God is wholly other. But some of the Gnostics who wrote these gospels contradict this . . . those who had gone on to receive *gnosis* [knowledge] had come to recognize Christ as the one sent from the Father of Truth, whose coming revealed to them that their own nature was identical with his – and with God's . . . The *Tripartite Tractate*, written by a follower of Valentinius, contrasts those who are Gnostics, 'children of the Father,' with those who are uninitiates, offspring of the demiurge. The Father's children, he says,

46. Pagels, *Gnostic Gospels,* p.40.
47. Tannahill, *Sex In History,* p.138.
48. Romer, *Testament,* PBS 10/91.

join together as equals, enjoying mutual love, spontaneously helping one another. But the demiurge's offspring – the ordinary Christians – 'wanted to command one another, outrivaling one another in their empty ambition'; they are inflated with 'lust for power,' 'each one imagining that he is superior to the others' . . . [Gnostics] refused to acknowledge such distinctions. Instead of ranking their members into superior and inferior 'orders' within a hierarchy, they followed the principle of strict equality. All initiates, men and women alike, participated equally in the drawing [of lots]; anyone might be selected to serve as *priest, bishop,* or *prophet* . . . Valentinian Christians . . . followed a practice which insured the equality of all participants. Their system allowed no hierarchy to form, and no fixed 'orders' of clergy. Since each person's role changed every day, occasions for envy against prominent persons were minimized."[49]

These ideals of the Gnostics were suppressed and condemned by dominator men with the same brutality used to wipe out the Goddess religions a thousand years earlier. When Irenaeus and Constantine edited the contents of the Bible, they deleted the best texts and published instead a MANual of *lessons in the supremacy of men* – heterosexual, dominator men.

> *It's man-made stuff . . . there's so many broken-down variations . . . but they're so cheeky, all the time adding in their own bits and pieces.*
> – Jimi[50]

KEY CLAUSES

Writings about domination became the key clauses around which the final draft of the Bible was constructed. Three centuries after the death of Jesus, a small fraction of the stories about him were published as the New Testament Bible of the Roman Empire. The selection process for its contents was determined by Roman men whose extensive edits fashioned the Bible into their own image.

> *The Bible teaches that women brought sin and death into the world . . . The Bible was written by man out of his love for domination.*
> – Elizabeth Cady Stanton[51]

Today's legal system overflows with long contractual tomes. Most of these lengthy contracts contain just a few key passages, the main points of the agreement – the *boilerplate* issues – which 95% of the surrounding contract serves to clarify and support. In a similar way, the many rules and beliefs of the male religions hide the key boilerplate ideas behind a deluge of minor clauses (like "don't eat pigs because they have divided hoofs" – Leviticus 11:7).

---

49. Pagels, *Gnostic Gospels,* pp.xxxvi, xx, 116, 40-41, 43.
50. Hit Parader 1/70.
51. *One Woman, One Vote,* PBS 12/18/95.

Of the tens of thousands of verses in the Bible, only eight can be interpreted as referring to homosexuality: two are mentioned in the Old Testament (Leviticus 18:22 and 20:13) and six more in the New Testament (Paul: Romans 1:24, 26-27, 31; Paul: I Timothy 1:10; and Paul: I Corinthians 6:9-10).

"There are verses that say you shall not wear clothing made out of two different kinds of fiber," notes Rev. Gary Tyman, "and verses that talk about cross breeding different species of animals, and verses that talk about not eating shellfish. I think it is disingenuous for Christians to pick out the [anti-gay] verses and then blindly ignore all the other verses that surround it."[52]

A maze of arcane details surrounding the key clauses in the Bible distracts readers from a few strategic decrees – key clauses that are at the core of heterosexual male religions:

1) Supremacy of men and requirement of women to serve male needs
2) Condemnation and persecution of homosexuals
3) Elitism: privileges for male heterosexuals
4) Worship/Warship

WARSHIP

> *The purpose of worship is to shift – from peripheral awareness to focal awareness – the mystery and wonder of the world. We sense it going on a lot, but we do not have it in focus of our attention. [Chanting monks] take what is in peripheral awareness – the overtones too faint for us to hear discretely – and elevate it to our direct consciousness. So they're doing in music exactly what worship was intended to do with the sacred: to get from peripheral to focal awareness.*   *– Houston Smith[53]*

"A purely negative evaluation of the effects of religion would be inaccurate," suggests Mary Daly. "It cannot be denied that many people, women and men, have achieved with the help of religion a kind of autonomy, charity and peace . . . [but] these qualities, and particularly this peace, have been attained at too high a price, that is, by leaping over inequities instead of working through these. Certainly, there is something deficient in harmony bought at the expense of insight, in solving problems by not seeing them . . . The church has been seen by some as essentially a *charismatic community*, in which such gifts as healing and prophecy are experienced. Unfortunately its apologists have failed to give due attention to the fact that the healing dispensed within the province of institutional religion has to a large extent been needed because of the destruction wrought by such religion. The healing dispensed institutionally . . . does not go to the

---

52. Need to Know, WXXI-TV Rochester, NY, 12/19/97.
53. *Houston Smith: Hinduism & Buddhism*, interview with B. Moyers, PBS 3/96.

cause of sickness. It is not preventive medicine. Rather, an elitism is perpetuated that feeds on illness of soul, mind, and body."[54]

When we worship, we are expending energy on something that's considered sacred and special. A religion can require the practice of *worship*, an activity which heightens awareness of "the mystery and wonder of the world...the sacred." But the way in which one group of people worships will distinguish them from people with other beliefs. A woman who eats meat on Friday doesn't comply with Vatican rules. A man who won't lay prostrate and face Mecca disobeys Muslim customs. Dominators fixate on such differences and care little for any increased sense of the "mystery and wonder of the world." Communal contemplation, and praise of the mystery, is replaced with a rejection of outsiders. Worship becomes *warship*.

Warship is a verb. It is a call to demonstrate *compliance* with beliefs and customs of a tribe – and battle against those who don't conform. Outsiders are "Other" – unlike us. The Others are excluded, obstructed and rejected. We who conform *deserve more* than the Others because our warship is "better." God approves of the way *we* pray.

> *Thou shalt have no other gods before me . . . Thou shalt not bow down thyself*
> *to them, nor serve them, for I the Lord thy God am a jealous God.*
> — Exodus 20:3,5

Rituals of submission appeal to dominators. Their religions use warship to define lines in the sand across which outsiders dare not tread. "By the year 200, the battle lines had been drawn," writes Pagels, "both orthodox and Gnostic Christians claimed to represent the true church and accused one another of being outsiders, false brethren, and hypocrites . . . each group attempted to define the church in ways that excluded the other . . . Gnostics defined the church precisely in terms of the quality of the interrelationships among its members . . . exploring the psyche became explicitly what it is for many people today implicitly – a religious quest. Some who seek their own interior direction, like the radical Gnostics, reject religious institutions as a hindrance to their progress . . . the Gnostic becomes a 'disciple of his [own] mind' . . . He learns what he needs to know by himself in meditative silence. Consequently he considers himself equal to everyone, maintaining his own independence of anyone else's authority . . . Whoever follows the direction of his own mind need not accept anyone else's advice . . . many Gnostics, like many artists, search for interior self-knowledge as the key to understanding universal truths . . . whoever explores human experience simultaneously discovers divine reality . . . Convinced that the only answers were to be found within, the Gnostics engaged in an intensely private interior journey."[55]

> *Blessed are the solitary and the chosen, for you will find the Kingdom. For*
> *you are from it, and to it you will return.*   — Jesus (Thomas:49)

---

54. Daly, *Beyond God the Father*, pp.153, 160-161.
55. Pagels, *Gnostic Gospels*, pp.104, 107, 123, 132, 134, 144.

Jimi Hendrix typified the Gnostic personality. Hendrix sensed that neither worship nor warship is *required* by the Creator.

> *People here are losing their peace of mind, they're getting so lost in all of these rules and regulations and uniforms that they're losing their peace of mind. If people would just take three to five minutes a day to be by themselves to find out what they want to do, by the end of the week they'd have something . . . that's how you can get yourself together and be friends with your neighbors, maybe even say hello and see if you can knock down all of those complexes.*   – Jimi[56]

Jimi ignored the requirements of worship and the rules of warship. He promoted a single belief – the Hendrixian creed:

> *As long as you are not harming another human being, what does it matter what you do? This I really believe: anybody should be able to think or do what they want as long as it doesn't hurt anybody else. But those old laws and ideas really do hurt people mentally. When natural feelings conflict against laws that were made hundreds of years ago – that's when you get hang-ups.*
>   – Jimi[57]

Jimi's wisdom mirrors Wicca's creed: "Do as you will. Harm none." But "old laws and ideas" train us to do what is willed by a hierarchy of men. When the Church merged with the Roman Empire under Constantine, people attracted to Jesus' vision of a classless society found themselves now groveling at the feet of kings. To call oneself Christian required tribute paid to the thrones of unjust monied men. The faith was revised by Rome to teach the opposite of what Jesus preached. Today, customs justify, and laws enshrine, our *right* to profit at the expense of anyone less lucky than us. In opposition with this is the teaching of Jesus about equal sharing of everything:

> *Those who call themselves kings like to order other people around. And their great leaders have full power over the people they rule, but don't act like them. If you want to be great, you must be the servant of all the others. And if you want to be first, you must be everyone's slave.*
>   – Jesus (Mark 10:42-44)

---

56. Circus 3/69.
57. Melody Maker 3/8/69.

FAIR PLAY VS. FAIR SHARES

Jesus opposed dominator hierarchy. Two thousand years after his death, the conflict continues in the economics of Fair Play vs. Fair Shares.

Fair Play = an individual's right to compete for the ownership of privately held wealth and resources.

Fair Shares = everyone's right of access to publicly owned resources and to equal opportunities for life and liberty.

> Fair Shares – "The Fair Shares perspective," explains William Ryan, ". . . concerns itself much more with equality of rights and of access, particularly the implicit rights to a reasonable share of society's resources, sufficient to sustain life at a decent standard of humanity and to preserve liberty and freedom from compulsion. Rather than focusing on the individual's pursuit of his own happiness, the advocate of Fair Shares is more committed to the principle that all members of the society obtain a reasonable portion of the goods that society produces...pursuit of private goals on the part of some individuals might even have to be bridled . . . Fair Shares . . . [is] an appropriate distribution throughout society of sufficient means for sustaining life and preserving liberty."[58]

> Fair Play – In opposition to Fair Shares is Fair Play, which equates life with a game played as competition, resulting in winners and losers. Those who lose have only themselves and the game to blame. "Fair Play," continues Ryan, "stresses that each person should be equally free from all but the most minimal necessary interference with his right to 'pursue happiness' . . . all are equally free to *pursue*, but have no guarantee of *attaining*, happiness . . . the emphasis on the individual's unencumbered pursuit of his own goals is summed up in the phrase 'equality of opportunity' . . . the ablest, most meritorious, ambitious, hardworking, and talented individuals will acquire the most, achieve the most, and become the leaders of society. The relative inequality that this implies is seen not only as tolerable, but as fair and just. Any effort to achieve what proponents of Fair Play refer to as 'equality of results' is seen as unjust, artificial."[59]

---

58. William Ryan, *Equality*, (New York: Pantheon Books, 1981), p.9.
59. Ibid. p.8.

We live under a system of Fair Play. Personal wealth is supposedly proportional with the merits of our achievements, our luck, or our inheritance. "The more meritorious person – merit being some combination of ability and constructive effort – *deserves* a greater reward," notes Ryan. "From this perspective it is perfectly consistent to suppose that *unequal* shares could well be *fair* shares; moreover, within such a framework, it is very unlikely indeed that equal shares could be fair shares, since individuals are not equally meritorious."[60]

Are rewards distributed fairly in our society according to the merits of each person? "Yes and no," answers Ryan. "Yes, we see some vague congruence here and there – some evidence of upward mobility, some kind of inequalities that can appear to be justified. But looking at the larger picture, we must answer with an unequivocal No! . . . When we assert that one group of persons is, on the average, four or five times more meritorious than another group, we are at the very outer margins of creditability . . . One struggles to imagine any measure of merit . . . that would manifest itself in nature in such a way that one sizeable group of persons would 'have' eight or ten or twenty times more of it – whatever 'it' might be – than another sizeable group has."[61]

MERIT TERRORIST

Making any achievement happen requires contributions from people other than the lone achiever. The quarterback who scores a touchdown couldn't have done it without the efforts of teammates. It can be argued that even the efforts of the opposing team are needed for the score. But our society rewards the achievements of individuals as if they happen in a vacuum: we tend to reward the achiever and ignore others who supported the effort. That we draw such distinctions between individual and group, between self and other, is an effect of what Daly calls, "The eternal masculine stereotype, [implying] hyper-rationality . . . 'objectivity,' aggressivity, the possession of dominating and manipulative attitudes toward persons and the environment, and the tendency to construct boundaries between the self (and those identified with the self) and 'the Other' . . . The eternal feminine . . . implies hyper-emotionalism, passivity, self-abnegation, etc."[62]

By contrast, in the matriarchal societies of history, the emphasis was not on boundaries and personal possessions – but rather on the group's happiness and shared power. In *Beyond God The Father,* Daly cites studies of ancient goddess cultures and notes that these matriarchies were "a very different kind of society from patriarchal culture, being egalitarian rather than hierarchical and authoritarian. Matriarchal culture recognized but one purpose in life: human felicity . . . not bent on the conquest of nature or of other human beings."[63]

But societies dominated by women were few and far between. "[In] the historical halls of fame," notes Tannahill, ". . . virtually every [woman in a position of power] owed

---

60. Ibid. p.10.
61. Ibid. pp.10-12.
62. Daly, *Beyond God the Father,* p.15.
63. Ibid. p.94.

her distinction to the accident of having been the daughter, wife, widow, or mistress of some great man . . . Matriarchy was historically rare . . . the mother-goddesses of history came to be credited with rather more power than they ever seem to have possessed."[64]

Dominator cultures denigrate sex in order to condemn and control women. Dominators create hierarchies of privilege for men whose merits are said to "deserve" reward. But how do people who inherit wealth *merit* their money? "The rich of one generation are almost all children of the rich of the previous generation," points out Ryan, "partly because more than half of significant wealth is inherited, partly because all the other prerogatives of the wealthy are sufficient to assure a comfortable future for Rockefeller and Du Pont toddlers . . . Such equal opportunities for advancing in life as do exist are darkly overshadowed by the many head starts and advantages provided to the families of wealth and privilege . . . a few thousand individuals are fully licensed to gather and retain wealth at the cost of the wasteful, shameful, and fraudulent impoverishment of many millions . . . I don't think many of us have strong objections to inequality of monetary income as such. A modest range, even as much as three or four to one, would, I suspect, be tolerable to almost everybody . . . The current range in annual incomes – from perhaps $3,000 to some unknown number of *millions* – is, however, excessive and intolerable, impossible to justify rationally, and plain inhuman. The problem of wealth is more fundamental. Most of the evils of inequality derive from the reality that a few thousand families control almost all the necessities and amenities of life, indeed the very conditions of life. The rest of us, some 200 million [Americans], have to pay tribute to them if we want even a slight illusion of life, liberty, and the pursuit of happiness . . . We need, rather, to accustom ourselves to a different method of holding resources, namely, holding them in common, to be *shared* amongst us all – not divided up and parceled out, but shared. This is the basic principle of Fair Shares, and it is not at all foreign to our daily experience . . . we share such resources as public parks and beaches . . . the public library [is] a tiny example of what Fair Shares equality is all about."[65]

Ralph Nader points out that one quarter of all children in America today live in poverty. "We have huge capital pools that aren't being put to productive uses," complains Nader, "they're being put into the 'paper economy' instead of the real economy that creates real jobs. We have a lot of capital in this country, pension money, for example, it's overwhelmingly controlled by corporations, banks, insurance companies, and funneled into speculative mergers and acquisitions instead of productive investments . . . massive pension money, and other of people's money, going to finance mergers and acquisitions and empire building creations that don't create any new wealth or new jobs, that make the people at the top and the investment bankers fantastically rich. We have a government that's supposed to be servicing us, instead they're shoveling out huge contracts, that aren't needed, to businesses: subsidies, giveaways, bail outs, you name it, monopolies as central power – and it's not able to serve the people. The whole corporate world, for

---

64. Tannahill, *Sex In History*, pp.325, 353.
65. Ryan, *Equality*, pp.18, 26, 30-1.

example, is bigger than poverty welfare. *The Wall Street Journal* itself estimated it at $140 billion a year. For what? This is supposed to be a sink or swim free enterprise system. Instead it's *corporate* socialism. When these corporations are ready to go bankrupt, because they are mismanaged, corrupt and speculative, they go to Washington. Only small business has the right to go bankrupt. The big guys go to Washington for a handout.

"The problem is that [Washington] is full of Think Tanks and trade associations who have universal health insurance, great pensions, great pay – they're never going to be challenged by *Nike* workers in Indonesia at $1.60 a day, and they're telling 80% of the American people, who have demonstrably experienced a declining standard of living in real terms for the last twenty years, that they are really better off!

"My remedy is this: people must be given control over what they own. They own $4 trillion of pension funds, they own the public land, they own huge amounts of mutual insurance assets, they own stock, they own the public airwaves – and they don't *control* any of it. Business corporations control it all. If you give people power you will democratize credit, to get more credit to small businesses and entrepreneurs in inner city areas. The more that big banks take control of our banking industry the less they loan to small business . . . The bottom 90% of the American people, in terms of wealth, is equal to the top 1%. There's a lot to squeeze out from the very super rich, who have thrived on handouts from the government, research and development from the government, all kinds of protection enabling their fortunes.

"Corporate welfare comes right out of your pocket, we call it Aid To Dependent Corporations, and there's no termination after two years, where you've got to get off it. What we have to focus on here is what are the corporations giving back? The corporations are profiting in genetic engineering, that was heavy government research input into that. Aerospace, heavy government research. In telecommunications, heavy government R & D. From NASA and the Pentagon, from the National Institutes of Health and so on. What are the corporations giving back? Instead they want to smash your right to use the courts, they want to force you to sign printed contracts – take it or leave it. No negotiation with your banks, insurance companies and HMOs and your employers. What are these corporations giving back to America? Are they basically global corporations who no longer pledge allegiance to the flag? We have growing disparity between the bosses at the top of the corporations and the workers, and a massive attack on our democracy and our law of contracts, our law of wrongful injury, and to have access to courts. Our democracy is being dismantled, that's the key point. Democracy is the greatest solution to problems that anybody has ever devised. We need more democracy, not less democracy, which is what we're getting."[66]

> *Government, in a democracy, is the only power that ordinary folks have to do battle with global monoliths that are dominating our economy and ruining our economy.*
> — Jim Hightower[67]

66. *Money, Class & Politics*, PBS 6/96.
67. The Phil Donahue Show, NBC 11/2/95.

Chapter 12: Separating Jesus from Christ

ﾟ

Today Christians refer to Jesus Christ almost as if Christ is his last name, but many of them realize its actually a title, it's the Greek word for a Messiah.
— James Tabor[1]

They got to be intelligent enough, to be precise enough, to realize the danger of words, because all they got is the word of God. They don't have God, they have the word. WORD = WERED – that which came to pass. I prove with my equations that they have to change the book. The book that's killing people is the Bible . . . They're saying that God said it, but they have no witnesses that He said it. But they say He said it so they could say something else, too, and make this world another place . . . They use the word "God" to put people to sleep. They got to write a blueprint, because somebody's following the blueprint. The Bible is the blueprint right now, it says what's going to happen in the future, but it doesn't have to be the only blueprint. They could make another blueprint, because people got a right to set their own destiny. — Sun Ra[2]

"The idea of Messiah looms very large for Christians," says historian Paula Fredrikson, "because the Greek word for Messiah, "Christ," became Jesus' last name, and that's how Christians define his function. But the Christian definition of Messiah is something that's generated *after* the lifetime of Jesus. We see the process of [defining Jesus as a Messiah] in the work of the evangelists, that's part of the goal of the gospel writers."[3]

The writers claimed Jesus as Messiah and gave him the name Christ. Three centuries later, Augustine and the Vatican link Jesus with original sin when they claim him as "Christ." This connection is an invention of the Church, and it is meant to reject flesh, especially the female body. But Jesus opposed anti-female Hebrew traditions. "As master and host," notes Crossan, "Jesus performs . . . the role of servant, and all share the same food as equals . . . Most of Jesus' . . . male followers would think more experientially of females as preparers and servers of the family food. Jesus took on himself the role not only of a servant but of female . . . Far from reclining and being served, Jesus himself serves the meal, serves, like any housewife, the same meal to all including himself . . . just as the female both serves food and becomes food, so Jesus would both have served

1. Mysteries of the Bible, *Messiahs*, A&E 8/10/97.
2. Interview with Charles Blass, Ascot Hotel, Copenhagen, 3/21/92, and NYC 10/24/91.
3. *Life & Times of Jesus*, The Learning Channel 12/94.

food here below and would become food hereafter . . . Long before Jesus was host, he was hostess."[4]

In the patriarchal society of the Hebrews, Jesus demonstrated a radical attitude towards women. "Some of them traveled with Jesus," explains David Barr, "which is a shocking thing to do. Women are supposed to protect the family honor, they are not to be with other men, and certainly not to leave home without their husbands or some male guardian going with them. So these are all kinds of countercultural, shocking, anti-family things that we see Jesus doing with women."[5]

> *Whoever does not hate his father and mother cannot become a disciple to*
> *me. And whoever does not hate his brothers and sisters cannot become a*
> *disciple to me.*   – Jesus (Luke 14:26)

Jesus and Christ represent two distinct beliefs that needn't be linked. Each developed separately and were originally unrelated to the other. But today we are trained to connect them, even though Messiah/Christ beliefs come from the Church, three centuries after Jesus died. As Fredrikson said, "The Christian definition of Messiah is something that is generated *after* the lifetime of Jesus."[6] Jesus of Nazareth would not identify with "Christ." The Messiah/Christ story teaches us that nature is sin. Society has outgrown this notion evolved from an age when males dominated our race. Today we can analyze the story to interpret history and psychoanalyze the past: a Messiah "justifies" the supremacy of men, just as Hindu beliefs promote the torture of women in India and Buddhist customs condone the murder of infant girls in China. Male religions define the human body in ways that enslave females.

> *Here comes a woman Sweat all down her back, for Birth or pleasure, she's*
> *on the right track. But for being free, she ain't supposed to plea, and don't*
> *rely on no man to try and understand.*   – Jimi[7]

The story of the Messiah/Christ condemns women in order to benefit heterosexual men. But the story of Jesus protests oppression, especially against weaker people. All scholars agree that Jesus preached *equality.*

> *Jesus said . . . the Kingdom . . . is, was, and always will be available to any*
> *who want it . . . That ecstatic vision and social program sought to rebuild*
> *a society upwards from its grass roots but on principles of religious and*
> *economic egalitarianism . . . with free healing . . . and free sharing.*
>   – John Crossan[8]

---

4. Crossan, *Historical Jesus*, p.404.
5. *Biography of Jesus*, A&E 4/95.
6. *Life & Times of Jesus*, The Learning Channel 12/94.
7. *Cherokee Mist – The Lost Writings of Jimi Hendrix*, p.84.
8. Crossan, *Historical Jesus*, p.xii.

Money is a form of stored energy credits, that's what it represents. A society rebuilt on the basis of equality and free sharing uses money as a means to achieve what is fair for everyone: *one shared level* of income and buying power. Everyone able to work has the right, the opportunity and the requirement to work. But all jobs should pay the same, a single income for everyone. What should *vary* from person to person is the amount of *time* spent on the job. The number of hours required to work any job is what needs to be determined by majority approval.

The degree to which we deviate from equal money for everyone is the degree to which justice comes undone. This is an insight of Jesus that the dominators make obscure. They obscure it with Roman Church logic that links Jesus, an advocate for equality, with *Christ*, a symbol of rejection of flesh and degradation of women.

The story of blues music, and of Voodoo's impact on the Messiah religions, is the hallmark of our time, explaining a collision of myths, fueled by renewed use of hallucinogens, and epitomized by the life of Hendrix.

> *From the first the music has felt like the attack on the institutions that it was actually attacking.*   – Michael Ventura[9]

> *Jesus took on through the mirror just ahead of me . . . He said . . . this was a good time to say what I forgot the last time, you know, what I meant to say. That's when I realized that he was as spaced out as me. Something about woman being the whole 1/2 of today and not being treated the way they should.*   – Jimi[10]

Hendrix identified with aspects of Jesus:

> *I've been Jesus Christ – 30 twice . . . Superman – C'mon, throw the Dice. Capt. Midnite, how do I look . . . King Out of Sight – Write a new Book.*
> – Jimi[11]

> *As my tears drop on my crystal ball, magnifies the reflections of Christ . . . he held a book with help from God – as reward he wipes our blood from his eyes – and the cross that he would use for his throne – represents not life but death. Is this the way all heroes go . . .*   – Jimi[12]

9. Ventura, *Hear That Long Snake Moan*, Whole Earth Review, Summer 1987, p.92.
10. *Cherokee Mist – The Lost Writings of Jimi Hendrix*, p.71, *I Escaped From the Roman Coliseum – May 18, 1969.*
11. Ibid. p.106, *Astro Man.*
12. Ibid. p.75, *As I Look Into My Crystal Ball.*

"Certain creative persons throughout the ages . . . found themselves at the edges of orthodoxy," writes Pagels. "All were fascinated by the figure of Christ...all returned constantly to Christian symbols to express their own experience. And yet they found themselves in revolt against orthodox institutions."[13]

> *The music gets louder and it gets rebellious because it's starting to form a religion, because you're not gonna find it in church . . . it's nothing but an institution . . . so then it moves on to trying to find yourself.*
> — Jimi[14]

To dominator MENtality Hendrix seems an unlikely super hero. Jimi too was amused by the irony of his position. He would imitate Mighty Mouse and sing *Here I come to save the day!* At other times he'd compare himself to *"Jesus Christ – 30 twice."* He recognized the teachings of Jesus to be instructions with which to organize society. If equality and tolerance had shaped human culture for the past two thousand years, the knowledge and technology we now need to survive would have been with us long ago. Instead, sensitive introspection in men and women was routinely brutalized by dominators. Our struggle to save the planet today is a race against time lost to obstructions and delays caused by persecution of intuitive seers.

> *The highest good is won only in the struggle against difficulties into which evil passions have brought us.*   — J.A. Stewart[15]

Hendrix understood that he was the only one who could publicize the need for weapons to throw off the Rock: *"Superman, C'mon, throw the Dice."* A unique group of people listen to Jimi. He could preach asteroid visions *"right into that little gap"* in the spaces between his listener's thoughts. But he had to escape the fate that dominators orchestrate for visionaries like Jesus, and like himself. Writing of his gladiator battles waged against misperception of his message, Jimi composed a poem titled "I Escaped From the Roman Coliseum," in which Jesus tells him, *"Sometimes you talk like the devil and he's in late and getting sorry for his trouble."*

"Well, I sure ain't you," replies Jimi, *"so what you want me to do? Go back to Earth and witness the royal change of the rubble? I'm trying to be saved on my own two feet, tell me some news so's I can throw it in the street."*[16] His career became a quest to find the right way to communicate the *"news,"* a message that would *"save"* Earth from the *"change of the rubble."*

---

13. Pagels, *Gnostic Gospels*, p.150.
14. Interview with Nancy Carter, L.A., 6/15/69, *Hendrix Speaks*, 1990 Rhino Records.
15. J.A. Stewart, *The Myths of Plato*, (New York: MacMillan and Co., 1905), p.453.
16. *Cherokee Mist – The Lost Writings of Jimi Hendrix*, p.71 *I Escaped From the Roman Coliseum – May 18, 1969.*

> *I wanted once to stay forever in California, but I hear God's even going to reclaim that soon. Sometimes I've wanted to go into the hills, but I stayed. Some people are meant to stay and carry messages.*   – Jimi[17]

Shortly before Hendrix died he was working on a piece titled *Astro Man and Strato-Woman – the Cosmic Lovers of the Universe*:

> *Please understand what I'm trying to say, I love the comics so it's easy to say . . . I had a dream just the other day that I was . . . ASTRO-MAN . . .*
> – Jimi[18]

Astro Man is a Superhero, like Jesus and Superman. *The Birth of a Super Hero* is the title of one of Jimi's favorite comic books, a 1966 Marvel Comics issue of *Spiderman*. Kept with this issue was Jimi's 30-page screenplay titled *Moondust*:

> *Scene leaves off at end of battle with man standing alone – cracking effect happens . . . A beam of light comes through [the] opening as flying saucers in formation appear on each side . . . He feels himself falling to the trembling ground and is still, although the catastrophe is still happening right before his half-closed eyes . . . MIDDLE PART OF THEME – ASTRAL TRAVEL – Before he feels himself leaving body . . . childhood situations flash before him.*   – Jimi[19]

Jimi takes his character through Venice and Rome and on to Atlantis where a voice from the sky announces "*a giant production of heaven.*" He compares heaven to a ship "*swirling through space looking for a steppingstone – getting Karma-dues,*" but its function is to "*clear every world of hate and repression.*" *Moondust* explains that Earth is the "*last to be called*" as Jimi's alter ego is "*now being drawn to Heaven.*"[20]

> *. . .and the story of the asteroid belt in our solar system is explained.*
> – Jimi [21]

Moondust goes on to explain the asteroid story in relation to the "*mixing of the races against the commander's rule*" and the "*coming together of Adam and Eve.*"[22]

---

17. Disc 9/12/70.

18. *Cherokee Mist – The Lost Writings of Jimi Hendrix*, p.106.

19 *Moondust*, p.28 was published as exhibit #479 in the catalogue for Sothebys sale 6258 *Animation Art and Rock 'n' Roll Memorabilia Dec. 14 and 17, 1991*.

20. *Moondust*, pp.29-30, which, while on public display at Sothebys in New York on Dec. 13, 1991, was read and noted by Charles Blass.

21. Ibid.

22. Ibid.

These scenes from *Moondust* relate with *The Birth of a Super Hero* as examples of the type of storyline that Jimi needed. The *Moondust* movie was intended to *"carry messages"* and its script explains our fate. So concerned were we that Adam command Eve – men over women throughout history, and white over black – that we didn't recognize our only real foe: *"the asteroid belt in our solar system."* By the time we see the threat, it's too late to do what we could have done long ago – protect the Earth. *Moondust* is a tragedy that need not have been.

The massive task of building a defense depends upon a pooling of resources among everyone everywhere. Our survival requires *"the mixing of races against the commanders rule."* Dominators prevent a society of equals from being organized. Jimi calls this *"the commanders rule"* – equality isn't happening. So many people who possess the greatest potential among us suffer death by neglect every day. Our dominator tradition is now *"getting Karma-dues"* for centuries spent fighting for special privileges kept hoarded away from conquered victims. Society complied with schemes to condemn sex and degrade women. This is what Jimi conflicted with. He knew that defeat of the dominators depends on *"the coming together of Adam and Eve."*

In a version of the song "Earth Blues,"[23] he sings of Jesus showing him *"a Queen in ebony in chains."*

> *Way up on the moon her boat traders painted on a tomb.*
> — Jimi[24]

Space age slave-masters take their trade all the way to the Moon. The 28-day lunar phases correspond with a female's monthly menstrual cycle. Jimi is saying that by enslaving in *"chains"* what is feminine yet vital, *"boat trader"* dominators lead us to ruin. In the song "Earth Blues" he sees the last of man seek refuge on the Moon, only to perish in a lunar *"tomb"* covered with dust: *"And across the surface these words were written 'First woman came from God's womb.'"*[25] In other words, woman was born not from a man's rib as the child of Adam. Rather, the "womb" of Creation is feminine, and the Goddess gives birth to life

> *Eve was born from Adam, the first among history's unmarried pregnant males . . . We have been locked in this Eden of his far too long. If we stay much longer, life will depart from this planet.* — Mary Daly[26]

"Earth Blues" is what Jimi called the time and energy we waste dominating each other, time and energy that could have saved the Earth. He sings of people struggling *"but*

---

23. *Straight Ahead* magazine #27 6/91, p.9.
24. Ibid.
25. Ibid.
26. Daly, *Beyond God the Father*, pp.195, 198.

not quite touching the Promised Land" and of "*precious years wasted.*" He asks for God's "*helping hand*" to achieve "*changes and rearranges.*" With flashing sirens warning "*Earth and Rock and Stone,*" he foresees "*the last time.*" Over a chorus of *LOVE, LOVE, LOVE* Jimi urges "*sisters and mamas*" to "*get it together for the Earth Blues coming at you.*"[27]

Male dominion over everything feminine thwarts the effort of everyone to advance towards our goal. Mother Earth today lays prone to disaster in order that men may enjoy the labor of slaves.

> *Jimi wanted me to paint a black woman and a white woman lying over each other in the shape of a cross . . . to symbolize that women are equal to men in the eyes of God.*   — Monika Dannemann[28]

> *When I was in Hawaii I seen a beautiful thing, a miracle. There were lots of rings around the Moon and the rings were all women's faces. I wish I could tell someone about it.*   — Jimi[29]

FLIMSY TWIGS

In the song "Astro Man," Hendrix sings of flying "*higher than that faggot Superman.*" Superman is not a gay character, and in Jimi's lyric "faggot" does not mean homosexual. Hendrix used the word faggot in its literal meaning, which is defined in Webster's Dictionary as "a bundle of twigs." Jimi associates faggot not with sexuality, but with *weakness*: bundles of twigs loosely connected and infirm, like the reasoning of male religions that condemn homosexuality. "Faggot Superman" means that the supreme hetero male icon is based on *weak thinking.* Dominators link homosexuality with disobedience to God and portray same sex attraction as a threat to civilization. They deny the truth that herd thinners are nature's way of reducing population and aiding the evolution of humans. They deny this because their intention is to persecute and dominate everything "feminine" in an effort to maximize their own access to sex. The reasoning of dominators is fraught with tenuous connections, as if the neural branches in their brains were unstable, like flimsy twigs, or literally "faggots."

Recent scientific studies have tested levels of mental energy expended when we attempt to comprehend concepts. Many people have difficulty grasping the links that form an idea such as "gays are herd thinners evolved out of stressed populations." Mental stress, such as stress produced when comprehending logic, causes damage to the hearts of people who have difficulty learning. The damage is in the form of *astimia*, which is reduced blood flow to the heart. Scientists are able to observe and measure this process. Dr. James Blumenthal of Duke University Medical Center reports, "People who test

---

27. Released on *Rainbow Bridge*, Reprise Records 10/71.
28. Dannemann, *The Inner World of Jimi Hendrix*, p.142.
29. Distant Drummer 4/17/69, p.9.

positive to mental stress have a two to threefold greater risk of suffering a future non fatal or fatal cardiac event."[30] A study published in the Journal of the American Medical Association shows that when some patients perform stressful mental tests, researchers observe serious defects in the pumping action of their hearts.[31]

For us to perceive how homosexuals benefit our race, we have to follow the logic of complex thinking, which means mental stress. And many people intuitively avoid mental exertion because of its damaging effects to their health.

> *Some people only use one-tenth of their brain capacity anyway, and there's so much more room to think other good ways.*   — Jimi[32]

And even when we do intellectually accept the *principle* that herd thinners are *intended* by nature, many people remain emotionally repulsed by homosexuality anyway. An unusual degree of mental strength is required to overcome years of conditioning aimed to berate gays.

PHILOSOPHICAL BATTLEGROUNDS

> *We know that Jesus was starting to get it together quite nicely, but that Ten Commandments thing was a drag. The bogey man isn't going to come and get you if you don't tie your shoe. You don't have to be afraid to make love to one of your boyfriends' wives.*   — Jimi[33]

Jimi's opinion of religion reflects the central conflict of his time: equality vs. sexual tyranny. Study of Hendrix brings us to rethink philosophies that we are trained to accept.

> *I'll take somebody like us to get it together, regardless of whether it's gonna be us, ourselves,...the **feeling** is there... The idea is to do it as strong as possible, to work out a certain **physical** change...Anybody can protest but not too many people can offer a decent answer. So we're gonna try to do that . . . give some kind of solutions for people to grasp . . . It's almost all philosophy, our music is, most of it, in a very hazy form, because it's still progressing. It's just like a little baby and it hasn't even reached the stage for it to walk by itself.*   — Jimi[34]

---

30. CBS Evening News 6/4/96.
31. Ibid.
32. Interview with Nancy Carter, L.A., 6/15/69, *Hendrix Speaks*, 1990 Rhino Records.
33. Distant Drummer 4/17/69, p.8.
34. Hopkins, *Hit & Run*, p.208, Brown, *Jimi Hendrix – In His Own Words*, p.81, from interview in London 1/7/69, and interview with Nancy Carter, L.A., 6/15/69, *Hendrix Speaks*.

It is necessary for men who control media to assert that philosophy *bores* the mass audience because rooted in the *philosophies* of world religions are explanations about how men maintain privileges over women. Even though talk about our beliefs makes up the majority of all dialogue in media, the public remains trained to shun discussion of *why* we believe what we do. Yet, it is *philosophy* that men use to rationalize their status and justify their persecution of women and gays. No wonder it's to the advantage of dominators that mainstream audiences be "bored" by philosophy.

Issues surrounding Hendrix and his life connect directly with everything that they aim to conceal. It is crucial for the men who control media to try and influence the way people perceive Jimi, in order to successfully suppress the message of Hendrix.

> *I've met one in a hundred people who let me talk about what I want to. Everybody asks me how old I am, if it's true I have Indian blood, how many women I've had, if I'm married, if I have a Rolls, or more of those jokes. The people who dig me don't want this at all. They want something different, to feel something inside, something real – revolution, struggle, rebellion.*
> — Jimi[35]

Jimi's story sets in relief his audience during the 1960s. Hendrix was Prophet-in-Chief of the freeks, a partnership culture modeled after the Diggers of England. Hendrix was the figurehead of what McKenna terms "the Archaic Revival" – a reemergence of communal equality, enhanced with ego-dissolving hallucinogens. Partnership societies have been suppressed since pre-history but were revived among freeks during the lifetime of Jimi. In the wake of this revival women fought for equality with men, and freeks heeded the shaman's example of hallucinogen-induced communion with Mother Earth.

> *Definitely I'm trying to change the world. I'd love to! I'd like to have my own country, an oasis for the gypsy-minded people. My goal is to erase all boundaries from the world. As long as I know there are people out there who aren't fully together I can't withdraw to lesser goals.* — Jimi[36]

During the Hendrix concert years (1966-1970), counterculture freeks countered a culture of profiteer business executives who orchestrated an orgy of blood money in Vietnam. It is Jimi's influence over this counterculture that links him with Vietnam. He composed war music, and in order to comprehend Hendrix, Vietnam must be discussed. My 1988 manuscript, *A Touch of Hendrix*, describes Vietnam as the battleground for equalitarian vs. elitist beliefs, and questions notions about who deserves what in society, and why.

35. Interview with Gigi Movilia, Rome, 5/68, cited in Shapiro's *Electric Gypsy*, (London: Heinemann, 1990) p.285.
36. Henderson, *Jimi Hendrix – Voodoo Child of the Aquarian Age*, p.257.

> *In South Vietnam it was only the "freedom" of wealthy elitists to profit that*
> *was being defended.*   *— A Touch of Hendrix, 1988*[37]

> *I don't want to say nothing about comparisons with other groups because*
> *if you do, that puts you higher or lower than them, and that's just the same*
> *old cycle . . . We're trying to give solutions to all the protests and the*
> *arguments that they're having about the world today, so we'll try to give our*
> *own little opinions about that in very simple words . . . What we're saying*
> *is not protesting but giving the answers or some kind of solution, instead of*
> *going towards the negative scene.*   *— Jimi*[38]

COMBINE SPIRIT WITH *BLUES*

"Spirit" denotes *perception* and *awareness* of our relationship with the Creator and Creation, spirit is our essence, our *soul*. "Blues" is a feeling of *physical movement*, a dance-based music derived from rhythms of the *body*. *Spiritual Blues* combines the two and interprets physical senses *as* expressions of God: spirit and flesh together as a human body-mind. In other words, sex and lust are as holy, and as unholy, as any Pope. If divinity is represented by Mass in church, it is also represented by sex in bed. Why we disagree with such ideas is explained in the philosophy named Spiritual Blues, a description of the way we're trained to pitch God against flesh so heterosexual men then dominate women and gays.

To experience our body-mind as a unified whole is the goal of Spiritual Blues. The spiritual mind and the sexual body express a single deity. Spiritual Blues reflect the reconciling of a lover's quarrel between Lucifer and God.

> *The background of our music is a Spiritual Blues thing. Blues is a part of*
> *America. We're making our music into Electric Church music; a new kind*
> *of Bible . . . one that will give you a physical feeling. We try to make our*
> *music so loose and hard-hitting so that it hits your soul hard enough to*
> *make it open. It's like shock therapy, or a can opener.*   *— Jimi*[39]

Spiritual Blues offers a clear view through the confusion of human history. Hendrix is its figurehead, connecting concepts with which to reconstruct our understanding of the past. Study of Jimi promotes *belief relief*, a means of being free from centuries of psychological hurt at the hands of man.

---

37. Fairchild, unpublished manuscript, (1988), p.44.
38. Distant Drummer 4/17/69, p.8, Stockholm Radio interview 1/9/69, Brown, *Jimi Hendrix — In His Own Words*, p.81, from interview in London 1/7/69.
39. Interview with Paul Zimmerman, New York 5/69, and East Village Other 1968, cited in Hopkins, *Hit & Run — The Jimi Hendrix Story*, p.170, and in Henderson, *Jimi Hendrix — Voodoo Child of the Aquarian Age*, p.256.

There are a few chosen people that are here to help get these people out of this certain sleepiness that they are in.   – Jimi[40]

Civilization has been completely asleep to the realization of just how serious is the threat of impacts. The sounds of Hendrix and the issues surrounding his life are like "shock therapy can-openers" prying apart our primary beliefs.

Prophets have been persons who establish a **breakthrough** *to a better cultural order and declare this break to be morally legitimate . . . the essential criterion of prophecy is whether or not the message is a call to* **break** *with an established order. Yet* **none** *of the major prophets called unambiguously for rejection of the sexist order, and in all cases their followers implemented this* [sexist] *system of social arrangements.*

– Mary Daly[41]

Spiritual Blues is a potent antidote for our establishMEnt-induced stupor of confused attitudes. Study of Jimi is an effective method for presenting concepts and directing attention to the hidden agenda of world religions. The life of Hendrix renders comprehensible the meaning of Spiritual Blues, and Spiritual Blues explains Jimi's life in a comprehensive way.

Jimi is history's most influential blues musician. His family's ancestry embodies the classic lineage of blues: *African* and *Irish* heritage. The Hendrix family tree fuses the Voodoo roots of blues with its Afro-Irish past. Voodoo is expressed in Jimi's image and in his lyrics. His autobiographic blues epic, "Voodoo Chile," establishes a unique link to British imperialism: Cromwell's crusade in Ireland enslaved Celtic pagans and sold them off to Caribbean colonies. There the Irish Celts mixed in with African slaves and learned new Voodoo ways. The cultural results of this union were rhythm & blues music imported to New Orleans. In the 1950s and '60s, R&B became rock, and it spread throughout America and Europe. A mass-movement of youth became *possessed*.

Two centuries earlier, Voodoo was the philosophy around which Hatian slaves unified to fight off foreign invaders. In a similar way Jimi's generation coalesced around rock. They worshiped crazed pied piper shaman musicians who convulsed to the Loas. Possession frenzy became the new standard for entertainment in the West. Voodoo-rooted music alters our attitudes as it dismantles taboos against sex. Like saints and priests of a new age, rock entertainers used their art to demonstrate the physical side of spirituality. Hendrix represents the extreme High Priest who leads the way away from society's Vatican past. In the 1960s, "generation gap" named the chasm between kids and pre-Elvis elders who grew up without rock. The invention of birth control pills sparked

---

40. San Diego Free Press 6/13/69.
41. Daly, *Beyond God the Father*, p.164.

an explosion of casual sex and *free love*. From 1966 to 1971, the five years of Jimi's peak popularity, VD among teens increased by one thousand percent.[42] To Victorian generations born before World War II, this sexual revolution, epitomized by Hendrix, seemed like a wave of alien mutations.

Afro, Irish and Cherokee lineage positions Jimi as an American child of Voodoo. He is the authentic shaman of world culture. The eternal appeal of his music will forever preserve the blues beat that kept ecstatic dance alive. Enshrined in his sounds are the altered perceptions of hallucinogen induced Voodoo possession, a celebration of the senses.

I want to show you the sound of emotion.

— Jimi[43]

"Voodoo Child (slight return)" is a tune he repeated anthem-like on stage to drive home the point: we *connect* with the Earth only when nature is alien no more. It was as if music had activated what we needed to be complete: a reunion of body/mind fragments. *"I pick up all the pieces and make an island"* sings Jimi in "Voodoo Child," a song about triumph over monumental obstacles:

I stand up next to a mountain
and I chop it down with the edge of my hand.

— Jimi"[44]

People say, "Ah yes, meteorites fall out of the sky, we accept that — a chunk this big, I accept that it falls out of the sky." But it was an intellectual leap to go from a fist-sized stone to a mountain, and have a mountain come down out of the sky.   — Eugene Shoemaker[45]

"Might even raise a little sand," sings Jimi in "Voodoo Child." He is a shaman whose life and art raise us up to chop a Rock down out of the sky.

When there are vast changes in the way the world goes it's usually something like art and music that changes it. Music is going to change the world next time.

— Jimi[46]

Eighteen days before he died, Hendrix returned to the British stage for the last time. His appearance at the August 1970 Isle of Wight festival climaxed Spiritual Blues

---

42. Carter, *Routine Circumcision- the Tragic Myth*, p.40.
43. "Have You Ever Been (to Electric Ladyland)", *Electirc Ladyland*, Reprise Records 10/68.
44. Ibid. "Voodoo Child (slight return)".
45. *Asteroids: Deadly Impact*, NBC National Geographic 2/26/97.
46. Rolling Stone 10/1/70.

symbolism when he opened the show with "God Save the Queen," the British anthem. As an African-American of part-Irish decent, Jimi channeled this music's deepest roots when "The Queen" came bleeding from his speakers: Cromwell's purge of Irish pagans brought slaves to the West Indies, and a new music brewed in the Caribbean. Rock 'n' roll Voodoo soon conquered America.

For his last British gig, Jimi brought body music blues back to the last bastion of paganism, because the Isle of Wight is known as the last county in Britain to be converted to Christianity. Its sleepy town of Freshwater, which hosted the festival, is said to be the last part of the Island to receive the religion.[47]

> *Thanks for waitin', it **has** been a long time, hasn't it?*
> — Jimi at Isle of Wight 1970 C.E.

47. *Mad, Mad World of East Afton*, Evening News (U.K.) 8/27/70.

Chapter 13: First Century

ॐ

We have a tradition that comes from the first millennium B.C.[E.], somewhere else, and we're handling that. It has not turned over and assimilated the qualities of our culture and the new themes that are possible and the new vision of the universe. It must be kept alive. The only people who can keep it alive are artists of one kind or another. That's the artist's function, the mythologizing of the environment and the world.
— Joseph Campbell[1]

One major thing is, the people lack, so to speak, a religious vocabulary, they don't understand what is meant by "Trinity" and "redemption" and "depravity" and any of the "need for salvation." Most people certainly no longer understand fully what is meant by these things, even if they know the words. The second thing is that the very notion of God, to the extent to which it still exists in peoples' minds, has changed. God is no longer someone who wants you to avoid sin, and who possibly might punish you for sinning. He's someone who forgives apriori everything and admits everything, perhaps except Hitler. Even those who, when you ask them do you believe in God? will say ' yes I do,' really don't, in many cases, believe in the God of the gospels, as far as I can see. They believe in a God that they have fashioned themselves.
— Ernest Van Den Haag[2]

I'm working on my own religion, which is life.
— Jimi [3]

When you are criticizing the philosophy of an epoch . . . there will be some fundamental assumptions which adherents of all the various systems within the epoch unconsciously presuppose. Such assumptions appear so obvious that people do not know what they are assuming because no other way of putting things has ever occurred to them.
— Alfred North Whitehead[4]

It is destructive for modern societies to number years and centuries according to a birth date for Christ. It's destructive because our year numerals all hark back, like a

1. The Power of Myth, *The First Storytellers*, PBS 3/88.
2. Firing Line, PBS 11/95.
3. Hit Parader 1/70.
4. Daly, *Beyond God the Father*, p.1.

reminder, to what the Messiah represents. Ingrained in our daily calendar remains a tale of male dominators, a subliminal message everyone gets when we see numbers like "1942."

DENNIS THE MENACE – YEAR OF THE DOMINATOR

Within five centuries after Jesus died, the stories he inspired had been transformed into the most popular religion of the western world. In 525 C.E., Pope John the First decreed that Christians should count calendar years beginning with the birth of Christ. A monk living in Rome named Dionysius Exiguus (Latin for "Dennis the Short") was assigned the task of determining when Christ was born. Dennis searched Church archives for clues, and for unknown reasons he concluded that the birth had occurred 754 years after the founding of Rome. That date was proclaimed Ano Domini (A.D.), Latin for "Year of Our Lord." "Ano" means year, and *domini* or *dominus* is Latin for "lord master" (the Greek word for *lord* is the same as the word for *master*). *Domini* means "master" – *domini* is the root word for *dominator*. Thus A.D. (Ano Domini) actually translates as "Year of the Dominator" – a title which Jesus would surely avoid.

Church officials were not unanimous in their agreement with Dennis the Short's conclusion regarding the year of Christ's birth. But they were under pressure from the Emperor to designate a date, so they went along with what Dennis said, even though there is no evidence to support Mr. Short's claim.

As for the day of the year, Dr. Ronald Hock of the University of Southern California points out that "The birth of Christ was originally celebrated along with the visit of the Magi and the Baptism on January 6th. We have evidence for that as early as the end of the second century, beginning of the third century. Others place the birth of Christ as late as April 21st or May 1st. The date of December 25th does not come around until the fourth century."[5]

In the fourth century, Church fathers announced that Christ's birthday was December 25, the same date as Constantine's birthday! The Church thus enshrined the Emperor like a proxy god. December 25 also marked the pagan festival of Sol Invictus, the Sun god. So the bishops hit three birds with one stone: birthday of Constantine, birthday of the Messiah, and celebration of Sol.

During the winter solstice in December, when days begin to grow longer, Sol the Sun god was worshipped by pagan peasants in frenzied rituals throughout Rome. It is the shortest day of the year, after which daylight increases a little bit every twenty-four hours. Ancient pagans thought that the Sun thus was reborn each year. The winter solstice marks the approach of spring, bringing renewal of crops and new life. Romans celebrated with green branches cut down in anticipation of the green crops to come. They placed candles on the branches in observance of the lengthening hours of sunlight that come with the spring. Gifts were exchanged as tokens of personal sacrifice, in thanks for the rebirth of Earth. The solstice was a time of great optimism and merrymaking.

---

5. *Birth of Christ*, Mysteries of the Bible, A&E 4/94.

The Church disapproved of its members celebrating with pagans, but nothing could stop Christians from joining in the popular holiday festivities of Rome. So, early in the fourth century, Church leaders decided to co-opt the Roman solstice festival by designating December 25 as the Messiah's birthday. They theorized that Christ's conception would have occurred during the spring solstice in March, start of the growing season. Nine months later he was born in December. This logic allowed the Church to subsume the Roman solstice ritual and incorporate it with the Christian religion each December, on Constantine's birthday. The faithful could now celebrate the Holiday ("Holy-day") and also claim the festival ritual as their own.

But neither the year nor the day that mark the birth of Christ are supported with historical evidence.

To randomly mark the passing years based on a Messiah symbol that denigrates nature is, in today's world, unacceptable. Marking time according to stories about Christ trains everyone to pay homage to "logic" about the supremacy of men and denigration of women. This is too flawed a symbol upon which to hang the inception of our everyday calendar. But this is not to say that the winter solstice shouldn't be celebrated.

KRISMAS

December 25 can instead be called Krismas, a day symbolized by Kris Kringle, a mythical combination of Jesus and St. Nicholas. The Dutch words for "Saint Nick" are *Sintre Clus*, which in English is pronounced Santa Claus. Nicholas was a fourth century Bishop from Mira who became legendary for protecting children and giving gifts to peasants. He became the most popular Saint among the masses of people in Europe during the Middle Ages. Nicholas represents equalitarian sharing. But then in 1969 the Pope of the Roman Catholic Church eliminated St. Nicholas' name from the official roster of Saint's Days because there are doubts about the existence of a real Nicholas. The first description of his life was written in 880 C.E., 500 years after his death. There is no evidence of his existence from the period in which he is said to have lived. But it is ironic that lack of such evidence should be a condition for excluding a religious figure from Vatican recognition, because, like St. Nicholas, there is no physical evidence to prove the existence of Christ either, and the first detailed description of Jesus' life that exists today dates from two hundred years after his death.

In the story *Miracle on 34th Street*, Santa Claus is put on trial in a New York City courtroom and asked to give his full name. Santa replies, "I am Kris Kringle." The origins of Kris Kringle begin with Martin Luther in the 16th century. When the German reformer created Protestantism, he banned worship of St. Nicholas. But the birthday of St. Nick, December 6, had become the most widely celebrated day of the year during the Middle Ages. Masses of people adored stories of Nicholas and how he cared for the downtrodden common folk. But Luther believed such worship should be reserved for Jesus alone. So he took the popular myths about Nick the gift giver and combined this with a baby angel called Kris Kringle – a winged cherub named after the Christ Child (pronounced "Krist Kindle" in German). Kris Kringle was said to fly around on December 25 and deliver gifts to good people.

Jesus, St. Nicholas, and Kris Kringle – the common theme that appeals to us about each of these stories is the spirit of giving. And gift giving was already enshrined by the Roman solstice festival each December. Therefore, today, we purge ourselves of Messiah ideas every December by celebrating not "Christmas," but *Krismas*.

Krismas conveys the combined stories of Kris Kringle, St. Nicholas and the baby Jesus as symbols of compassion and giving. By using the term "Krismas," we show allegiance to these values and celebrate the ancient solstice festival of giving. At the same time, we convey rejection of a Messiah/Christ which demeans women with claims that nature-is-bad and sex-is-sin. We can once again celebrate the winter ritual of gift giving, Santa Claus and all, without the Messiah associated with it. So, next December light up a Krismas tree, and separate Jesus from Christ.

The symbol for the new tradition of Krismas is a winged cherub with a broken arm, representing the selfless sacrifice of giving, like the injured cherub Hendrix kept as a statue in his apartment.[6]

<u>EIGHTH DAY OF KRISMAS</u>

> *Ye shall circumcise the flesh of your foreskin, and it shall be a token of the covenant betwixt me and you. And <u>he that is eight days old shall be circumcised</u>.*   – Genesis 17:11-12

> *The exceptionally early age at which Jews performed the rite takes it entirely out of the category of initiation ceremonies among them, and proves it to be of religious or symbolic nature.*   – Joseph Jacobs[7]

As noted earlier, the origins of circumcision in Hebrew law make no mention of hygiene as the *reason* for removing foreskins from boys. Although the custom became a stamp of identification for the Jewish people, Nicholas Carter suggests that its purpose was instead to purge male infants of the "unclean" blood of mothers. "A Biblical injunction in Leviticus (17:10) prohibited Jews from eating blood . . . [in] kosher food . . . all blood vessels had to be removed to make it ritually acceptable . . . Because of her sexual nature, woman was taboo as far as holy things were concerned. Jewish law prohibited sexual intercourse during menstruation or any other discharge of blood from the vagina, and for <u>a period of seven days</u> after the cessation of the flow of blood

6. New Musical Express 9/9/67, see Chapter 1 p.17, ft. #70.
7. Carter, *Routine Circumcision – the Tragic Myth*, p.12.

(Leviticus 18:19)…it was decreed that everything she would lie or sit upon would be unclean… Circumcision could have an additional motivation in a sacrifice of blood as an expiation because of the fear of blood pollution. Since the mother, during her period of ritual purification following childbirth, must, of necessity, touch the child – indeed, since the shedding of blood is part of the birth process – what must be done to save the child from blood pollution?: 'And <u>on the eighth day</u> the flesh of his foreskin shall be circumcised.'"[8]

> *Periah is the tearing of the inner lining of the foreskin which still adheres to the gland, so as to lay it wholly bare. This was (and is) done by the operater – the **mohel**, the professional circumciser – with his thumb-nail and index finger. [An] essential part of the ritual is **mesisah**, the sucking of blood from the wound . . . it was necessary for the mohel to clean the wound by taking the penis into his mouth. In the case of a young adult male . . . the bleeding would have been copious.* — A.N. Wilson[9]

In the Jewish tradition, the mesisah ritual has been regarded as being imbued with magical powers, and often, when a mohel died, the prepuces of the infants he had circumcised were buried with him to drive away evil spirits.

<u>FEAST OF PREPUCE</u>

Christians designate December 25 as the birthday of Christ. The <u>eighth day</u> following December 25 is <u>January 1st</u>, this is the day on which Jesus was circumcised. For the past fourteen centuries, the Catholic Church has celebrated the First of January as the Feast of the Circumcision of Christ, a.k.a. New Year's Day. This is the ritual around which most modern world calendars observe New Year!

> *There are some things about society you have absolutely no way of discovering unless you're in a crisis . . . There are lots of secret rules by which power maintains itself. Only when you challenge it, force the crisis, do you discover the true nature of society. And only at the time it chooses to teach you. Occasionally you can use your intellect to guess at the plan, but in general the secrets of power are taught in darkened police cells, back alleys, and on the street.* — Abbie Hoffman[10]

"Prepuce" is the medical term for a foreskin – the bit of tissue at the tip of the penis to which much of the world unwittingly pays homage each New Year. As Carter explains, "An

8. Ibid. p.14.
9. Wilson, *Paul – The Mind of the Apostle,* p.131.
10. Abbie Hoffman, *Soon to be a Major Motion Picture,* (New York, Perigee Books, 1980), p.1.

example of phallic worship during the Middle Ages involved the Holy Prepuce of Jesus Christ (one of twelve said to be in existence at that time) which belonged to the Abbey Church of Columbus, in the diocese of Chartres, France. This relic was said to posses the miraculous power of rendering all sterile women fruitful . . . The cross is known to have symbolized the phallus and testicles for ages . . . One form of the cross, the Egyptian Ankh, shows the male and female organs in conjunction. The Tree of Life, which figures prominently in the Old Testament, was a common symbol of the 'female principle.'"[11]

Potency fantasies of Church Fathers caused them to imagine a preserved piece of old foreskin as possessing the power to impregnate females. The Prepuce of Jesus, circumcised eight days after Christmas, is the basis of New Year's Day every January 1st. But our calendar can instead be based on a miracle that is universally relevant to today. The arrival of Hendrix into our world represents such a miraculous happening.

HENDRIX EVENT – THE BIRTH OF LIGHT

> *I hate to be put as only a guitar player, or only as a song writer, or only as a tap dancer. I like to move around . . . People let a lot of old time laws rule them . . . I'd like for them to get easier in their minds a little bit.*
>
> – Jimi[12]

The birth of Jimi on November 27, 1942 C.E. is the key moment and central event in human history. At the time that Jimi was born in Seattle, something happened in England, a miracle that only Winston Churchill and a few of the Allied commanders of World War II knew about. It was a secret that would alter the course of history: the *Ultra Secret* – the breaking of the unbreakable Nazi communications code. Every message that Hitler and his generals sent to each other through their code machine named *Enigma* was suddenly deciphered by Operation Ultra, a group of codebreakers. Hitler's secret information was then shared instantly with Churchill and his generals. This decoding feat in England marks the miraculous entrance of Hendrix into the world in November 1942.

November 1942 brought a breakthrough for the Allies at Alamein. This was the first Allied victory of the war, the victory for which Britain had waited so long. On Churchill's instructions church bells, which had been silent since the start of the war, rang throughout Britain in November. But the ground war was the lesser of worries for the Allies that autumn. In England, not much stood in the way of Hitler but a small Royal airforce and its antiquated Navy. "The Battle of the Atlantic was the dominating factor all throughout the war," said Churchill. "Never for one moment could we forget that everything happening elsewhere, on land, at sea, or in the air, depended ultimately on its outcome, and amidst all other cares, we

11. Carter, *Routine Circumcision – the Tragic Myth*, pp.18, 23.
12. Brown, *Hendrix – The Final Days*, p.86, from an interview with Keith Altham, London, 9/11/70, Henderson, *Jimi Hendrix – Voodoo Child of the Aquarian Age*, p.256, Village Voice 1968.

viewed its changing fortunes day by day with hope or anticipation. Amid the torrent of violent events one anxiety reigned supreme . . . Dominating all our power to carry on the war, or even keep ourselves alive, lay our mastery of the ocean routes and the free approach and entry of our ports."[13]

> *The chief hidden factors that helped the Allies win* [the Battle of the Atlantic]: *they intercepted, solved, and read the coded radio messages between Admiral Karl Donitz, Hitler's commander of the U-boats, enabling the Allies to divert their convoys around wolfpacks and sink the subs. This was of fundamental importance because whoever won the Battle of the Atlantic would win the war. The struggle between Allied ships bringing supplies to Britain and German submarines seeking to sever that lifeline was the longest battle of the greatest war of all time. The Germans used a cipher machine called the Enigma to put messages into secret form...the Enigma used by the German navy . . . withstood British codebreaking for the first two years of the war. It was not until the British captured key documents from German warships that they were able to break the naval Enigma continuously.*   — David Kahn[14]

Some of the brightest minds from Britain and the U.S. gathered in Bletchley Park near London: an assembly of mathematicians, musicians, chess players and crossword puzzle experts. Most of them were students brought to Bletchley from nearby Oxford and Cambridge to do their part in solving the mother of all puzzles up to that time: the Nazi Enigma machine. "When the U-boats returned to the north Atlantic in the autumn of 1942," writes F.H. Hinsley, "after months in which they had been concentrated off the American coast, they were using a new Enigma key, Shark, that was unreadable. The result was reflected in a huge increase in Allied shipping losses on the convoy routes."[15]

David Kahn recalls, "North Atlantic sinkings, which totaled some 600,000 tons in the last half of 1941, more than quadrupled to 2,600,000 tons in the last half of 1942. And each of the nearly 500 ships sunk in those six months meant more freezing deaths in the middle of the ocean . . . at the highest levels fears grew that the lack of intelligence, combined with the growing number of U-boats, would sink more ships than could be built. The tonnage left would not suffice to maintain rations and sustain industry in the United Kingdom, much less bring over troops, supplies, weapons, and ammunition to carry the war to Hitler . . . the supreme commanders looked with growing impatience to Bletchley Park for its contribution. On November 22, 1942, the

---

13. David Kahn, *Seizing the Enigma – The Race to Break the German U-Boat Codes 1939-1943*, (Houghton Mifflin, 1991), p.ix.
14. Ibid. pp.ix-x.
15. F.H. Hinsley and Alan Stripp, *Codebreakers - The Inside Story of Bletchley Park*, (Oxford Univ. Press, 1993), p.6.

O.I.C. urged BP, with British understatement, to focus 'a little more attention' on the four-rotor Enigma. The U-boat war was, it said in a silent scream, 'the one campaign which Bletchley Park are not at present influencing to any marked extent – and it is the only one in which the war can be lost unless BP do help.' Unbeknownst to the O.I.C., however, that help was already on the way."[16]

> *Here I come to save the day.* – Jimi imitates Mighty Mouse[17]

At the start of the Battle of Alameim, the British destroyer H.M.S. *Petard* was ordered to hunt for submarines in the eastern Mediterranean near Alexandria. One of the *Petard*'s depth charges crippled U-boat #559 of the Nazi fleet. The submarine surfaced and the Nazis abandoned it. Crewmen from the *Petard* investigated the damaged sub. Kahn describes how "First Lieutenant Anthony Fasson, a Scot, and [Colin] Grazier had dived naked into the sea . . . so [did] the fifteen-year-old canteen assistant, Tommy Brown . . . Fasson . . . using a machine gun, smashed open cabinets in the captain's cabin and . . . took out some documents. Tommy Brown . . . carried these precious papers up the conning tower and gave them to the men in the whaler . . . Fasson and Grazier [were told] to get out at once . . . They had just started up when, unexpectedly and swiftly, the submarine sank . . . They went down with the submarine . . . The whaler with its precious documents came alongside the *Petard* and was hoisted on the run . . . The *Petard* continued to Haifa, where the valuable documents were given to naval intelligence officers."[18]

The documents from U-559 were taken to Bletchley Park. "This was on November 24, 1942," writes Robert Harris. "More than nine and a half months into the blackout . . . a small package . . . was the haul for which Fasson and Grazier had died, still in its original covering, as it had been passed out of the sinking U-boat . . . they'd found something waterproof to wrap it in. The smallest exposure to water would have dissolved the ink. To have plucked it from a drowning submarine, at night, in a high sea . . . it was enough to make even a mathematician believe in miracles . . . Two little pamphlets, printed in Gothic lettering on pink blotting paper . . . At first glance they scarcely looked worth the cost of two men's lives: two little pamphlets, the Short Signal Book and the Short Weather Cipher Book, printed in soluble ink . . . But to Bletchley they were beyond price, worth more than all the sunken treasure ever raised in history . . . It was the back door into Shark . . . It was a perfect crib. A cryptanalyst's dream . . . we'd been given a key. The weather code was the key that unlocked the door."[19]

16. Kahn, *Seizing the Enigma*, p.217.
17. "Astro Man" released on *Cry of Love*, Reprise Records 2/71.
18. Kahn, *Seizing the Enigma*, pp.224-6.
19. Robert Harris, *Enigma*, (New York, Random House, 1995), pp.24, 150, 74.

"Nov. 24, 1942, nine and a half months into the blackout."

The "blackout" at Bletchley Park began earlier that year in the winter of 1942, when the Nazis introduced unbreakable codes for the Enigma machine. The Allies could not read messages between Hitler and his U-boats. A blackout began which lasted until Jimi Hendrix was born nine months later in November. Then came the miraculous breakthrough: Enigma was solved.

It was Thanksgiving Day in America when Lucille Hendrix went into labor. Jimi was born the following morning. Thankfully, the Allies, at this time, received the key that ended the blackout and saved the world from enslavement to Nazi dominators. The key to the code had desperately been sought for an expectant nine-month period of feverish calculations at Bletchley Park. During the blackout, a feeding frenzy of Nazi U-boats was winning the war. If ever we were in need of divine intervention to deliver us from evil, this was it. But right after the blackout began in late winter 1942, when hope for the world was at its most black, Jimi was conceived in Seattle. It happened nine months prior to the Enigma breakthrough, and this "Hendrix conception" coincided with a strange intersection in America.

MARCH 6, 1942

The most influential founder of blues in America is Robert Johnson. While Hitler was seizing power in Europe in the 1930s, Johnson wrote "Crossroads Blues," which made famous the legend of a bluesman who visits a country crossroads at midnight to be transformed and imbued with supernatural Voodoo. Johnson recorded "Crossroad Blues" on Nov. 27, 1936. On that day, six years later, Jimi Hendrix was born.

Hendrix too was transformed during his youth when he learned to play blues in the South.[20] In a song called "Voodoo Chile," Jimi sings about his supernatural experience. Hendrix became the successor to Robert Johnson in American blues. Johnson died in 1938, murdered by poison in a Mississippi jukejoint. On March 6, 1942, the most powerful tornado ever to hit the Delta wiped that jukejoint off the face of the Earth. Nine days short of nine months later, Jimi was born on November 27. It was as if that twister over Johnson's death site marked a crossroads time warp of the Hendrix conception. Reincarnated, the blues were personified in Jimi. His conception intersects a blackout that began in Europe as Hitler's Enigma code concealed Nazi secrets for the next nine months.

But Robert's storm wasn't over. On the anniversary of Johnson's death thirty years later (August 16, 1968), Jimi debuted his version of the National Anthem just south of the Mason-Dixon line in Columbia, Maryland. One year later he played the Anthem at Woodstock, and Hurricane Camille, the strongest storm ever seen in the west, blew up the Delta's birthplace of the blues in Mississippi, while Jimi played "Voodoo Chile" and kissed the sky onstage at Woodstock, long after Robert cut "Crossroads" on his birthday.

---

20. *Jimi Hendrix :Blues* CD booklet, MCA 4/94 pp.4-5.

SHAMAN'S MAGIC ATOMS

The atoms I exhale are mixed into the atmosphere and can be inhaled by
a plant or someone else. Thus we are related, you and I and Buddha and
Jesus Christ!   – Tom Gehrels[21]

Millennial or revolutionary prophets, or, more simply, magicians and prophets
. . . their activities represent, in many ways, an extremely radical challenge to
any established religiopolitical system . . . the charismatic or the holy man. . .
the more ordinary term for what they describe is magician. . . one who can
make divine power present directly through personal miracle . . . magic
renders transcendental power present concretely, physically, sensibly, tangibly
. . . Magic, like myth, is a word and a process that demands reclamation from
the language of sneer and jeer. Magic is used here as a neutral description for
an authentic religious phenomenon. . . There is . . . an ideological need to
protect religion and its miracles from magic and its effects . . . The spectrum
. . . from religion to magic . . . a miracle worker to a magician, is not one of
description but prescription, not one of differentiation but of acclamation.
And the discriminant is the political one of official, approved, and accepted, as
against unofficial, unapproved, or unaccepted activities . . . religion and
magic, the religious miracle and the magical effect, are in no way
*substantively distinct . . . the prescriptive distinction that states that **we***
*practice religion but **they** practice magic should be seen for what it is, a*
political validation of the approved and the official against the unapproved
and the unofficial.   – John Crossan[22]

"The human body is actually a river of intelligence, of energy, and of information," says Deepak Chopra, "and it is constantly renewing itself in every moment of your existence . . . It has been estimated that even with one breath that you breath in you take in ten to the par of twenty-two atoms from the universe, a huge amount of raw material that comes from everywhere in existence and ends up as your heart cells, your brain cells, your kidney cells and so on. With each breath that you breathe out you breathe out ten to the par of twenty-two atoms and these have their origins in every cell of your body. You are literally breathing out bits and pieces of your heart and kidney and brain tissue . . . Scientists have speculated, based on mathematical calculations, as a result of radioactive isotope studies, that right at this moment you may have in your physical body at least a million atoms that were once in the body of Christ, or Buddah, or Mahatma Gandhi, or Genghis Khan, of Saddam Hussein, or anyone else that you care to think about. In just the last three weeks, a quadrillion – which is ten followed by fifteen zeros

21. The New York Times Magazine 7/28/96, p.19.
22. Crossan, *Historical Jesus*, pp.137, 305, 310.

– a quadrillion atoms have circulated through your body that have circulated through the body of every other living species on our planet. Think of a tree in Africa, a squirrel in Siberia, a pheasant in China, and you have in your physical body raw material that was floating there three weeks ago."[23]

THE HENDRIX EFFECT

Jimi Hendrix embodied evolutionary change in the biochemistry of humans and of the Earth. Jimi functioned like a potent supernatural hallucinogen affecting our planet. It was as if a mutational strain was manifest in human form, introduced into the environment, and all atoms which passed through him were supercharged a quantum leap up the evolutionary scale.

From the moment of his conception, a gradual build-up effect commenced. As the atoms that came into contact with Jimi, even while he was still in the womb, made their way back through the atmosphere and around the world, every living thing they passed through experienced the *Hendrix Effect*: heightened perception and intuition. It was as if the planet itself is an egg cell that had suddenly been fertilized. The conception and presence of Hendrix instantly altered Earth's biosphere. The whole nature of everything changed.

> *Only one sperm can be successful . . . The successful sperm binds to the egg's*
> *surface. An explosive charge of enzymes in its head bores through the shell*
> *. . . a chemical signal sweeps across the egg. With lightning speed the shell of*
> *the egg hardens to prevent other sperm from entering it . . . It's the signal*
> *for the egg to start dividing.*   *– BODY ATLAS[24]*

Following the Hendrix Conception on March 6, 1942, an increasing accumulation of atoms on Earth were exposed to the Hendrix Effect and then went on to circulate through the globe during the Enigma blackout of 1942, while Nazi atrocities escalated. Bodies piled up in death camps. Civilization was pregnant with expectation, waiting for the Allies to deliver the Enigma formula. Then came the *beltch* from Bletchley Park – a broken code, relief. By the ninth month after Jimi was conceived, enough atoms had circulated through his unborn body, become supercharged, and made their way back through the cells of all living things. Civilization and the Earth were transformed, Jimi was born, the code was broken, all in the same moment of history. This Enigma coincidence shines as an eternal Star of Bethlehem.

The presence of Hendrix quickly influenced events, producing a super boost of creative intuition in all non-dominator people. Axis powers collapsed in reaction as Nazi's withered in submission. Like Superman under kryptonite, the Third Reich grew dizzy and weak in proportion to the growth of Jimi.

---

23. *Body, Mind & Soul – The Mystery and the Magic*, PBS 8/95.
24. *Reproduction*, Body Atlas, The Learning Channel 12/94.

Following the Allied victory at Alameim in November, Churchill ordered churchbells to ring in England. A miracle was manifest in the land. Bletchley Park received the missing link, retrieved by Anthony Fasson's superhuman salvage of key Nazi documents. The Enigma code cracked wide open as Jimi emerged from the womb. Out of this heightened state our fertilized Earth produced its climax: after nine months of expectant blackout, the Gian mind of the living globe gave birth to *enlightenment.*

> *Enigma is a very sophisticated cipher system. And SHARK is the ultimate*
> *refinement . . . If it is true, as someone once said, that genius is "a zigzag*
> *of lightning across the brain" then, in that instant, Jerico knew what genius*
> *was. He saw the solution lit up like a landscape before him. After that,*
> *everything happened quickly . . . they broke the SHARK traffic . . . sending*
> *the translated decrypts down the line to London. They were indeed the*
> *crown jewels. Messages to raise the hairs on the back of your neck.*
> — Robert Harris[25]

Fred Winterbotham oversaw project Ultra and passed Hitler's intercepted messages on to Churchill. Winterbotham said that the Prime Minister regarded Ultra as "absolutely vital." For example, with data from the Enigma, Churchill received advance warning of German plans to bomb Coventry, England. But any attempt to evacuate the city would have alerted Hitler that the code had been broken. Churchill weighed the cost of casualties against losing information from Ultra. Coventry was sacrificed so that the code breaking would remain hidden from Hitler.

"The cypher breaking operation was accomplished by a team of brilliant mathematicians and cryptographers," recalls Winterbotham, "this near miracle . . . the supremely important source of Intelligence information, which General Eisenhower described just after the end of the Second World War as a decisive factor in the Allied victory . . . Ultra was indeed an almost incredibly valuable source of Intelligence . . . with the art of cracking enemy cyphers . . . the theoretically unbreakable German cypher machine Enigma – which gave birth eventually to Ultra – that art took on a completely new dimension; and surely no other act in the history of officially sponsored skullduggery ever had comparably fruitful results . . . Ultra . . . [and] its almost fabulous influence on Allied strategy . . . I well remember the deep anxiety of . . . [the Air Staff and the Secret Service] lest this gift from the gods should fall into enemy hands . . . Ultra . . . was a real war-winner. *From the end of November onwards* the picture given by Ultra included not only the German forces in Tunisia commanded by Walter Nehring, but also Rommel's Afrika Korps retreating from Cyrenaica in the East."[26]

---

25. Robert Harris, *Enigma*, (New York, Random House, 1995), pp.73, 27.
26. F.W. Winterbotham, *The Ultra Secret*, (New York: Harper & Row, 1974), pp.vii, xi, vii, 97.

NOVEMBER 27– CRITICAL JUNCTURE

> *From late 1942 onwards* no general seems to have disregarded the
> guidance of Ultra . . . by then it had proved its worth as an absolute reliable
> source . . . 11 Brigade was approaching Tebourba inside Tunisia, which they
> captured on **27 November** [Jimi's birthday]. *That day we got orders to
> follow the Army into Tunisia . . . It was at this critical juncture that log-
> reading and traffic-analysis* [codebreakers] *really came into their own.
> Without their help and the help of direction-finding we would have been
> completely at sea.*
> — F.H. Hinsley[27]

Peter Talbacarassi was a young Oxford scholar from Germany when he joined the Ultra Secret team. "Ultra was *the* decisive element in the battle of the Atlantic," said Talbacarassi, "and this is extremely important because the battle of the Atlantic was decisive about the war as a *whole*. If we hadn't won the Battle of the Atlantic in the winter of '42-'43, England could have been knocked out. If we had been knocked out, and France had already been knocked out, then what happens to the Americans? You can't cross the Atlantic because the U-boats are still there, and if you *do* cross it, where do you go? The fact that **we broke the U-boat code in November of '42** and could therefore sink these U-boats much faster than they could arrive on the scene, if you know where they were, I mean what chance did they have? This was decisive not only for the battle of the Atlantic, but for the *war*."[28]

American General Mark Clark recalls, "When I did receive Ultra, particularly at Anzio, it was like manna from heaven. It was like somebody sending me intelligence on a silver platter that I couldn't get any other way."[29] Without intelligence intercepted by Ultra, the D-Day invasion of Europe at Normandy would have been delayed by at least two years. Eisenhower later said, "Ultra was of priceless value at Normandy, it saved thousands of Allied lives and was decisive to Allied victory."[30]

Solving the Enigma jigsaw turned the tide of the war against Hitler. Bright days lay ahead. Civilization awakened from Dark Ages as the rising Sun cast its first ray over the life of Jimi Hendrix. The age of Spiritual Blues dawned as ten millennia of dominator brutality, climaxed by the Nazis, began to fade from the Earth.

> *Theodore Roszak writes of "the full and hideous flowering of the politics of
> masculine dominance" . . . associating war with "the manly and
> adventurous virtues" . . . This masculine metaphysical madness was lived
> out in Nazism and Fascism.*
> — Mary Daly[31]

---

27. Hinsley and Stripp, *Codebreakers - The Inside Story of Bletchley Park*, pp.40,219.
28. *Ultra Secret*, CBS News 60 Minutes 6/5/94.
29. Ibid.
30. Ibid., and Winterbotham, *The Ultra Secret*, p.xi.
31. Daly, *Beyond God the Father*, p.120.

World War II was a drama played out against the specter of dominator delusions. Hitler lashed out at Jews, communists and Bolshiviks, calling them all "degenerates."

> *Hitler also seized the idea of the culture being infected by degenerates –*
> *modernism in art was the symptom. There was a sign of what is going*
> *wrong with society: that's why you don't have a job, that's why you're*
> *standing in a bread line, that's why you're paying a million marks for a loaf*
> *of bread – it's because of **that** kind of sickness in society, which is*
> *symbolized by **this** kind of art. That became a very powerful argument.*
> – Sander Gilman[32]

Forms of art in Germany that deviated from classical traditions were attacked. Abstraction and dissonance were forbidden. Nazis jeered jazz music and outlawed the use of muted horns, claiming that the effect "turns the noble sounds of wind and brass instruments into a Jewish pre-Messianic howl."[33] The SS condemned expressionist painter Emil Nolde. Nolde's fascination with dark-skinned people in nature settings was labeled "degenerate." His famous altarpiece, "The Life of Christ," was displayed as an example of degenerate art, flanked by Nazi commentary: "Insolent mockery of the Divine."

In a campaign to establish styles and attitudes preferred by Nazis, Hitler built a museum in Munich called the House of German Art. In 1937, the museum opened with a lavish pageant called Two Thousand Years of German Culture. It may as well have been called Two Thousand Years of Dominators. "There were enormous spaces and these muscle bound [men], huge big figures and relatively few people in there," recalls art historian Peter Guenther. "It was really kind of a frightening affair, and the thing which disturbed me, as a seventeen year old, was the enormous numbers of nudes. Not only male nudes – muscle backed – but also pink females, in large numbers. They were like mannequins, with no movement and no expression and no character. Basically, to me, that was far closer to pornography than anything from the expressionists. With the expressionists they were all moving, they were dancing or swimming or jumping or running or doing something, because they were out in nature. They had taken off this bourgeoisie clothing and they were full of the joy of life. As far as women were concerned, if you look at the Nazi depiction, there were really only two roles: either they were nudes or they were mothers. And the other thing, if you really want to look at the two sides of the coin of what is war, look at the Nazis and look at the expressionists and you'll find out who is who. The German expressionists were all against the war, there was not an expressionist who was not against the war. The Nazis considered war as the greatest accomplishment of mankind. They honored victory under all circumstances. Even if you died, you died in victory and therefore you were a martyr."[34]

---

32. *Degenerate Art*, PBS 12/19/95.
33. Ibid.
34. Ibid.

Art critic Robert Hughes reviewed the exhibits at the House of German Art and concluded, "It is perfectly hypocritical art. It is hypocritical about the body, it is hypocritical about politics, it is hypocritical about every damned thing you can imagine . . . Anybody can understand a whacking great surfer with giant pecs holding up a sword . . . [by contrast] expressionism was art which above all celebrated inwardness. And that which was inward must be outlawed – this is the essence of totalitarianism, so therefore the object is to sweep all these little inward thoughts out of their secret chambers and expose them to the light of ridicule, like spraying Raid on a bunch of cockroaches...I remember when I was a kid seeing the newsreels of the liberation of the camps, the starved corpses...and it always comes back to me when I look at the distortion and elongation in certain German expressionist pictures, as though the esthetic distortions of expressionism had been made real and concrete and absolute on the real suffering human body by the Nazis. As though this was some kind of climactic work of art which ended up mimicking what the Nazis had attempted to repress."[35]

Dominator art ridicules sensitivity in men and rejects any suggestion of introspective spirit or troubled soul. Nazis deem men unsensuous and women *only* sensuous.

> *Particularly the Hebrews really wipe out the goddess . . .it's an extreme case that we have in the Bible, and our own Western subjugation of the female is really a function of biblical thinking.*
>
> – Joseph Campbell[36]

Could the hatred of Jews that engendered the Nazi holocaust be the result of a subconscious revolt against Hebrew Creation myths? Bible stories taught everyone to reject flesh and enslave nature. Nazis snapped under the pressure of being trained by their faith to feel guilt and shame about sex. A religion may give men advantages over women, but at the cost of alienating people from their own bodies. Sexual urges were forced into a netherworld of unspoken restrictions, waiting to explode. Sigmund Freud explored the intensity of dangerous alienation in Germany when he asserted that circumcised Jews and woman are despised by Nazis because both have part, or all, of the penis missing.[37]

Attitudes were produced that were not just unnatural, they were *anti*-natural. Everyone loses peace of mind when the body is made into an object of shame. TreMENdous resentMENt against this had built up in the huMAN subconscious for MANy generations. The Nazis, without even being fully aware of what was driving their aggression, were "out to get" the source of this sexual pressure that had driven Hitler, and much of western culture, to madness.

35. Ibid.
36. The Power of Myth, *Love and the Goddess*, PBS 3/88.
37. Carter, *Routine Circumcision – the Tragic Myth*, p.87.

In May 1995, researchers at Brown University reported a study that revealed that Jewish men show sharply higher rates of depression than non-Jewish men. Within a one-year period 13 percent of Jewish men in the study showed signs of major depression, compared with 5.4 percent among non-Jewish men.[38] Could a tradition of rejecting flesh and condemning life account for much of the anxiety underlying such widespread depression in Jewish men?

Unnatural tension over sex stems from the Messiah myth. Tension escalated for centuries and then exploded as the Nazi holocaust against Jews. At the climax of this epic drama, Jimi Hendrix appeared on Earth. In every sense Hendrix delivers us from dominators. His Irish-African ancestry is a mix of cultures that practiced body abandon and possession dance. With this lineage Jimi's Voodoo blues undermines ideas about nature being sinful. This music *relieves* beliefs like those that drove Nazis to attack Jews. This is why, two decades after World War II, Jimi was received in Europe like a new Savior. At the height of the holocaust in 1942, the presence of Hendrix marks the start of civilization's awakening from Dark Ages. With his birth, the tide was turned.

But every time we think of the "21st Century," we subconsciously make a regressive connection: twenty-one centuries of *Christ*:

Christ = Messiah = Original Sin = Sex Denigrate = Control of Women

It is through Jimi's life that we find the language and connections with which to unravel what happened. Hendrix thus becomes our point of reference for the disMANtling of male-supremacy religions: not necessarily *anti*christ, but *un*christ.

> *...the idea that the "antichrist" must be something "evil." What if this is not the case at all? What if the idea has risen out of the male's unconscious dread that women rise up and assert the power robbed from us? What if it in fact points to a mode of being and presence that is beyond patriarchy's definitions of good and evil?*   — Mary Daly[39]

THE NEW VIEW – A UNION OF URGES – FUTURE AND PAST

> *Whatever happens, it should have a chance to be brought into the open, if it's a new idea, a new invention, or a new way of thinking, it should at least be brought into the open and be respected as being new and probably a decent change or a help for the human race. We shouldn't have to keep carrying the same old burdens around.*   — Jimi[40]

---

38. WROC-TV News, Rochester, NY 5/95.

39. Daly, *Beyond God the Father*, p.96.

40. Henderson, *Jimi Hendrix – Voodoo Child of the Aquarian Age*, p.481, from an interview with Keith Altham, London 9/11/70.

It isn't yet possible today to separate Jesus from Christ. Two thousand years have been devoted to connecting these two stories without anyone understanding the Messiah myth.

> *It may be that we will witness a remythologizing of religion . . . replaced by*
> *the emergence of imagery that is not hierarchical . . . This means that no*
> *adequate models can be taken from the past.*   — Mary Daly[41]

Major religions of the world today are examples of male resistance to female regulation of sex. Female intermittent receptivity to sex, as opposed to the typical male's ongoing sexual quest, allowed women of pre-history to determine when mating occurred. World religions were designed to instead empower men with the regulation of sex by casting women as creatures of sin, outside of God's favor.

> *Wives, submit yourselves unto your own husbands, as it is fit in the Lord.*
>   — Paul: Colossians 3:18

> *Wives, accept the authority of your husbands, even if some of them do not*
> *obey the Word.*   — Paul: – I Peter 3:1

Through *Rock Prophecy,* future generations can now be made aware of this "religious" trick within dominator civilizations.

> *With any new civilization that you might find yourself involved in, or you might*
> *see growing, they have to have their own officers and police and governments*
> *and all that . . . You just take the best from all politics, or all religions, or all*
> *countries, and you just do the best with that.*   — Jimi[42]

Through confusion that has plagued our race, we begin to see clearly how the Hendrix Event connects future and past. *Rock Prophecy* reveals Jimi's vision of a defenseless Earth, our progress squandered beneath the heels of dominator men in pursuit of private privileges. As civilization today awakens to our fate, we start to mark time in *Hendrix Correct* terms:

> *In the beginning there was The Endless Bummer,*
> *the eternal void known as The Big Drag . . .*

Prior to Jimi's birth, the HIStory of MANkind was, for most people, most of the time, a really Big Drag. The basic requirements for psychedelic life – LSD, penicillin, and birth control pills – were unknown before the lifetime of Hendrix. People wandered in a barren black and white wasteland of the mind, slaves to the ways of subjugating one another.

41. Daly, *Beyond God the Father*, p.71.
42. Brown, *Hendrix – The Final Days*, p.94-5, from an interview with Keith Altham, London 9/11/70.

More than 15,000 years have passed since partnership societies based on psychoactive plants created cultures in which the drudgery of life was punctuated with rituals of hallucinogen induced ecstasy. After the Fall of these Edens, HIStory turned into a bummer for almost everyone. The drag reached an apex under Nazi dominators. And then a miracle – Jimi appeared.

The Big Drag is over. Hendrix is the World Shaman through whom we see the meaning of Spiritual Blues and define our goals according to Nature's Way of Creation.

> *We really can create a caring, refeminized, ecosensitive world . . . We can begin this restructuring of thought by declaring legitimate what we have denied for so long. Let us declare Nature to be legitimate. The notion of illegal plants is obnoxious and ridiculous in the first place . . . The last best hope for dissolving the steep walls of cultural inflexibility that appear to be channeling us toward true ruin is a renewed shamanism. By reestablishing channels of direct communication with the Other, the mind behind nature, through the use of hallucinogenic plants, we will obtain a new set of lenses to see our way in the world.*   – Terrence McKenna[43]

The Hendrix story functions like the corrective lens on the repaired Hubble Space Telescope: through a Hendrix Perspective we see clearly what has happened and what is happening. The mythology of Jimi provides our connection to Creation's Way – the ultimate world religion, an *equality* religion – the freeing of the *freek*s.

> *What all the myths have to deal with is transformation of consciousness: you were thinking in **this** way, and you have now to think in **that** way.*   – Joseph Campbell[44]

Hendrix represents the enlightenment with which civilization awakens from Dark Ages. In observance of this miracle, time marking jargon is now described in Hendrix Correct terms:

Columbus arrived in the New World 450 years Pre-Jimi.
The Civil War ended 77 years Pre-Jimi.
The Great Depression began 13 years Pre-Jimi.
The start of WWII dates from 3 years Pre-Jimi.

Jimi was born in the First Century, Year 1 of the Uncommon Era.
Apollo 11 landed on the Moon in 26 U.E.
Rock Prophecy was written in 53 U.E.

---

43. McKenna, *Food of the Gods*, p.98.
44. The Power of Myth, *The Hero's Adventure*, PBS 3/88.

One hundred years after *Rock Prophecy*, calendars will read:

Second Century, Year 153 of the Uncommon Era, etc.

NEW YEAR'S DAY THANKS

Thanksgiving Days are positioned like bookends around Jimi's first and last birthdays. Lucille Hendrix, Jimi's mother, went into labor on Thanksgiving Thursday. Twenty-seven years later, on November 27, Jimi celebrated his last birthday on Thanksgiving Thursday. Thursday was designated *Jupiter Day* by ancient Babylonians who named the days of the week after the planets.[45]

> *The Romans called the fourth day of the week . . . 'Jupiter Day.' When the Germanic peoples took over their system of naming days after the gods, or the planets they represented, they replaced Jupiter, the Roman sky-god, with the Germanic god of thunder, Thor.*
>
> – John Ayto[46]

The last "Thor-day," or Thursday, in November is Thanksgiving Day, which often falls on Jimi's birthday. Thursday is Jupiter Day and Jupiter is the ruling planet of Sagittarius, Jimi's astrological sign. The symbol for Sagittarius is the centaur, a creature half man and half horse. A centaur represents the centering of nature and spirit together as one unified being. This is the hallmark of Hendrix, the central figurehead of Spiritual Blues, a philosophy of body-mind union in celebration of nature. In observance of this Hendrix Event, and to give thanks for our deliverance from Dark Ages of the Big Drag, we combine Thanksgiving Day and New Years Day into a single holiday each November 27.

So it is written in the First Century of Light, in the Uncommon Era.

---

45. *Shadows and Signs*, Wonders of the Universe, The Learning Channel 6/95.
46. John Ayto, *Dictionary of Word Origins*, (New York: Arcade Publishing, 1990), p.530.

Chapter 14: Creation's Way

ॐ

In reality Jesus started off a lot of wars, not he himself but the people who supported his cause. That's why Christianity is a thing of the past. Religion is the thing, and it has to be found within yourself. You have to live with peace of mind. Music is my life, you have to be honest, it's about life and feelings.
— Jimi[1]

The word "religion" comes from the Latin term *religio*, meaning "bond." Religio is derived from the verb *religare*, which means "to tie back" or "link back." In religion we find myths and explanations that link our world back to the beginning of time, to the start of Creation. It is in this sense that the Hendrix story conforms to the meaning of religion, because the issues and explanations surrounding Hendrix trigger a chain reaction of insights that link back to the world's creeds and exposes the psychological *intent* behind these stories.

I don't go by comparisons. I just go by the truthness or the falseness of the whole thing, the intentions of whatever it might be. — Jimi[2]

Through Jimi's life a continuum of issues connects like dominos in a row. His story touches one by one the key ideas of modern thinking in our world and enables us to construct an understanding of the past. The philosophy is called Spiritual Blues, and it forms the basis of faith in *Creation's Way – the Equality Religion*. Like other world religions, Creation's Way celebrates miracles that manifest as *coincidence*.

A coincidence is an imprint of divine mystery, a signpost just beyond probability. With each incident of coincidence we are reminded of just how much more there is to life than meets the eye. But taking too seriously a series of coincidences has long been the bane of objective logic. From the three-dimensional view of modern rationalism, people who attach meaning to coincidences are deemed "superstitious" and "irrational." But many people are unaware of just how pervasive this issue is in our lives. If we were to study any number of TV dramas and sit-coms, we'd find their story lines comprised of unexpected numbers of coincidences. Most of these shows use coincidence as the main structural pillars in their scripts. People who look at me askew for pointing out coincidences related to Jimi are usually the same people who sit transfixed before sit-coms written entirely around incidents of coincidence. Once one becomes aware of this issue, you'll see it everywhere.

---

1. Morgenposten 9/6/70.
2. Brown, *Jimi Hendrix – In His Own Words*, p.73, from an interview in Harlem 9/5/69.

But finding meaning in numbers and dates and incidents that coincide isn't much different from searching for a higher purpose to the random chaos of existence. Imagine the devout Elvis fan who points out how the King and Jesus were both Capricorns who started out in trios and ended up with 12 cronies. More obsessed mystics notice that the names Jesus H. Christ and Elvis Presley both contain 12 letters (!). With a little stretch of the imagination, coincidences can be found almost anywhere.

But a certain leap of faith is required for logical western rationalists to determine that, at some point, probability has been breached and the phenomenon in question is in fact inexplicably mysterious. For example, consider something pretty basic, like life on Earth. We can't deny that it is quite a coincidence that our "third stone" just *randomly* happened to end up 93-million miles (on average) from the Sun. A fraction closer and life would burn away, a fraction further away and molecular evolution would've frozen solid.

An even stranger coincidence is found in the Moon's diameter, which is an exact fit over the Sun's disk when seen during a total eclipse from Earth.

But when an extended series of simultaneous, related events appear to defy the laws of probability, belief in a random and meaningless universe can be called into question. We then consider the issue of divine intervention and wonder whether these strange strokes of fate might be guided on our behalf by hidden hands. Like split-second glimpses into the unknown, coincidences excite the imagination. Seemingly random happenings hint at an unseen grand design.

In one sense, the topic of coincidence falls into a sub-category of miracles. The same instinct that makes us take note of a coincidence also instructs us to recognize the miraculous. We are a species seeking to experience transcendent reality, to *see* the origins of life. What we regard as miracles are what we recognize as divine presence. Each year millions of people flock to sites of unexplained coincidences and proclaim the incident to be proof of holy visitations. Through spontaneous synchronizing of related events, we sense a divine presence in the world.

The issue of coincidence with regard to Hendrix was first described in a manuscript written by his artist girlfriend, Monika Dannemann, during the months following his death. She quotes Jimi as saying, "*God's real name has been lost over the ages. His real name has nine letters . . . Number 9 symbolizes the reality of God here on Earth . . . 6 means life and love. But 9 is the highest spiritual number that exists.*"[3]

Monika analyzed numbers and dates associated with Jimi's life and wrote, "It was not by accident that his birth, life and death added up to the number 9. His [astrological] sign (9 rays), his age 27 (2+7 = 9), his death on the 18th (1+8 = 9), the month of September – the 9th month, and 9 sleeping pills [the number of Vesperex tablets missing from Monika's packet, which caused Jimi's death on Sept. 18, 1970]. . . I realized all this through the knowledge he'd given me of numbers."[4]

3. UniVibes #8 11/92 p.32, from pp.27, 85 of Dannemann's 1971 manuscript, edited by Richard Levey.
4. UniVibes #8 11/92 p.32, from p.100 of Dannemann's 1971 manuscript, edited by Richard Levey.

In his autobiography, *I Used to Be an Animal, but I'm All Right Now*, singer Eric Burdon describes finding instructions that Hendrix had written for Monika. "We unearthed the plans he'd left for Monika's paintings," wrote Burdon. "He'd made her promise that she would use her skills to execute the paintings and drawings that he'd left behind . . . Later we were to find, whilst examining the sketches, that all the numbers, all the measurements, were all in nines and sixes, nine inches, six millimeters, six-feet, sixty-nine millimeters, ninety-six inches and so on."[5]

Sharon Lawrence is a journalist who knew Jimi and reported his interest in digits. "He showed me a tattered, faded book published at the turn of the century," recalls Sharon, "a standard reference book on numerology. *This is important. I've read it dozens of times. You should read it. I'm a nine,*' he said softly, as though he were confiding a rare and special secret. *'It's a powerful number and it can be very good or very bad. Nines are meant to accomplish things in this world.*'"[6]

Not since the "Paul is Dead" rumor of 1969 have I been so moved to decode cryptic significance from rock star minutia.

OBSESSED WITH DETAILS

While studying numerology, I realized that critics who accuse me of being "obsessed" for noticing number patterns in Jimi's story might also accuse many biblical scholars of being obsessed too. For example, Frank Higgins points out that some scholars consider Freemasonry to be the parent of all religions. Higgins reports that "the key to the entire secret [Freemasonry] system, concealed from the masses by the priesthood. . .is found in the ancient method of using identical characters for letters and numbers, a system called Gematria."[7]

"Gematria," writes numerologist Julia Line, "is the name given to the profound magico-philosophical science of reducing words to numbers in order to decode the information believed to be implicit within them. The numerical value of any word can be found simply by adding up the numbers of letters of which it is composed . . . The Qabalistic Gematria . . . a major contributory factor to present-day numerology . . . uses the twenty-two letters of the Hebrew alphabet, and their corresponding numbers, to decode hidden meanings in the scriptures or to discover a person's essential character and destiny by name analysis."[8]

Numerologist Annemarie Schimmel further explains, "The Arabic alphabet follows the old Semitic sequence of letters, called *abjad*, and since each letter has a twofold meaning, one can easily develop relations between names, meaningful words, and numbers (as has been done in the Cabala for centuries) . . . the Jewish Cabala, which is based upon a highly complicated number mysticism, whereby the primordial One divides itself into 10 *sefirot* (from *safar*, or *number*), which are mysteriously connected with each other and work

---

5. Eric Burdon, *I Used to be an Animal, but I'm Alright Now*, (London, Faber & Faber 1986), p.217.
6. *Castles Made of Sand – Remembering Jimi Hendrix*, San Francisco Examiner 11/25/90, p.16.
7. Arielyvon Taylor & H. Warren Hyer, *Numerology – Its Facts and Secrets*, p.36.
8. Julia Line, *Discover Numerology – Understanding and Using the Power of Numbers*, (Sterling Publishing, 1985), pp.9, 15.

together, with the 22 letters of the Hebrew alphabet serving as 'bridges' between them . . . Since Hebrew letters also serve as numbers, the figure of the sefirot and its derivations lead to fascinating relations . . . The number 666 in the Book of Revelation is a model case: numerous interpreters have found in it the names of persons who seemed to personify the 'Beast' of their own time."[9]

"The symbolism of numbers features prominently in religious creeds and doctrines throughout the world," writes Line. "Many passages and occasionally whole books in the Old and New Testament of the Bible can be interpreted numerically. Religious truths were hidden within the texts from the eyes of the unbeliever while still allowing the encoded Christian message to be understood by the chosen few."[10]

There are no numbers in the Hebrew alphabet. Letters are used instead, and each letter has a corresponding numerical value. "Alaf," the first letter, is 1. "Hey," the fifth letter, is 5, and so on. "When you read a word you're also reading a number," says Rabbi David Wolper, "so there is a practice called Gematria where you count up the numbers of different words and see how they correspond to the numbers of other words. It becomes very intricate and very interesting, and to many, profoundly significant."[11]

"When a Jewish mystic looks at the Bible," explains Rabbi Johathan Omer-Man, "he or she doesn't look at the same narrative as an ordinary reader does. He looks for tiny signs in the use of language, the way the letters appear, in order to understand what is the level of existence beneath this. And so we are always looking for strange phrases or the way the letters are used, sometimes even the shapes of the letters, to give us clues, to give us intimations of what lies behind. And when we do, we discover the most incredible riches."[12]

Hebrew mystics believed that the letters were designed by God and each one contains hidden meanings. "The rabbis come up with interpretations that seem very far from the text," notes Wolper. "They do that because the assumption is that God isn't redundant and if God is in that text, every letter, every word, every mark on the page has many, many different significances."[13]

In modern times, scholars use computers to search for repeating patterns of letters throughout the Bible. Using the principles of Gematria, some researchers claim to have decoded hidden prophecies foreshadowing World War II, the holocaust and AIDS. However, as Professor Lawrence Shiffmann points out, "Something like twenty five percent of the words in the Hebrew Bible are of disputed meaning. There's no way that we're ever going to know all the facts regarding the entire environment that was devised or was composed. We're never going to know everything about the Bible. The Bible perhaps is one of the permanent mysteries of mankind and perhaps that is why it is so successful, because the way in which the Bible operates is that it brings us to a kind of eternal study."[14]

---

9. Annemarie Schimmel, *The Mystery of Numbers*, (Oxford University Press, 1993), pp.5, 17.

10. Line, *Discover Numerology*, p.15.

11. *Who Wrote the Bible?*, A&E 3/95.

12. Ibid.

13. Ibid.

14. Ibid.

A scholar can spend a lifetime analyzing remote and bizarre tangents surrounding the Bible and few, if any, establishment journalists will label that scholar "obsessed." The key clauses by which the Bible dictates male supremacy and persecution of gays are insulated by a lengthy maze of texts and elaborate rituals that divert attention away from the key clauses. For example, students of the Torah, the first five books of the Bible, concentrate on the 613 commandments contained in the Torah. The number of days in a year, 365, are subtracted from 613 and that leaves 248, which is the number of text columns written in Hebrew that make up the standard Torah. "It must be written as Moses has written it," explains Hebrew scholar Eric Ray. "Only in Hebrew and in the same way that he wrote it, with the columns of letters so that you have eventually the number of columns that come together with the days of the year to make up all the commandments. There are 613 commandments which are in the Torah, and there are 248 columns, and 365 days [in a year]. The two together [248 + 365] becomes 613, which are the number of commandments which are in the Torah."[15]

The maze of details gets even more arcane when students must learn how the 248 columns correspond to the individual pieces of a human skeleton and how 365 of the "negative" commandments in the text are numbered after nerves and blood vessels in the human body (!). Diverted in this dense forest of distractions, scholars often blow a lifetime concentrating on obscure details that were designed to de-emphasize the core intention of the Torah's key clause: condemn all people who are not male heterosexuals. The attention of Bible students is diverted away from this camouflaged rule hidden within loads of complex information. Many come away from years of study feeling that God *rewards* us for persecuting gay people and dominating women.

To devote decades to daily study of such texts is the establishment's idea of time well spent, or at least time spent out of the way of the ruling class that controls us.

> *The main [media] thing for [the public] is to divert them, to get them . . .*
> *involved in fundamentalist stuff, or something, just get them away from*
> *things that matter.* — Noam Chomsky[16]

Journalists won't label any scholar's endless Bible study as "obsessed" because the Bible legitimizes male privilege, and men control the media. On the other hand, when I devote *any* amount of time to the study of Jimi Hendrix, most of those same journalists will leap to their keyboards and punch out "O-B-S-E-S-S-E-D." They *especially* rush to tag that label onto anyone who takes Jimi *seriously*, and they are often paid well to do so. The establishMENt associates Jimi with cannabis and hallucinogens – the dreaded feminine partnership drugs, symbols of the planet/plant Goddess. Dominator eyes glaze over at the MENtion of Hendrix. Anyone who *studies* Jimi is ridiculed into oblivion beneath the heels of dominator media. Charges of "obsessed" are followed by "worship,"

15. *Who Wrote the Bible?*, *"Torah,"* A&E 3/95.
16. *Manufacturing Consent*, 1992, PBS 9/95.

and then "fan," as in fan*atic*. In the worst sense of that word will any Hendrix "scholar" be portrayed by the men who control media, because Jimi has the effect of lessening their dominator grip on society. Hendrix too easily leads to direct questioning of, and challenge to, hierarchy. Study of his life is therefore not "approved."

This competition between who gets to pin the label – "scholar" or "fanatic" – is similar to the battle to distinguish religion and its miracles from magic and its tricks. Although religion and magic are fundamentally the same, the former is acclaimed by those who benefit from religion and the latter is likewise condemned. As Crossan points out, "The prescriptive distinction that states that *we* practice religion but *they* practice magic should be seen for what it is, a political validation of the approved and the official against the unapproved and the unofficial."[17]

To even suggest a connection between Hendrix and numerology is considered evidence of obsession and possible grounds for psychiatric confinement/medication. But a lifetime blown on deciphering the outer limits of Gematria minutia brings praise and reward from the halls of male authority.

> *The discriminant is the political one of official, approved, and accepted, as against unofficial, unapproved, or unaccepted activities.*
> — John Crossan[18]

"With Gematria providing the cipher," writes Julia Line, "and the Pythagoreans method of interpreting numbers by the qualities assigned to them, plus a few additional contributions from Judaism and Christianity, numerology was created."[19]

As with Islam, Judaism, and Christianity, numerology too is a belief system created by men and used to degrade women. Schimmel notes, "The Pythagoreans went so far as to divide everything in the universe into two categories: the odd numbers belong to the right side, which is associated with the limited, the masculine, the straight, with light and goodness . . . while even numbers belong to the sphere of the infinite, the unlimited (as they are infinitely divisible), the manifold, the left side, the female, the moving, the crooked, darkness, evil . . . For Plato, all even numbers were of ill omen, and V.C. Hopper states correctly: 'As if the feminine numbers were not already sufficiently in disfavor, the stigma of infinity is attached to them, apparently by analogy to the line.' Virgil claims: 'The deity is pleased with the odd number,' and the same idea is taken up in the Islamic tradition, where it is said, 'Verily God is an odd number (*witr*, that is, 'One') and loved the odd numbers.'"[20]

---

17. Crossan, *Historical Jesus*, p.310.
18. Ibid. p.308.
19. Line, *Discover Numerology*, p.9.
20. Schimmel, *The Mystery of Numbers*, p.13.

Historically, odd numbers represent the male, and the "eldest of odds" is number *three*:

> *The eldest of odds, God's number properly . . .*
> *Heaven's dearest number, whose inclosed center*
> *doth equally from both extremes extend,*
> *the first that hath a beginning, midst, and end . . .*
>
> – Du Bartes[21]

Greek Hellenists imagined human beings to be split into threefold divisions of body, soul and spirit. From this belief, Islam and Judeo-Christian religions have constructed the Fall of Man at the hands of sinful nature and wicked women. *Even* numbers represent the *female*: EVil EVen numbers. The primary even number is two. Two divides the One, the number of God. The damage caused by this split is unified by number three, as in the Christian Trinity. Three, the eldest odd, sign of the child. "The triad leads to a new integration," writes Schimmel, "one that does not negate the duality preceding it but rather, overcomes it, just as the child is a binding element that unites the male and the female parents . . . From time immemorial thinkers have tried to explain the unfolding of the One into multiplicity with special reference to the 3. Lao-tzu says: 'The Tao produces unity, unity produces duality, duality produces trinity, and the triad produces all things.' The Pythagoreans likewise postulated that the unqualified unity was divided into 2 opposing powers to create the world and then turn into tri-unity to produce life."[22]

In our three-dimensional world, life seems to have been created from groups of three: length-width-height, solids-liquids-gas, animal-mineral-plant. All shades of the rainbow are derived from three primary colors: red-yellow-blue. Time itself is composed of past-present-future. *In Mysteries of the Bible Numerically Revealed*, John Yunger points out that in the New Testament, the number three is associated with the resurrection and re-birth of Jesus.[23]

"Numerologists believe," notes Julia Line, "that we are born at a certain date, hour and minute not merely by chance, but in order to learn important lessons and to perform specific tasks during our lifetimes and that the conditions and vibrations prevailing at the precise moment of our birth must be favorable if we are to fulfill our mission in life."[24] When Jimi was born, Jupiter, the *sky father*, was the ruling planet of his astrological chart. "Jupiter represents the ability to expand through growth and also by understanding," writes Line, adding that the most widely used planetary/number correspondences designate Jupiter as "Number 3."[25]

21. Ibid. p.58.
22. Ibid. pp.58-9.
23. John Yunger, *Mysteries Of The Bible Numerically Revealed*, letter from author 12/24/92.
24. Line, *Discover Numerology*, p.9.
25. Ibid. p.52.

Chapter 15: Multiples of Three[1]

ॐ

*Earth, why is it named Earth? It's the third planet from the Sun, and it is
number three – you spell it phonetically: T-H-R-E-E and you turn it
backwards and you've got E-r-t-h. That's why it's named Earth, because it's
number Three.*
                                                                    – Sun Ra[2]

When lining up the Hendrix numbers, it quickly becomes apparent that the *key* is
number three – *Multiples of Three*. In the citings described ahead, notice how
sequences progress in triplicate leaps: 3, 6, 9, 12, 15, 18, etc. *Multiples of Three* means
identifying how these numbers represent aspects of Jimi's life.

One might wonder why, after proclaiming today the First Century, does this book
refer to Common Era year numerals, dated by the arrival of a Messiah. The reason is that
Jimi existed in a culture which designates the birth of Christ as Year One (scholars believe
Jesus was born at least four years earlier). The Gregorian calendar (since 1582 C.E.) has
ingrained its influence into our collective psyche for more than four centuries. For this
reason, the upcoming discussion of numbers associated with Hendrix includes Gregorian
calendar dates. Modern society is conditioned with year and century counts that originate
in the Messiah story. Year titles for "20th Century" and earlier are cited in this context for
their numerological effects.

Like Columbus in search of the New World in 1492, 1942 is the year when our search
for Multiples of Three begins with Jimi's birth. 42 is itself a multiple of three (3x14 = 42).
Had it been a leap year, 1942 would have contained 366 (3x122 = 366) days. The year of
Jimi's birth brought the return of an astrological cycle known as the Saturn/Uranus
conjunction. Approximately every 45 years (3x15 = 45), Saturn (the planet representing
status quo institutional conservatism) reaches an alignment with its polar opposite, Uranus
(the planet representing revolutionary change). "Of all the planets," writes astrologer Lyn

---

1. *Multiples of Three*, including the Saturn/Uranus conjunction at Jimi's birth, was reported for the first time in
my manuscript, *A Touch of Hendrix* in 1988. Ideas from Chapter 13 of *Rock Prophecy*, including information
about the Saturn/Uranus conjunction, were also reported in my article titled *Multiples of Three* which was
published in the November 1992 issue of *UniVibes* magazine. In 1995 I worked on the Exhibit-A Hendrix
Exhibition world tour and the book which resulted from that project, titled *The Ultimate Experience* (London:
Boxtree Press, 1995), mentions the Saturn/Uranus conjunction that I'd reported back in 1992.
2. Interview with Charles Blass, NYC 10/24/91.

Birkbeck, "the radical and idealistic Uranus is most truly opposed by Saturn, with the latter's conservative and pragmatic nature. So whenever they are forced together by conjunction, approximately every forty-five to forty-six years, the resultant effect of Saturn's immovable object meeting Uranus' irresistible force is usually quite noticeable."[3]

Saturn-Uranus conjunctions are periods in which the nature of institutions themselves evolve and noticeably change under the effects of opposing influences: Uranus – a new order, versus Saturn – an existing order. Whereas Saturn represents immovable rigidity, Uranus represents movement and restlessness. Prior to 1942, their conjunction in 1897 heralded the end of the Victorian era, on the cusp of turn-of-the-century revolutions in physics (Einstein), psychology (Freud), and art (Picasso). Blues were born in Mississippi during the conjunction of a century ago.

The effects of planet alignments are felt before and after their actual conjunction. Birkbeck points out that "such a planetary event as this is not merely confined to the year of its exactitude, but spreads over several years either way."[4]

At the time of the 1942 conjunction of Saturn and Uranus, World War II was transforming global institutions, while Jimi Hendrix was born on the 27th (3x9 = 27) day of November (Sagittarius). These landmark events were presided over by an alignment of Earth, Saturn and Uranus. "1942," wrote Birkbeck, "[brought] the breaking down (Uranus) of class and sexual barriers (all Saturn) that were created, respectively, by the [wartime] military mixing and movement of men from their accustomed environments, and by the surfacing of latent abilities [among] women having to work in a 'mans world' of arms manufacturing, and farming, etc., and, finally, by the international warring itself. Of course, following upon more freedom came new barriers and restrictions, which is a very compact but frustrating expression of Saturn and Uranus. The major example of this was the [1945] division of Germany into East and West, with its all too perfect but sinister symbol – the Berlin Wall, which is essentially, but not solely, an opposition of interests between the free enterprise (Uranus) of the West and the tight state control (Saturn) of the USSR/Communist Bloc . . . just as there was an enormous spurt of progress during WWII, it is very likely that major breakthroughs are going to happen a few years hence."[5] Birkbeck wrote this analysis prior to the 1988 conjunction of Saturn-Uranus, and her prediction proved correct. A year later, in 1989, the Berlin Wall came down, the Soviet Union dissolved and communism reformed.

Astrologer Tim Lyons writes that when the 1942 Saturn-Uranus cycle that kicked off with Jimi's birth returned in 1988, both Saturn and Uranus were astrologically located "in future-oriented Sagittarius, emphasizing the need to discover new principles and a broader view."[6] Like Birkbeck, Lyons also accurately predicted the effects of this

3. Lyn Birkbeck, *The Saturn-Uranus Conjunction – Its Spiritual and Historical Significance*, Horoscope 2/88, p.17.

4. Ibid.

5. Ibid. pp.18-19.

6. Tim Lyons, *The Saturn-Uranus Conjunction – Approaching the Gate*, American Astrology, 2/88, p.30.

conjunction on the years that followed in the early 1990s: "We are changing our thinking about the world political system as it has developed since World War II," he wrote in 1988. "The governmental structures (Saturn) are obviously reaching their breaking point (Uranus), and we are faced with profound changes in the social status quo, in governmental privilege, and in our whole relationship to the socio-political development of the past four decades."[7]

Both Lyons' and Birkbeck's predictions proved true when in the '90s there came an end to four decades of Democratic control of the U.S. Congress, reform of the welfare state, a rise of armed anti-government militias, the New World Order, and rollbacks in perks for government officials. "Uranus is creative space; Saturn is fear and contraction," notes Lyons. "The combination of these two planets urges us to look anew at our need to unite form with freedom, past with future, solidity with space, fear with insight . . . discipline begets a flash of insight which becomes the ground for further discipline . . . the lightning bolt of Uranus needs to be grounded and put to use, while being allowed to destroy what needs to be destroyed . . . humanity seems to take the wrong approach to Saturn and Uranus. Instead of having the appropriate structure grow naturally from our free insight (which would make our laws an expression of wisdom and freedom), we build structures that are contrary to that natural insight, eventually forcing our need for freedom (Uranus) to revolt against the structures of that status quo (Saturn) . . . What needs to be let go of is our set of preconceptions about how things should be."[8]

During the 1942 conjunction of Saturn and Uranus, when Hendrix was born, the "structures that are contrary to natural insight" began to crumble. Those "structures" were attitudes about sexuality and sin and their relation with ideas about a Messiah/Christ. The old notions climaxed in 1942 with an unnatural structure called the Third Reich.

In the aftermath of the 1942 conjunction, Pope Pious XII stunned religious leaders and academics by reversing the Vatican's centuries old intolerance of inquiry into the origins of the Bible. In 1943, the Pope issued a new edict that encouraged scholars to fully investigate the question of who wrote the sacred texts. This Vatican decree initiated unprecedented research into the history and events surrounding the formation of the Holy Book. And then a new age of understanding was christened in that same year by the discovery of the Dead Sea Scrolls. The two thousand year old Scrolls provide a clearer picture than ever before of life in the Middle East during the time of Jesus, enabling new interpretations of scripture.

> *John Allegro was among the first team of scholars to study the Dead Sea Scrolls, and he concluded the writings reveal that the Christian religion was founded by druggies who worshipped shrooms. Drug taking, orgiastic mystery cults worshipped a certain sacred mushroom, said Allegro, and he*

7. Ibid. p.28.
8. Ibid. pp.28-30.

> *went on to claim that Jesus Christ had not been a man, but a code name for*
> *that mushroom.* — Tom Robbins[9]

Allegro's theory exemplifies the idea of a lighting bolt (Uranus) by which "discipline begets a flash of insight which becomes the ground for further discipline." After years of study, he arrived at the insights presented in his book *The Sacred Mushroom and the Cross*, alleging that the entire Bible is a carefully coded document of sacred mushroom mysticism. The secrets, wrote Allegro, "if they were not to be lost forever had to be committed to writing, and yet, if found, must give nothing away."[10]

Prior to the discovery of the Dead Sea Scrolls, during the approach of the 1942 conjunction when the effects of a Saturn-Uranus alignment were building in force, Dr. Albert Hoffman synthesized LSD in his Swiss laboratory for the first time. Initial tests of the compound on animals proved insignificant. Hoffman stored the vial of LSD away. Then on the afternoon of April 16, 1 U.E. (1943), a few months after the birth of Jimi, and with the effects of the Saturn-Uranus conjunction in full bloom, Hoffman recalls, "I had a strange feeling that it would be worthwhile to carry out more profound studies with this compound."[11] The first human LSD trip, perhaps the single most transformational event of the first century, followed when Hoffman ingested the drug.

The shattering effects of the conjunction in the year 1 U.E. kicked off a restructuring of civilization. Hendrix was born that year under the sign of Sagittarius. And under Sagittarius the next Saturn-Uranus conjunction occurred 46 years later, in February 1988, while I was writing about Jimi's Prophecy for the first time in my manuscript titled *A Touch of Hendrix*.[12]

About that conjunction Lyn Birkbeck wrote, "One particular area of scientific discovery will be concerning the dual nature of Man as represented by the sign in which the 1988 conjunction of Saturn and Uranus takes place – Sagittarius [Jimi]. This dual nature implies the animal and divine aspects of being, for that is what the centaur, Sagittarius' symbol, represents . . . the combined effect of the Saturn-Uranus conjunction will definitely implement a turning point in Mankind's world view – be that view literal, psychological, or both. The sign of this conjunction's placement, Sagittarius, governs religious beliefs . . . Since disruptive Uranus has been travelling through Sagittarius since 1981, certain churchmen and theologians have been disrupting such Christian tenants as the Immaculate Conception, the Resurrection, and whether or not Jesus Christ was really the Son of God. On this issue we may close by saying that the greatest and most far reaching change to take place over the next few years will be Mans idea of what 'God' actually means in practical (Saturn) and symbolic (Uranus) terms."[13]

9. High Times 12/76, p.95.
10. Ibid.
11. Martin Lee & Bruce Shalin, *Acid Dreams – the CIA, LSD and the Sixties Rebellion*, (New York, Grove Press 1985), p.xiv.
12. *A Touch of Hendrix*, unpublished manuscript (1988), p.351.
13. Birkbeck, *The Saturn-Uranus Conjunction – Its Spiritual and Historical Significance*, p.20.

After the date of Jimi's birth, the next incident of Multiples of Three picks up with his arrival in England on the 24th (3x8 = 24) day of the 9th month in '66. Twelve days later his Experience trio was formed on the same day that LSD was banned in America – Oct. 6, '66 – a date with triple sixes, an omen of biblical proportions:

> *You need wisdom to understand the number of the beast! But if you are smart enough, you can figure this out. Its number is six hundred and sixty six, and it stands for a person.*   – Revelation 13:18

The Number of the Beast is also called the Apocalyptic Number. Julia Line notes, "The beast is regarded by some to be the antichrist who will one day gain dominion over the whole world . . . The number 666 was thought to represent the numerical value of some proper name, written in either Hebrew or Greek letters. Diverse attempts have been mainly to identify the beast with historical characters including Mohammed, Luther and Napoleon I. The most popular identification, however, is with the Roman Emperor Nero."[14]

Nero ruled Rome (54-68 C.E.) two decades after the death of Jesus. He was the first great persecutor of Christians in Rome, slaughtering thousands by feeding them to lions in the Coliseum.

> *I escaped from the Roman Coliseum...*   – Jimi[15]

Exactly nineteen centuries later, counterculture *freeks* paralleled early Christians as new saints to suffer persecution beneath the heels of dominators.

Freeks were about being *free*: free love, free living, shared communality, non-authoritarian equals. What the world knew as "hippies" was an *equalitarian* subculture, and as such they bore direct comparison with Christians in Rome, or rather with peasants in Jerusalem during the time of Jesus. For example, whereas the peasants in Jerusalem staged a great rebellion during the years 66-70 C.E., exactly nineteen centuries later in 1966-1970 C.E. the freeks staged a great rebellion during the Hendrix concert years. These were the days of a cultural revolution that swept the world, creating a great surge towards freedom and equality.

> *The two periods of greatest movement toward equality occurred at opposite points of the business cycle: during the years of the Great Depression and during the boom of the late 1960s . . . the high-water mark of equality being attained in the years 1968-1970 . . . from the middle to the end of the 1960s . . . unemployment . . . during the spurt towards equality in the late 1960s,*

---

14. Line, *Discover Numerology*, p.16.
15. *Cherokee Mist – The Lost Writings of Jimi Hendrix*, p.71.

> *it was consistently below 4 percent . . . Since then, as we have started to slip backward toward greater inequality . . . corporate profits, which had declined from about $82 billion in 1966 to $69 billion in 1970, bounced up . . . there has been a sharp decline from the high point of 1970 [back] to the equality balance of the early 1960s . . . Persons were sent to state and federal prisons at a rate that peaked at about 50 per 100,000 of population around 1960-1961. Beginning about 1964, the rate began to drop rapidly, reaching a low of 38 in 1969 and then, as the counterattack on equality began, rising sharply to a high of over 60 in the late 1970s . . . During the years from 1963 to 1969 an average of more than 150 civil disorders a year were counted, almost three times the average for the preceding five years. As we moved into the 1970s and the movement toward equality began to be beaten back, there was a sharp falloff in this kind of collective activity, dwindling to only 17 disorders in 1973.*   – William Ryan[16]

The peak years of the hippie counterculture are marked at their start by the simultaneous birth of the Experience and ban on acid on October 6, 1966, and at their end by the death of Hendrix on September 18, 1970. Within those four years from '66 to '70 a revolution transpired. Likewise, from 66 to 70, nineteen hundred years earlier, C.E., the great Jewish revolt against Rome raged.

> *. . . deprivation led to the massive peasant involvement in the double social and political revolution that began in 66 C.E. . . . Mass crucifixions also framed the beginning and ending of the First Roman Jewish War. In the early summer of 66 C.E., Florus, then Roman governor of the Jewish homeland, ordered his troops to attack inside the city itself . . . Four years later, in the early summer of 70 C.E., Titus' army had completely encircled Jerusalem and the siege was being pressed toward its awful consummation . . . the Temple's actual destruction in 70 C.E.*   – John Crossan[17]

Nineteen centuries later, in 1970, came the destruction of Jimi and music from his studio, a modern Temple for rebels. During the construction of his studio, Jimi originally named it "Electric Temple."[18] The death of Hendrix *is* the destruction of the Temple. During the four years preceding the Temple's destruction in '70 C.E., modern Zealots in America and Vietnam fought against the armies and police of the establishMENt. 20th century rebels called Yippies swept into the media spotlight during the winter of '67 and the spring of '68...

---

16. Ryan, *Equality*, pp.162-3, 177, 165, 172, 167.
17. Crossan, *Jesus – A Revolutionary Biography*, pp.126, 132, and *Historical Jesus* p.220.
18. *Cherokee Mist – The Lost Writings of Jimi Hendrix*, p.66.

> *The Zealots . . . were a coalition of bandit groups that swept into Jerusalem*
> *between the winter of 67 and the spring of 68 as Vespasian's scorched-earth*
> *strategy tightened the noose inexorably around the capital. They were, as*
> *Richard Horsley put it, "peasants-turned-brigands-turned-Zealots". . . and*
> *with Zealots arrived not only social revolution but the. . . reign of terror as*
> *well . . . the Zealots . . . fought within [Jerusalem] for overall control of the*
> *rebellion in 68 C.E.*   – John Crossan[19]

Likewise, '68 is the year when Yippies fought for overall control of the rebellion in the new Jerusalem on the streets of Chicago. That year's Democratic National Convention inspired the incarnation of Zealots exactly nineteen centuries after 68 C.E. And 1968 was the peak year of Jimi's popularity.

Like a new Trinity, our modern savior joined the Experience trio on that fateful date when the acid sacrament was banned, the day of triple sixes: Oct. 6, '66. *Freeks* recognized the ban on acid as handiwork of the beast. On this darkest day during the Vietnam holocaust, when all hope for gentle people seemed crushed beneath the heels of a new Nero, the Experience appeared. It was as if the deity had intervened directly to bestow a means with which to subvert the anti-LSD decree. Persecution of Christians under Nero had begun in the mid 60s C.E. Likewise, in the mid 1960s C.E., nineteen centuries later, persecution of *freeks* began with a ban on acid. Haight Ashbury hippies overruled the establishMENt's new LSD law by staging a pagan *Love Rally* at the gates of City Hell.

Jimi's career, and the new Zealot rebellion, peaked in 1968, which is the only Hendrix concert year for which the sum divides equally into 3 (3 x 656 = 1968). This was also the year in which the third (and last) Experience album of new songs was released. Then, after midnight on the 30th day of the 6th month of '69, the Experience disbanded. During that same month "If 6 Was 9" became the first Hendrix song featured in a Hollywood film – '69's *Easy Rider*.

Eighteen months after last performing in Britain, Hendrix returned to England on the 27th day of August. He was 27 years old, having been born of the 27th day (3x9=27). But most of the incidents in Jimi's life characterized by Multiples of Three occur in the 9th month of 1970 – September, the only month spelled with 9 letters. On the 3rd day of the 9th month in Copenhagen, Jimi played his third-to-last concert. Three days later, his final concert occurred at a "Love & Peace Festival" in Germany, on the 6th day of the 9th month – "If 6 Was 9":

> *He talked for a while about a song he had written called "If Six Was Nine"*
> *. . . Jimi said that these numbers together are a very powerful force, and he*
> *drew them within each other. It looked like a spiral when he added more*

---

19. Crossan, *Historical Jesus*, p 213, and *Jesus – A Revolutionary Biography*, p.143.

rays, the individual rays as well as the whole form spinning to the right. He
said the sign with nine rays in it is the symbol of a very high spiritual power
which is coming towards Earth. — Monika Dannemann[20]

What Monika didn't understand was that the drawing Jimi fashioned by combining the two numerals, 6 and 9, is a sketch of the asteroid.[21] The drawing appears in her book and the "rays" spiraling out are its illustrious tail burning bright as it enters our atmosphere. At the bottom of his sketch he drew the Earth in the distance, with the Electric Love asteroid approaching through clouds. At the top he placed a long arrow, indicating a collision course straight ahead.

Jimi's sketch of the Rock is a composite combination of the figures 6 and 9, numbers which correlate with the length and width of Haley's Comet – measured at 6 miles by 9 miles when it passed Earth in 1986. This is the omen ratio with which Jimi alerts us to the size of Electric Love. If it's big enough to knock our globe off its axis, it has to be 900 miles long and 600 miles wide. Electric Love will leave us in pieces.

The *Love & Pieces* Festival on the 6th day of the 9th month was Jimi's last gig – *If 6 Was 9*. Twelve days later, on the morning of September 18 ($3 \times 6 = 18$), Hendrix died. He was with Monika at the time. If you count up the number of days that she made contact with Jimi, as described in her 1970 manuscript, the total is 18 days: 12 days in 1969 and 6 days in 1970.[22] When she called for the ambulance on that 18th and last day, the number she dialed was 999 – which is the number for emergency help in London. It was 18 minutes past the hour when that call was made. Nine minutes later the ambulance arrived at 27 ($3 \times 9 = 27$) minutes past the hour. Eighteen minutes later, the ambulance departed the Samarkand Hotel with Jimi. It arrived at St. Mary Abbots Hospital at 3 minutes past 12 ($1+2 = 3+3 = 6+6 = 12$) o'clock – a drive of 18 ($3+3 = 6 \times 3 = 18$) minutes. Forty-two ($3 \times 14 = 42$) minutes later, at 45 ($3 \times 15 = 45$) minutes past 12 o'clock, Jimi Hendrix was certified dead.

Born on the 27th, died at 27 on the 18th day of the 9th month – exactly three years and three months after his breakthrough at the Monterey Pop Festival. After just three brief years, the ministry of Jimi, like that of Jesus, was cut short.

The next event with a Multiple of Three coincidence happened a decade later in 1980 C.E. ($3 \times 660 = 1980$) when the posthumous Hendrix album *Nine to the Universe* was released. The age of the Universe was not known during Jimi's lifetime, when he ascribed *nine* "to the Universe."

The latest word is that the universe may be only 9 or 10 billion years old . . .
Scientists used to agree that the universe was about 15 billion years old, in

20. Dannemann, *The Inner World of Jimi Hendrix*, p.133.

21. Ibid.

22. Most of the dates are in dispute, which may be one reason why Monika's 1995 book omits mention of the specific dates on which she claimed to have seen Jimi.

1994 new observations shaved off some five billion years.
                                                        – Wonders of the Universe[23]

A team of astronomers . . . used data to calculate a Hubble parameter
between 61 and 77 kilometers per second per megaparsec, or about 9.5
billion years . . . the universe is only 9 billion years old.
                                                        – Patricia Barnes-Svarney[24]

At the Carnegie Observatories in Pasadena, California, a team of scientists led by Wendy Freedman used the Hubble space telescope to measure the distance to stars called Cepheid Variables. These stars pulsate in cycles that relate to their brightness; the brightness can be used to measure distance, and therefore age too. Calculations at Carnegie in 1995, more than a quarter century after Jimi wrote *Nine to the Universe*, place the age of the universe at approximately 9 billion years old.[25]

With each incidence of coincidence we are reminded of how much more to life there is than meets the eye. Coincidence characterizes the events of Jimi's life. In the Multiples of Three scheme of things it is fitting that he identified himself as "*a nine*" – number 9 is the *super multiple*, comprised as it is of *triple* threes (3+3+3 = 9). "A very special place belongs to the 9," asserts Annemarie Schimmel. "In Christian circles the 9 was generally connected with the concept of the Trinity."[26] Jimi's number is nine and his life intersects Multiples of Three. And Trinity is a key link to the meaning of Jimi.

Constantine's "Trinity" requires us to believe in Eve and Eden, it enshrines Jesus as Messiah sent by a Father God to save us from sins of the flesh. These are linked concepts, *intentionally* connected by Constantine's Church. Only by worshipping the Messiah is our original sin forgiven. The "Trinity" places Jesus in a myth that vilifies sensuality, a myth written to pitch women against men. Jimi is in opposition with this denigration of sex represented by the Trinity. As the figurehead of Afro-Irish Voodoo blues, Hendrix represents possession of the body by natural forces. The *meaning* of Jimi sets in relief the *idea* of Constantine's Trinity.

THE HENDRIX EVENT

Jimi's lineage positions him as the archetype for possession and Voodoo blues. His story conflicts with ideas of a Messiah who rejects flesh and condemns sex. Issues surrounding Jimi explain why women and gays are targets for religions written by heterosexual men. Comprehending Hendrix means realizing that it is Jimi who frees the slaves trained by culture cults called "religion." Our chains break when we grasp the

---

23. *Big Bang Big Mystery*, Wonders of the Universe, The Learning Channel 6/95.
24. Barnes-Svarney, *Asteroid – Earth Destroyer or New Frontier?* p.31.
25. The Osgood File, CBS Radio Network 5/10/96.
26. Schimmel, *The Mystery of Numbers*, pp.27, 178.

issues and explanations generated by Hendrix. His story re-interprets the myths of religion. Through a Hendrix Perspective the next generation can at last be *deprogrammed*. This is the Hendrix Event, the long-awaited revelation about *how* the religions of the world connect rejection of flesh with privileges for men, revelations of intent behind the Messiah idea, now to be discussed and discarded.

When we comprehend Hendrix, the issues around Jimi raise the Christ figure into a new view, one from which we can dismantle damage done. Through Spiritual Blues, we *undo* the Messiah mess—not necessarily *anti*christ, but *un*christ.

> *Religious symbols fade and die when the cultural situation that gave rise to them and supported them ceases to give them plausibility.*
>
> — Mary Daly[27]

> *Here comes a woman, wrapped up in chains,*
> *Forget about the man, he put your life in pain.*
> *If you want to be free, come along with me.*
>
> — Jimi[28]

The mythology of Jimi interprets world religions, and like the faiths it explains it contains unique numerology. Numbers are patterned throughout Jimi's life in a sequence key of nine times three (9x3 = 27), the triple three (3x3 = 9) super multiple Trinity. His birthdate/death age – *27* – is a triplet multiple too: 3x9 = 27 is 2+7 = 9x3 = 27. Even his death date – 18th day – has a chain of threes: 1+8 = 9÷3 = 3+3 = 6x3 = 18. The nine ties together all of these Multiples of Three digit cycles: 9+9 = 18 is 1+8 = 9 x 3 = 27÷3 = 9.

Jimi's nine, a *trinity-of-three*, marks the vortex of a storm: his life's trajectory intersects a crossroads where key changes mysteriously came together and left imprints till the end of time.[29]

> *I represent everything as far as I'm concerned.* – Jimi[30]

27. Daly, *Beyond God the Father*, p.15.
28. "Message To Love," released on the *Band of Gypsys* album, Capitol Records 4/70.
29. My 1988 manuscript, *A Touch of Hendrix*, details historical stories around the dates of Jimi's trajectory along a timeline of related events.
30. Hall and Clark, *The Superstars – In Their Own Words*, p.19.

Chapter 16: Memory of the Future

Claire Sylvia is one of the longer living heart/lung transplant survivors. In her book *A Change of Heart*, she describes how after transplant surgery, traits and characteristics of the man whose heart she received suddenly developed in her. She experienced unfamiliar cravings and preferences that she later learned match those of the donor whose heart she now lives with. "The heart is more than a pump," says Claire, "it comes with it's own rhythm – unique to each of us – it's own cellular structure that has a memory, that records things that have happened to us so that, if our heart is passed on to someone else, those memories that have been imbued in the heart will become of the person who is now living with it."[1]

> *Cardiologists are now looking at cellular memory in transplant patients.*
> – Deepak Chopra[2]

Swiss psychiatrist Carl Jung envisioned a "collective unconscious" of the human race in which each one of us carries in our subconscious memories the combined experiences of all people who have lived before us. Deepak Chopra speaks of an expanded version of collective memory called the *holographic model* of memory: "a three-dimensional projection of memory . . . all of it is in every bit of it. Every bit of the hologram is the whole thing from a different perspective. Scientists are suggesting that holographic memory is what the body is, that you and I have not only personal memories, but impersonal memories that go back a long time . . . being non-local, spaceless and timeless, it goes back eons of time . . . that each cell is a hologram of the entire universe, both personal and impersonal memory . . . As this lifetime's experience, from the fetus to the adult, we replicate the experience of our species and other species . . . we have the memories of everything that has happened in the entire evolutionary history of not only mankind, but other species as well."[3]

In the 1953 novel *Childhood's End*, Arthur Clarke describes a future in which our civilization is under the control of an unseen alien race called the Overlords. For fifty-five years, the aliens rule human society from spacecrafts "as mankind waited for the

1. Claire Sylvia and William Novak, *A Change of Heart*, (New York: Little Brown, 1997), pp.3, 6, 92, and ABC News 20/20, 5/16/97.
2. *Body, Mind & Soul – The Mystery and the Magic*, PBS 8/95.
3. Ibid.

Overlords to show themselves and to step down from their gleaming ships."[4]

"The Overlords have brought security, peace and prosperity to the world," writes Clarke. "The majority of the people seem content to let the Overlords run the world as they please." Finally the day arrives when the aliens show themselves: "It was a tribute to the Overlord's psychology, and to their careful years of preparation, that only a few people fainted . . . There was no mistake. The leathery wings, the little horns, the barbed tail – all were there. The most terrible of all legends had come to life, out of the unknown past. Yet now it stood smiling, in ebon majesty."[5]

Overlords resemble devils; they represent our memory of the future. "Cause and event could reverse their normal sequence," observes Clarke. "There must be such a thing as a racial memory, and that memory was somehow independent of time. To it, the future and the past were one. That was why, thousands of years ago, men had already glimpsed a distorted image of the Overlords, through a mist of fear and terror."[6]

"Has anyone done an experiment that shows the existence of time?" asks Chopra. "No respectable physicist since the year 1913 has used the word time by itself. They talk about space-time continuum, because time, as we experience it, is a psychological event, is a concept that we have invented in order to explain our experience of change. Reality is much more flexible than people realize, even the reality of time [is] programmed by our past belief, which we inherited from our parents and our cultural tradition, and our indoctrination by society – the 'hypnosis' of social conditioning. We remain localized in the boundaries handed down from generation to generation. We refuse to see that reality is open to revision. Nothing has to be accepted just because we inherited it . . . Can it be that time will wait for one man and overtake another depending on what each one expects?"[7]

> *There are experiments that have been done on sort of the timing of consciousness, and they seem to lead to a very odd picture which doesn't even quite make consistent sense . . . There is something very odd about consciousness, and somehow, almost as though the future affects the past in some way, although a very tiny, limited scale, but something maybe of the order of a reasonable fraction of a second.*   – Roger Penrose[8]

> *You feared and recognized us, as we knew that you would. It was not precisely a memory . . . for that memory was not of the past, but of the future – of those closing years when your race knew that everything was finished . . . and because we were there, we became identified with your race's death. Yes, even while it was ten thousand years in the future! It was*

4. Arthur C. Clarke, *Childhood's End*, (New York: Ballantine Books, 1953), p.20.
5. Ibid. pp.15, 68.
6. Ibid. p.68.
7. Deepak Chopra, *Higher Self*, audio lecture tape.
8. *A Brief History of Time*, Triton Films 1991, produced by Gordon Freedman.

*as if a distorted echo had reverberated round the closed circle of time, from
the future to the past. Call it not a memory, but a premonition.*
                                                                     – The Overlords[9]

Is it tomorrow, or just the end of time?   – Jimi[10]

ROCK OF AGES

It is no accident that Hendrix communicates in a medium called "rock." It is no
coincidence that rock music evolved parallel with the unmooring of society from centuries
of belief in the sinfulness of sex. During the years when Jimi grew up, generations clashed
over attitudes towards love. Rock music came to spearhead a collision of myths: nature and
sex as expressions of the deity versus a Messiah God who punishes us, especially women and
gays, because we're too physical. The Hendrix years saw a climax of these tensions stemming
from centuries spent when men set rules and beliefs against anything feminine. Persecution
of intuitive, sensitive people impeded society's advance toward knowledge and technology.
An elite class of unjust monied men, the so-called "rich," silenced the seers who knew where
to place the blame for our fate. Any seer who could understand the phenomenon of rocks
injuring Earth could also see reasons why inequalities among us prevent any attempt at
defense. Opportunities that would have saved us were squandered so that the "rich" may
enjoy privileges that none deserve.

Now, through the medium of rock, a Prophecy predicts our rendezvous with a Rock.
Jimi envisioned Earth *asteroid destroyed* in a future that echos the past. Cause and effect
have "reversed their normal sequence" because our collective memory is independent of
time. That our race now speaks the term "rock music" signals that we have "already
glimpsed a distorted image" of the Rock.

Rock music is a memory of the future. *Rock Prophecy* provides the missing link. Rock
of Ages refers to a recurring impact of our planet by asteroids throughout eons and ages. A
memory record of the evolutionary past, imprinted in each cell of our species, activates this
explanation in response to the presence of rock music. Electronic rock became manifest
during the lifetime of Jimi and is epitomized by his image.

*Jimi spoke of his plans for the future . . . his next double album, which he
wanted to call . . .* **Rock of Ages**.   – Monika Dannemann[11]

We have evolved to become responsive to rock and to sense from it this intrinsic
vision of the Rock, as if the awareness is evoked from our subconscious by certain

---

9. Clarke, *Childhood's End*, p.207.
10. "Purple Haze" released on *Are You Experienced?* Reprise Records 9/67.
11. Dannemann, *The Inner World of Jimi Hendrix*, p.154.

sounds that our species has been evolved to respond to, sounds rooted in rhythm and blues. For millennia this instinct has lain dormant in the human brain, awaiting the presence of electronic rock to trigger an evolution of awareness.

> *Purple haze all in my brain, lately things don't seem the same.*
> — Jimi[12]

> *According to Ayurveda, the human body is a manifestation of sound. More specifically, our bodies are expressions of primordial sound, or ancient natural sounds expressing themselves in rhythms and synchronicities and frequencies of vibration. These frequencies of vibration become the energy fields that ultimately become the matter of our bodies.* — Deepak Chopra[13]

Most of humanity accepts the word "rock" to refer to music, as if from these sounds we subliminally anticipate a Rock. An ancient impact is etched into our cellular memory; it's what impelled Jimi to transmit his prediction through sound. Each cell in our bodies is a hologram of memories from our race that go back to the days of dinosaurs and beyond. An individual life, from fetus to adult, mirrors the evolution of our species. Our subconscious mind carries memory of everything that's happened in the history of Earth. We remember the Rock, the ancient light in the sky, the light that extinguished life. It is a memory of the *future* – of what the Overlords called "those closing years when your race knew that everything was finished."[14]

Rock music grew out of blues. But blues evolved a century ago as an overflow release of animist instinct, blues became a release for imported families of African slaves stifled by Christian customs against sex in the west. The root of this music is in the story of Eden and the Messiah – anti-sex, anti-female – a war of myths. The slaves needed a way to be human in a culture that stifled life. The created blues, which fueled rock, and the conflict was carried on in sounds that transmit Jimi's Prophecy. The music is called *rock* because it "became identified with your race's death."[15] Rock music carries the memory of a coming impact. It carries *Rock Prophecy*.

Mankind had only so much time within which to erect a defense against asteroids. Like a biological clock, we were programmed by the Earth to wake up to this realization. The planet's psychoactive plants acted to implant this image in our minds, but society resisted nature and natural hallucinogens. The effects of the plants inspire compassion and equal partnership among people; hallucinogens were designed by Earth for this purpose. But dominator men, in a race to ease their own access to sex, sought to control everything feminine and gentle.

---

12. "Purple Haze" released on *Are You Experienced?* Reprise Records 9/67.
13. *Body, Mind & Soul – The Mystery and the Magic*, PBS 8/95.
14. Clarke, *Childhood's End*, p.207.
15. Ibid.

Ancient asteroids that severely injured Earth have left etched in the cells of our bodies a craving for sound that activates awareness of the Rock, even while the arrival of Electric Love was many years away, "as if a distorted echo had reverberated round the closed circle of time, from the future to the past."[16] Not until the lifetime of Hendrix did technology advance past setbacks to a point where rock music was possible. Our need for rock sound was finally satisfied. In Jimi's music we hear at last the Earth's scream, a release of the ancient noise that awaits us.

Biblical predictions of Armageddon reflect memories of the collision, a collective recollection of the ancient impact.

> *As the lightning cometh out of the east, and shineth even unto the west; so shall also the coming of the Son of man ... The Sun will become dark, and the moon will no longer shine. The stars will fall, and the powers in the sky will be shaken ... then shall all the tribes of the Earth mourn, and they shall see the Son of man coming in the clouds of heaven with power and great glory ... At the sound of a loud trumpet, he will send his angels ...* – Jesus (Matthew 24:27-31)

The Rock of Ages transcends time. In "Up From the Skies," Jimi refers to our subconscious collective memories of pre-history as "*the rooms behind your minds*" and asks if we have a "*vacuum there?*" – an unawareness of the Rock that shapes our evolution.

> *Is it just remains from vibrations and echoes long ago?*
> *Things like 'Love the World' and 'Let your fancy flow.'*
> – Jimi [17]

Deepak Chopra reminds us that "our bodies are expressions of primordial sound, or ancient natural sounds expressing themselves in rhythms and synchronicities and frequencies of vibration."[18] Hendrix sensed these sound patterns to be the source of our evolutionary "*flow*" which "*echoes*" the "*vibrations*" of a "*long ago*" asteroid impact. "Love" is a verb that expresses procreation and nurture. Jimi christened the Rock with the name *Love*, therefore "Love" and "Rock" now have double meanings: each is a *noun* that refers to the asteroid and each is a *verb*, i.e. "to *love* the world" or "to *rock* the cradle." Rock music is like an evolutionary alarm clock meant to activate awareness of "Love". Jimi is the link through which this mutation was made.

In "Up From the Skies" he sings about what Earth was like "*before the days of ice*" and explains "*this is why I'm so concerned.*" Earth once spun in orbit closer to the Sun and ice never formed at the poles. An asteroid struck and knocked us into a colder orbit where we remain today.

---

16. Ibid.
17. *Cherokee Mist – The Lost Writings of Jimi Hendrix*, p.18, *Up From the Skies.*
18. *Body, Mind & Soul – The Mystery and the Magic*, PBS 8/95.

Some scientists also believe that larger impactors were responsible for the ultimate rotation of a planet. At one time during its formation, Venus may have spun in the "correct" rotation, similar to the other planets. A major collision with a huge asteroid could have changed all that, creating the opposite-from-normal rotation (or maybe all the planets were struck by larger objects, changing their rotation; but based on the overall spin of the solar system, Venus is the actual oddball). The axis of a planet could have changed in much the same way, the large impactor turning the planet away from an up-and-down axis line. — Patricia Barnes-Svarney[19]

> *I come back to find the stars misplaced,*
> *And the smell of a world that has burned.*
> *Maybe it's just a change of climate.*
>
> — Jimi [20]

When asked to explain these lyrics from "Up From the Skies" Jimi replied, "It's a story of a guy who's been on Earth before, but on a different turning of the axis, and now he's come back to find this scene happening, like the axis of the Earth, if it changes, it changes the whole face of the Earth. Why keep living in the old, in the past? These buildings ain't going to be here for all that long, so why be like that?"[21]

There's a lot of lost people around and like there are only leaders in times of crisis. That's just what's happening now. It's not just a fad that's going on, it's very serious. If you revert back in time, there's Egypt. It's very dusty now, but it used to be green. — Jimi[22]

We are in times of crisis, anticipating an impact. Jimi is the seer who shows us. Our human future was sold out because contributions from half the race were wasted. Under repression from world religions, sensitive and feminine people held critical visions that went unexpressed.

Christian theology widely asserted that women were inferior, weak, depraved, and vicious. The logical consequences of this opinion were worked out in a brutal set of social arrangements that shortened and crushed the lives of women . . . It is female talent that has been lost to ourselves and the species. It is men who have sapped the life force of women. — Mary Daly[23]

19. Svarney, *Asteroid – Earth Destroyer or New Frontier?* p.209.
20. *Cherokee Mist – The Lost Writings of Jimi Hendrix*, p.18, *Up From the Skies*, and "Up From the Skies" released on *Axis:Bold as Love*, Track Records 12/67.
21. Hall and Clark, *The Superstars – In Their Own Words*, p.131.
22. San Diego Free Press 6/13/69.
23. Daly, *Beyond God the Father*, p 95, 173

The race to build a defense against asteroids is lost.

> *All they're doing is making themselves weaker and weaker until their*
> *negatives come and just take them away. That's what is going to happen,*
> *then you're going to have no world to live on. The establishment is going to*
> *crumble away.*   – Jimi[24]

The coming of Love finds Earth unprotected. When Hendrix spoke of the Prophecy he said that people "are going to feel" the change that will come to Earth, "in many ways they are a lot of the reason for causing it."[25] We will *cause* Earth's collision with the asteroid by our *inability* to cooperate as equals and mobilize world resources in time to protect ourselves from the Rock.

> *Where be these enemies? Capulet, Montegue, See what a scourge is laid upon*
> *your hate, that heaven finds means to kill your joys with* **Love***.*
>   – William Shakespear[26]

> *You know where all the earthquakes happening stem from is bad vibrations,*
> *they get very heavy sometimes, you know? If you want to save your state, get*
> *your hearts together.*   – Jimi[27]

THE BIG BONG THEORY

> *The world's gonna go like topsy-turvy soon because humans forget that they*
> *are part of Earth-matter too, so they have bad vibrations floating around*
> *now. So there's gonna be a big physical change.*   – Jimi[28]

> *Nature might be an organism whose interconnected components act upon*
> *and communicate with one another through the release of chemical signals*
> *into the environment . . . Alkaloids in plants, specifically the hallucinogenic*
> *compounds . . . catalyzed the emergence of human self-reflection . . . The*
> *hallucinogens function as interspecies chemical messengers . . .*
> *information transfer from one species to the other . . . Hallucinogens acted*
> *as catalysts in the development of imagination, fueling the creation of*
> *internal stratagems and hopes that may well have synergized the emergence*
> *of language and religion . . . Where plant hallucinogens do not occur, such*

24. L.A. Free Press 1969.
25. Ibid.
26. William Shakespeare, *Romeo and Juliet.*
27. 4/26/69 L.A. Forum Concert CD, booklet text by M. Fairchild, *Lifelines – The Jimi Hendrix Story*, disc IV, Warner Records 11/90.
28. Brown, *Jimi Hendrix – In His Own Words*, p.65, from an interview in Beverly Hills, CA 6/69.

transfers of information take place with great slowness, but in the presence of hallucinogens a culture is quickly introduced to ever more novel information, sensory input, and behavior and thus is bootstrapped to higher and higher states of self-reflection. — Terrence McKenna[29]

Jimi predicts that the world will soon go "topsy-turvy" because we forget that we are "part of Earth-matter." Modern societies forgot about the communion with our planet that happens when we eat psychoactive plants. Feminine sensibilities and communal nurturing are produced by use of hallucinogens. Relaxed and benevolent moods produced by mushrooms, weeds, seeds, bark and cactus — and insights unique to these moods — have been suppressed. McKenna writes, "The natural world had come to be seen, by late Roman times, as a demonic and imprisoning shell. This was the spiritual legacy of the destruction of the partnership model of self and society and its replacement with the dominator model . . . [with] values based on a dominator hierarchy accustomed to suppressing consciousness and awareness . . . The orgiastic psychedelic religion that worshiped the Mother Goddess made the Catal culture anathema to the new dominator style of warfare and hierarchy . . . [which] trampled...the last great partnership civilization. Plunder replaced pastoralism . . . human god-kings replaced the religion of the Goddess . . . This is but the most recent effort to profiteer from and frustrate our species' deeply instinctual need to make contact with the Gaian mind of the living planet . . . the Western tradition has suffered a long, sustained break with the sociosymbiotic relationship to the feminine and the mysteries of organic life that can be realized through shamanic use of hallucinogenic plants . . . The global triumph of Western values means we, as a species, have wandered into a state of prolonged neurosis because of the absence of a connection to the unconscious. Gaining access to the unconscious through plant hallucinogen use reaffirms our original bond to the living planet . . . Life lived in the absence of the psychedelic experience . . . is life trivialized, life denied, life enslaved to the ego and its fear of dissolution in the mysterious matrix of feeling that is all around us . . . Returning to the balance of the planetary partnership style means trading the point of view of the egoistic dominator for the intuitional, feeling-toned understanding of the maternal matrix . . . we need a new paradigmatic image that can take us rapidly forward and through the historical choke point that we can feel impeding and resisting a more expansive, more humane, more caring dimension that is insisting on being born."[30]

The men who control media train the public to accept competitive customs that prevent us from mounting the collective effort necessary to develop a defense against asteroids. Locked in this straight-jacket MENtality, we are oblivious to our fate. From the perspective of the biosphere, the *purpose* for human intelligence having been evolved by Earth is to create a defense against asteroids. Humans are collectively a protective mutation evolved by Gaia to produce enough destructive capacity to shatter rocks. That's what all living planets (with water based life forms) do. This is why people are fascinated

29. McKenna, *Food of the Gods*, pp.41, 24.
30. Ibid. pp.146, 237, 89, 245, 62-63, 252, 92, 253

with flight and with explosives, and speed. We've been programmed to seek out and destroy globe-threatening asteroids. We are meant to function as the "teeth" of the planet.

> *The whole planet as an organism – you see, if you will think of ourselves as coming* **out** *of the Earth, rather than as being thrown* **in** *here from somewhere else, but thrown* **out of** *the Earth – we* **are** *the Earth, we are the consciousness of the Earth, these are the eyes of the Earth, and this is the voice of the Earth – what else?*   – Joseph Campbell[31]

With awareness and respect we care for our planet, but the human race does not "worship" the Earth. Rather, it is the Earth that *worships us*. We are the saviors of the planet; saving it is our function. Mother Earth pays tribute to us in the form of special mushrooms, leaves, seeds, cactus and bark. Through these psychoactive plants the planet activates people in unique ways. The biosphere has evolved such chemicals as a language with which Earth can communicate with us. The altered states they induce connect us with Gaia. They are what McKenna calls our "umbilicus to the feminine mind of the planet."

> *The music flows from the air; that's why I can connect with a spirit. And when* [people] *come down off this natural high, they see clearer, feel different things, don't think of pain and hurting the next person. You think of getting your own thing together.*   – Jimi[32]

It is through our dedication to asteroid defense that the biosphere stands a chance of survival, our only chance of existing *Stone Free* and without rings, like the rings of debris around Saturn's rainbow black eye. *"Each stone they touch they shall learn more and more of the purpose of living and giving and receiving,"* wrote Jimi.[33] The natural order for society is for all members to share all resources equally among people so that everyone's efforts can be aimed at the Rock.

> *We know how to tackle the problem, we know the magnitude of the problem, and in fact it's just another great challenge for the human race to take on its shoulders and say "Hey, we can tackle this, we can do this." Life has been here on this planet for three and a half billion years and many, many times there have been extinction events. But now at long last a species has evolved which is smart enough, and has the technology to actually intercede and make sure that these things don't happen again. We are that species.*
>   – Ducan Steel[34]

---

31. The Power of Myth, *The Hero's Adventure*, PBS 3/88.
32. Life 10/3/69.
33. *Cherokee Mist – The Lost Writings of Jimi Hendrix*, p.115 *Terra Revolution and Venus*.
34. *Doomsday: What Can We Do?*, Fox 2/14/97.

But instincts that inspire fascination with flight and with bombs also inspire aggression in us. To fulfill our mission of asteroid avoidance, we evolved as creatures dedicated to destruction. Yet, as a species, we also support our collective efforts with expressions of nurture and compassion. It's the nurturing *accommodator* trait in us that is cultivated by the Earth through plant hallucinogens meant for us to ingest. The effects of these chemicals on our senses open access to more comprehensive perspectives. From insights gained in these states, we perceive reasons why we behave the way we do.

Jimi called the hallucinogen experience a "sixth sense, or Free Soul."[35] Without it, our goal of avoiding asteroids would have remained unformulated. Without the calming effects of psychoactive plants, our instinct for destruction would have destroyed us ages ago. Some people are more susceptible to the effects of these chemicals than other people. A spectrum of reactions enables the variety of ideas needed to create a defense for our world.

> *There's a line in the Koran [where Allah] says . . . 'If We had wished, We could have made you one people, but as it is, We have made you many, therefore, vie among yourselves in good works.' I think it's a wonderful formula; it doesn't say why We made you many, but I think the truth of the matter is that the one and the many together add up to a more glorious totality than if we had the one only . . . There is a happy ending that blossoms from difficulty that must be surmounted.*   – Houston Smith[36]

Throughout history, our purpose was sensed by shamans and seers. In dominator cultures these people were brutalized and removed from society, their visions persecuted with them into oblivion. The suppression of benefits, which would have resulted from what they knew, has set back our advance towards technology we now need. Our society has little time left within which to arm the planet, and dominators stand in our way. Their aggressive competitive MENtality seeks to silence all calls for equality. In the absence of equality, our race fought and crawled its way through HIStory. Our combative ancestors squandered opportunities which, if acted upon, would have helped save us today.

> *Nature, far from being endless warfare among species, is an endless dance of diplomacy. And diplomacy is largely a matter of language. Nature appears to maximize mutual cooperation and mutual coordination of goals. To be indispensable to the organisms with which one shares an environment – that is the strategy that ensures successful breeding and continual survival.*
>   – Terrence McKenna[37]

---

35. Hall and Clark, *The Superstars – In Their Own Words*, p.22.
36. *Houston Smith: Islam*, w/Bill Moyers, PBS 4/96.
37. McKenna, *Food of the Gods*, p 41.

Deepak Chopra warns that our society of people who seek to compete against each other is "creating an epidemic of cardiovascular disease, compromised immune systems, the epidemic of cancer, and degenerative disorders. But even more importantly it has given rise to a legacy of war and hatred and perdition and conquest and subjugation and ecological devastation. We have become the predators of the planet Earth. And just like other predators before us we are risking our own extinction, and risking the extinction of Mother Earth and this wonderful universe . . . The universe has chosen us to take care of it. We are a privileged species."[38]

> *The driving force of modern industrial civilization has been individual material gain, in other words it's accepted as legitimate, and even praiseworthy, on the grounds that private license yields public benefits, in the classic formulation. It has long been understood very well that a society that is based on this principle will destroy itself in time. It can only persist with whatever suffering and injustice it entails as long as it is possible to pretend that the destructive forces that humans create are limited.*
>
> — Noam Chomsky[39]

> *Our fight/flight response gave rise to a predator psychology which was useful in a certain phase of our evolution . . . Everyone who is familiar with Darwinian evolution is familiar with the expression "survival of the fittest." And that phrase was probably very relevant and pertinent when we lived as hunter-gatherer tribes in forests and had to be wary of predators. But we have become the biggest predator on our planet. If you know the history of predators, you know that this ultimately leads to their extinction.*
>
> — Deepak Chopra[40]

FIFTY YEARS NOTICE

On March 26, 53 U.E. (1996 C.E.), a full year after I began writing *Rock Prophecy*, a newly discovered comet named Hyakutake reached its closest approach to Earth. That night ABC News reported, "After a comet smashed into Jupiter recently, Congress asked NASA if there is any way to defend ourselves against a big one coming our way? And surprisingly, there is. During the cold war Russian and American scientists devised and tested all kinds of solutions just now being published."

"There's a macho way to do it and then there's a gentle way to do it," explained Neil Tyson of the Hayden Planetarium. The macho way is to send a missile into deep space, find the object and, using nuclear weapons, blow it up or bump it off course. "But the kinder,

38. Deepak Chopra, *The Way of the Wizard*, PBS 11/95.
39. *Manufacturing Consent*, 1992, PBS 9/95.
40. *Body, Mind & Soul – The Mystery and the Magic*, PBS 8/95.

gentler solution," said Tyson, "would be, if you can catch it early enough in its orbit, to fly up to it and attach a little rocket to it . . . and slowly nudge it out of harms way, like a little tugboat. [However] I wouldn't feel comfortable without at least fifty years notice." Asked what would happen if a comet aimed at Earth should appear suddenly, such as Hyakutake, which was spotted only two months earlier. Tyson answered, "I know of no way that we can stop it."[41]

Attaching a "little tugboat" to a flaming asteroid racing past at 50,000 mph is a bit optimistic. Compounding the problem of our technological unpreparedness for such a task is the feeble attempt that society exerts in even looking for Earth threatening asteroids and comets. Air Force Col. Mike Bodenheimer, Chief of NORAD's Aerospace Warning Division, warns, "NORAD has limited capability to see an incoming asteroid. Our systems would not pick that up until very close to the in gain, and then you'd have only a few moments until collision with the Earth. Just as we have no defense against an intercontinental ballistic missile, we would have no weapon capable of going into space to intercept this particular object."[42]

Dr. David Morrison, Director of Space for NASA-Ames, explains, "If something sneaks up on us there is very little we can do. In fact today, the most likely situation is zero warning. The next impact of a mile wide object will probably happen without any prior discovery of it at all. The first thing you'll know is that you'll feel the ground shake and see a plume of fire coming up over the horizon."[43]

Clark Chapman points out that "the only real network of telescopes that scans the skies has been designed and built by the military."[44] And the military has not been looking for comets or asteroids. They've been tracking "enemy" satellites and watching for nuclear missiles, like a case of technology held hostage by misplaced aggression.

> *Some people only use one-tenth of their brain capacity anyway, and*
> *there's so much more room to think other good ways and try to turn them*
> *on regardless.*   – Jimi[45]

On Halloween 52 U.E. (1995 C.E.), five months after the first draft of *Rock Prophecy* was copyrighted at the Library of Congress, PBS television premiered an episode of *NOVA* titled "Doomsday Asteroid." This program reports, "The military has begun to release data from other meteor explosions. Now some scientists believe there may be far more rocks out there than previously thought. And we have no defense against them . . . But in 1983 President Reagan proposed spending billions of dollars on another threat from the skies, a nuclear attack . . . Reagan proposed a radical new defense that would destroy nuclear weapons before they strike. When the network detects the launch of a Soviet ICBM, computers acquire the missile track and send interceptors to destroy

41. ABC World News 3/26/96.
42. *Doomsday: What Can We Do?*, Fox 2/14/97.
43. *Asteroids: Deadly Impact*, 2/26/97 NBC National Geographic.
44. Nova, *Doomsday Asteroid*, PBS 10/31/95.
45. Interview with Nancy Carter, L.A., 6/15/69, *Hendrix Speaks*, 1990 Rhino Records.

the missile during its initial boost phase. The program known as the Strategic Defense Initiative, or SDI, would have set up an elaborate missile defense system. It would be built around satellites in space armed with interceptor rockets that would track down and destroy nuclear warheads. The program is nicknamed Star Wars . . . Weapons designers wondered if they could apply their skills to a related problem: saving the Earth from an asteroid impact. But is such a feat even possible?"[46]

Jimi Hendrix was decades ahead of these scientists. Somehow, Hendrix understood the extent of the threat more than a dozen years before the public ever heard of SDI theories in 1983. "Do you realize," he asked in 1969, "that they have a laser beam that you could put in satellites that'll circle the world and it'll stop any rockets from being let off anywhere in the world? But NOOO, they don't want to hear about these new ideas, they want to hear about the old ones, like spend all this money and get a big missile system. Do you realize they have inventions now that make it so you don't have to think about defense problems now, forever? They have a plan where they have a laser-beam and a chain of satellites around the world and any rocket released, this will automatically blow it up, anywhere in the world, through a certain chart plan. All this is true. There's scientists working on this now. This is so much of a better idea to spend all that money on, than to spend all that money on the anti-ballistic scene. That's nothing but hogwash; he just wants his brothers, sisters, fathers and mothers to have a job, that's all."[47]

On May 19, 54 U.E. (1996 C.E.), while I was battling with hundreds of media dominators intent on obstructing publication of this book, an asteroid a half mile wide nearly collided with Earth, coming almost as close as the Moon . . .

> *The machines that we built would never save us, that's what they say.*
>
> — Jimi[48]

T.H.E.M.

Hendrix is a classic case of the shaman seer marginalized and persecuted by dominator culture. A message about our planet's survival is communicated through Jimi and the establishMENt won't listen. Discussion is obstructed, and because of this we miss our window of opportunity to organize in time any defense.

> *The elite, who benefit from a static, hierarchical cultural climate and who would be threatened by total openness to the future . . . having managed to blame "the Hellenic influence" for Christian servility to oppressive powers,*

---

46. Nova, *Doomsday Asteroid*, PBS 10/31/95.

47. Brown, *Jimi Hendrix – In His Own Words*, p.89 (from Beverly Hills interview 6/69), and interview with Nancy Carter, L.A., 6/15/69, *Hendrix Speaks*.

48. "1983 (a merman I should turn to be)" released on *Electric Ladyland*, Reprise Records 10/68.

> *they now offer us the "future" of incorporation with Yahweh & Son . . . The institutional fathers are still running the show in the Name of the "Future," which is another word for past. Bachofen pointed out that the patriarchal principle is one of restrictions and that after the crushing of the original matriarchy, which was characterized by openness to others, the principle of hierarchy took over.* — Mary Daly[49]

As has happened throughout the HIStory of civilization, in a rush to confiscate elite privileges for a tiny few, the common good of us all was traded away for the benefit of T.H.E.M. – The Hierarchy of Elitist Men. "They choke their own selves," complained Jimi. "They get so greedy with the money that they don't want to give it up. That's silly, that's just nothin' but a drug, matter of fact it's one of the worst drugs. There's other ways how you can live. They're *so* block-minded.[50]

". . . I don't think what I say is abstract. It's reality. What's unreal is all those people living in cement beehives with no color and making themselves look like their gig and slaving themselves for that one last dollar and crying with millions in their pockets and constantly playing war games and making bets. They're losing themselves in big ego scenes and being above another man in some kind of form. I spend most of my time just writing songs and so forth, and not making too much contact with people because they don't know how to act. They act just like the pigs that run these places, you know, countries. They base everything on the status thing, that's why there are people starving, because humans haven't got their priorities right. I don't feel like talking to most people because they're just bullshitting."[51]

> *Ride . . . the Waves of my Interpreture. Music, Sound . . . truth and life, regardless of your questionable timid compromises, which I intend to erase, which I will erase, without a hint of reward, as I am only a messenger and you a sheep in process of evolution, almost at death with yourself, and on the staircase of birth. Soon you may almost forget the smell of your family.* — Jimi[52]

49. Daly, *Beyond God the Father*, p.184.
50. Interview with Nancy Carter, L.A., 6/15/69, *Hendrix Speaks*, 1990 Rhino Records.
51. Life 10/3/69, International Times 3/28/69 - London interview with Jane de Mendelssohn.
52. *Cherokee Mist – The Lost Writings of Jimi Hendrix*, p.128.

Chapter 17: Retarded History

ॐ

Every one of the mythologies that has come to us has come into being in the context of a given, specific society. Now those [ancient] societies were for the most part pressed, there was no margin for allowance, everybody had to conform, and the disciplines through which conformity was enforced were very serious and ruthless . . . the individual was being shaped . . . to the demands of that society . . . the laws are given and strictly enforced. Anyone who can't follow is licked, [i.e.] in the Australian initiations, little boys who did not do as they were told, who just had ideas of their own, were killed and eaten. This is one way to get rid of juvenile delinquents, but it's also a way to eliminate some creative possibilities. The societies as a result were relatively static . . . We train a person to develop his imperfections, his peculiar nuances of personality and talents, that thing which was never in the world before is what we want people to become . . . The problem . . . [is] the imagery that will enable a person to develop himself without violating the requirements of the society . . . Our society just does not afford the individual the 'play' in its traditions that is now necessary for people to find themselves. We ask people to find themselves. So this is exactly those ages of transition. We're a little late because everything is delayed in our culture.

— Joseph Campbell[1]

The eighteenth century Southerner, however unattractive he may look from the viewpoint of the twentieth century, was simply a man of his time – a time that was still, except in a few areas of a few great cities, rough, ruthless, and wholly self-seeking. The modern WASP sometimes condemns his ancestors for not having known better. But in terms of their time, there was no reason why they should have known better.

— Reay Tannahill[2]

Contrary to apologists for the "rough, ruthless, and wholly self-seeking" men of HIStory, the fact is that dominators *did* receive reasons why they should have "known better" than to exploit and brutalize weaker victims. The teachings of Jesus, along with other

---

1. *The Function of Mythology, World Mythology,* Lecture at Esalen 8/69, Big Sur Tapes.
2. Tannahill, *Sex In History,* p.318-9.

prophets, condemn domination. Every tortured scream beneath dominator boots – every starving child's cry, every mutilated gay who sought only to aid a neighbor – was proof plenty that our ancestors knew what they were doing. There is no excuse for this abuse. The price for it is a smashed planet. Never before has this equation been so formulated.

When the message of Jesus was rewritten by Constantine and Augustine into a creed for male dominators, the Roman Empire fell, countries crumbled into centuries of Dark Ages. "Medieval Europe was one of the most constipated, neurotic, and woman-hating societies ever to exist," concludes McKenna. "It was a society dying to escape from itself, a society obsessed with moral rectitude and sexual repression."[3]

The sexual classes – women and gays – and especially the sensitive and intuitive seers among them, were silenced. Insights from these people were lost. Progress was impeded. HIStory is retarded. The struggle of seers to communicate their visions was obstructed. "It takes time to keep people down," says Pastor Dixie Petrey, "and if you're going to try to keep over fifty percent of the group down it takes a lot of energy to do that, energy that could better be used for building rather than destroying."[4]

Retarded History occurs when opportunities to advance knowledge and technology are lost or obstructed. A classic example of Retarded History is the story of Spanish *Conquistadors*, the *conquering* dominators who plundered the Maya Indians.

A thousand years ago in what is now Central America, a civilization of 12 million corn farmers came to an end. "At the end of the classic Maya period warfare escalated and became much more disruptive than at any other time period," explains archaeologist Arlen Chase. "Besides warfare becoming more destructive there were also new sacrificial patterns . . . rather than simply taking captives and putting them to work, they were taking captives and cutting off their heads and building skull platforms."[5]

Historian Arthur Demerset describes how the Maya became "victims of their own success, and as [the cities] grew and became more vibrant and more attractive, eventually all of this nice fertile farmland was covered by houses. They were basically cutting themselves off from their own food source. As time went by all of the forest was eliminated, this caused wide scale erosion, which eventually resulted in less rainfall and people just weren't able to live there anymore."[6]

"The Maya are a good example of a civilization that was living right on the edge of their ecological balance," observes archaeologist Diane Chase. "They were doing a good job of growing crops, of catching water and all the rest of it, but there are times when all it takes is a little bit of change and everything is thrown out of balance . . . At the end of the classic Maya period agriculture probably failed and the warfare was a bit too aggressive."[7]

3. McKenna, *Food of the Gods*, p.170.
4. P.O.V., *Battle For the Minds*, PBS 6/10/97.
5. *Lost Kingdoms of the Maya*, written by Patrick Prentice, PBS 1/93.
6. Ibid.
7. *Searching for the Maya*, writers: Marshall Riggan & Robert Schyberg, Pyramid Films Ltd. 1995, PBS 11/25/96.

Then in the 16th century the Spanish Conquistadors invaded the Indians. "The advent of the Europeans in the New World effectively ended pre-Columbian civilization," concludes Arlen Chase, "and it ended civilization not so much because the Europeans were militarily superior, but because Europeans introduced diseases that did away with pre-Columbian populations within a relatively short time span."[8] Survivors were forced by the Spanish to convert to Catholicism. But Mayan society had reached an unusually advanced state. The culture's obsession with time was enshrined in a precious calendar.

Because of the Spanish invasion, our understanding of what the calendar communicates was nearly lost forever. "Research into Maya documents was very long delayed," wrote Otto Muck. "The religious fanaticism of the conquering Spaniards had, among other regrettable effects, that of obliterating the civilizations of Mesoamerica, which were far superior to the Spanish. Their records and their history were destroyed. Barely anything that could be easily deciphered has been preserved."[9]

"Don Juan de Zumarrage, first Bishop of Mexico, destroyed every scrap of writing he could find in a gigantic auto-da-fe," notes historian C.W. Ceram. "The other bishops and priests followed his example; the soldiers, with no less zeal, demolished everything that was left...the records and pictures that might have told us so much were incinerated . . . of Mayan documents from preconquistador times exactly three manuscripts are left to us."[10] The surviving texts are almanacs filled with astrological information.

> *The men and women who wrote the almanacs were scribes well versed in astronomy. Using a sophisticated mathematics they calculated the movements of the night sky thousands of years into the past and thousands of years into the future. They knew that the universe moves in cycles, some very large, some very small. They even predicted eclipses of the Sun. They seemed to have been fascinated by the relationship between time and the events in their own lives.* — Patrick Prentice[11]

"The Indians had wailed pitifully when ignorant bishops consigned their writings to the bonfire," writes Adrian Gilbert. "In doing so they were destroying some of the greatest scientific creations that the human mind has ever achieved, and the records of hundreds of years of astronomical research . . . The first-ever history of Mexico in Spanish . . . spoke of an ancient Mexican calendar that had vanished at the time of the conquest. With the help of this calendar the Aztec priests had, so it was said, been able to keep an accurate chronology over very long periods of time. It . . . recorded solstices, equinoxes and the movements of the planet Venus . . . five pages of the Dresden [text] were given over to computations

---

8. Ibid.
9. Muck, *The Secret of Atlantis*, p.243.
10. Ibid.
11. *Lost Kingdoms of the Maya*, PBS 1/93.

concerning Venus. It seems that the Maya were not so much concerned with the day-to-day movements of the planet but with its average cycle over long periods of time."[12]

Otto Muck's analysis of Mayan texts dates that calendar back eleven thousand years to the moment that the Carolina Meteorite crashed into the Atlantic Ocean. We would have learned much more from the Maya if their manuscripts hadn't been destroyed by the Spaniards. We would have known centuries ago about the ancient asteroid whose path is steered towards Earth by the orbit of Venus. The Maya discovered this. And then Spanish dominators reigned destruction on the Indians. The result is Retarded History – research impeded, knowledge obstructed.

> *The Maya were among those who recognized adolescent homosexuality, and, indeed, favored it over heterosexuality ... One study of modern tribes (made in 1952) showed that two-thirds of them considered adolescent homosexuality as normal and acceptable, and other researchers have found it institutionalized among the Cubeo on the Amazon, and the Mohaves and Zuni, among others, in North America ... The Maya, however, also recognized and tolerated – as the Aztecs and the Incas did not – the type of adult homosexuality that is permanent and genetic. As luck would have it, it was the Maya that Spain encountered first in the civilizations of the New World.*
> — Reay Tannahill[13]

A pro-gay civilization held the keys to our understanding of asteroids, and anti-sex dominators silenced them. The Mayan *Book of the Chilam Balams* preserves the legend of the Great Snake in the sky crashing to Earth in pieces:

> *A fiery rain fell, ashes fell, rocks and trees crashed to the ground. He smashed trees and rocks asunder ... And the Great Snake was torn from the sky ... and skin and pieces of its bones fell onto the Earth ... and arrows struck orphans and old men, widow and widowers who were alive, yet did not have the strength to live. And they were buried on the sandy seashore. Then the waters rose in a terrible flood. And the Great Snake in the sky fell in and the dry land sank into the sea.* — Chilam Balams

The Spaniards destroyed the books of the Maya. For the next four centuries, until Otto Muck's research was published, no one realized that the "Great Snake" was a Mayan metaphor for the ancient asteroid. The rock's "fiery rain" and flaming tail had mystified the ancient Indians and inspired their legend of a snake in the sky. What other insights were lost at the hands of Spanish savages?

---

12. Adrian Gilbert & Maurice Cotterell, *The Mayan Prophecies,* (Rockport: Element Books, 1995) pp.34, 11,38.
13. Tannahill, *Sex In History,* p.292.

> *Those who translated the Maya cycles at face value . . . misunderstood the Maya intellect. Such a misunderstanding implies that the Maya were less intellectually developed than ourselves. Only when we become as intellectually developed as the Maya, therefore, can we ever begin to understand just how advanced they were . . . We are beginning to understand that they had knowledge vital not only for their own time but for the very survival of the human race in our own.*
>
> — Adrian Gilbert[14]

Like the books of the Maya, the wisdom of millions of individual seers was lost throughout the ages. Anyone whose insights threatened the privileges of "rich" dominators was persecuted or murdered. The most intuitive minds of our species could not survive the brutality of men driven to crush and control all things introspective and sensitive, crushed because what the seers saw were ways in which straight men scripted religions with rules that confiscate all rights away from women and gays. As Mary Daly states, "Our self-destructive use of brawn need not have been."[15] We are all victims of Retarded HIStory.

<u>DOUBLE ZERO</u>

Today we face the climactic Retarded History incident wrought by T.H.E.M. It's the super boo-boo, two-digit year designation dates plaguing nearly all of the world's computer systems. Back in the 1960s and 1970s, in order to save space and money, early computer programmers entered year digits in just two digits instead of four (instead of 1970, they used "70," and so on.) As a result, at the stroke of the year 2000, most computers were set to register the year as "00." Many computers would assume that 00 means the year 1900. Others would misunderstand the numbers and shut down. Computer consultant Kevin Schick warned, "This problem will be one of the largest problems ever to face the business community."[16] Ninety percent of all businesses in the late 1990s paid huge sums of money to change their software before the year 2000. *Newsweek* magazine called it "the most ambitious and costly technology project in history, one where the payoff comes not in amassing riches or extending Web access, but in securing raw survival."

The "solution" involved going through every line of data in every computer program worldwide and changing all of the two-digit dates to four-digit dates that can accommodate "2000." The cost of this is estimated at $600 billion. "That tab doesn't include litigation," reports *Newsweek*. "Reasonable extrapolations about litigation take you over $1 trillion."[17]

---

14. Gilbert & Cotterell, *The Mayan Prophecies*, pp.290, 2.
15. Daly, *Beyond God the Father*, p.174.
16. NBC Nightly News, Robert Hager, 4/14/96.
17. Newsweek 6/2/97.

The U.S. government alone spent $30 billion to change its software. Experts estimate that more than 5 percent of all businesses will go bust.[18] Computer Horizons is a consulting firm which estimates the average cost to businesses will be $10 million to $200 million. One insurance executive said, "This is money that we *have to spend*, this is money that, without spending it, could cause *major catastrophe*."[19]

The irony is that the business world does not "have to spend" and *waste* such sums of money. All that is required is for world governments to decree a change in our modern calendar. There will be no need to switch software from "two digit" to "four digit" dates if we agree to a new calendar based on the birth of Hendrix. As of this writing we are in the year 56 of the first century, the Uncommon Era. Adding date digits to computer programs isn't necessary until we reach three digits in the year 100 U.E. The time and energy now being spent to change computer dates for the year "2000" is diverting resources away from creating anti-asteroid technology.

A TV news report about the change of computer dates ended with a warning that if the $600 billion switch to four-digit numbers isn't finished by the year 2000, then "instead of being a time for big celebration, the millennium could become a big zero, in fact two zeros, getting a brand new century off to a nothing start."[20] But if society wastes such time and energy to keep a calendar based on the Messiah/Christ, then "major catastrophe" and a "nothing start" will result instead from our lack of defense against the Rock. To spend billions on an unnecessary software change, when all that is needed is to declare this the first century, constitutes the ultimate Retarded History incident.

Jimi Hendrix represents the dividing line between life and death in the final days of the human age. *Rock Prophecy* spells out our options. Hendrix foresaw the impacts that ignited Jupiter in 51 U.E. (1994 C.E.). Jupiter is the ruling planet of Sagittarius, Jimi's astrological sign. Astrologer Roger Bacon notes that Jupiter also rules the *ninth house* of the horoscope as "major fortune."[21] The number nine, therefore, can sometimes be considered a lucky number. The ninth house is the house of wisdom, books, and the worship of God. It refers to faith, religion, and divinity.[22] Jimi studied numerology and he regarded the nine as the number that represents himself. But numerologist Annemarie Schimmel cautions that "the number 9 can be variously interpreted. At times, the purely negative aspect is stressed . . . [Jesus] died at the ninth hour of the day (from sunrise, i.e., 3:00 p.m.). This hour was the *none*, subsequently marked by a special monastic devotion, while the word itself has become our *noon*."

In *Mysteries of the Bible Numerically Revealed*, John Yunger concludes that nine is the number associated with judgement,[23] and numerologist Petrus Bungus equates

18. Ibid.
19. NBC Nightly News, Robert Hager, 4/14/96.
20. Ibid.
21. Schimmel, *The Mystery of Numbers,* p.178.
22. Ibid.
23. John Yunger, *Mysteries Of The Bible Numerically Revealed,* letter from author 12/24/92.

nine with pain and sadness, noting that the sixth verse of the ninth Psalm contains a prediction of the antichrist:[24]

> *O thou enemy, destructions are come to a perpetual end; and thou hast*
> *destroyed cities; their memorial is perished with them.*   – Psalm 9:6

At the end of civilization, our vast libraries "memorialize" the reasons why our progress was halted for so long. HIStory is filled with evidence that reveals how advances have been set back for centuries at the hands of men who brutalized and let die those that possessed precious perceptions.

> *Number 9 was worshipped by the Maya. Nine 'Lords of the Night' are painted*
> *on the tomb walls and the Temple of Inscriptions, similarly, nine codes*
> *appear along each side of the Lid of Palenque . . . All relevant numbers*
> *compound to 9 . . . Magic number of the Maya.*   – Adrian Gilbert[25]

> *I'm a nine* – Jimi[26]

We await the *disaster* – a word from two Latin terms: "dis" (ill) and "astrum" (star), meaning *malevolent astral influence*. It is the abyss of our unseen dreams, the nadir depths of our subliminal fears, what only our genes are aware of, suddenly exposed in the form of Jimi's story, his house of wisdom, books, faith, religion and divinity, the ninth hour of the day, the *none*. Not necessarily antichrist, but *unchrist*.

> *Heaven in reality is a rocket-ship, always swirling through space looking for*
> *a steppingstone . . . but needing to clear every world of hate and repression.*
>   – Jimi[27]

FORERUNNERS OF A FUTURE GENE POOL

An evolutionary mutation today transforms the gene pool of humans. Hendrix represents the forefront of this wave. A small fraction of our race carries this trait of altered perceptions. Sensing the Rock's return, Gaia is spawning a new breed of freeks to be her natural defense. We are the forerunners of tomorrow's world, a human order free from inequality and aware of our purpose. We bear witness to the last gasp of dominators at the brink of extinction.

---

24. Schimmel, *The Mystery of Numbers*, p.164.
25. Gilbert & Cotterell, *The Mayan Prophecies*, pp.289, 306.
26. *Castles Made of Sand – Remembering Jimi Hendrix*, San Francisco Examiner, 11/25/90, p.16.
27. *Moondust*, p.29, seen on public display at Sothebys in New York during the week prior to auction in Dec. 1991. While on display, page 29 was noted by Charles Blass.

> *There are a few chosen people that are here to help get these people out of this certain sleepiness that they are in . . . you may not necessarily be one of the chosen few ones to help.* — Jimi[28]

Hendrix is the non-dominator common denominator: a central mutation around which Mother Earth directs our metamorphosis. Freeks see Jimi as a lightning rod igniting our enlightenment. His birth marks the start of a revolutionary evolution in the human gene pool. As the numbers of freeks increase during the Uncommon Era, their rising tide will wash our species free from the obstructions of T.H.E.M.

> *It's the other folks, you know, the people that are dying off slowly but surely. Anybody as evil as that dies one day or another. Not too many people know, you know, but it's good like that, because then we can sneak in through the back door, and the next thing you know[29]. . . all of a sudden kids come along with a different set of brain cells and the establishment doesn't know what to do. The walls are crumbling and the establishment doesn't want to let go. We're trying to save the kids, to create a buffer between young and old. Our music is shock therapy to help them realize a little more of what their goals should be[30] . . . A lot of these old people, they want to make themselves old, so they tie-up their brains and, in the process, they try to build their own heavens: they want to be written down in war history, they want to be written down in money history, and those things are nothin' but jokes, in the next few years they're gonna all be jokes, and those people are gonna be jokes. Some of them should be put in cages now, to be looked at, because they're gettin' very rare.* — Jimi[31]

The arrival of the Rock confirms everything Hendrix said, but proof of our fate will come too late to save this world. Out of the rubble, in the aftermath, many centuries ahead, the next wave of humans to evolve will be freeks. We are their forerunners, we battle savages in the first century and leave behind this text: *Rock Prophecy* explains the fate of our race, thanks be to Jimi. Let us give praise each Thanksgiving New Year, every November 27.

The savages of the first century are braintrained to hate nature. Anti-female ancient faiths maintain their hierarchies, threatened by everything that isn't T.H.E.M. Hendrix realized that we dig our own graves with the energy we spend attempting to dominate others.

---

28. San Diego Free Press 6/13/69.
29. Interview at the Palladium, Hollywood, CA 3/69, portions of this interview are published in Brown's *Jimi Hendrix – In His Own Words,* pp.54, 58, 63.
30. Village Voice 1968, cited in Henderson, *Jimi Hendrix,* p.256.
31. Interview with Nancy Carter, L.A., 6/15/69, *Hendrix Speaks,* 1990 Rhino Records.

Your home isn't America, it's the Earth, but things are precarious.... Brand name religions like Buddhism and Zen are just clashes. The Catholic Church is spreading and vomiting over the Earth. The Church of England is the biggest landowner in England. Younger people, their minds are a little more keener, so since they can't get release and respect from the older people then they go into other things and their music gets louder and it gets rebellious because it's starting to form a religion. You're not gonna find it in Church. A lot of kids don't find nothing in Church – it's nothin' but an institution, so they're not gonna find nothing there.   *– Jimi[32]*

Burn away the Bible for too many finger prints of man smudge the once true hope that we may <u>live</u> again. Now it's the hand book of the war machine which has wrecked even our age . . . which is now crippled from spiritual pain. Burn down the religions, divided in which they stand . . . for what they preach is money and games for there's only one God . . . and that is in the spirit of every man . . . not a different disguise for each corner of the same land. These are not words of blind protest. These words are born from long ago clashes with today. Atomic power can light our homes forever . . . but instead it's used for Continental SIZE Graves . . . Only 1/100,000,000th of the human mind we find ourselves using. The rest we foolishly throw away. So ignorant we are, as long as the money rolls . . . Hold off those world wide happy tones. There's more money to be made from killings and spades . . . forget your conscience, come have a bone.   *– Jimi[33]*

Jimi used his music to warn the freeks who listen. The music survives and carries his message beyond the reach of men whose brutal *"finger prints . . . smudge the once true hope that we may live again."*

"I'd have to have a voice," he said. "I'd try to use my music as a machine to move these people to get changes done…The belief comes in through electricity to the people. We plan for our sound to go inside the soul of the person and see if we can awaken some kind of thing in their mind, because there are so many sleeping people. Soon I believe that they're going to have to rely on music to get some peace of mind or satisfaction, direction, actually. People want release any kind of way nowadays. The idea is to release in the proper form. Then they'll feel like going into another world, a clearer world.

"Music is gonna be here regardless and it's gonna influence a whole lotta people's minds because that's part of their Church now. People don't realize that music has *so much* to do with what's happening today. And you're *not* gonna stop the music . . . It's

32. Ibid, and Distant Drummer 4/17/69.
33. *Burn Down the Churches*, from Sothebys' lot #384. The first page is shown in the catalogue for Sothebys sale 6258 *Animation Art and Rock 'n' Roll Memorabilia Dec. 14 and 17, 1991*. Excerpts here are from the five remaining handwritten pages which were published in Jimpress magazine 6/99, pp.7-10.

getting to be more spiritual than anything now. It's just like how you go to a gospel church. We're trying to get the same thing through modern-day music."[34]

I am Electric Religion! – Jimi[35]

BLACK GOLD

"As I Looked into My Crystal Ball" is a poem in which Hendrix asks, *"Why would such Heavenly beings . . . want to desert Earth? But as I watched I understood."* He describes the *"burnt out minds. . . who searched for the hurting truth of space, and the dizziness they felt inside – reflected off the spinning slave pebble Earth."* He compares inadequate attempts by authorities, who will try too late to stop the Rock, to an army of ants caught by surprise: *"Ego Armies marched antly into view. Only to be blown apart – As the Sun whispered it's secret through space."* Finally, we are left with the unimaginable horror of an uninhabitable planet: *"Down on Earth we lost 3 continents, their fiery soul snuffed out by ice and Nature's rains and pieces . . . As the axis turns in its womb, frozen flowers and animals try to hold positions they had before."*[36]

Love is being tested here. Love for our WHOLE world. Not just our families.
– Jimi[37]

We are failing the test: our inability to coexist as a single human family means that the world will not be left "whole."

In another poem titled "Black Gold," Hendrix warns *"it's up to us to straighten out this mess – we got to go through Hell, and then that's the last of this miserable test."* Racial hatreds work in favor of dominators who, Jimi notes, *"don't want us to mix."*[38]

They make black and white fight against each other so they can take over at each end. If they get the Black Panthers fighting the hippies, who are really the young whites, then we'll be right back where we started off twenty years ago. That's what they're trying to do.   – Jimi[39]

Hendrix warns T.H.E.M. that human achievements are meaningless on a vulnerable planet. *"Let them go to the Moon,"* he wrote, *"let them go to Saturn . . . that's where*

---

34. New England Scene 11/68, The Dick Cavett Show, ABC 8/69, Life 10/3/69, interview with Nancy Carter, L.A. 6/15/69, *Hendrix Speaks*, 1990 Rhino Records, and interview with Flip Wilson broadcast on The Tonight Show, NBC 7/10/69.

35. Interview in London 1/69, printed in Royal Albert Hall concert program notes.

36. *Cherokee Mist – The Lost Writings of Jimi Hendrix*, pp.74-5.

37. Ibid. p.117.

38. Ibid. *Black Gold*, p.91.

39. Chris Welch, *Hendrix*, (New York: Delilah/Putnam Books, 1973), p.32.

they'll learn." On the Moon we see evidence of impacts. Around Saturn we see rings of debris and dust, such as will circle Earth after the collision. During the lifetime of Hendrix, we were still able to prevent the disaster. Jimi searched for a way to communicate this; he asked himself *"what can we know about happiness?"* The answer he wrote in "Black Gold" is *"Invent a word called Love."* He named the asteroid Love to signify its potential to unite all races under a single purpose. Ignore this warning, he writes, and *"NO ONE on Earth will escape."*[40]

In "Black Gold," Jimi calls for *"no more slaves"* under dominator hierarchy, because *"when the Earth opens up"* our divided cultures *"will pass sentence upon themselves."* Asteroids have *"killed so many worlds before . . . Realize before it's too late"* or else we will know why *"Atlantis cried."*[41]

Jimi's "Black Gold" poem foresees reasons for our fall: dominators dismiss the Prophecy until the asteroid approaches in the sky *"and then"* writes Hendrix, *"they blame our mistakes on God . . . because God will protect us when it comes to dooms day."*[42] Leaders of greed will claim the Rock in the name of male religions and say it is sent as God's punishment for our sins.

> *It is characteristic of the male, when an incident or event is sufficiently disagreeable, to pretend that in point of fact it never actually happened . . . this statement . . . does say something about the phallic mentality into which the dominant elite in our world have been socialized.*
>
> — Edmond Cahn[43]

"We better ALL realize," Jimi warns in "Black Gold." He threatens us to *"get our places before GOD tells us to our face"* – our name is *"PAST – the Human Race."* Solar winds will illuminate Electric Love: *"The Sun knows as the Wind Blows and the fire Grows towards the far Shores"*;[44] lit up by the Sun, the Rock's fiery tail grows longer over the ocean's horizons, as it approaches impact with land.

> *We're gonna have this thing called "Horizon, Between Here and Horizon," or something that pertains to that. And that goes into certain things like "Room Full of Mirrors." Then we have this other one called "Astro Man," talking about living in peace of mind. Well "Astro Man" will leave you in pieces.*
>
> — Jimi[45]

---

40. *Cherokee Mist – The Lost Writings of Jimi Hendrix*, pp.91-2 *Black Gold*.

41. Ibid. pp.92-4.

42. Ibid. p.92.

43. Daly, *Beyond God the Father*, p.121.

44. *Cherokee Mist – The Lost Writings of Jimi Hendrix*, p.94 *Black Gold*.

45. Chris Welch, *Hendrix*, p.92, from interview with Keith Altham, London, 9/11/70.

Hendrix saw the Rock appearing Up From the Skies Between Here and Horizon. He saw himself as Astro Man, a messenger whose instructions will either leave people with *"peace of mind,"* or, if unheeded, leave us *"in pieces."*

When humanity has perished, the legacy of what happened to us will be left explained only in *Rock Prophecy*, buried as "Black Gold" amidst rubble, in the bruised eye of a lopsided planet ringed black and blue after impact.

> *Out beyond ideas of right-doing and wrong-doing there is a field. I'll meet you there.* — Rumi

> *Good and Evil lay side by side...If I don't meet you no more in this world, I'll meet you in the next one.* — Jimi [46]

Jimi's mission was to prepare us for *"the end of time,"*[47] the end of the human age, *"not a good scene or a bad scene, this is the truth"*[48] – a reality we must face. His message is for us to make peace with extinction, with a fate we have sown and will reap. Our time is nearly up, the human race is HIStory, the age of man is *Past*.

> *They got to get off this planet and get on another planet . . . That's what the grave is named after – "gravity." See, this planet could be a black hole . . . it does drain the life out of people . . . the gravity here is so great on this planet that it draws people down into the ground. They can't survive here . . . this planet is in the valley of the shadow of death.* — Sun Ra[49]

> *Perfect is death. It's a physical death. Termination.*
> — Jimi[50]

46. "Have You Ever Been (to Electric Ladyland)" and ""Voodoo Child (slight return)," released on *Electric Ladyland*, Reprise Records 10/68.
47. "Purple Haze" released on *Are You Experienced?*, Reprise Records 9/67.
48. *Cherokee Mist – The Lost Writings of Jimi Hendrix*, p.70 *Valleys of Neptune*.
49. Interview with Charles Blass, Ascot Hotel, Copenhagen 3/21/92.
50. Hall and Clark, *The Superstars – In Their Own Words*, p.26.

Chapter 18: Newest Testament

♪

It is no coincidence that income among Americans was closest to relative equality during the years when Jimi's career was at its peak. "The high-water mark of equality [was] attained in the years 1968-1970," writes William Ryan. "As we moved into the 1970s and the movement toward equality began to be beaten back, there was a sharp falloff."[1] The years between Jimi's birth and death, 1942-1970, are characterized by an inspired flight of the human spirit. More people than ever before were transformed for the better in the presence of the Hendrix Effect. Once Jimi was gone, society regressed back into heavy metal pits of hierarchy and greed, reaching the depths of obscenity under the Reagan Regime in the '80s.

> *Over the decade of the 1980s almost 100% of the growth in household wealth went to just the top 20 percent of households. This has almost never happened in our history except perhaps in the 1920s. In terms of shared wealth the top one percent has increased its share from about 33 percent in 1983 up to 39 percent in 1989 . . . The income of the average family has basically been stagnate for the past 15-20 years and has actually started to decline in the 1990s . . . We in the U.S. are now the most unequal country in the industrialized world in terms of wealth and in terms of income. I think this is creating important and potentially dangerous social divisions in our country . . . The 1980s was a period of very rapid economic growth and the great majority of people did not benefit from this. There is a feeling of disenfranchisement and it's partially reflected in the growth of the paramilitary organizations and this feeling that government can do no good, blaming immigrants and the welfare population for the faltering conditions of the middle class . . . My proposed wealth tax takes a relatively small bite out of the wealth of the wealthy . . . If you look at the full array of taxes paid in our society what you find is that the tax burden is pretty much proportional to income . . . each income group is paying about the same percentage of its income, and this is very antithetical to our original notion of some kind of progressive taxation . . . It's the poor in this country who've been most hurt by this rising inequality and for [Capitol Hill] to try to decrease the benefits that they pay to the poor . . . even further is a political*

---

1. Ryan, *Equality,* pp.162, 167.

> *catastrophe and a social catastrophe. If anything, benefit levels should be*
> *raised for the poor.*   — Edward Wolf, Professor of Economics[2]

Dominators today hoard resources away from people weaker than themselves. Everyone with less brawn, brains, and luck than T.H.E.M. is a victim. In the summer of 1999, during the peak of the media's so-called "economy boom," the number of people requesting emergency food from food banks in America jumped by 14 percent. During the previous year 20 million Americans requested that help, and a third of those people were employed,[3] but they were working at jobs that paid slave labor wages in the wake of a decade of corporate "downsizing."

Unequal incomes inspire crime and aggression. Any benefit gained from inequality is outweighed by the way it retards progress and corrupts judgement. We should all be racing to build a defense against asteroids and the quickest, most effective way to attempt it is to mobilize everyone as equals around this task. A cooperative society must be willed into existence today. The way to eliminate divisions, obstructions, hate and violence is to achieve agreement among the majority of people for relatively equal income, or at least a maximum wage. Income equality should be a main ethic and central tenant of society, equal fair shares of everything, to the degree that we agree it should be.

DECISIONS BY INSTANT POLL

> *Every corporation, every special interest, whether you like them or not, is entitled to ensure that its message is heard, but you can't get away from the fact that the influence of money so distorts free speech that it's no longer an honest and fair debate among competing ideas. It's who has the money to frame the issue, because if you don't have the money to frame the issue then whether you're right or wrong isn't going to matter in the long run.*   — Matthew Myers[4]

> *We inadvertently create a situation in which, by virtue of privileging those with money we make it very difficult for those without to be heard at all... [In the past, both sides of an issue] would each have a stump. We are now in an environment in which the tobacco industry buys the stump and gets up and makes their statement. The anti-tobacco people don't have the money to buy the stump and in effect the tobacco industry has bought this that the other side can't afford. We've now made "Freedom of Speech" into "Freedom of Speech if you can afford to buy the access to speak."*
>   — Kathleen Hall Jamieson[5]

---

2. McNeil/Lehrer News Hour, PBS 9/27?/95.

3. ABC World News 6/24/99.

4. Matthew Myers, council for non-profit group: Campaign for Tobacco-Free Kids, "Free Speech For Sale", PBS 6/8/99.

5. Kathleen Hall Jamieson, Dean of Annanberg School of Communication at U. of PA., "Free Speech For Sale", PBS 6/8/99.

When personal incomes are the same, or nearly the same, business and institutions are then free to compete in *ideas*. Wealth accumulates around the most effective and efficient plans, not around people who "own" any plan or technology. Technology today makes possible the instant mass polling of whole populations. Proposals to use public money to fund research and development projects can be decided upon by voter referendums. "Government" by such means is for the first time possible today.

Decision-making is taken out of the hands of an elite class of string-pullers. Governments, corporations and media will instead exist to present debates, poll the population and oversee transfers of funds for projects that the majority of people agree to. Each person shares relatively equal income from the results. "Government" thus becomes a service that dispenses choices for work opportunities to every person able to work.

People relate to each other best when everyone's personal income is relatively the same. Only token differences in income, agreed upon by the majority of us, should be accepted. We should all be thinking in terms of slim differences in incomes among us, a narrow range of difference, with a maximum income no more than double or (rarely) triple the standard income shared by most. This is the prescription for a healthy society organized to achieve optimal advances. Wealth then concentrates only around those *ideas* that most effectively meet needs in a market of freely competing proposals.

"We can have this 'left right' debate but the true political spectrum in this country is not left to right," says Jim Hightower, "it's top to bottom, and most people aren't ideological at all. We're a little bit of this and a little bit of that, depending on the issue. What's missing is that the vast majority of people are not even within shouting distance of the powers at the top, whether those are Democrats or Republicans, and these are the people that are left out of the debate in Washington and the debate in the national media. And that's the danger of these media conglomerates taking it over, because their power is at the core of the trouble that America is in today . . . [The media] is not addressing real power. They want us to focus on Washington, as though that's the central power in the United States, rather than focusing on the real power, which is the Wall Street corporations. Actually, government, in a democracy, is the only power that ordinary folks have to do battle with global monoliths that are dominating our economy and ruining our economy."[6]

Our population is today trained to accept without question that some people deserve more money than others. Making this inequality appear universally accepted is the primary message of the Affluence Controlled Media Influence (A.C.M.I.). The aim of the ACMI is to justify reasonings with which we have aGREED to GREED.

> *There's the real mass media, the kinds that are aimed at the guys who get a six pack, the purpose of those media is just to dull people's minds. For the 80%, or whatever they are, the main thing for them is to divert them, to get them to watch national football and to worry about the motherless child with*

---

6. The Phil Donahue Show, NBC 11/2/95.

six heads, or whatever you pick up at the supermarket stands, or look at astrology, or get involved in fundamentalist stuff, or something – just get them away from things that matter, and for that it's important to reduce their capacity to think. Take sports, that's another crucial example of the indoctrination system, because it offers people something to pay attention to that has no importance and keeps them from worrying about things that matter to their lives, that they might have some idea about doing something about ... [sports] is a way of building up irrational attitudes of submission to authority and group cohesion behind leadership elements ... that's why energy is devoted to supporting [sports] and creating a basis for them, and why advertisers are willing to pay for them. – Noam Chomsky[7]

"Many people yearn to be introduced to the facts concerning their true identity," reflects McKenna. "This essential identity is explicitly addressed by a plant hallucinogen. Not to know one's true identity is to be a mad, disensouled thing – a golem. And, indeed, this image, sickeningly Orwellian, applies to the mass of human beings now living in the high tech industrial democracies. Their authenticity lies in their ability to obey and follow mass style changes that are conveyed through the media. Immersed in junk food, trash media, and cryptofascist politics, they are condemned to toxic lives of low awareness. Sedated by the prescripted daily television fix, they are a living dead, lost to all but the act of consuming ... if we sufficiently reconstructed our image of self and world, we could make out of psychopharmacology the stuff of our grandest hopes and dreams. Instead, pharmacology has become the demonic handmaiden of an unchecked descent into regimentation and erosion of civil liberties ... Plants are the missing links in the search to understand the human mind and its place in nature."[8]

Prohibition of psychoactive plants has created a society of alienated people addicted to aggression. Unequal income among us creates unending resentments. Income equality for all and free access to our planet's plants are requirements for a happy society. These are the creeds to fight for.

Within a system of income equality, what achievers deserve is reputation and respect. No one need hold notions about anyone "meriting" money more than anyone else. A shared experience of equal incomes leaves us free to distinguish ourselves without rationalizing lies about why some people deserve more money than others.

We can't "work hard" unless we are *lucky* enough to be able to endure "hard work." "Merit" is *always* just luck. People who insist that the lucky among us be entitled to more money must be enlightened about how unequal incomes cause aggravation and grief. Some people inherit wealth, but how do they *merit* that "unearned" money? To suggest that anyone *deserves* more money than the rest of us because of "birthright" is a violence provoking notion.

7. *Manufacturing Consent* 1992, PBS 9/95.
8. McKenna, *Food of the Gods*, p.265.

Some people point to 5000 years of recorded human conflicts and call it proof that humans are aggressive by nature. But those conflicts are proof that inequality doesn't work. Advancement of our whole society was retarded because of the fighting. Equality solves our problems, but unfair laws from unjust monied men stand in the way of peace for everyone. Police armies of the "rich" are like mercenaries paid to enforce unjust laws.

And after ages of delays we finally arrive at where we should have been many centuries ago. Today a change to a culture of equality can finally be made. Dominators are doing everything they can to train us to think this isn't possible. But if it ain't equality, it's hate. And we as a people become more free with every dominator we impede, by any means that impedes T.H.E.M.

NOT NECESSARILY "EASTERN STANDARD TIME"

To suggest that anyone has the right to possess dozens, or hundreds, or thousands of times more money than others is a radical and extremist idea. The effects of inequity lead us to the brink of extinction. Dominators call equality impractical and *Rock Prophecy* is condemned by T.H.E.M., but objections have no effect on the asteroid coming at us. The politics of equality once offered us a chance to organize our resources and protect the planet. Today's civilization lost that opportunity, we're left defenseless, our energies spent on an elite few, and yet we were warned. The possibility of survival existed and we missed it.

When the asteroid lands, dominators will deny the Prophecy still. Suffering under radical lack of expanded perceptions, they can't fathom that Hendrix sensed our destiny. They are to blame for shaping a society of people derelict in their duty to protect Earth. So to a defenseless world *Love* now comes.

> *Love come shine over the sea…*
> *I take my spirit and smash my mirror…*   – Jimi[9]

We possess the potential to erect weapons against rocks, but we instead weaken Mother Earth as she lay prone to impact. Within this cosmic shooting gallery, our resources were wasted on a privileged few. Clawing against each other in pursuit of the B*est*, men erected cultures of cults in deference to *unnatural* extremes: Rich-*est*, Strong-*est*, Smart-*est*, Pretti-*est*, Tall-*est*, Great-*est*. To the bitter end they are obsessed with *est*, driven to revere the uncommon radical extremes of inequity, to worship the Rich-*est*, to desire the Rare-*est*, to kow-tow to the Great-*est*. It was inevitable that a program called "*est*" be erected to train people to blame themselves for the hurt we endure in a rat race to be B*est*.

In the early 1970s, a man took his name, "Erhard," and fashioned an acronym around *e.s.t.*: Erhard Seminars Training. The death of Hendrix marked the start of this consumer craze in which millions underwent 60-hour sessions of *est*. Whereas during

---

9. "Room Full of Mirrors" from *Rainbow Bridge*, Reprise Records, 10/71.

Jimi's concert years we reached our most equal state, in the absence of the Hendrix Effect we slipped back towards animal status. *est* is an early symptom of decline.

William Greene describes *est* sessions: "People are not allowed to smoke, eat, be aware of time, stand up, talk, go to the bathroom . . . *est* staff and volunteers become like aggressive animals . . . the trainer remains with the 250 uncomfortable-looking people. He stands at the front of the room . . . looking like a military convert, he begins screaming. Swearing. Calling everyone assholes. Machines. Liars. Hopeless assholes, unable to make life work . . . 'You are confused. You are poor slobs. You are all so confused about life, so filled up with beliefs and concepts, that you don't even realize that you're a fucking machine. Assholes' . . . Hour after hour the trainees are bombarded with this verbal flagellation . . . people begin to cry . . . someone throws up . . . it is a combination of philosophy and filthy language, designed to confuse and scare the trainee . . . often during the training, people are afraid. Fear is another very big factor in causing an individual to vomit . . . The main tenet of *est* is that you have to take responsibility for your life. Your problems can't be due to someone else's actions. This is repeated over and over again in the training."[10]

est was hyped by the media to a public trained to blame themselves for a society based on greed. *est* offered in-your-face theater for a culture weaned on TV. *est* sessions affect the mood of trainees; being traumatized for 60 hours alters moods enough for people to conclude they'd paid for "results." But like Gestalt Therapy, *est* rhetoric is based on dogma about "personal responsibility." *est* takes *responsibility* to extremes. "*est*ians believe they are responsible for such far-removed events as plane crashes and wars, and ultimately whatever one person does to another person" – including muggings and murders on distant continents.[11]

The effect of *est* is to divert attention away from the cause of our problems. For example, the Bible calls gay people "abominations" and "reprobate." All over the world, kids grow up with the message that "God" condemns gay people. The kids become teens who taunt and brutalize anyone they think God "dislikes." Then *est* persuades the hated gays to blame themselves for injuries the kids inflict. Blame yourself for your problem.

> Never mind that the Bible singles out homosexuals to condemn.
> Never mind that we're trained when we're young to internalize emotional attachments to Bible stories.
> Never mind that people use the Bible, the foundation of Western culture, to justify hatred of gays.
> Never mind that gays are often discriminated against, inundated with hate, and forced into poverty.
> Forget all this – *est* instead tells us that we are each responsible for whatever happens in our lives, so blame yourselves.

---

10. William Greene, *est - 4 Days To Make Your Life Work*, (New York: Simon & Schuster, 1976), pp.38-9, 44, 57-8, 145, 160.
11. Ibid. p.145.

est represents essential dominator philosophy. Dominator media adores *est* because it allows hate-rosexual men to be the brutal*est* sadists, without blame. *est* empowers dominators because it diverts the victim from identifying the victimizer. We won't imagine a Bible story hurting us if we're blaming ourselves for being hurt. Dominators cherish this aspect of *est*: victims blaming themselves for being victimized – dominators stay blameless. This is how the men who control media train us to accept "responsibility."

> *Knowing that you are totally responsible for everything in your*
> *life can be a very frightening experience.* — William Greene[12]

We're told to blame ourselves and "forgive" others. It's more *convenient* for the ruling class if we all "forgive" those who take things from us. "Forgiveness" is an idea dominators created to make it easier for T.H.E.M. to control us – they say we're better off forgiving those who wreck our lives. But "forgiving" is *for giving back* the unfairness, *for giving* it back to those who are unfair to us.

In the aftermath of Jimi's death, *est* was the ideal therapy for dominator culture, something we've been trained to relate to all of our lives. Even the name was perfect: "est" acts like a subliminal ad for elitist privilege. Everyone is trained to agree that certain people deserve the *est* in life: the great-*est* and the b*est*. *est* was the darling of men who control media.

"People are yelling and screaming about how awful *est* is and how aggressive the staff and volunteers are," observed Greene, "yet they are going ahead and taking the training and loving it . . . Everyone, at one time or another, has suffered a serious threat to his ego when he chances upon a person who is smarter, more efficient, or more successful than he...the situation will be so acute as to create a pain . . . most individuals are operating out of a need to survive. They need to avoid the risk of learning from someone who is smarter than they . . . Time after time, graduates stated that they were resentful of Erhard's salary, or his car, or the devotion and following that he has acquired . . . 'I have my racket and Erhard has his,' one graduate said. 'It's just that his is working better. If he is making millions of dollars, God bless him, he deserves it.'"[13]

Again, the major aim of elitist media is to convince us that some people *deserve* wealth. Countless news stories trained the nation to take interest in *est*.

NEW-EST TESTAMENT OF THE HENDRIX MILLENNIUM

But *est* trainees were deceived because *equity* is *best*. There is no *quality* without *E-quality*:

QUALity   eQUALs   eQUALity

12. Ibid.
13. Ibid. pp.157, 174, 136.

In observance of this ultimate equation, *Rock Prophecy* completes the link to the New-*est* Testament. *Rock Prophecy* defines the faith of Creation's Way and interprets HIStory in terms of Spiritual Blues. Through Hendrix connections we understand the system that enslaves us. It is Jimi who frees the slaves.

Digging beneath the surface we see a meaning: after the asteroid lands, new life on this planet will evolve and dig out nuggets from the rubble, unearthing treasures that Jimi called Black Gold. Black Gold is *Rock Prophecy*, a Rosetta Stone holding keys with which to translate what happened – the single explanation, the one link.

> *A person should try to get . . . a certain faith with one link. There's no whole lot of religions, just one link. There's only a few chosen people that supposedly are to get this across . . . Some people should just be lent to start ideas, and others should carry them out.*   – Jimi[14]

> *Something like a great fiery mountain was thrown into the sea . . . There fell a great star from heaven, burning like a torch, and it fell upon the third part of the rivers, and upon the fountains of the waters . . . the third part of the Sun was smitten, and the third part of the Moon, and the third part of the stars; so as the third part of them was darkened, and the day shone not for a third part of it, and the night likewise. And I beheld and heard an angel flying through the midst of heaven, saying with a loud voice, Woe, woe, woe, to the inhabiters of the Earth.*   – Revelation 8:10-13

For a thousand years after the impact, our planet's atmosphere will remain inhospitable for life. After these ten dead centuries of the Hendrix Millennium, creatures will emerge from the Dark Age. From *Rock Prophecy* they'll learn of our destruction by Love. And a new civilization will be built, and this civilization too will meet the same fate, and the civilization after that, for many times more into a distant future of many Hendrix Millennia, until one society evolves to a state of equality from which global defense against asteroids can be achieved.

From the view of geologic time, near-extinctions after impacts every ten or every hundred thousand years happen in the blink of an eye. Hendrix understood this at the end of his life, just hours before death, in the last words he wrote:

> *The story of life is quicker than the wink of an eye,*
> *the story of Love is hello and good-bye, until we meet again.*
>   – Jimi[15]

---

14. San Diego Free Press 6/13/69, and Shapiro, *Electric Gypsy*, (Heinemann 1990), p.462, from an interview with Keith Altham, London 9/11/70.

15. *Cherokee Mist – The Lost Writings of Jimi Hendrix*, p.135, *The Story of Life*.

Civilizations will come and go every so many asteroid-ended centuries, because people progress only so far before "*the story of Love*" – the arrival of another Rock – says "*hello*" and we say "*good-bye*," until we evolve again, out of the rubble, and start the cycle all over.

> *The axis of the Earth, if it changes, it changes the whole face of the Earth, like*
> *every few thousand years, so that new civilizations come every time it changes.*
> — Jimi[16]

Today's society is but one more link in this progression over eons of time. This is Creation's Way of evolution. An end to one civilization's span of centuries on Earth does not affect the process; in fact, the galaxies don't even notice. After all, the cosmos has all the time in the universe. Our world today is in a precarious state. That we are expendable is a message Hendrix couched in metaphors in his song "Castles Are Made of Sand."

> *There was a young girl who's heart was a frown*
> *because she was crippled for life and couldn't speak a sound*
> *… but then a sight she'd never seen made her jump and say,*
> *"Look, a golden winged ship is passing my way."*
> *And it really didn't have to stop, it just kept on going,*
> *and so castles made of sand slip into the sea…*
> — Jimi [17]

Several thousand years of Retarded History result today in our transitional civilization. We are destined to watch our own extinction. All the castles and plans and dreams and hopes lapse back into their unformed origins and begin to evolve again from scratch, out of a fatal crater on the face of Earth, a scar that we could have prevented.

> *The Maya believed that there had been four other creations before our own*
> *. . . These early races were incapable of fulfilling what was to be the prime*
> *purpose of humanity: to cultivate the Earth . . . They were therefore*
> *destroyed, only a few individuals remaining.* — Adrian Gilbert[18]

OBITUARY RITUAL

Through medieval Dark Ages, the interpretation of biblical script was exclusively in the hands of Vatican authorities who could read Latin, the language into which the Bible was translated from Hebrew and Greek by Jerome of Dalmatia in 382 C.E. Then in 1524, William Tyndale sought to translate the Bible into English for the first time, but authorities

---

16. Stockholm Radio 1/8/68, BBC Radio One interview 10/6/67.
17. Released on *Axis: Bold As Love*, Track Records 12/67.
18. Gilbert & Cotterell, *The Mayan Prophecies*, p.80.

in England obstructed his effort. Tyndale fled to Germany where he completed the first English translation of the New Testament. Church authorities in Cologne forbade him to print the text. He fled to Worms and there published the Bible in English in February 1526. During the following month, copies circulated in England. For the first time, masses of Britons were able to assess for themselves the meaning of scripture, without having Church clergy dictate interpretations.

Over the following decade 18,000 copies of the English Bible circulated. But Cuthbert Tunstall, the dominator Bishop of London, bought up most of the books and destroyed them. A medieval think tank then published Sir Thomas More's rebuttal to Tyndale's work. More's propaganda denounced Tyndale's translation of the Bible as "not worthy to be called Christ's testament, but either Tyndale's own testament or the testament of his master antichrist."[19] Tyndale was then hunted down and burned at the stake on October 6, 1536, exactly 430 years prior to the birth of the Experience and the banning of acid.

*It is the winners who write history – **their** way.*   – Elaine Pagels

During the centuries prior to Tyndale, almost no one in society had access to the Bible. Whatever effect the book might have had was retarded throughout the Dark Ages, while Vatican dominators proclaimed their version of Jesus. Only a select few could actually read the Bible. And most of the Gnostic gospels had completely disappeared. In 367 C.E., Athanasius, the Archbishop of Alexandria, ordered that all "heretical" texts not included in Constantine's Bible be destroyed. Gospels of the Gnostic sects were gathered up and burned. But several monks from St. Pachomius collected the condemned texts and buried them in a jar in the cliffs overlooking the monastery at Nag Hammadi in Egypt. For the next 1600 years, the *real* story of the deity remained hidden here in these condemned and hidden gospels.

It wasn't until after the birth of Hendrix and the defeat of the Nazis that the world discovered these buried books. A few months following the end of World War II, an Arab peasant, digging for soft soil to fertilize his crops, unearthed the lost Gnostic gospels. "The effort of the majority to destroy every trace of heretical 'blasphemy' proved so successful that, until the discoveries at Nag Hammadi, nearly all our information concerning alternative forms of early Christianity came from the massive orthodox attacks upon them," notes Pagels.[20] "Had they been discovered 1000 years earlier, the Gnostic texts almost certainly would have been burned for their heresy. But they remained hidden until the twentieth century, when our own cultural experience has given us a new perspective on the issues they raise."[21]

Publication of these texts didn't come easy even in a century with new perspectives. The old perspective of "winners" seeking to advance their own spin on history had delayed for decades circulation of the recovered gospels. "The Gnostic find from Nag

---

19. *The Oxford Companion to the Bible*, p.759.
20. Pagels, *Gnostic Gospels*, p.xxiv.
21. Ibid. p.151.

Hammadi has been beset from the beginning to this day by a persistent curse of political roadblocks, litigations, and, most of all, scholarly jealousies and 'firstmanship,'" wrote scholar Hans Jonas nearly twenty years after the books were discovered.[22]

Like the death of Tyndale, the suppression of the Gnostic gospels is another landmark tragedy of Retarded History. The martyred Mayan Indians, Tyndale, and the Gnostic gospels form a trilogy of lessons[23] that set a precedent for establishMENt persecution of *Rock Prophecy*, the New-est Testament book of Creation's Way – the *equality* religion. The fate of our race is explained in these pages and blame is placed on T.H.E.M. Dominators will pay to confiscate copies of this book, just as Tyndale's bibles were gathered and burned.

> *The worshippers of the Yahweh of patriarchy, as they come to realize the potential of this Antichurch to bring about the transference of consciousness into another world, can be expected to use all of the tools of violence at their command. For the social reality that they attempt to link with "Ultimate Reality" is precarious, and the danger of anomy or of "conversion" is a threat that lurks always behind the irrational dogmatism of the High Priests of war.* — Mary Daly[24]

It was no accidental coincidence that riots at Woodstock '99 began when promoters tried to show a film of Hendrix playing the National Anthem three decades earlier.

> *Satan . . . the root* ***stn*** *means "one who opposes, obstructs, or acts as adversary." (The Greek term* ***diabolos***, *later translated "devil," literally means "one who throws something across one's path.")* — Elaine Pagels[25]

THE NEW NAG HAMMADI

An Inquisition will invoke dominator laws to obstruct circulation of *Rock Prophecy*. Jimi's prediction will be denounced on all grounds. The establishMENt will persecute those who promote this book. So bear witness to the New-est Testament: every November 27 New Year, write your name in *Rock Prophecy* and bury the book in a safe place, a sacred place, a place where, like the Nag Hammadi library, the dominators won't find it, and where a future race can dig Black Gold out from beneath the debris of shattered Earth and fathom what happened to humanity. *Rock Prophecy* conveys our fate.

Burial of this text represents graves tended for victims who remain nameless in HIStory,

---

22. H. Jonas, Journal of Religion (1961), p.262.
23. Another example is the burning of the great Library of Ptolemy I in Alexandria by Roman dominators in 47 B.C.E.
24. Daly, *Beyond God the Father*, p.143.
25. Pagels, *The Origin of Satan*, p.39.

all of the seers and sages who were left to die or be killed because they held perceptions unacceptable to He. Our legacy is explained here. Through these Black Gold burials we become defeaters of greed, the enemies of T.H.E.M. and Saviors of Mother Earth.

> *Men forget. They must, therefore, be reminded over and over again . . .*
> *Religious ritual has been a crucial instrument of this process of*
> *"reminding."*   – Peter Berger[26]

> *They forgot, did not believe, or just snuffed the feelings or thoughts off to*
> *continue with their crazy soul. Searching, always trying to satisfy their lust and*
> *desires, but before appreciating they were to create new ones.*   – Jimi[27]

And let us forever remember the persecution of freeks under savages of the first century. We bury this book and thereby relate to all beings who pass this way, past charred remains of dark shattered continents, that here is Black Gold, among this scattered rubble of broken stones is found *Rock Prophecy*. Thus, the scriptures of Jimi bear eternal witness to the example of man. The tragedy on our planet transmits this lesson of infinite benefit for all living things, everywhere, forever.

New Year ceremonial burials of *Rock Prophecy* convene with these words of the Equalitarian Prayer:

> *We are accommodators, they are dominators,*
> *we nurture, they exploit.*
> *We seek freedom from inequality for all people,*
> *they have aGREED to GREED.*

> *Equality is the Law of All, money is the means,*
> *share everything equally between all people.*

> *You and the next deserve the same*
> *those who take more deserve shame*
> *Teach an elitist in equity's name*
> *our labor of Love, Creation's Way*

---

26. Peter Berger, *The Sacred Canopy: Elements of a Sociological Theory of Religion* (New York: Doubleday, 1967), p.40.
27. *Cherokee Mist – The Lost Writings of Jimi Hendrix*, p.115 *Terra Revolution and Venus*.

We must not be afraid of paths chosen by God.
                                                                                    — Jimi[28]

The day of the Lord will come like a thief,
and then the heavens will pass away with a loud noise,
and the elements will be dissolved with fire,
and the Earth and the works that are upon it will be burned up.
                                                                        — II Peter 3:9-10

A solar wind is blowing our way. The seers tried to warn us and were silenced throughout HIStory. It is *she* who warned and was ignored. It is *she* we did not hear: "The wind!" cries Mary. "The *WIND*!" screams Mary.[29]

. . . it whispers no, this will be the last. — Jimi[30]

When the Rock appears streaking towards Earth through our solar system, there will be enough time before impact for everyone to realize that we could have been saved. But because of the removal of Jimi, and the persecution of *Rock Prophecy*, the world of T.H.E.M. is condemned to death. Mother Gaia dies. The Savior returns to crucify the brutes, not necessarily antichrist, but unchrist.

So it is written, because it was done.

28. Ibid. p.117.
29. "The Wind Cries Mary" released on *Are You Experienced?*, Reprise Records 9/67.
30. Ibid.

Epilogue: The Inversion

ॐ

A drug is something that causes unexamined, obsessive, and habitual behavior. You don't examine obsessive behavior, you just do it. You let nothing get in the way of your gratification. This is the kind of life that we are being sold at every level. To watch, to consume, and to watch and consume yet more. The psychedelic option is off in a tiny corner, never mentioned; yet it represents the only counterflow directed against a tendency to leave people in designer-states of consciousness. Not their own designs, but the designs of Madison Ave., of the Pentagon, of the Fortune 500 corporations. This isn't just a metaphor, it is really happening to us . . . the creation of the public as herd . . . the public live in a golden moment created by a credit system which binds them ineluctably to a web of illusions that is never critiqued. — Terrence McKenna[1]

Many other factors induce the media to conform to the requirements of the state-corporate nexus. To confront power is costly and difficult; high standards of evidence and argument are imposed, and critical analysis is naturally not welcomed by those who are in a position to react vigorously and to determine the array of rewards and punishments. Conformity to a "patriotic agenda," in contrast, imposes no such costs. Charges against official enemies barely require substantiation; they are, furthermore, protected from correction, which can be dismissed as apologetics for the criminals or as missing the forest for the trees. The system protects itself with indignation against a challenge to the right of deceit in the service of power, and the very idea of subjecting the ideological system to rational inquiry elicits incomprehension or outrage, though it is often masked in other terms. — Noam Chomsky[2]

In the 1980s, I performed Jimi Hendrix music in a hometown band called EXP. For years nightclub owners refused to book us. "People don't want to hear Hendrix," insisted the guys who ran the clubs. But I kept trying to get gigs and one day a band that was booked at a club cancelled their date. I was in the club at the time and the owner let EXP

---

1. McKenna, *Food of the Gods*, pp.253-254.
2. Chomsky, *Necessary Illusions – Thought Control in Democratic Societies*, pp.8-9.

have the gig because it was convenient for him, being a weekday when no other group was available on short notice. A radio ad mentioned that a "Hendrix band" would be performing that night. Five hundred people showed up to hear us, a sizable crowd for Thursday night in Rochester. EXP played well. People were enthused.

The next day I went back to the club to line up another gig, but the owner refused. He resented the fact that we'd drawn so many people to his club to hear *that* kind of music. Even though we were able to earn profits for his business, he didn't *want* crowds to enjoy "Hendrix music." He dismissed us all, as a class.

From then on I saw a meaning in the inverted Strat that Jimi played (Hendrix was left handed and used a right-handed guitar flipped upside down): to me it represents something I call the *Inversion*. Inversion describes negative rejection of someone when helping that person is beneficial to you. In other words, the Inversion is an irrational urge to silence or annihilate something that can do you some good.

> *It's like a hospital, when a patient might be kickin', he doesn't want an operation, he knows good and well it might be good for him in the long run, but he's scared and he's kickin' around in the bed and the nurses are trying to strap him down. Well, I'm the nurses trying to get him together and prove to him that this* **is** *right.*
> — Jimi[3]

At its worst, the Inversion is such illogical hatred of someone or something that the persecutors will go to extremes, including harming themselves, in order to obstruct the object of their hatred.

The more well known I became for my writings about Hendrix the more I experienced the Inversion. It's like the more natural you are with a talent, the more you'll be blocked from expressing it. Dominators get maximum satisfaction out of silencing those who have most to say. The stories I wrote that were published with the core collection of official Hendrix CDs reached more than six million people. Dominators dismiss us all as a class. We're written off, we "don't matter." As far as dominators are concerned, we can jump out of the camps and into the ovens.

When was the last time that six million people were written off? No matter how many readers want to see *Rock Prophecy*, the men who control media will obstruct discussion of this book. Their "rejections" of the Prophecy are examples of the Inversion, Retarded HIStory in action. The more insightful the perception, the more brutal the suppression of it. Such setbacks and obstacles to the advance of knowledge and awareness today leave us vulnerable to the Rock. Had the seers not been persecuted, we would have long ago prepared a defense against asteroids. What was beneficial for us was obstructed and rejected – that's the Inversion.

Jimi focused on the Inversion a few days before he died. He drew a sketch.[4] At the top of the page are the letters "GOD DOG" next to a drawing of a hill with three crosses – the

---

3. Interview with Nancy Carter, L.A., 6/15/69, *Hendrix Speaks*, 1990 Rhino Records.
4. Dannemann, *The Inner World of Jimi Hendrix*, p.152.

Crucifixion. Jimi wrote "devil" and "lived" underneath to show how, like "GOD DOG," the spelling of devil is a reversal of lived. Next to this he wrote: "6 Modern Man" above a swastika, symbol of Nazi dominators. Then Jimi wrote "Hemingway" next to it. Ernest Hemingway was the most famous writer of macho dominator stories when Jimi was growing up. The *Oxford Companion to English Literature* cites Hemingway for his "deliberate cultivation of the brutal and the primitive."[5] Hemingway novels celebrate war, bullfighting and big game hunting. Jimi's drawing couples the name of Hemingway with the swastika. Then he sketched a scene of the crucifixion and above it wrote "6 Modern Man."

"Six is the number for man," writes John Yunger, author of *Mysteries of the Bible Numerically Revealed*.[6] Jimi associates "6 Modern Man" with ancient Romans who crucified Jesus. He put these themes together in his sketch. Beneath a scene of the Crucifixion he wrote, "devil." The devil's number is 666, threefold that of "6 Modern Man." Hendrix connects these scenes with extinction. Dominators (i.e., Hemingway, the swastika, Modern Man) silence the seers (i.e., Jesus, Jimi, etc.). We've lost what the seers tried to tell us. The advance of humanity is impeded. History is Retarded.

The swastika associates with "Axis powers," the coalition during World War II between Nazi Germany, Italy, Japan and Baltic countries. The battle of Axis nations against the Allies reached a turning point when the Enigma code was broken at the moment of Jimi's birth. Hendrix grew up obsessed with a vision of the *Axis*. He titled his second album *Axis:Bold As Love*. When he was young, dominators were called "Axis" forces. It was as if society sensed a connection between the brutality of Axis nations, and the axis of our planet. Aggression prevents us from uniting against an asteroid, therefore, the Rock will hit and the axis of Earth will invert – Axis:Bowled (Over By) Love. The poles of the globe remain stable only if we find a way to stop the Rock from knocking our planet off its axis. But dominators obstruct the most perceptive among us and retard our efforts.

> *They show you how to kill – and if you don't they will . . .The Axis gonna put them slaves they killed so many worlds before – but they will pass sentence upon themselves when the Earth opens up."*   – Jimi [7]

Inspired by subliminal memories of an ancient impact, and in anticipation of the asteroid, our culture named a music "rock." Humans are evolved to respond to rock as a host medium. Through it we become conscious of our collective memory of the future. Jimi's Prophecy is delivered through rock music, which makes manifest our awareness of the influence of future impact.

Likewise Jimi's fixation with the term "Axis" represents a memory of the future, too. The Nazi coalition came to be called "Axis" nations, as if society sensed from Nazi men

---

5. *The Oxford Companion to English Literature*, (Oxford Univ. Press, 1996) p.456.

6. Letter to author, 12/24/92.

7. *Cherokee Mist – The Lost Writings of Jimi Hendrix*, pp.91, 94, *Black Gold*.

Earth-threatening consequences as a result of their aggression. As if because of such behavior we anticipate a shift in the axis of our world,

Impact is imminent, yet dominators suppress *Rock Prophecy* because this book explains why civilization dies at the hands of Modern Man. *"Just ask the Axis,"* sings Jimi, *"he knows everything."*[8]

> *You got to find out everything now, because that's the only way you're going to survive, you got to know everything.*   — Sun Ra[9]

Our survival depends on equality between people, but everyone who understands this is persecuted by dominators. Because the Hendrix story contains these connections, issues surrounding Jimi are a threat to T.H.E.M. Anyone who tries to communicate the Prophecy is obstructed. The men who control media instead flood the market with "Hendrix books" that cater to a fringe group of fans who like to look at pictures and lists of "facts." Any attempt to explain how Hendrix connects with HIStory is viciously resisted. The Prophecy is kept hidden from the public.

> *Hendrix's only exposure is in the back room of someone else's home, where he is secretly admired and treated as a novelty. But never is he brought to the front room for all to see and appreciate. Hence, there has been miserly validation of Jimi's impact . . . Jimi put some companies on the business map, and still there is labor under the misrepresentation of what Jimi Hendrix is all about.*   — Billy Cox[10]

NONE KNOW ANY OF ITS WORTH

> *Cultural, political and intellectual movements of note almost always start small – with one ardent individual or a small group of impassioned people. At first these initiators are unknown to the rest of us. As they begin to focus attention on themselves, we may well regard them as nuts. But gradually the ideas they've championed catch on, often becoming so widely accepted after a time that new small groups form in rebellion against them.*
> — Judith Applebaum[11]

The worldwide Hendrix network is dominated by dominators. This collectors' network is infested with men who compete with each other to obstruct their "opponents" and credit themselves for research achieved by others. The worst of T.H.E.M. surface in

---

8. "Bold As Love" released on *Axis:Bold As Love*, Track Records 12/67.
9. Interview with Charles Blass, Ascot Hotel, Copenhagen 3/21/92
10. Guitar for the Practicing Musician Presents Jimi Hendrix/Stevie Ray Vaughn, 1992, p.24.
11. Applebaum, *How to Get Happily Published*, p.65.

an obscure newsletter called *Grimpress*, put out by Eve Ramrod. *Grimpress* is a hate-rag that makes the burnt offerings of Cain seem like Vatican art treasures. Having *Grimpress* label you "trivial" and "trainspotter" is like having the thousand pound circus lady call you "fat."

> *The spirit of envy was watching to destroy our blessings . . . At length it reached the bishops themselves, and arrayed them in angry hostility against each other, on pretense of a jealous regard for the doctrines of Divine truth . . . the churches were everywhere distracted by divisions . . . [the Emperor] recommended them . . . not to be jealous, if any one of their number should appear pre-eminent for wisdom and eloquence, but to esteem the excellence of one a blessing common to all. On the other hand he reminded them that the more gifted should forbear to exalt themselves to the prejudice of their humbler brethren, since it is God's prerogative to judge of real superiority. Rather should they considerately condescend to the weaker.*
>
> — Euseibus[12]

The men who control media take treMENdous pleasure in obstructing publication of what I know about Jimi. Explanation of the Inversion itself is met with denials and derision from dominators. They say they can't care less who sees *Rock Prophecy*; but they're like tobacco companies claiming cigarettes don't harm your health. The establishMENt maintains armies of psychiatrists paid to label all descriptions of the Inversion "*paranoid*." "Paranoid" is the most condemning heresy that dominators affix to us through their media Inquisitions. Continents of credibility are leveled under the "p" word.

> *There is nothing more remote to discussing what we have been discussing than a "conspiracy theory." If I give an analysis of the economic system and I point out that GM tries to maximize profits and market shares, that's not a "conspiracy theory," that's an "institutional analysis," it has nothing to do with conspiracies. That is precisely the sense in which we're talking about the media. The phrase "conspiracy theory" is one that's constantly brought up, and its effect is to discourage institutional analysis.*
>
> — Noam Chomsky[13]

Patterns to the issues described in this book are labeled "paranoid" by men who control media. Dominators can dismiss these descriptions so long as they obstruct

12. *Nicene and Post-Nicene Fathers of the Christian Church*, ed: Schaff and Wace, *Eusebius: Church History & Life of Constantine the Great*, pp.515, 526.
13. *Manufacturing Consent*, 1992, PBS 9/95.

publication of my reports. For example, there are dozens of incidents in which editors of magazines have published uninformed and inaccurate attacks on my work. My written corrections and rebuttals to these attacks are ignored by editors, left unpublished and unseen by readers. What follows are some typical examples, just a few of my obstructed and unpublished replies to attacks on my research. These are letters from me that editors refused to let readers see, thus allowing the magazine's errors to stand as monuments to the Inversion.

MUSICIAN TRIP

During 1991-92, Jimi's British girlfriend, Kathy Etchingham, compiled a lot of new information about the death of Hendrix and submitted her files to England's Attorney General's office. Then in September 1992, *Straight Ahead* magazine published an article of mine titled "The Etchingham and Mitchell Files." This was the first published account of the new details regarding Jimi's death. It was an explosive article, containing first-ever interviews with the ambulance attendants who retrieved Jimi's body on the morning of September 18, 27 U.E. (1970). Incredibly, the two attendants, Reg Jones and John Saua, had never before been interviewed nor questioned about Jimi's death. Their identities were unknown to researchers until Kathy Etchingham and Dee Mitchell tracked them down in England in 49 U.E. (1991).

My article in *Straight Ahead* in September 1992 also contained the first published interview with Dr. Martin Siefert. Siefert had tended to Jimi's dead body upon its arrival at the hospital. My article also included new testimony from Officer Ian Smith, who was present at the death scene.

In December 1992, three months after "The Etchingham and Mitchell Files" was published, *Straight Ahead* ran an interview I conducted with Kathy Etchingham titled "Why Take Five Hours To Call An Ambulance?" In this interview, Kathy's statements frame the key issues that had come to light about Jimi's death as a result of the new testimony from the ambulance attendants and Dr. Seifert. The evidence suggests that Hendrix was fighting for his life much earlier in the morning on his last day than everyone had been led to believe by Monika Dannemann, the girl Jimi was with when he died. Incredibly, for two decades Monika was the single person upon whose testimony everyone had relied for the story of Jimi's death.

"Why Take Five Hours To Call An Ambulance?" contains key information about the toxicologist's report concerning rice grains that were found in Jimi's stomach during autopsy. Kathy had interviewed the toxicologist and discovered that descriptions of the partially digested rice grains in the autopsy report suggest Jimi died much earlier in the morning than was previously thought.

In February 1993, two months after "Why Take Five Hours To Call An Ambulance?" came out, *Straight Ahead* published my follow-up article titled "Christians In Rome." At this point, throughout the world, only four articles had been published detailing the new information about Jimi's death, and three of them were written by me.[14] My three articles spearheaded the tip of an iceberg that became a media avalanche.

In November 51 U.E. (1993), Scotland Yard announced that British officials had agreed to investigate the death of Hendrix. Their decision was based on the information that Kathy presented a year earlier to the Attorney General. The announcement made front-page headlines around the world: "Hendrix Death Case Re-Opened!" A frenzy of reports deluged the airwaves.

On Thursday, December 16, 51 U.E. (1993), London's newspaper *Mail On Sunday* dispatched a reporter named Sharon Churcher to see me in Rochester, New York (USA). We spent the day together going over details and information regarding the Scotland Yard investigation.

> "How do you know about my involvement?" I asked Sharon during our taped interview.
>
> "From an anonymous source," she replied.
>
> "I write and consult for the official Hendrix production company in Hollywood," I told her.
>
> "I know you do, I was told about you from one of my best industry sources, who frankly said you are the Oracle."
>
> "Well," I said, "there were only four articles that were published, and I'd written three of them, the most concise descriptions. The last one I wrote sums up what's at stake and points out discrepancies in Eric Burdon's testimony [about Jimi's death] and Monika Dannemann's testimony. It's titled 'Christians In Rome.'"
>
> "You were very gutsy to do this given the libel laws," Sharon told me. "I'd be terrified. Everyone's been frightened for years of libel. What we want to do in the *Mail On Sunday* is a big wrap-up piece on the whole thing and how it's been re-opened. Have you talked to anyone in London?"
>
> "Yes, Scotland Yard, I've been helping them out and passing along information."
>
> "I can't tell you my sources," Sharon said, "but I was told by somebody who knows this case that they owe everything to you."

It was my "Christians In Rome" article that tipped the scale in favor of British authorities deciding to investigate the information about Jimi's death. Since I was the writer for the official production company for Jimi Hendrix, Are You Experienced? Ltd., my readership was exceeding six million people worldwide because of my booklets included with official Hendrix CDs. Kathy Etchingham was wise to enlist my involvement in her efforts to bring news of Jimi's death to the attention of British authorities, because

---

14. My 3 articles were published in Straight Ahead magazine, the first of which was reprinted in the Hendrix newsletter Voodoo Chile. The fourth article on Jimi's death, the one not by me, is in the November 1992 issue of Rock World (U.K.).

after my articles were published, London's Attorney General's office believed that the facts surrounding Jimi's death in Britain were being scrutinized and publicized in an *official* way by the "estate" of Hendrix (I worked for the official Hendrix production company). And my articles expressed *anger,* pointing with resentment to "an inept British inquest" which botched the original police inquiry into the circumstances of Jimi's death. My "Christians In Rome" article ends with a plea for people to write letters and demand a proper investigation. British officials took notice.

Below is my article from the Feb. '93 issue of *Straight Ahead,* which kicked off the media blitz:

CHRISTIANS IN ROME

In an interview for KPFA radio, broadcast on Jimi's birthday in 1982, Eric Burdon discussed the morning that Jimi died and said, "The only thing I remember specifically and clearly is [Monika's] car was parked outside and it was a *cold* morning and the *fog* was in the back window of the car, and [Jimi] had written in the window on the car, on his way down to the apartment the night before, he'd written '*LOVE*' on the back window of the car. And I remember standing outside looking at the window of the car, you know, and I knew it was his handwriting."

In light of new evidence indicating that Jimi died before 5:30 a.m that morning, the above comments are of interest because we must wonder just how early it was when Burdon *arrived* at Monika Dannemann's flat and noticed "fog" on the car windows. On the day that Jimi died (Sept. 18, 1970), the temperature in London reached 74 degrees. One would expect that night "fog" would be burned away by the morning sun well *before* 9 a.m. If Burdon saw fog, he must have been at Jimi's death scene earlier. It will be of interest to obtain hourly temperature readings of London weather for that morning and determine precisely *how* early it was that Burdon arrived there. [Prior to Burdon's statement about the window fog everyone had been <u>led to believe by Monika that she didn't realize Jimi was in trouble until past 11 a.m.</u> that morning. Keep this in mind while reading what follows.]

In addition to Burdon's statement, we should also re-examine an interview that Amsterdam radio conducted with Monika on Sept. 19, 1975. "We stayed home till about 12 o'clock," Monika said of that last night with Jimi, "and then I drove him to a flat of some friends of his, and he stayed there for about half an hour, and then I picked him up again. We talked till about 7 o'clock in the morning, and then I started to sleep, and <u>I woke up about 9 o'clock</u> and Jimi was still asleep and I just couldn't sleep, but after a while I realized that he got sick. Well, at first I tried to wake him up and I just couldn't, he didn't wake up, so I called the ambulance, which came after 10 minutes, and they checked him and I asked them if he would be alright again and they said yes, sure, there's nothing special about it, he'll be OK again. *While we were driving in the ambulance they seated Jimi on a chair, but with his head backwards*, which I found out only later that this was the worst position they could have put him in because he couldn't breath properly, because he had been sick. We got to the hospital and immediately got Jimi in a special room. At first they said to me he will be alright. I went to the doctors to ask what happened and they said he'd be alright, and then about a half an hour later they told me he was dead . . . I do believe that he got poisoned."[15]

Contradicting Monika, both of the ambulance attendants who arrived on the scene that morning said that the flat was *empty* except for Jimi's *dead* body. Neither of these men have any recollection of ever having laid eyes on Monika. This is supported by the fact that they had to call the police. When a body is found in an empty flat, it is standard procedure for London Ambulance Service attendants to immediately call the police before anything at the scene is moved. The attendants were unable to identify the body, there was no one there to even say that this was Jimi Hendrix. And both attendants insist that they handled Jimi's body properly, laying him *flat* inside the ambulance, not *upright* "seated on a chair," as charged by Monika.

In addition, both of the attendants, as well as Ian Smith (the police officer who was called to the scene) swear that *no one else* rode along in the ambulance with Jimi's body, as Monika claims she did. What's more, Dr. Seifert, who tended to Jimi's body when it arrived at the hospital, insists that there was "no woman at admissions." Referring to Monika's claim that she was told at the hospital that Jimi was alright, and her claim to have gone in to view Jimi's body after being told of his death, Dr. Seifert insists, "No nurse went out to say we'd revived him . . .and no one would have been allowed to look at him or stand over him. That would never have been done."

Clearly, lies have been/are being told about the circumstances surrounding the death of Hendrix. In the face of all of these opposing accounts of that morning it is infuriating that the original 1970 inquest was such a botched up investigation. For more than 22 years we were left only with Monika's story of what happened. We have been led to regard the two ambulance attendants as everything from inept fools to criminally negligent conspirators. Having finally been tracked down and interviewed (as they should have been in 1970), the question is obvious:

---

15. Interview with C. Glebbeek, Amsterdam Radio 9/19/75.

have these men been both libeled and slandered before an international audience for over two decades? What's more, has the general public's view of Jimi as the "drug addict zombie responsible for his own death" been the result of a cover up by "other hands" that were at play that morning? We don't know how Monika's nine sleeping pills got into Jimi's system. But in the absence for so many years of so many crucial testimonies to cross reference, public perception of his death remains outrageously manipulated.

If any one of the people with him early in the morning on Sept. 18, 1970 were more responsible for what happened (accident or foul play) than we've been led to believe, they have, until now, been successful in *shifting* that responsibility onto Jimi and forever condemned him to a public stigma of "irresponsible drug addict." Has Jimi been so pathetically sacrificed?...**If 20th century authorities refuse to complete their inexcusably botched 1970 inquest properly they can count on us to describe their folly in detail for Jimi's billions of future fans to look back and condemn what has been wrought.**

Can any of us even believe that the mainstream media, especially in the United States, has been so conspiratorially ignoring this story? **An inept British inquest set the stage for Jimi's media crucifixion** and establishment watchdogs everywhere remain blind or asleep. The wall separating Hendrix fact from fiction is as high as the Tower of Babel, and in its shadow we are left to rail at the authorities like early Christian in Rome. We *are* early Christians in Rome . . .

Every one of us can spare an hour of our time to write a letter to the Attorney General's Office in London to help persuade them to do the right thing and re-open this inquest. The millions of people who have responded to Jimi, and the billions more who will respond, deserve this. But most of all, Jimi deserves this.

write to:
Mr. J.D. Kellock
The Legal Secretariat to the Law Officers
Attorney General's Chamber
9 Buckingham Gate
London SW1E 6JP England

Because my article for *Straight Ahead* included a mailing address for British authorities, the charges I'd made came to the attention of England's Attorney General, Sir Nicholas Lyell. British officials saw that I was the writer for the official Hendrix company.

They realized that Kathy Etchingham, Jimi's girlfriend who gathered evidence about his death, was not acting alone and without access to the media. Through me, the writer for the "estate," Scotland Yard and the Attorney General sensed that what we said about their treatment of Jimi's death would be circulated worldwide.

"Christians In Rome" made accusations against an "inept British inquest setting the stage for Jimi's media crucifixion." Framing Jimi's death in terms unflattering to British police work, and spreading these charges to an international audience, was one thing. But having this come from me – the writer for the Hendrix company – put things in a different light. Since *I* was angry, British authorities perceived that Jimi's *"estate"* was angry.

Pressure to stage an official 1993 investigation mounted in response to my article. To save face, the authorities had to look into my charges of British ineptness. It was a matter of pride and honor; hence the widely publicized winter 1993-'94 Scotland Yard investigation into the death of Hendrix.

The February 1996 cover story of *Musician* magazine is an expose of research surrounding Jimi's death. Almost all of the points in the story had long ago been reported in the early 1990s. But this 1996 *Musician* article titled "Killing Floor" contained several key insights and connections that were discovered by me. And *Musician* claimed to be unaware of my work. I wasn't credited in their article.

When their story about Jimi's death came out in January 1996, I sent the following letter to *Musician*.. The magazine's editor refused to print this when they ran reply letters about their Hendrix story in two subsequent issues:

MY OBSTRUCTED JANUARY 1996 LETTER TO MUSICIAN:

I had influence in the accumulation of data about Jimi's death, much more than many of the people mentioned and credited in your article titled "Killing Floor" [*Musician* Feb. 1996]. Several of the main insights and connections presented in your story were discovered by me. The connections I contributed to the Hendrix death investigation are:

1) I was the first to notice and report Eric Burdon's published and recorded memory about the time of day [he arrived at Jimi's death scene, very early in the morning]. The Burdon link is my insight, Steve Roby expanded upon it in his interview with Burdon [*Straight Ahead* Aug. 1995]. The 1990 edition of *Electric Gypsy* [Hendrix bio] doesn't mention Burdon saying he got a call about Jimi [being near death] at "first light" [crack of

dawn]. When Harry Shapiro [author of *Electric Gypsy*] was revising *Electric Gypsy* for a new 1992 version of the Hendrix biography, I told Kathy Etchingham [in May 1991] about Eric Burdon's autobiography and what Burdon says about Jimi's death. Burdon's quotes in his book about learning that Jimi was in trouble "at first light" were then brought to Shapiro's attention via Kathy. When Shapiro used this information in his 1992 revised edition of *Electric Gypsy* he added, (p. 473) "Admittedly, a musician's 'crack of dawn' could be anything up to midday."

Shapiro cast doubt on Burden's memory of that morning. When this *Electric Gypsy* revision was published in late-1992, I then wrote an article titled "Christians In Rome" for [*Straight Ahead*]. Since Shapiro had cast doubt on Burdon's memory, my article pointed out additional information from Burdon about the "window fog." My point is that Burdon's memory can be pinned down more accurately (than in *Electric Gypsy*) by the temperature in London the morning Jimi died, since Burdon was at the scene while it was still cold enough for car windows to be fogged. Therefore Monika couldn't have been telling the truth about when she noticed Jimi was in trouble.

2) I was the first to notice and report the discrepancy in Monika's 1975 interview about waking at "9 a.m." when Jimi died. My "Christians In Rome" article was the first and only source to reveal the 1975 radio interview in which Monika said she woke up "at 9 a.m." – a contradiction to her other statements about the time that she awoke. The 1975 interview with Monika is extremely obscure. Researchers learned of its significance from me. When Scotland Yard was deciding whether or not to re-open the inquest, the information I provided about Eric Burdon and Monika helped persuade them to investigate.

3) I wrote the first series of articles which reported the new details of Jimi's death. Kathy Etchingham had compiled most of the new information and submitted it to England's Attorney General. My article titled "The Etchingham and Mitchell Files," which appeared in *Straight Ahead* in September 1992, was the first published account of the new details of Jimi's death. Two months later, in December 1992, *Straight Ahead* published my follow-up article, an interview I did with Kathy titled "Why Take Five Hours To Call An Ambulance?" This article was then followed by "Christians In Rome."

In early 1993 only four articles had been published on the new information about Jimi's death: my three articles in *Straight Ahead*, and a four-page report in *Rock World* magazine. Then, in November

1993, Scotland Yard announced that British officials would investigate the information that Kathy had presented to the Attorney General. It was my "Christians In Rome" article that tipped the scale in favor of investigating the information compiled by Kathy.

I was the writer for Are You Experienced? Ltd., the official Hendrix company. After my articles were published, London's Attorney General's Office perceived how treatment in Britain of the facts surrounding Jimi's death was being scrutinized and publicized in an official way by someone from the Hendrix production company. "Christians In Rome" included an address for British authorities. Thus the charges I made came to the attention of England's Attorney General, Sir Nicholas Lyell. With resentment I pointed to "an inept British inquest" which botched the 1970 inquiry into Jimi's death. My article ended with a plea for readers to write letters and demand a proper investigation.

4) In summer 1994 Kathy Etchingham and I completed a 60 page manuscript which details the Scotland Yard investigation. This manuscript remains the most comprehensive analysis of the information surrounding Jimi's death. It has not found a publisher. The media elite aim to see that a stigma of "drug overdose" and "responsible for his own death" sticks to Jimi. *Musician* [Feb. 1996] claims that we have to "hold Hendrix himself responsible for actions that brought his life to an end." Has this view of Jimi been the result of a cover-up by "other hands" that were at play on that morning in 1970? We don't know how Monika's nine sleeping pills got into Jimi's body. In the absence for so many years of so many crucial testimonies to cross reference, public perception of his death is manipulated.

My 1992 article points out: "if any one of the people with him . . . were more responsible for what happened . . . they have . . . shifted that responsibility onto Jimi and forever condemned him . . . Future generations will . . . condemn what they have wrought."

Four years later *Musician* asks, "What's at stake? The image of who Hendrix actually was, and the story future generations will accept as the true account of his final days . . . New evidence in the form of testimony delivered to British authorities and to *Musician*, raises questions about Dannemann's story."[16]

I am the source connection for much of that key "testimony delivered." Without my work much less would've been "delivered."

---

16. Musician 2/96, p.40.

In June 1995, David Henderson, author of the first authoritative Hendrix biography, phoned me. "I want to ask you about that thing you wrote in *Straight Ahead*, 'Christians In Rome,'" said David, "where you were talking about the Dannemann case and Etchingham and the ambulance attendants. Is there an update on that?"

I told David about three people that Jimi and Monika had spent time with on the afternoon before Jimi's death: Philip Harvey, Penny Ravenshill and Anne Day. Kathy Etchingham had interviewed these people in the spring of 1995, and in June she told Steve Roby (of *Straight Ahead* magazine) that they described how Monika was very abusive to Jimi just hours before his death. Roby then went ahead and published the interviews in *Straight Ahead* (without crediting Kathy for conducting the interviews and making them available to him).

I related these developments to David Henderson. But he had called to ask me about "Christians In Rome" because, after reading my article, he realized the significance of Eric Burdon's statement about being at Jimi's death scene so early in the morning on that day, early enough to recall fog on the windows. Then David told me, "That interview with Burdon is from 1982, that was the interview that we did, me and Bari Scott from KPFA. It was a produced tape. I did the interview. We went and saw Eric and did it in New York at the Ritz where he was playing."

I said to David, "For some reason there was a delay [in calling the ambulance for Jimi]. Monika has changed the time when she says she woke up and left the flat. She's changed that over the years in different interviews . . . The ambulance drivers now waver on the point [of Jimi being dead when they arrived], saying that he was not dead at the scene, that he died en route to the hospital, which is just as bad, because if he was still alive at Monika's flat, and Monika and Eric were there all that while [since early morning], what were they doing to cause that delay [in waiting until 11:18 a.m to call for help] if Jimi was still alive when the ambulance got there? Evidence points to the fact that people were there for hours with him while he was in trouble. Trying to revive him? we don't know, we can't say, we can say just that there is doubt here on a lot of different accounts."[17]

These issues had all been summed up in 1992 in "Christians In Rome."

During the 1993-94 Scotland Yard investigation Kathy Etchingham and I worked on a manuscript titled *The Hendrix-Etchingham Story*. On August 10, 51 U.E. (1994), we copyrighted our manuscript. It remains the most detailed and comprehensive analysis of the information surrounding Jimi's death. When it is eventually published, everyone who is interested in the fate of Hendrix will get the clearest picture of what happened on his last day.

Ironically, one hundred American publishers obstructed publication of *The Hendrix-Etchingham Story*. There exists treMENdous pleasure among the media elite over widespread misperceptions of Jimi's death.

> *Ultimately, one has to hold Hendrix himself responsible for actions that brought his life to an end.*   – Musician 1996

17. Author's conversation with David Henderson, 6/95.

Musician doesn't get it.

Has the general public's view of Jimi as the "drug addict zombie responsible for his own death" been the result of a cover-up by "other hands" that were at play that morning? We don't know how Monika's nine sleeping pills got into Jimi's body. But in the absence for so many years of so many crucial testimonies to cross reference, public perception of his death remains outrageously manipulated.   – "Christians In Rome" 1992

Rock Prophecy explains what so threatens T.H.E.M. about Hendrix.

New evidence in the form of testimony delivered to British authorities and to Musician, raises questions about Dannemann's story.
                                                                 – Musician 1996

I am the source connection for much of that "testimony delivered," and I was not identified nor credited by *Musician* magazine. And then the editor of that magazine refused to publish my letter (shown above) when *Musician* ran responses to their article about Jimi's death. Readers were unable to see the truth. How petty can an editor get? Is he in *that* much need of crediting himself with quality research?

In 55 U.E. (1997), a collector gathered much of the data about Jimi's death into a book put out by an English publisher. Again my work went unacknowledged.

On Jimi's 53rd birthday (November 27, 1995), David Henderson phoned me to read a dedication he wrote for the new revised edition of his Hendrix biography: "Thanks especially to Michael Fairchild for his important chronological notes, and also for his new information regarding Jimi Hendrix's death."[18]

                                                                          – Amen

GUITAR GREASER RAG

In autumn 1994, my article for *Guitar Shop* magazine[19] mentioned Jimi's last known use on stage of a sound effect device called the Octavia. In winter 1995, *Guitar Shop* published a letter[20] which suggested that I was wrong. The letter claimed that Jimi's last known use of the Octavia was not at his May 2, 1970 show in Madison, Wisconsin (as I pointed out in my article), but rather the Octavia is heard at Jimi's Isle of Wight concert on August 30, 1970 during the song "Red House."

But *Guitar Shop* magazine is incorrect. I sent a letter to the editor and he refused to correct the error.

---

18. David Henderson, *The Life of Jimi Hendrix – 'Scuse Me While I Kiss the Sky*, Bantam trade edition, 4/96, p.xi.
19. *Jimi's Voodoo Rig*, Guitar Shop, Fall 1994, p.35.
20. Guitar Shop, Spring 1995, p.6.

MY OBSTRUCTED MAY 52 U.E. (1995) LETTER TO GUITAR SHOP:

The sound [you] refer to is not an Octavia. The best photo of Jimi's Octavia on stage is the Joe Sia "crotch" shot from the Fillmore (see *GS* Fall '94 p. 82). The white slanted box in the foreground is Jimi's Octavia. Hendrix photo archivist Ben Valkhoff analyzed photos from the Isle of Wight and found no evidence of an Octavia on stage there. In addition, in scenes from the 1990 film, *Hendrix at the Isle of Wight* (I was a consultant on that film and producer Alan Douglas didn't list me in the film's credits! You silly asshole, Alan), at the end of the song "Spanish Castle Magic," and in the first solo of the song "All Along the Watchtower," we see scenes which reveal that Jimi used only the wah-wah pedal, Fuzz Face, and UniVibe devices on stage at the Isle of Wight concert. He is also playing a Gibson Flying V guitar during "Red House" with unusual WEM PA amps. When the fuzz is turned off, and the wah-wah is on, weird treble squeals result. It sounds almost like an Octavia effect, but lacks the distinctive Octavia "crunch" sound.

Guitar transcriber Douglas Nobel analyzed the Isle of Wight "Red House" passage (CD time: 7:58-8:32) in question and agrees that this solo lacks Octavia. The tone that [*Guitar Shop*] refers to for this "Red House" passage is heard also from Jimi's guitar during the mid-section of "Machine Gun" at the Isle of Wight show. No Octavia is used there either. The camera shows Jimi's foot on the wah-wah pedal instead.

I think it is the WEM PA amps that caused the "squeal tone" at Isle of Wight during those passages. The tone is similar to the Octavia squeal tone. Either the WEM amps, or the weird PA circuitry (which caused tones at that show to sound overly high-end or overly low-end) is the source of the guitar's squeal. But the Octavia was not used there. Jimi's last known use of Octavia on stage remains Madison, May 2, 1970. [as I originally noted in my article.]

The above letter concerns a technical point about Jimi's music that is of little interest to most people. But with regards to accuracy in chronicling information about Hendrix, it is important to know when he last used the Octavia sound effect,[21] because he pioneered its use and for decades many people have associated that sound with him.

I cite this dispute as an example of the Inversion: in this case *accuracy* ceases to be of concern. Some editors care only to "one up" and *dominate* the debate. By obstructing my letter, *Guitar Shop* leads readers to think Jimi plays Octavia at Isle of Wight.

---

21. The next night in St. Paul Jimi plugged in the Octavia at the start of his concert and tested the sound, but didn't end up using it during any songs that night.

Unnecessary error. Retarded History in the works.

But the next example is even more *domineering*:

UNAVIBER GOOSE STEPS ON APOLLO 13

Houston, we have a problem. Authorities are perplexed over the recent wave of Unaviber mail attacks against innocent Hendrix fans. Several people were somewhat perplexed by in-your-face bloody lies when they unwittingly opened Unaviber envelopes sent from Ireland. Our hearts go out to those poor unfortunates who sustained misinformation from this brutal and mindless attack.

The following letter is my reply to attacks on my work by *Unaviber* magazine, mailed out of Ireland. Publication of my letter was obstructed by the editor. (The magazine is named after a "Univibe," which is another sound effect device used by Jimi.)

SUPPRESSED JUNE 52 U.E. (1995) LETTER TO UNAVIBER:

In my booklet for MCA's 1995 worldwide release of the Hendrix CD titled *Voodoo Soup* I wrote about the track titled "The New Rising Sun." I considered the date that this song was recorded by noting, "Jimi's guitar is filtered through either a Univibe unit, or, less likely, through a rotating Leslie Speaker. However, whereas the Leslie was available in 1968, the Univibe dates back only to winter '69."[22]

Since "The New Rising Sun" was recorded at TTG Studios in October 1968, and since the Univibe effect wasn't available until 1969, I speculate in my CD booklet that "Jimi may have later in 1969 fed 'New Rising Sun' tapes through a Univibe in another studio...or there is a chance that the master tape of 'New Rising Sun' was [made in '69 and] mistakenly stored away in a 1968 TTG Studios box."[23]

Unaviber magazine then published the following: "According to Fairchild's liner-notes, the track was recorded at TTG Studios in Hollywood on 23 October 1968. His further explanations get rather hazy and speculative...there are hints of possibly storing the tape in an incorrectly labeled box."[24]

The date "Oct. 23" is written on the box which contains the master tape of "New Rising Sun." And my explanation of the recording date, based on the presence of Univibe, is not "hazy," it's insightful.

The editor of *Unaviber* magazine, "Julius," is not an expert on Jimi's Univibe sound effect. His magazine's review of my work claims

---

22. *Voodoo Soup* CD booklet, MCA Records 4/95, p.11.
23. Ibid.
24. Univibes #18, 5/95, p.3.

that the Univibe device "was not available until <u>late</u> '69."[25] This is incorrect. The Univibe is heard on Hendrix recordings from August 1969 and also on Jimi's "Mannish Boy" sessions in April '69. A month prior to those sessions, on March 5, 1969, London journalist Valery Mabbs interviewed Hendrix for *Record Mirror* and her article describes Jimi's "new sound effect." [from *early* 1969, not "late '69."]

Unaviber is also mistaken in the assertion that "The New Rising Sun" is "based on the idea of 'Electric Ladyland'" [another Hendrix song]. There is no structural resemblance between these two songs. The only musical similarities are embellished trills that Jimi laces over chord changes.

Unaviber then "corrects me" by informing readers that "New Rising Sun" has "nothing whatsoever to do with [the song] known as 'Hey Baby.'" But I never said that it did. The master tape of this music, used for the *Voodoo Soup* CD, was found in a box with the title "The New Rising Sun" written on it. Another song called "Hey Baby (Land of the New Rising Sun)" appears on the *Rainbow Bridge* album (1971). The only feature that these two songs have in common is the *title* "New Rising Sun," not the music. *Unaviber* corrects me for the magazine's own error.

My *Voodoo Soup* text also points out Jimi's switch from using a dark rosewood guitar neck to a light colored maplewood neck. Unaviber regards this observation as "triviality, and even absurdity." But Jimi's switch in guitar necks supports the theme of my story for these reasons:

1) Prior to October 1968 there are only rare and isolated incidents of Hendrix using the light colored maplewood guitar neck. Most photos show a dark rosewood neck. The period when he switched to light colored maplewood necks and consistently used them began in October 1968 with the first recording sessions for his fourth studio album, which is the subject of *Voodoo Soup* – the fourth studio album that Jimi didn't complete, which he called *First Ray of the New Rising Sun*.

2) My text for *Voodoo Soup* focuses on the meaning of "The New Rising Sun" and sets up, in the first paragraph, a "light vs. dark" theme that runs throughout the booklet. Jimi's switch to a "light" colored guitar neck in October 1968 happened at the same time that he introduced the song "The New Rising Sun." My booklet notes turn this coincidence into a metaphor: the start of the maplewood neck period in October '68 is a starting point for Jimi's album, *First Ray of the New Rising Sun*. My text calls his "light" guitar neck a "scepter with which Jimi ignites a Rising Sun crusade."[26] Here's why:

25. Ibid.
26. *Voodoo Soup* CD booklet, MCA Records 4/95, p.21.

From October 1968 until his death <u>two years</u> later, Jimi used light colored maplewood necks almost exclusively on his black and white Strats. This is the *two year* period during which he was creating his fourth studio album (*Voodoo Soup* is a 1995 speculation of what that fourth, unfinished, album might have been). The time period for the songs on *Voodoo Soup* is the same as the time period for the light colored guitar neck. Jimi's fourth album was originally titled *First Ray of the New Rising Sun* – which is an image of *light*. On stage during this two year period he now performed with a light colored guitar neck. It seems "absurd" not to point out these symbols. The theme of "light vs. dark" is central to explaining the Rising Sun concept. It is not "trivial" to write about a related change in his guitar color which distinctly marks this period.

In my CD booklet I point out a way for people to realize that when they see photos of Hendrix playing a black or white guitar with a light color maplewood neck, they will know that the picture dates from the period of Jimi's fourth and last studio album. People who read my booklet learn that photos of him using a light neck were taken during the last two years of his life, which is the *subject* of *Voodoo Soup*: music from his *last two years*.

Unaviber then asks, "Why on earth (in space?) does Fairchild link the release of (the song "Steppingstone") with the disablement of the Apollo 13 mission?" The reason is because my CD booklet for *Voodoo Soup* is mostly about *outer space ideas*, such as: Sands of Mars, Jupiter Sun, 2001: A Space Odyssey, Flying Saucer, The New Rising Sun, 2010: Odyssey 2, etc. With this "space" theme, the coincidence of the Apollo 13 fiasco occurring on the same day that "Steppingstone" (a song on *Voodoo Soup*) was released, warrants mention in my notes about "Steppingstone". The major Apollo Moon missions occurred during the Hendrix concert years. Jimi's image and popularity were affected and influenced by a technology revolution epitomized by NASA. Any connection between Hendrix and the exploration of space fits the subject of *Voodoo Soup*.

But that's not the only reason I cite the Apollo 13 mission. My CD booklet text reads: "the 'Steppingstone' disc came out on April 13, 1970, the same day that Apollo 13 became disabled in space. Jimi's record never charted."[27] There is an obvious Apollo 13/April 13 corollary here. 13 is the most unlucky number, and on unlucky April 13 the unlucky Apollo 13 mission was launched at the 13th hour. Three

---

27. Ibid. p.14.

astronauts were nearly killed by bad luck. And on this unlucky day Jimi's most unlucky record, "Steppingstone," was released.

My booklet points out that "Steppingstone" was originally titled "Sky Blues Today." Both of these titles associate with Apollo: the spacecraft was a steppingstone through a blue sky, to the moon (a "stone" we'll step over to reach the planets.) "Sky Blues Today" and "Steppingstone" are images that lend themselves to association with Apollo. That's why my CD booklet about space themes "links" Apollo 13 with the release of "Steppingstone".

And by citing Apollo 13/April 13 I was able to imprint in readers' minds what a unique time period this was when lunar trips were made. When I was writing the booklet for *Voodoo Soup* in early 1995 I read an article about an upcoming major film with Tom Hanks then in production. I read that the movie would be called *Apollo 13*, a film about the mission that went haywire on the April 13 day in 1970 when "Steppingstone" was released. (Later in 1995 *Apollo 13* became a hit movie, earning several Oscar nominations and winning one in 1996.)

But in early 1995 I thought to myself: later this year the Apollo 13 mission will be portrayed by a major film. Won't it be noteworthy for Jimi's fans to see this movie and realize that on the day when NASA nearly crashed, so did Jimi's "unlucky" record. I can convey this in my booklet with a 17-word mention of the Apollo 13/April 13 coincidence, and it also fits the outer space/sky/stone metaphors of my story too. Perceptive readers will enjoy it.

But NOOOOOOoooo – *Unaviber* didn't "get it." The rag's review asked me a Direct Question: "Why on earth (in space?) does Fairchild link the release of "Steppingstone" with the disablement of the Apollo 13 mission?" And then Julius, the editor, refused to publish my answer! It's as if the intent of *Unaviber* magazine is to print opinions that (imperceptively) discredit me.

Here's another fact of Hendrix history in my letter that Julius refused to publish:

Unaviber's review of *Voodoo Soup* notes that on the track titled "The New Rising Sun" we hear "those celestial sounds and those funny plucked notes which have never appeared on any other Hendrix production but one: the infamous 'God Save The Queen,' which later proved to have been played entirely by one David Henderson."[28]

The review implies that when the song "God Save The Queen" (this music is unrelated to the version mentioned earlier played at the Isle of Wight concert.) was included on an official CD release that I worked on (*Lifelines,* Warner Records 1990),

---

28. Univibes #18, 5/95, p.3.

that I didn't recognize a track of *fake* Hendrix music. The playing of a teenager named Dave Henderson was released on a Hendrix CD and credited as Jimi's music! *Unaviber* brings this up in their *Voodoo Soup* review in a context of *blaming* me for it. But if anyone recognized fake Hendrix music it was *me*.

I first heard "God Save the Queen" in March 44 U.E. (1987). On hearing it I said to friends, "This music is NOT played by Hendrix." To my amazement, some researchers disagreed. In fact, in 1988 three well-known Hendrix experts each told me that they believed Jimi did play the music now known as "God Save The Queen." But, as a guitarist, it was obvious to me that the music lacked Jimi's technique. Then in 1988, this music was chosen by producer Alan Douglas to be included on an official Hendrix CD titled *Live & Unreleased*.

A year later I began working for the Hendrix production company run by Mr. Douglas. Warner Records was interested in a Hendrix project called *Best of the Bootlegs*. That summer I asked producer Bruce Gary about the songs being considered for this release. When Bruce announced "God Save The Queen" I interrupted and said, "But that's not Jimi playing." On October 12, 1989, I sent this memo to the Hendrix production company that I worked for:

> *From the first time I heard this "God Save the Queen" piece I did not believe it was Jimi on guitar at all. Besides the modal runs during the acoustic section sounding completely foreign to Jimi's style, there is the sloppy, off-the-beat phrasing of the "God Save the Queen" melody itself. It sounds to me like a mid-1970s MXR Flanger unit is being used (and poorly at that). This (MXR) unit had not been developed by Sept. 1970 [when Jimi died] . . . Is it possible that this is [a session musician] playing in a "Hendrix style"?*

The following summer, 1990, I was working on *Lifelines*, a Hendrix CD set from Warner Records. I was amazed to learn that the producers were yet again including "God Save the Queen" on an official release! My first suggestion was to delete it. On July 31, 1990 I faxed to AYE? Ltd. this memo regarding changes for *Lifelines*:

> *In the errors list is the "God Save The Queen" segment, with the acoustic intro. This was also used for the Reference Library Series. The player is NOT Jimi. The phase-shifter/flange effect on this is technology from a post-Hendrix period. To me this music doesn't sound like Jimi's attack, nor his strum style, nor his rhythm, nor his modal patterns. When I first heard it I thought it might be [a studio musician].*

My objections went unheeded and the *Lifelines* CD was released in December 1990 with "God Save The Queen" tracks included! [and subsequently became the target of litigation against Warner Records from the guy who actually played the guitar. And the people who owned and controlled Jimi's music never even knew of my attempts to prevent Alan Douglas and Bruce Gary from making this mistake in the first place.]

Unaviber wouldn't let me make any of the above points to the readership I had built up with that magazine over the years. The editor promotes imperceptive attacks on my work and then prevents me from answering direct questions asked of me by obstructing publication of the above rebuttal. The release of fake Hendrix on an official album is a serious incident. I can prove that I tried to prevent this mistake, yet Unaviber used the opportunity to raise the issue in a context of blaming me for it and then covering up the truth in order to discredit me. Univibes is bad vibes.

I sent my letter to the editor and the turd instead used his rag to smear me with lies. With these dominator tactics, his magazine sets a goose-stepper standard for anti-scholarship. Julius follows in the footsteps of Irenaeus, excluding all but his own narrow accountant's MENtality, a silly fixation on "the MAN, the Music, and the Memorabilia" – while oblivious to any Meaning.

Even worse, in the summer of 1995, Are You Experienced? Ltd. began an official Hendrix website on the Internet called *Room Full of Mirrors*. I was asked to write a column for this website, and I submitted several articles that appeared on the Internet. Then in July 1995, after *Unaviber* had obstructed my reply to their review of *Voodoo Soup*, I gave my letter to the then-official Hendrix website, which was controlled by Alan Douglas, producer for AYE? Ltd. It was Alan whom I had warned not to release the fake Hendrix music on official CD releases, so my article about his boo-boo never appeared on the website he controlled.

I was prevented from reporting the truth in *Unaviber, Guitar Shop* and *Musician* magazines. And again I was blocked. It's as if the editors are determined that I be *blamed* for something I fought to correct. My work was stepped upon, like one of Jimi's Univibe pedals trampled beneath SS boots.

HEIL CHILE

> *You ask what is our policy? I will say it is to wage war by sea, land and air with all our might and with all of the strength that God can give us, to wage war against a monstrous tyranny . . . If we fail, then the whole world, including all that we have known and cared for, will sink into the abyss of a new dark age . . . How long will he resist? We cannot say how long that wicked man will torture and afflict the nations . . . You do your worst, and we will do our best!*
>   – Winston Churchill[29]

> *Friends, Romans, countrymen, WATCH OUT FOR YOUR EARS! I come to bury Caesar, not to praise him. The evil that men do lives after them; the good is oft*

---

29. Speeches of Churchill, (M.P.I. Home Video, 1990).

interred with their bones. So let it be with Caesar . . . And why should Caesar be a tyrant, then? . . . What trash is Rome, what rubbish, and what offal when it serves for the base matter to illuminate so vile a thing as Caesar!
                                            – "Little Caesars" by Billy Shakespear[30]

CENSORSHIP EVENTS

The "marketplace of ideas," built during the nineteenth and twentieth centuries, effectively disseminates the beliefs and ideas of the upper classes while subverting the ideological and cultural independence of the lower classes . . . In the United States, in particular, the ability of the upper and upper-middle classes to dominate the marketplace of ideas has generally allowed these strata to shape the entire society's perception of political reality and the range of realistic political and social possibilities.
                                            – Benjamin Ginsberg[31]

Those segments of the media that can reach a substantial audience are major corporations and are closely integrated with even larger conglomerates. Like other businesses, they sell a product to buyers. Their market is advertisers, and the "product" is audiences, with a bias towards more wealthy audiences, which improve advertising rates . . . The major media – particularly the elite media that set the agenda that others generally follow – are corporations "selling" privileged audiences to other businesses . . . Those who occupy managerial positions in the media, or gain status within them as commentators, belong to the same privileged elites, and might be expected to share the perceptions, aspirations, and attitudes of their associates, reflecting their own class interests as well. Journalists entering the system are unlikely to make their way unless they conform to these ideological pressures, generally by internalizing the values. It is not easy to say one thing and believe another – and those who fail to conform will tend to be weeded out by familiar mechanisms . . . What you have is institutions, big corporations, that are selling relatively privileged audiences to other businesses. What comes out is a picture of the world, a perception of the world, that satisfies the needs and the interests and the perceptions of the sellers and the buyers.   – Noam Chomsky[32]

The above Chomsky passage is excerpted from his 1989 book *Necessary Illusions*. In 1988, a year before this book came out, I had described in my manuscript *A Touch*

---

30. William Shakespeare, *Julius Caesar*.
31. Chomsky, *Necessary Illusions – Thought Control in Democratic Societies*, p.7.
32. Ibid. pp.7-8, and *Manufacturing Consent*, 1992, PBS 9/95.

of Hendrix how "American television engages viewers with programming designed to rationalize and reinforce inequity as a sacred inevitability. The common theme broadcast by networks is the acceptance of elitism: the notion that talent, personality, skill, luck, stamina, or certain abilities *should allow* access to uncommon material wealth. This opinion is what network executives and their advertising clients promote. Financial elitism, and the system of laws sustaining its unfairness, is rarely challenged on TV because of censorship imposed by self-serving rich network owners and advertisers. Financial equality for all is a topic forbidden to be rationalized or portrayed in a positive way through TV program plot and content. Rich elitists present a TV culture modeled after their own pursuit of greed, while viewers are enticed to emulate puppet personalities carefully selected by wealthy string pullers."[33]

With few exceptions, the electronic media is a showcase example for training the public to endure something we really don't like – inequality. We're trained to endure and *accept* extreme privileges for some people and not others. Our media weeds out discussions about equality. How equality can remedy most human problems is a foreign thought to most people. Instead, "celebrities" and commentators are promoted to us *only if* they themselves agree that some people deserve *more* than others. This is a litmus test celebrities must pass, and it's never assessed overtly by string pullers, who instead probe their "stars" subtly via wink 'n' nod conversation.

Rock Prophecy represents equality. So most of the public will be kept in the dark about Jimi's predictions. If the establishMENt is ever forced to acknowledge *Rock Prophecy* the media will trot out critics and pay T.H.E.M. well to take pot shots at this book.

So here's a blanket disclaimer for these crackpot reviewer jerks:

You're just puppets of the unjust monied. May your sphincters grow taste buds, and dribble your shitty opinions.

[When you see one of these assholes slam this book in a review, just copy this response on to toilet paper to send F.Y.I.]

Jeff Cohen, director of Fairness and Accuracy In Reporting (F.A.I.R.), explains, "As the media concentrates in the hands of fewer and fewer corporations, there's less and less outlet for any voice that will be critical of big business, whether it's pro-labor or pro-middle class consumer . . . Between General Electric, which owns NBC, and Westinghouse, which [owns] CBS – they play a big role in building about 80 percent of the nuclear power plants in the world. What people have to understand is that these corporations are very, very political. They have big lobbying operations in Washington and they give money to both political parties to reduce the policy options in Washington

---

33. *A Touch of Hendrix,* unpublished manuscript, (1988), p.30.

and they give money to sponsor television news pundit shows so they can narrow the debate in the news media as well . . . The fact is, corporations are running a lot of what goes on in Washington. When General Electric lobbyists drafted the corporate tax law of 1981 and reduced G.E.'s corporate tax to below zero, do you think that was discussed on any of these shows? . . . What's telling is that in the media there are no pundits who are real advocates for the middle class and the working class. Where's the debate? On television you tend to have a debate between corporate centrists and the far right . . . There *is* a left, but you just don't see it on TV . . . All over television you have political movement conservatives. When they're not on the air trying to recruit to the right wing, they're off the air strategizing with right wing groups and trying to build the conservative movement . . . Where are the progressives on American TV? They don't exist . . . While the correspondents are focusing on the minutiae of Washington, focusing you on a certain stage, what's happening on the side of the stage is big money interests are drafting legislation, getting legislation passed, putting up the money for the campaigns, and those are the same corporations that fund the pundit shows."[34]

Donna Edwards, director of the Center for a New Democracy, points out, "We get all of our news information from about 29 sources, which is not an awful lot. On top of that, because corporations own these media outlets, there is control over content. There is control over advertising. There is control over the kind of information and analysis we get."[35]

> *The culture-vulture elite can censor and determine media that trains viewers to approve of unfair inequities; a culture that worships the uncommon . . . Consumers are endlessly enticed to revere and imitate the celebrated rich. The aggressive nastiness with which business owners restrict access to jobs becomes praise worthy . . . The world's resources have been confiscated by the rich who hoard our valuables behind mercenary police-armies. Laws enacted by the rich sustain a class hierarchy of vastly unequal living standards. Pent up rage from the victims of this system is ritualistically vented through televised mega-doses of violent sports and sadistic crime dramas. The system produces a craving for violence against a scapegoat group of victims.*   *– A Touch of Hendrix,* 1988[36]

"One company can own every TV station in the country . . . up to 35 percent," notes Cohen. "In one recent act of censorship, CNN refused to take ads criticizing the telecommunications deregulations bill. Those were advocacy ads that would say that the Consumer Federation of America says that this new law will cause consumers to lose billions of dollars in cable TV and phone company rates, and CNN won't run those ads."[37]

---

34. The Phil Donahue Show, NBC 11/2/95.
35. Ibid.
36. *A Touch of Hendrix*, unpublished manuscript, (1988), p.266,
37. The Phil Donahue Show, NBC 11/2/95.

> *[Broadcast media] got $70 billion worth of free airwaves. The then-head of the Federal Communications Commission called it the biggest corporate give away this century. So this [media] industry has been dumping tens of millions of dollars into the process around the time of this key legislation and we've had no public discussion about it, the public can't get upset about it because they don't know about it, because these guys control the airwaves, they have quote-unquote "free speech."*
>
> — Charles Lewis[38]

The men who control media staged a blackout of discussion on the digital spectrum issue so that they wouldn't be charged fair market value for the spectrum that broadcast companies are receiving for free from the public. The digital spectrum is a $70 billion public asset which media moguls strong armed Washington legislators into handing over to them for free!

Burt Neuborne of the Brennan Center for Justice asks, "Whether the people who have the money are going to so dominate the ability to express their opinions that people who don't have the money are going to be turned into listeners, not speakers...a relatively small slice of the world gets to decide what gets said and all the rest of us sit like groundlings in the audience and grunt about whether we like it or not. That's what we're going to unless we can find a way to increase the ability of people without large amounts of money to either get access to the media or to get access to the political process, or to in some way break through the huge screen that money creates these days, so that they can get their voices heard as well. The First Amendment is aspirational, it's romantic, it says that the purpose is to create a world in which people can speak freely and equally to one another, therefore there's an obligation to step in at some point and even the playing field so that individuals can actually have real discussions and real debates, because what we've now got is not a real democracy with real debate, we've got a plutocracy in which money talks."[39]

"You have to look for the publications that aren't owned," says Cohen. "Half a dozen corporations control most of the content of cable. It doesn't matter if there are 500 stations. Vladimir Pozner used to be in the Soviet media. He said, 'We had more daily newspapers in Moscow than you have in New York City. We had all these different magazines, but they all came from one owner, the Communist Party and the state.' That's what we are approaching here: five owners or so and they're owning all of these different channels . . . TCI and Time-Warner, two big cable operators, between them they bring the cable wire into about half of the cable homes in the country, and for a long time they've had a big chunk of Turner Broadcasting and CNN. Every time there's an effort by someone to start a new all-news channel that would compete with CNN, since you can't get a news channel on or any new channel on cable unless you go through the gate keepers, those

---

38. Charles Lewis, Center for Public Integrity, The News Hour, PBS 6/4/99.
39. *Free Speech for Sale,* produced & directed by Kathleen Hughes & Tom Casciato, 1999, PBS 6/8/99.

who bring the wire to your homes – TCI and Time-Warner didn't want anyone to compete with them – so there's no alternative. Now, if you ask the public, 'Would you like to have more than one all-news channel on cable?' the public would say sure, but you never get that option. Wouldn't you like to see an all-consumer rights channel hosted by Ralph Nader? Wouldn't you like to see an environmental channel that's maybe run by Greenpeace? They don't have a chance of getting on the air when TCI and Time-Warner are the gate keepers that control what new channels get on cable."[40]

> *The way the country's being run, you see badness, you can see evil right in front of your face as soon as you turn on the TV.*   – Jimi[41]

PAYING TRIBUTE TO THE RICH

Men who control the media weed out people who disagree with the existence of a privileged "rich" class. The goal of elitists is to leave dissenters without means of support: no jobs and no welfare. They force "unwanted" people to vie in crime and then throw them in prison concentration camps where victims are infected with AIDS – *Administered* Immune Deficiency Syndrome.

Laws written by the unjust monied, the so-called "rich," enact a silent genocide of death by neglect, herding impoverished victims into crime-ridden ghettos where "poor people" are enticed to kill each other off. And the media underreports/distorts this story, but mainly doesn't cover it at all.

Most of our lives are spent dodging the dominators: we are corralled into workplace gladiator rings each day to battle teeth-gnashing workers trained to subjugate as many people as possible. Everyone is threatened into submission and forced like slaves to pay tribute to men who own money. But money is confiscated from the public with laws written by the "rich" and enforced by mercenary police armies. Civilization today is a waking nightmare of refugees seeking shelter from the M.A.N. – the Mean And Nasty, a testosterone-overload hierarchy. We are the victims of a class-based, status hell, Sieg Heil Hierarchy.

> *This is the ultimate consequences of having broken off the symbiotic relationship with the Gaian matrix of the planet. This is the consequence of lack of partnership; this is the legacy of imbalance between the sexes; this is the terminal phase of a long descent into meaninglessness and toxic existential confusion.*   – Terrence McKenna[42]

---

40. The Phil Donahue Show, NBC 11/2/95.
41. New England Scene 11/68.
42. McKenna, *Food of the Gods*, p.254.

PREDICTIONS FOR THE A.C.M.I. *(AFFLUENCE CONTROLLED MEDIA INFLUENCE)*

> *They didn't take me off the air because people **weren't** listening. They took*
> *me off because the people **were** listening . . . When I got bounced, ABC said,*
> *"You didn't generate advertising revenues" . . . I pointed right back to them*
> *that ABC had an offer from the Teamsters Union to buy $20,000 worth of*
> *ads. They rejected that on the basis that it would be "advocacy" advertising*
> *and they can't have any advocacy. So corporations can put their viewpoint*
> *forward and that's not "advocacy." But a union, working people coming*
> *together who want to put a viewpoint forward, they are not accepted.*
> – Jim Hightower[43]

Dominators will suppress *Rock Prophecy*. Ads for this book will be obstructed from publication and denied means of being seen or circulated. But as the Prophecy becomes known in the underground, the A.C.M.I. will roll into action with propaganda "reviews" designed to label the text "paranoid" and "lunatic." All attempts at an accurate explanation of the Prophecy will be stifled by the men who control the media. Spin doctors will twist every word. They'll focus on my use of the term "dominator" and take pains to reverse that label onto me. And if discussion of the Prophecy reaches a public arena, elitist media will portray me as the "dominator" who *wants* an asteroid disaster just so I can say, "See, I told ya so." Imagine T.H.E.M. reading Poe's "Conqueror Worm" and declaring, "Edgar *wants* you to die just so his poem can come true!" That's not my attitude. My message is that impact is inevitable, so adjust your priorities accordingly. *Rock Prophecy* is a philosophical horror story, I'm just its messenger. But as the asteroid looms into view as foreseen by Jimi, the evil media, in the final stages of decay, will title me "antichrist" and lay blame for our fate at my feet.

> *White collar conservatives . . . they're hoping soon my kind will drop and die.*
> – Jimi[44]

"The U.S. media are alone in that you must meet the *condition of concision*," warns Chomsky. "You've got to say things between two commercials or in 600 words, and that's a very important fact because the beauty of concision, saying a couple of sentences between two commercials, the beauty of that is that you can only repeat conventional thoughts. If I get on *Nightline* and say Gaddafi is a terrorist, Khomeini is a murderer, the Russians invaded Afghanistan – [for] all this stuff I don't need any evidence. Everybody just nods. On the other hand, suppose you say something that just isn't regurgitating conventional pieties? Suppose you say something that's just the least bit unexpected or controversial? Suppose you say 'The biggest international

---

43. The Phil Donahue Show, NBC 11/2/95.
44. "If 6 Was 9" released on Axis:Bold As Love, Track Records 12/67.

terrorist operations that are known are the ones run out of Washington,' or 'The U.S invaded South Vietnam . . . The Bible is probably the most genocidal book in the total cannon. Education is a system of imposed ignorance . . .' Well, people will quite reasonably expect to know what you mean. Why did you say that? I never heard that before. If you say that, you better have a reason, you better have some evidence, in fact you better have a lot of evidence because that's a pretty startling comment. And you can't give evidence if you're stuck with concision. That's the genius of this structural constraint."[45]

> *The prose demanded by the middle class is preeminently that of institutional advertising . . . [suggesting] the indispensability of cliche to middle class understanding. Where the more fortunately educated read to be surprised, the middle class reads to have its notions confirmed, and deviations from customary verbal formulas disconcert and annoy it.*
> — Paul Fussel[46]

Explanations about how major religions of the world were designed to empower heterosexual men while justifying privileges for the lucki-*est* among T.H.E.M. is what elitist media is most concerned to conceal. The belief system fed to the "mass class" by the elites deletes all calls for equality. The concept of equal money for everyone doesn't even register among the hypnotized public. The fight for fairness is omitted from HIStory like nutrition is removed from processed bread.

Equal access for everyone to everything (as far as is possible) is the solution to human suffering and the single idea that dominators must suppress. Common-sense fairness has been made to seem strange to most people, to a point where discussion of it will "disconcert and annoy." Instead of equality, HIStory transmits elitism. Intolerable unfairness is inflicted on masses of worker-slaves, people who never get enough time to analyze what's happening. Conditioned with the "constraint of concision," they struggle beneath the wheel of dominator overlords who keep us all running ragged on a work-a-day treadmill.

WINDOWS 53 – THE NEWEST CONSTANTINE

> *Satan finally offers Jesus "all the kingdoms of this world and their glory," which Satan claims as his own. Thus Matthew, following Mark's lead, implies that political success and power . . . may evince a pact with the devil – and not . . . marks of divine favor.*
> — Elaine Pagels[47]

---

45. Manufacturing Consent 1992, PBS 9/95.
46. Fussel, Paul, *Class*, (New York: Ballantine, 1983), p.168.
47. Pagels, *The Origin of Satan*, p.81.

Like Constantine's reconstruction of Jesus, with Bethlehem temples in the prophet's hometown, Paul Allen's Experience Music Project in Seattle likewise presents an interpretation of Jimi, gaudy "cathedral" and all. Already there are troubling signs.

An early project that Mr. Allen's EMP became publicly associated with is the ten hour PBS TV series titled *The History of Rock and Roll*, which aired in 1995. The EMP was a sponsor of this documentary; their name and logo precede and follow each of the ten hour-long TV segments. A large audience first learned of the EMP through this TV series. But if you look at the Hendrix segment in *The History of Rock and Roll*, it starts with a clip from a 1965 TV show in which Jimi is seen playing in a back-up band with another black guitar player. As we watch the screen we see the *other* black guitarist highlighted to indicate Jimi! It's as if, you know, "all them guitar pickers look alike!" And this is the show that *introduced* the Experience Music Project to a national TV audience. From my experience with the complex database of information and misinformation surrounding Jimi, I shudder to think of how the EMP will portray Hendrix.

On Jimi's 50th birthday (1992), a copyright registration went into effect for my 62-page manuscript titled *The Festivals*. This unpublished text is about the four major festivals that Hendrix headlined (Monterey, Woodstock, Atlanta, and Isle of Wight). The manuscript was commissioned for a CD-ROM project produced by the Hendrix company, then located in Hollywood. The project was shelved when the people I worked for began fighting the lawsuit (financed by Paul Allen's money). But on January 6, 1993, before litigation hit the fan, I thought the CD-ROM program was due for release when I sent a copy of *The Festivals* to Paul Allen at the EMP. I sent it as an example of my work. In the first chapter of *The Festivals*, I describe Hendrix setting fire to his Stratocaster guitar at the Monterey Pop Festival and point out how "No other single act in the history of rock music so connects this art form with its roots."[48]

Two years later, in 1995, Paul Allen's EMP sponsored *The History of Rock and Roll* TV series and for each of the episodes, the logo at the beginning, accompanied by Hendrix music, is a Stratocaster guitar bursting into flames. It's as if the producers are implying that Jimi setting fire to his guitar at the Monterey festival is the single act in the "history of rock and roll" that most connects this art form with its roots (!). The EMP logo appears every time the flaming guitar is shown. When I see this I think of my manuscript sent to the EMP.

Much of my copyrighted writings at the Library of Congress contain research and conclusions about the Hendrix story, writings that for many years have been obstructed from publication. Projects about Jimi use concepts from these writings without crediting me.

I initiated Paul Allen's museum's purchase of thousands of world-class Hendrix items. It took years of work for me to get into a position where I could orchestrate this. But, as is discussed in this book's Introduction, after arranging for a cornerstone collection to become part of Mr. Allen's museum, I was told to expect no compensation from the billionaire's project. Then the lawsuit, financed by Mr. Allen's loan, against the

---

48. *Festival Notes*, unpublished manuscript 11/9/92, p.16.

Hendrix production company I worked for, resulted in my unemployment. I had contributed much to the success of Hendrix releases from 1989-1995, and I was in line to be the next Creative Director for the estate. After the lawsuit was settled, my position was given to a Japanese American woman (no blood relative of Jimi Hendrix) and my contributions to Jimi's legacy then underwent persecutions and revisions. The result has been a pathetic decline in public interest in "Hendrix releases." Never again will we see a Jimi CD rise high in the charts, as they did when I was able to help orchestrate their success. Subsequent releases have been so embarrassingly bad that dominators have triumphed in the total marginalization of Hendrix light years away form any public concern at all.

The legal system which scripts laws to allow this whole tragedy to happen demonstrates the Inversion. (My attempt to find legal help to confront Paul Allen's Hendrix museum is a story that makes us crave for the relative "freedom" of old Soviet controlled media.) Unfortunately, a heavy price will be paid for these evil circumstances. I've tried to communicate Jimi's prediction of destruction, but the Inversion obstructs us and seals our fate.

> *There was a rich man who had much money. He said, "I shall put my money to use so that I may sow, reap, plant, and fill my storehouse with produce, with the result that I shall lack nothing." Such were his intentions, but that same night he died.*   — Jesus (Thomas:63)

Paul Allen has contributed at least $1 million to the Search for Extraterrestrial Intelligence Institute in Mountain View, California. S.E.T.I. uses radiotelescopes to search for alien life forms. "It's the kind of interesting question the human race should be investing in," said Allen, "is there intelligent life out there?"[49] But those telescopes should instead focus on the alienated life forms at the EMP and inquire whether there is intelligent life on Earth. How ironic it is that I am the one who figured out Jimi's asteroid prediction, yet the museum project dedicated to the Hendrix legacy refuses to help me, despite the work I did for them, while Paul Allen scans the skies for objects in space. And then his DreamWorks and NBC interests pump out pumped up movies and reports about asteroids, after I was left unemployed by the lawsuit he financed.

Bear in mind that in 1995 there was a very hostile lawsuit going on which had been financed by Paul Allen against the Hendrix production company that employed me. Why *wouldn't* Paul Allen's legal "team" monitor my writings that were being registered and filed at the Library of Congress? It is *legal and permitted* for anyone to read material on file of the LOC. And after all, I was the main conceptualist for Mr. Allen's opponents at the Hendrix company in Hollywood, the company being sued with his money. It would seem inept or incompetent NOT to investigate my publicly available writings on file at the LOC, since I was a "mouthpiece" for Are You Experienced? Ltd. Is this how the asteroid story made its way to the top of the list of world media in the late 20th century? A topic that Paul Allen, media mogul, "stumbled upon" during the Hendrix lawsuit investigations?

There are three issues to consider regarding the EMP:

1) I orchestrated the acquisition of some of the worlds best Hendrix collections for them. Nearly a half million dollars were paid for the material I lead them to.

2) The EMP refused to pay me anything, and Paul Allen began financing the lawsuit against the company I worked for, and was in line to be Creative Director of. As a result of the lawsuit settlement, my job was given to a Japanese American woman and I was left unemployed. The EMP refused to help.

3) During the 1995 litigation I was writing the story of Jimi's prediction of an asteroid impact and I registered the story at the LOC. After litigation ended, NBC and DreamWorks, media companies in partnership with Paul Allen, began churning out highly publicized stories and reports about asteroids.

The reasons why Mr. Allen's EMP disfavors me, so we were told, will be published later...

The Inversion of Retarded HIStory will climax as my persecutors deny any truth to *Rock Prophecy*. And when the telescopes of the Search for Extraterrestrial Intelligence finally spot the Rock, all people on Earth will become spectators to their own globally televised live extinction, broadcast on MSNBC.

Dominators will use every trick in the book to suppress this text. When they realize that the Prophecy of Hendrix is correct, they will prevent the public from understanding the issues described in these pages. If our race is to perish from the Rock, dominators will be damned if they'll let anyone know that it was Hendrix who tried to prevent it.

> *Throughout the seventies and eighties the need to deny the impact of the sixties took on something of the flavor of a mass obsession.*
> — Terrence McKenna[50]

After expending so much energy to deny the significance of Jimi, dominators won't think twice about damaging anyone who informs the public about the contents of this book. The Prophecy will be denied and Hendrix instead portrayed as another dismissable guitar greaser clown. But if *Rock Prophecy* succeeds in reaching its audience, I will then be labeled the antichrist and figuratively burned at the stake by an establishMENt Inquisition.

---

50. McKenna, *Food of the Gods*, p.240.

THE ERUPTION OF MT. RAINIER

In 55 U.E. (1997), Paul Allen wanted to buy the Seattle Seahawks football team if he could persuade taxpayers to contribute $300 million for a new Roman Coliseum-like arena. ABC News called the proposal "a partnership in which mostly the public will pay and the very private Allen would profit."[51]

Many politicians defend construction of new sports stadiums, pretending that the unnecessary expenditures are "economic development." But most studies prove otherwise. "If they really were focusing on creating jobs and economic growth," says Prof. Roger Noll of Stanford University, "they'd go for other kinds of industrial developments or commercial developments. They would not go for sports stadiums."[52]

> *They try to build their own heavens, they want to be written down in war history, they want to be written down in money history, and those things are nothin' but jokes, in the next few years they're gonna all be jokes and those people are gonna be jokes. Some of them should be put in cages now to be looked at, because they're getting very rare.* — Jimi[53]

> *Big money interests are drafting legislation, getting legislation passed, putting up the money for the campaigns, and those are the same corporations that fund the pundit shows.* — Jeff Cohen[54]

With Constantine-like ambitions, EMPeror Allen financed a referendum vote to approve public tax money for his coliseum arena in Washington State. He paid millions more for a media campaign to support his crusade.[55] But 23 years ago Washington State taxpayers financed a "stadium of the future," the King Dome. Today that stadium is still $130 million in the hole. A whole generation is left with debt.

> *Together we can leave something for future generations.* — Paul Allen[56]

> *The institutional fathers are still running the show in the Name of the "Future," which is another word for past.* — Mary Daly[57]

---

51. ABC World News 6/16/97.
52. Ibid.
53. Interview with Nancy Carter, L.A., 6/15/69, *Hendrix Speaks*, 1990 Rhino Records.
54. The Phil Donahue Show, NBC 11/2/95.
55. ABC World News 6/16/97.
56. Ibid.
57. Daly, *Beyond God the Father*, p.184.

> *We are PAST: the Human Race . . . why keep living in the old, in the past?*
> *These buildings ain't gonna be there for all that long, so why be like that?*
> — Jimi[58]

Just as the Roman Coliseum was due to open in July of 1999, the Mayor of Seattle appeared on national TV news to address a "homeless emergency" in the city. About 5500 people in Jimi's hometown have no place to live, and on any given night half of them are turned away from shelters and forced to sleep in the streets. Many of these victims erected tents in the shadow of Paul Allen's dominator coliseum monstrosity, as if begging for crumbs from the evil EMPeror's plate. "These are our urban refugees," pleaded Mayor Paul Schell, "how can we not help them? In many ways we're probably the richest city in the country right now on a per capita basis... but the fact is that we've got longer food lines than we've ever had before and more people looking for places to stay...this can't be."[59] Mercenary police armies of the "rich" harass the shelterless victims and slap them with fines for trespassing into the sight of dominators.

On the same day that Seattle's mayor begged for mercy, the U.S. Attorney General declared suicide to be a major public health threat in America, becoming the 8th leading cause of death, and the *third* leading cause of death among African-American men.

MASTER

> *The Greek word for "master" is the same as that for "Lord."*
> — John Crossan[60]

EMPeror Allen owned nearly half of TicketMaster, the largest distributor of live entertainment tickets in America. While under his control, in 53 U.E. (1995), Allen's company was charged with being a monopoly that gouges consumers through its service fees. Instead of buying tickets directly from a box office, millions of people were required to order tickets through TicketMaster and pay mandatory service fees. A 1995 survey by the U.S. Public Interest Research Group found that for 80 entertainment events across the country, TicketMaster added to ticket prices an average of 27 percent in fees. TicketMaster made an estimated $240 million from these service fees in 1994. By the mid-1990s, Mr. Allen's company controlled two thirds of the 10 million concert seats in America.[61]

"TicketMaster has a monopoly and has gone about its business to obtain a monopoly," said Seattle attorney Steve Bermann, who helped to mount a class action suit against TicketMaster. "I think evidence will show, for the purpose of being able to raise

---

58. *Cherokee Mist – The Lost Writings of Jimi Hendrix*, p.94 *Black Gold.* and Hall and Clark, *The Superstars – In Their Own Words*, p.131.
59. News Hour, PBS 7/28/99.
60. Crossan, *Historical Jesus*, p.254.
61. McNeil/Lerher News Hour, PBS 10/12/95.

prices artificially, TicketMaster has bought up or taken steps to exclude every market entry, has locked up the market through exclusive arrangements, and has boycotted anyone who tried to lower the prices."[62]

Paul Allen's TicketMaster controlled more than 90 percent of ticketing in Seattle. Books and ideas can be "controlled" too.

Stone Gossard of Seattle's Pearl Jam rock band testified before Congress about TicketMaster practices. "Something is vastly wrong," said the musician, "when the system under which a ticket distribution company can dictate the mark up on the price of a concert ticket and prevent a band from using another less expensive approach to distributing tickets and even effectively preclude a band from performing at a particular arena if it does not want to use TicketMaster."[63]

Fred Rosen, then TicketMaster CEO, counterargued, "We're an extension of the box office, we're not in lieu of the box office, we're an alternative of the box office, and we call it a convenience charge because you don't have to go to the box office if you choose not to. So you sit down and you negotiate a contract and various factors are involved in it."[64]

Jim Weyermann, deputy director of the Seattle Center in 1995, negotiated a three-year deal with TicketMaster in 1995 which gave the company exclusive rights to sell seats at the Seattle Center. The deal raised TicketMaster's control of all ticketing in the Seattle market to *over 90 percent*. The Center's director claimed that the service fees reflect the cost of doing business. "If you don't want to pay the service fee, then don't go," said Weyermann. "I mean, that's America . . . In the entertainment industry you have to be tough. You have to be thick skinned and you have to be willing to do what it takes to run your business profitably, or someone else will eat you for lunch."[65]

A 1996 *USA Today* article about EMPeror Allen's EMP museum reported, "Jimi memorabilia is plentiful . . . Budget can't be a great concern when your benefactor is a billionaire."[66] *USA Today* said that when the EMP staff goes to work (which includes the Hendrix collection that I worked to make available to them) "it's a bit like Christmas morning . . . [the curator] calls music 'an essential food group.' He gorges every day."

HUNGER STRIKE FOR RIGHTEOUSNESS

Let dominators eat cake for lunch and gorge themselves on Molotov cocktails from the Third World, but I'm one consumer they won't consume. No nourishment will remain for the leeches after I engage a hunger strike at the altar of a Roman Coliseum in Seattle. When an organization is in place to shepherd and protect *The Five Books of Michael*, I

---

62. Ibid.
63. Ibid.
64. Ibid.
65. Ibid.
66. USA Today, 3/15/96, section D, p.2.

will refuse food and strike for righteousness, to protest the EMPeror's refusal to compensate me for my work.

For the boycott of all we christen thee Dominator Museum. May your walls house the fossilized remains of days when people suffered under laws that sustain inequity. May the garbage children starving in the sewers of Bucharest invade your nightmares, they deserve as much as you.

> *Do not seek riches from a man you do not know, lest it only add to your poverty. If God has ordained that you die in your poverty, so he has appointed it, but do not corrupt your spirit because of it.*
> — Dead Sea Scroll #42416

EQUALITY PARTY

> *The two top classes . . . have very few ideas. One of the few is that capital must never be "invaded," as it likes to put it. Another is that a jacket and tie are never to be omitted. But other than those, it has no very extensive stock of beliefs.* — Paul Fussel[67]

Publishers and producers resist investment in messages about equal money income among people. It's the single idea they are most concerned to weed out. Challenges to unfair privileges enjoyed by unjust monied people are not tolerated in our unfree media. I call their privileges unfair and they "reject" (obstruct) my reports.

There must be a grassroots organization of working people who band together to circulate *Rock Prophecy*. This book reports the story that the A.C.M.I. most needs to suppress. As soon as these thoughts are expressed in the media, hordes of braintrained dominators crawl out of the woodwork to complain and demand that I be silenced. Freeks must speak out about *Rock Prophecy* because dominators write letters of condemnation to media officials and other "authorities" and demand that we be stopped.

> *In the normal course of events . . . a writer's audience is apt to remain silent (people almost never volunteer comments on what they've read unless it made them mad).* — Judith Applebaum[68]

> *In any walk of life people only write in when they perceive something to be bad.* — Jimpress[69]

---

67. Fussel, *Class*, p.170.
68. Applebaum, *How to Get Happily Published*, p.223.
69. Jimpress #32, 10/94, p.13.

The Affluence Controlled Media Influence will invoke laws to obstruct *Rock Prophecy*. As a refugee from dominator tyranny, I seek political asylum among freeks. I must find safe haven and explain what I see. It is up to fair-minded people who see this book to protect the text and circulate it to as many readers as possible. We're in a battle for the planet. The murderers of Earth will see our world destroyed before they allow fair sharing in the way that Jesus proclaimed, in the way that will save us.

> *When we pay attention to these values that society has always held sacred, then order emerges out of chaos . . . When values disintegrate, everything disintegrates – health disintegrates, poverty attains dominance over affluence, societies and civilizations crumble.* – Deepak Chopra[70]

WHAT YOU CAN DO

> *We are not going to have "a mythology," we are going to have individual mythologies, little cluster mythologies, people of similar readinesses who get together and are helping each other.* – Joseph Campbell[71]

1) Initiate discussion of *Rock Prophecy* with everyone you know.

2) Identify politicians, businesspeople, celebrities and media representatives who believe that any person deserves more than double the money of anyone else.

3) Boycott the businesses of these people. Seek to convey to everyone the idea that all humans deserve nearly equal amounts of personal income.

4) Organize public gatherings and marches to demonstrate in favor of a maximum wage.

5) For people unfamiliar with the means by which media is manipulated and controlled by unjust monied men, good introductions are the 1992 film *Manufacturing Consent* and the 1999 documentary *Free Speech for Sale*. *Manufacturing Consent* is a film about Noam Chomsky and it's often available in libraries. *Free Speech for Sale* is available from Public Affairs Television, Inc. P.O. Box 2284, S. Burlington, VT 05407.

---

70 Deepak Chopra, *Creating Affluence*, (San Rafael: Amber-Allen Publishing, 1993), p.55.
71. *The Function of Mythology, World Mythology*, Lecture at Esalen 8/69, Big Sur Tapes.

6) Anyone who can offer constructive editorial suggestions and/or corrections to any section of this book, please contact First Century Press, P.O. Box 39606, Rochester, NY 14604. 716 244-5552.

7) Notify First Century Press of any store or shop where *Rock Prophecy* can be distributed.

8) Help First Century Press document the persecution of *Rock Prophecy*. Keep track of incidences of obstruction and false portrayals of the Prophecy. Everything will be described on line at www.rockprophecy.com. Today's dominators will be forever condemned by future generations of the Hendrix Millennium.

9) Protect *Rock Prophecy*, circulate it, and every November 27 Thanksgiving New Year, organize groups of the faithful to take copies of this book to different secret locations and plant the Newest Testament like seed in the ground, where no dominator can retrieve and destroy the truth.

I seek to communicate with everyone who can help create the Equality Party, a political organization dedicated to advancing the cause of fairness.

TEN CONNECTIONS

1) Everyone deserves the same, those who take more deserve shame.

2) Earth communicates with us via psychoactive plants: mushrooms, bark, seeds, leaves, and cactus.

3) Human beings are Earth's defense against asteroids.

4) Hendrix sensed the approach of a Rock and named it Electric Love.

5) The birth of Hendrix marks the start of the Uncommon Era. The simultaneous breakthrough of Project Ultra broke the Nazi Enigma code and initiated an age when gentle people can be free from domination.

6) Christ = Messiah = original sin = denigration of sex = control of women. All major world religions are schemes of male supremacy.

7) Dominators have silenced the seers and retarded history, set back human advances towards the anti-asteroid technology that would have saved our doomed, transitional civilization.

8) Gays are nature's herd thinners, averting births and aiding our race.

9) Worship = warship. Irenaeus destroyed the original gospels and replaced them with anti-gay/anti-female rewrites.

10) For each elite pleasure at equity's expense, expect three times the pain on the afterlife plane.